ART UNDER ATTACK

HISTORIES OF BRITISH ICONOCLASM

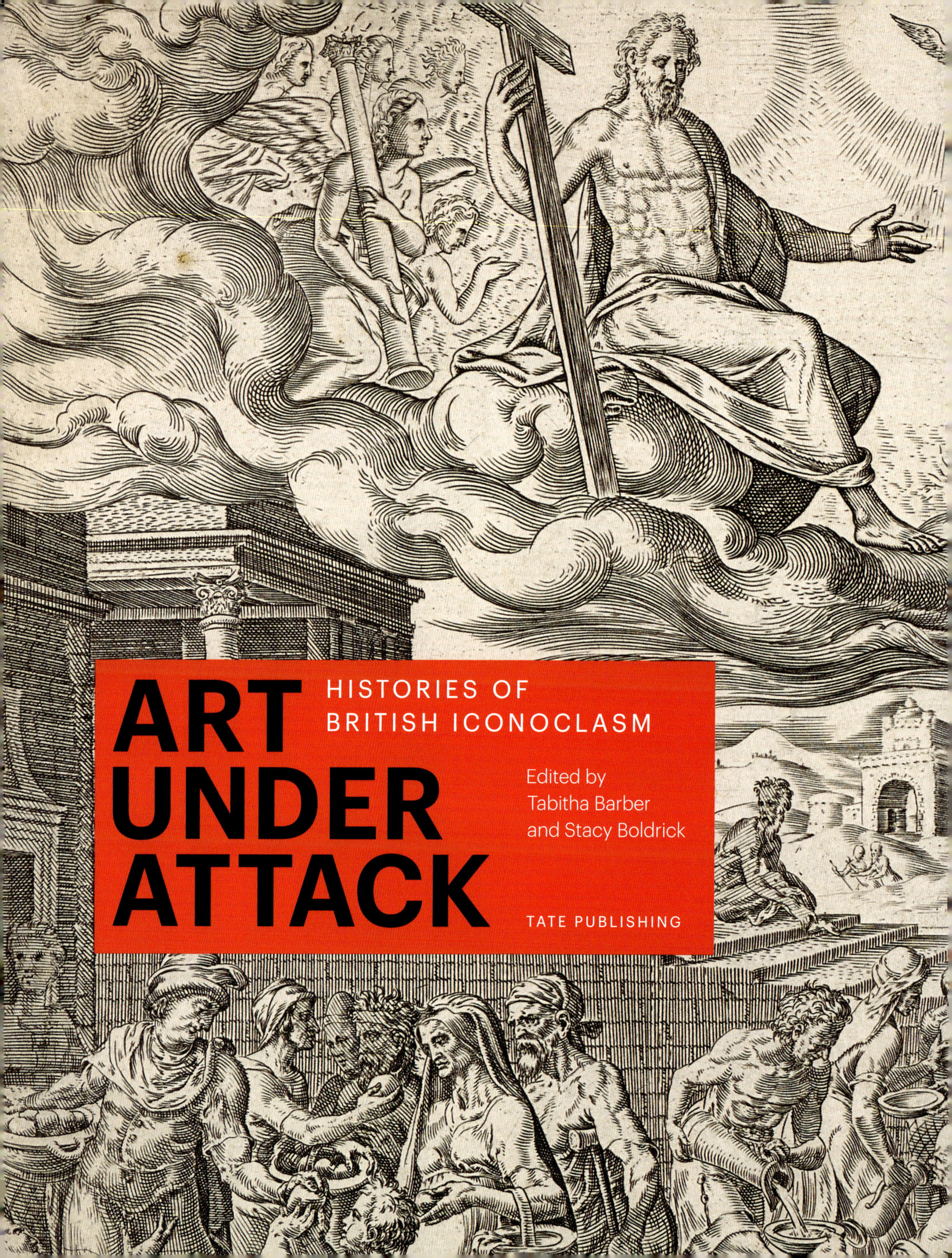

ART UNDER ATTACK

HISTORIES OF BRITISH ICONOCLASM

Edited by
Tabitha Barber
and Stacy Boldrick

TATE PUBLISHING

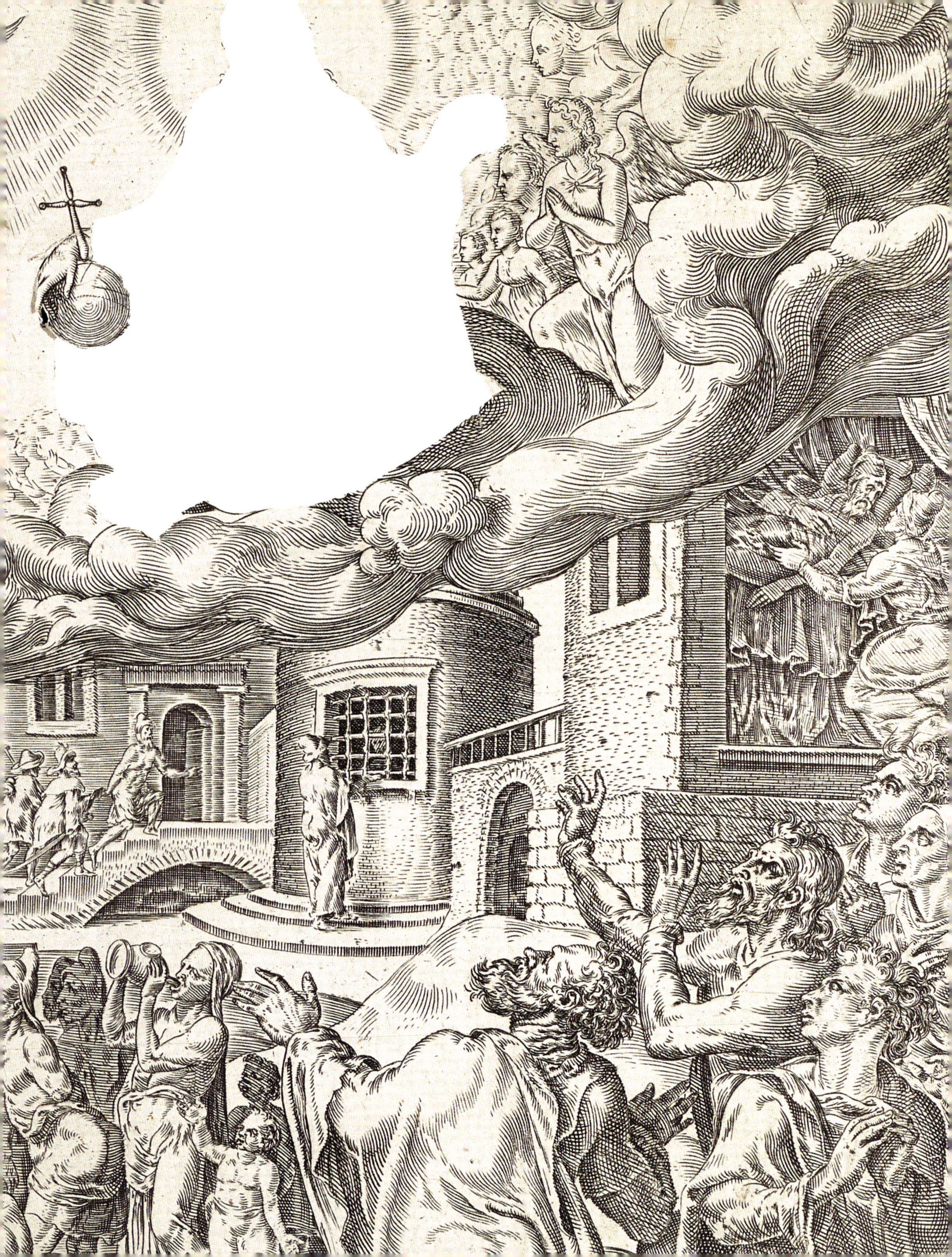

CONTENTS

CONTRIBUTORS

AW Andrew Wilson
LM Lena Mohamed
MGS M.G. Sullivan
RK Ruth Kenny
RW Richard Williams
SB Stacy Boldrick
SH Susan Harrison
TB Tabitha Barber

II POLITICS

III AESTHETICS

FOREWORD

The earliest work in the Tate collection is a work from 1545. This is not an accident. That our collection begins here is in large part due to the fact that Henry VIII's Dissolution of the Monasteries in 1538, the break with Rome and the increasingly hard-line Protestant interpretation of imagery, not only in Henry's reign but more especially during those of Edward VI and Elizabeth I, was hugely disruptive of the production of images in England.

Our collection is post-Reformation and, in net distinction to most European collections, mirrors the slow rise of a class of patronage quite separate from that of the Church. The newly established Church of England had little need of art, and the artistic legacy housed within the fabric of the many previously Roman Catholic communities was either looted, destroyed or concealed.

This is why it seemed apposite for Tate Britain to mount an exhibition which examines what is not in our collection, and why. We are so used in Britain to seeing fine art as separate from the Church, in both material and iconographic terms, that it may not seem such an obvious question. But if we look more closely at our collections, noting their early reliance on foreign artists, trained in countries where religious patronage was the norm, and if we look at our churches, without their polychrome sculptures and icons, and relate this to a later taste for the pure and the plain, we start to see why such an exhibition is especially pertinent for a national institution that even hopes to represent 500 years of British art.

Iconoclasm, as has been well demonstrated in recent studies, is as much about changing the meaning of an image as about destroying it completely. Politically inspired iconoclasm makes this especially clear, and examples abound within any colonial or patriarchal system. Even if the word might literally refer to breaking, the intentions of those who attack art often depend on at least partial if not complete recognition of the original. Nonetheless, one of the reasons why it is difficult to put on an exhibition on the subject is that art which has been attacked is more prone to breakage and dispersal. Our curators have found various ways in which to speak of the original, and these different media in themselves broaden out our usual scope and range.

Another way in which this exhibition departs from the conventional is that it covers a long period of time and as such has involved a number of curators with different specialisms. I was delighted that it was possible for Stacy Boldrick, an acknowledged historian of iconoclasm and a medieval art historian who also follows contemporary art, to work alongside Tabitha Barber, our Curator of British Art 1550–1750. They have benefited at Tate Britain from the input of Ruth Kenny, Sofia Karamani, Jenny Powell, Philippa Simpson and Andrew Wilson, and from numerous external advisors, notably Leslie Brubaker, Richard Clay and James Simpson. I would additionally like to thank Dario Gamboni and Nick Penny for their important support of the project at particularly difficult stages, and Fiona Bradley for her understanding. For 'Art under Attack' has been a difficult project, and iconoclasm is a difficult subject, not least in its definition. Recent attempts to embrace its plurality – its creative as well as its destructive dimensions – have been staged at Karlsruhe and elsewhere, but this is the first such exhibition to concentrate on a very particularly British aspect of the subject, which has profoundly shaped the nature of our heritage. We acknowledge the artists who have deployed destruction in art, as well those artists and institutions whose work has been attacked. To all those who have been ready to help us explore this delicate history, with loans that may be seen rarely in this kind of context, or which resonate differently here, we are profoundly grateful.

This exhibition has been made possible by the provision of insurance through the Government Indemnity Scheme. Tate Britain would like to thank HM Government for providing Government Indemnity and the Department for Culture, Media and Sport and Arts Council England for arranging the indemnity.

PENELOPE CURTIS
Director, Tate Britain

ACKNOWLEDGEMENTS

Iconoclasm is a wide and far-reaching subject and to explore 500 years of contentious objects and their historical contexts requires the expertise of more than two curators. Many individuals – more than can be named here – have willingly shared their knowledge and goodwill, directing us to crucial material which otherwise we might have missed. To all of them we extend infinite thanks.

This exhibition would not have been possible without the exceptional generosity of our lenders. We are especially grateful to the Master and Members of the Worshipful Company of Mercers who have lent for the first time the statue of the Dead Christ. Glass has been removed from the windows of Canterbury Cathedral especially for the show, and other cathedrals and parish churches have trusted us with their unique and fragile objects. National and international institutions as well as private owners of broken fragments have responded with enthusiasm to loan requests which initially must have seemed strange and curious. We cannot name everyone individually, but we express gratitude to all of our lenders and all those involved with the loans. Jo Bartholomew, Susan Harrison, Jane Ruddell and Leonie Seliger deserve special thanks. In addition, we thank all of the artists and gallerists, especially those who informed particular stages of the exhibition, namely Jake and Dinos Chapman, Ivor Davies, Kate Davis, Michael Landy, Gustav Metzger, Lucy Skaer and Michael Wilkinson.

Several people have helped us to identify and locate suitable objects, and have provided vital information which has transformed our understanding of them. As well as colleagues at Tate and The Fruitmarket Gallery, we extend thanks to Paul Binski, Spike Bucklow, Fiona Bradley, Mary Clark, John Crook, Richard Fawcett, Stephen Feeke, Ben Jones, Adrian Le Harivel, Todd Longstaffe-Gowan, Julian Luxford, Matthew Power, Kiffy Stainer-Hutchins, Brandon Taylor, Pauline Plummer, Richard Williams, Paul Williamson and Lucy Wrapson. In stimulating meetings in London and Indiana, AHRC Iconoclasms Network members articulated and formulated insights into iconoclasm which significantly shaped our approach, and extended our understanding. The catalogue authors contributed to building a narrative about iconoclasm and Britain over the centuries. We thank all of these individuals.

The project team at Tate Britain has involved many contributors from beginning to end. Thanks go to Sofia Karamani, Lena Mohamed, Jenny Powell and Philippa Simpson; to Andrew Wilson, whose role in shaping the Destruction in Art section was invaluable; to Ruth Kenny, who has approached a complex project with intelligence and focus. At Tate Britain we thank Gerry Alabone, Jennifer Batchelor, Ricky Bowtell, Rachel Crome, Dan Crompton, Sionaigh Durrant, Claartje van Haaften, Adrian Glew, Juleigh Gordon-Orr, Geoff Hoskins, Carolyn Kerr, Nigel Llewellyn, Hans Biorn Lian, Andy Shiel, Sam Taylor, Liam Tebbs and Natasha Walker; in Tate Publishing, Rebecca Fortey, Miranda Harrison, Bill Jones, Miriam Perez and Johanna Stephenson; for his catalogue design Philip Lewis; and for the exhibition design Biba Dow, Alun Jones and Markus Nurkkala of Dow Jones Architects, and Joseph Kohlmaier and Stefan Kraus of Polimekanos.

Iconoclasm's questions are indeed endless and all consuming; family and friends have been especially forbearing over the past two years. To them we owe ultimate thanks.

TABITHA BARBER AND STACY BOLDRICK

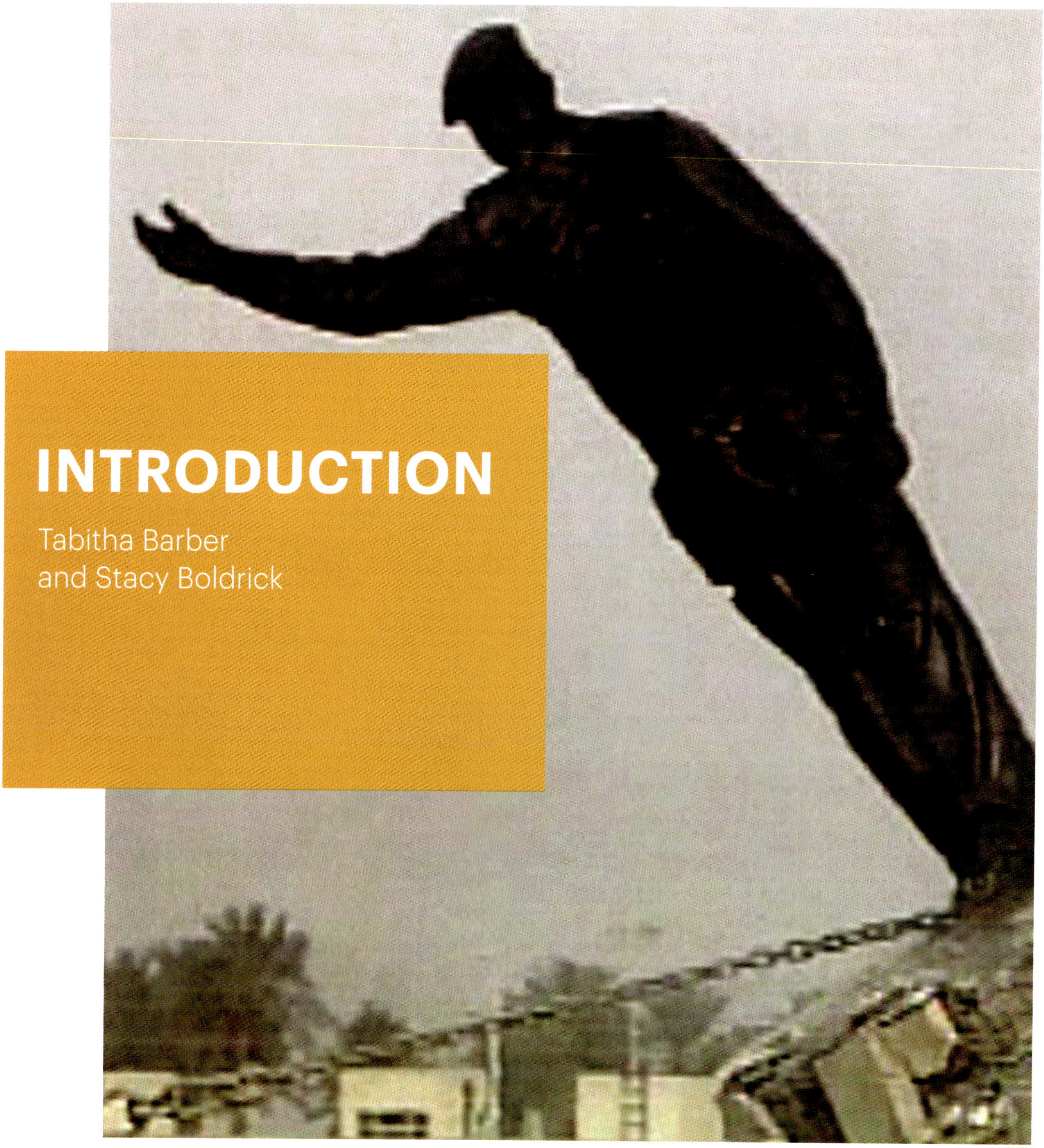

INTRODUCTION

Tabitha Barber
and Stacy Boldrick

On 29 March 2003 BBC News reported the destruction by British troops of two monuments to Saddam Hussein in Basra, southern Iraq. One of them was a 6m-high black cast-iron statue showing the Iraqi leader in a greatcoat with his right arm raised in the air. 'It just sort of crumpled', said the tank commander, 'there was a big flash and sparks everywhere and it disappeared, it was gone. I wish it was the real thing.' This deliberate action, aimed at striking a 'psychological blow' at the dictator's supporters, is an instance of modern-day iconoclasm, or image breaking. Like the famous toppling of Saddam Hussein's statue in Baghdad, an event that most people can vividly bring to mind, the action was purposeful, calculated and symbolic and the reason for it understood. Such actions, and the motivations of iconoclasts – what stimulates and drives the impulse to destroy, deface and break (and in the process remake) images – are the concerns of this present survey.

Iconoclasm is a word with many meanings and its application can be enormous in scope. The word 'iconoclastic', meaning revolutionary or anti-establishment, is now so ubiquitous that it has become more mainstream than groundbreaking. Iconoclasm can be literally understood, however, as 'image breaking', from icon (Greek *eikon* or image), and clasm (from *klastes*, literally breaker). It is this definition – iconoclasm as an act of physical destruction – that informs this study, and which is applied to attacks on images in a British context. Part of all cultures, iconoclasm is a global phenomenon with a long history, but this survey is the first to focus on British iconoclasm stretching over nearly five hundred years. Iconoclasm in Britain is most commonly understood in the context of attacks on religious art during the Reformation. Here, iconoclasm and its definition have been expanded to cover both religious and secular forms of actions against images, ranging from the sixteenth century to the present day. One of the aims of this survey is to demonstrate that iconoclasm is not just a feature of Britain's historical past but is an ongoing reality, and that the methods and motives of iconoclasts, and the meanings of their actions, have many parallels across the centuries.

The three sections of this book – Religion, Politics and Aesthetics – and the subsections and specific case histories within them explore how religious, political and aesthetic controversy can become arenas for assaults on art. They explore the sixteenth-century state-administered prohibition of old ways of worship and the aim to purge both churches and minds of the sin of idolatry; the iconoclastic zeal of seventeenth-century Puritan reformers, whose violent actions were enshrined in legislation; the symbolic statue-breaking that is an aspect of political difference and which accompanies political change; the targeted attacks on cultural heritage by the Suffragettes at the beginning of the twentieth century; and attacks on art by individuals stimulated by a moral or aesthetic outrage. Finally, focus shifts to look at the actions of artists themselves: the idea of destruction as creation explored by artists in the Destruction in Art Symposium in 1966; and the contemporary use of destruction to transform images and materials.

Iconoclasm is not random, but embodies conflict and has a purpose and an intention. Destruction without a rationale is not necessarily iconoclasm. By looking at particular moments in history, we can see instead that each iconoclastic act has a motive, a strategy and a goal, and very often, official approval. The motivations of iconoclasts arise out of specific historical contexts, but their actions are commonly aimed against images that have symbolic value – that represent the ruling authority or prevailing viewpoint that they wish to challenge, whether

1
The Dead Christ *c.*1500–20 (detail)
Limestone
197 × 68.6
The Mercers' Company, London

2
View of Sir Francis Chantrey's 1837 statue of the Duke of Sutherland
Ben Bhraggie, Sutherland, Highlands of Scotland

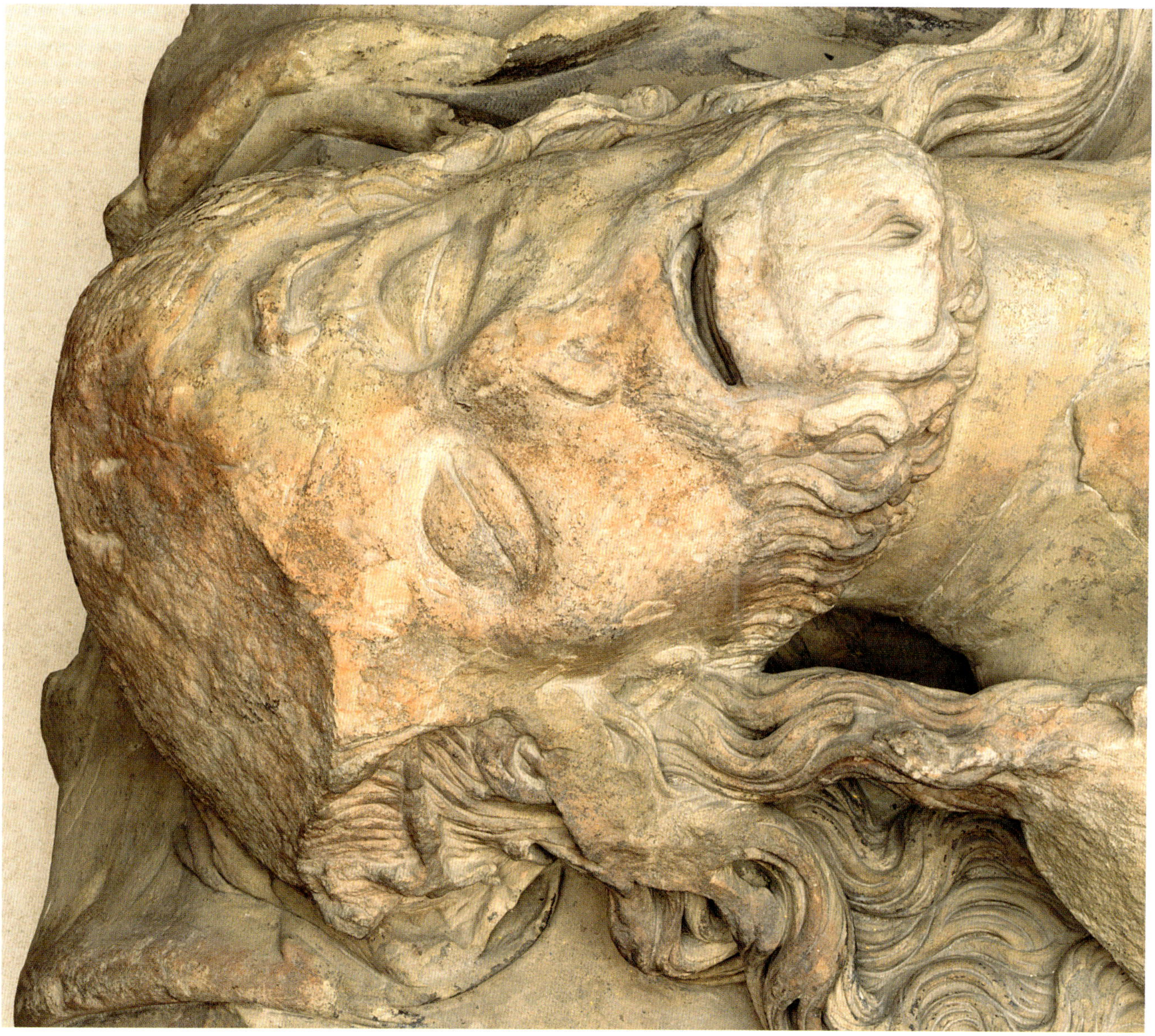

it be the Church of Rome or figures of British rule in Dublin.

This survey, which accompanies an exhibition, necessarily focuses on the material remains of iconoclasm, predominantly fragments. It contends that they themselves have power. Through iconoclasm's various actions – scratching, defacing, obliterating, relocating, beheading, spitting or burning – an object is taken from its original context and is transformed, and becomes instead symbolic of the act of iconoclasm, or what it was that the iconoclast intended to remove. Iconoclasm, however, can also occupy the realm of words and ideas. While the exhibition focuses on the tangible remains of objects that have been physically attacked, here we can discuss more widely the history of symbolic, verbal vitriol that plays a substantial role.

The *Dead Christ* (pp 68–9), a major loan to the exhibition and an incredible survivor of pre-Reformation sculpture, exemplifies the immense power and hold over people that images could, and still can, possess. It was this power that reformers found dangerous and wished to eradicate. It is a harrowing portrayal of Christ removed from the cross, lying with the visible signs of rigor mortis, his mouth slightly ajar, a thorn penetrating his brow and with blood flowing from his wounds. Confronted by it today, its sensual pull and emotional impact are still such that the dreadful spectre of idolatry – confusion between the real and the represented, or the worship of an image instead of God – is near enough to be imagined. The compulsive need to brutally remove the limbs (the symbols of his wounds) and crown of thorns can be understood.

Similarly, one can understand the discontent created by the colossal statue of the Duke of Sutherland, which stands 100ft tall on top of Ben

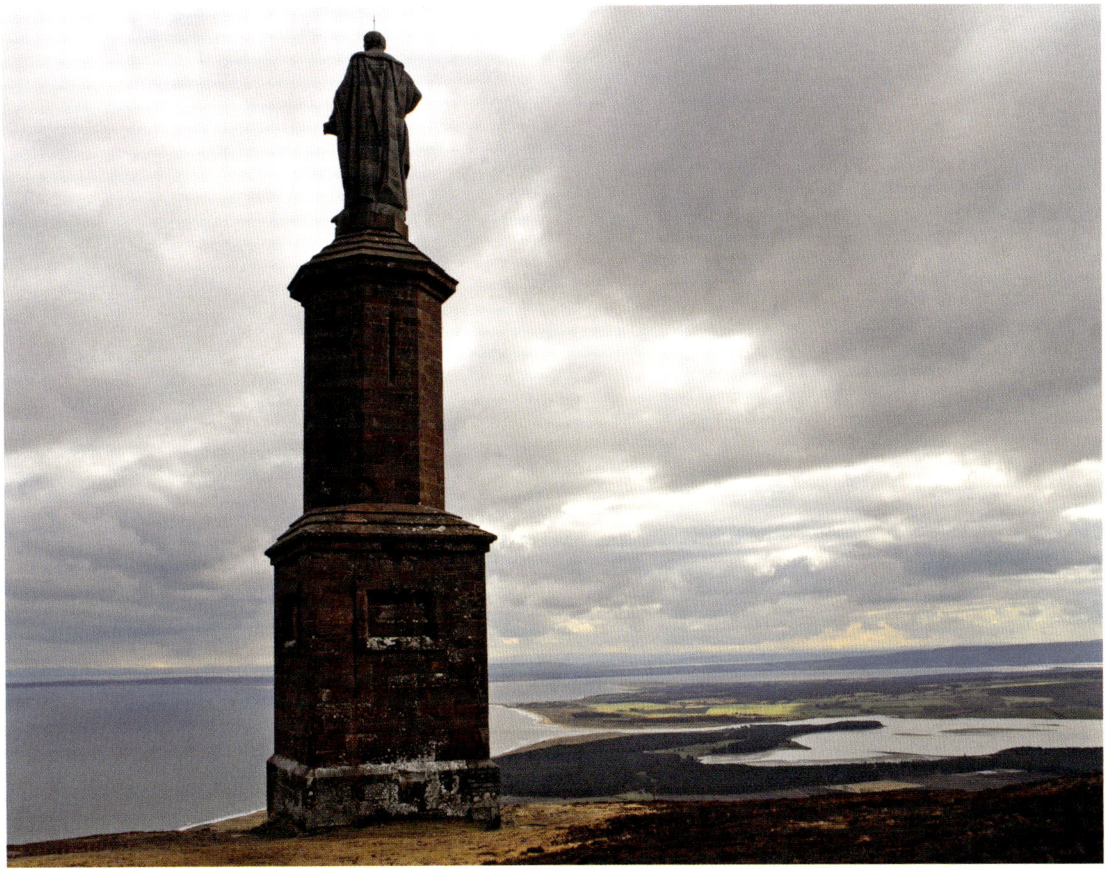

Bhraggie in Golspie, east Sutherland (ill.2). Through its sheer size, audacious imposition of itself on the landscape and desire to be respected, this nineteenth-century monument still has the capacity to provoke. Representing a figure closely associated with the Highland Clearances, attempts at its toppling and calls for its blowing up are active today. In *The Independent* (9 October 1994) it was imagined in a fragmented state, its pieces lying scattered in the heather as a symbolic statement against the man it represents. That contested historical figures continue to prompt action against their images (long after their death) is further illustrated by how Prince Frederick Duleep Singh (1886–1926) treated his portrait of Oliver Cromwell (ill.3). A monarchist with romantic Jacobite sympathies, Duleep Singh hung the portrait upside down in his gallery of royal portraits at Blo Norton Hall, Norfolk. A humorous yet clear mark of disrespect, by inverting it he turned it from a portrait that commemorated Cromwell into one that dishonoured him.

One example of aesthetic iconoclasm is the splashing of dye on Carl Andre's sculpture *Equivalent VIII* 1966, eventually known as 'The Bricks'. Ridicule and anger were directed at the sculpture's ordinary materials, lack of craftsmanship and its low cost and high price, which were a prelude to the physical attack during an economic slump. It became a target for the press and the taxpaying public, dissatisfied with the government-funded purchase of what seemed to be 120 bricks rather than a work of art. Verbal vitriol and misunderstanding led to the physical attack on *Equivalent VIII* and it became an icon for those with contempt for contemporary art.

Iconoclastic acts are often talked about in dramatic and traumatic terms. They are outrages, abuses and assaults, and can indeed be violations of works of art, but iconoclasm is not only that. Iconoclasts largely understand the object they are

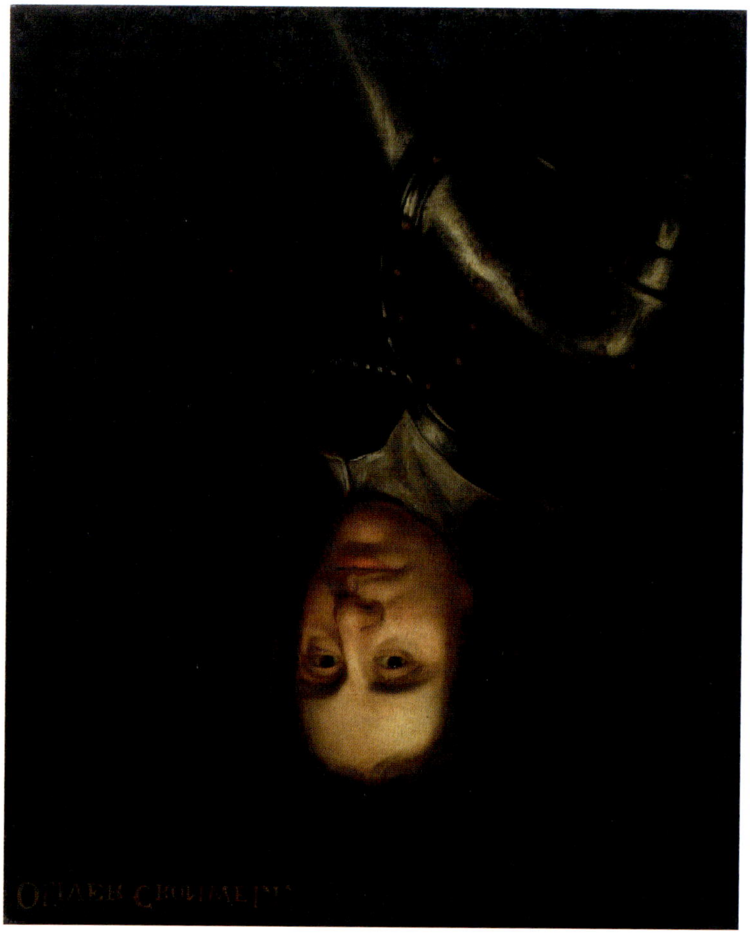

3
British School
Oliver Cromwell, 17th century
Oil paint on canvas
75 × 62
Inverness Museum and Art Gallery

Formerly in the collection at Blo Norton Hall, Norfolk, the portrait was hung upside down in the 19th century as a monarchist protest

attacking and what it represents, and their actions are strategic and rational, although acts can appear mindless when rationales are not clearly expressed. While some iconoclastic acts are violent, others are subversive and playful. Iconoclasm can also be carefully administered in an attempt to destroy the offending elements without harming the precious and valuable ones. In contemporary art today, iconoclasm is exploratory and inquisitive in nature, critically re-evaluating and reconfiguring the work. This survey looks at the material evidence for iconoclasm and its intentions, actions and remains. It is asking questions about when, how and why it was done, and also who did it.

Iconoclasm, and iconoclastic motives, can be greatly misunderstood because the historical motive for destruction is lost and forgotten. Museum labels can omit references to damage, and conservation can expertly erase from view traces of past harm. This survey, through its narratives of destruction, highlights the significance to the history of an object its story of dispute and attack, and also the importance of the specific circumstances behind that action. We hope to confound conventional expectations of iconoclasm – thinking of it as violent, aggressive and thoughtless – and to look again at the contested relationship of art and material objects. Iconoclasm is a coming together of art, politics and social history. Art, as symbol, will always attract conflict, for today's admired icons can readily become tomorrow's terrible idols. The work of iconoclasm is never finished; iconoclasm never ends.

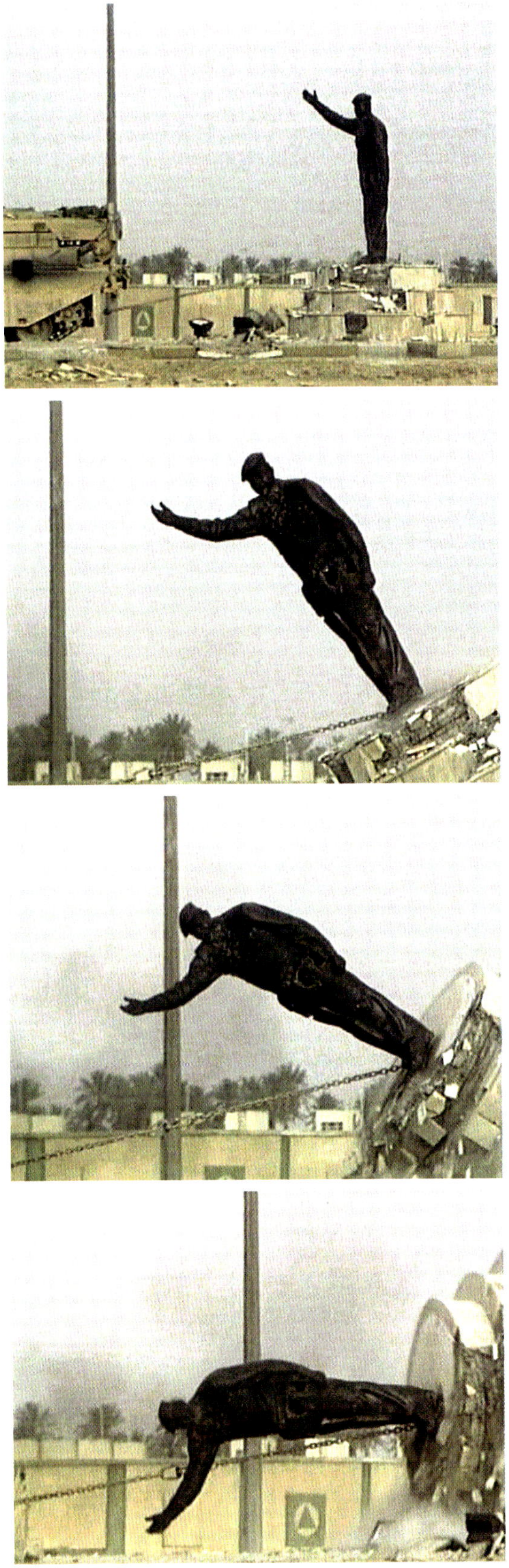

4
Video grabs showing British forces using a tank to topple a statue of Saddam Hussein on the outskirts of Basra, southern Iraq, 5 April 2003

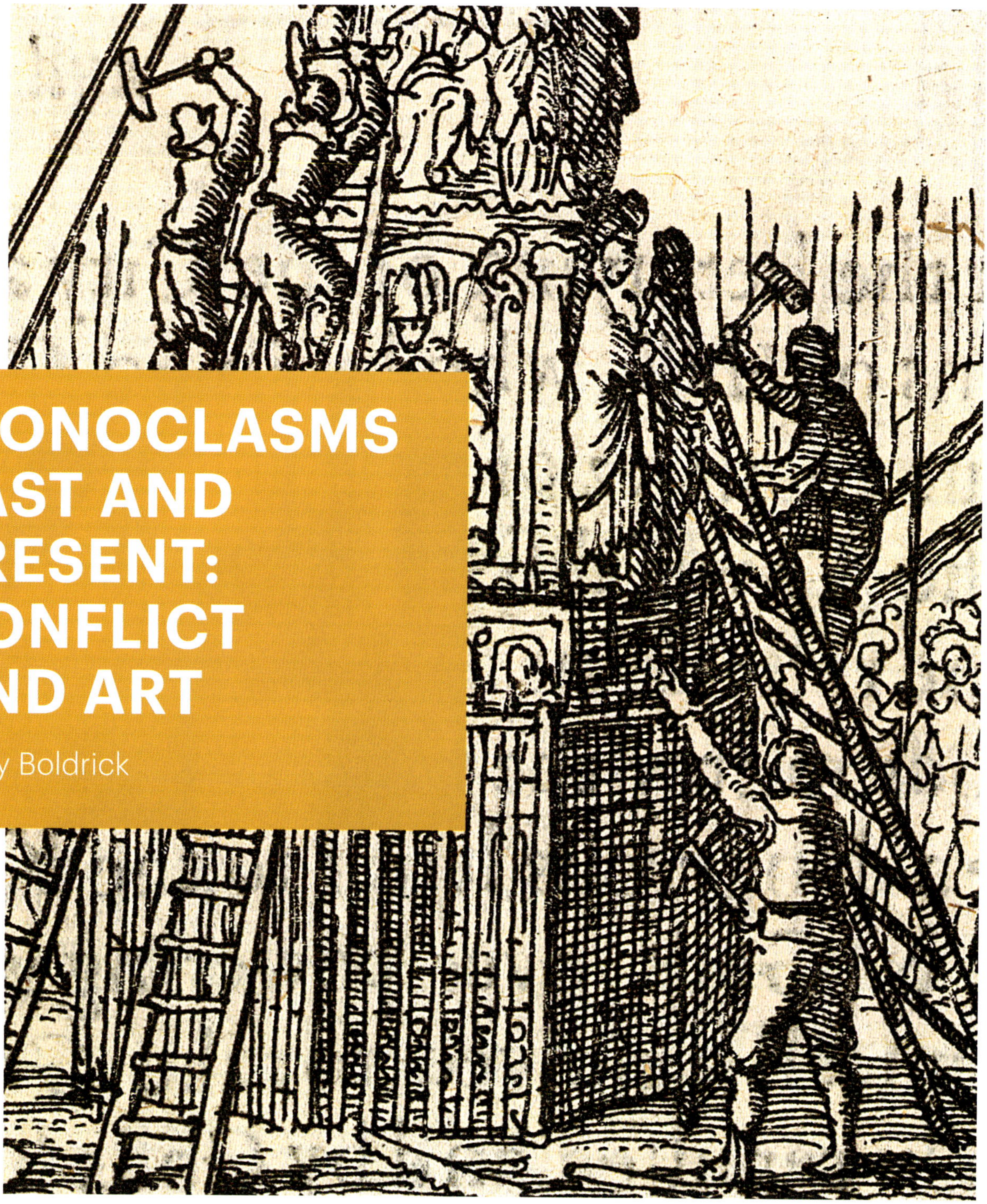

ICONOCLASMS PAST AND PRESENT: CONFLICT AND ART

Stacy Boldrick

[W]hen students scoff at the idea of a magical relation between a picture and what it represents, ask them to take a photograph of their mother and cut out the eyes.[1]

Iconoclasm is always an acknowledgement of the power of the image.[2]

Images and art objects invariably elicit positive and negative reactions. From monumental statues to religious sculptures, from coins to painted portraits, images have attracted acts of veneration as well as desecration and degradation, many of them physical, their handling ranging in degrees and forms, including stroking, striking, slicing, smashing, slashing, spitting, obliterating, kissing, rubbing, scratching, counter-stamping, beheading, burying, dismembering, dismantling, toppling, inverting, bending, hiding, blocking out, writing upon, blowing up, marking, painting, whitewashing, erasing, improving, removing and recycling. Strong beliefs can unleash radical actions. Each engagement with an image or art object arises out of a unique set of circumstances and historical contexts, but they often occur when representations elide with the things they represent: when boundaries between image and subject or idea blur in the viewer's mind, not as a result of confusion that the image might actually be alive, but as a result of belief, out of a dedication to what seems to the individual to be a greater purpose.[3]

There are many reasons why images and works of art are, or were, struck or smashed. Firstly, it is in the nature of certain pieces to elicit significant, intense responses. The most powerful images and works of art resonate with an array of meanings and can never be completely understood, contained or controlled because the experience of looking at an image for any length of time is strange: variable, unfixable and inconsistent.[4] Historically, physical engagements with artworks have come from isolated individuals as well as from political regimes – from below or above, outside or within positions of power – as a way of controlling not only images, but also the things they represent; breaking images can begin a process of forgetting about those things. The *Virgin Mary Feeding the Christ Child (Maria Lactans)* c.1520 is one of several surviving fragments from two or three alabaster altarpieces in Whittlesford parish church smashed during the reign of Edward VI (1547–53) because they signified an 'old' religion and an 'old' regime (ill.44).[5] Found in the south chancel wall in the late nineteenth century, the shattered fragments represent a single incident from a period of iconoclasm orchestrated from above: the authorised annihilation of almost all medieval religious sculpture in England over the course of the Reformation.[6] By contrast, a lead fragment from an equestrian monument of King George III (ill.77) remains as an example of iconoclasm 'from below', when New Yorkers and George Washington's troops toppled the monument in 1776, an exultant response to the announcement of independence from Great Britain, an act of protest and revolt.[7] From above or below, both of these acts fractured sculptures, leaving behind ruins and traces of their initial states.[8]

The survival of these remains, valued as precious historic relics, symbolic trophies or spoils of war, expresses desires to preserve either the image or the act of destruction, or to reclaim the materials for a new context.[9] Thus iconoclasm's subjects encompass not only the destruction of images but also the dynamics of their contestation and survival – they are critical moments in the lives of the objects themselves.[10] Iconoclasm helps us to understand art, or the power of art, by showing us a range and depth of physical responses which individuals, groups or regimes have applied to inanimate things throughout history, as an expression of critical ideas. Such responses are, according to W.J.T. Mitchell, 'creative destructions' in which 'a secondary image of defacement or annihilation is created at the same moment that the "target" image is attacked'.[11] The icons of iconoclasm are many and varied, ranging from the ruins of Fountains Abbey, the Bamiyan Buddhas, Stari Most (the Old Bridge at Mostar) and the World Trade Center Towers to Robert Rauschenberg's *Erased de Kooning Drawing*, Jamie Reid's design for the album cover of the Sex Pistols' *God Save the Queen* (ill.5) and the reworked Goya etchings of Jake and Dinos Chapman (p.166). The spontaneous defacement of the Winston Churchill monument in London's Parliament Square during the anti-capitalist May Day demonstrations in 2000 was unplanned, but the image of the attacked statue has come to represent the protests and even anti-capitalism itself (ill.6).[12]

Contested ownership or control over important images can make them iconoclastic targets. Motivations for breaking images are multifarious and frequently very specific or impossible to understand fully.[13] When a social group or regime commits an act of iconoclasm, a broad rationale may be institutionalised and shared by many, but seldom by all members of an organisation or nation. The viewer may understand that the image or object is not alive but nevertheless projects on to it a sense of animism associated with the person or abstract idea it represents. These complex passions for precious objects are addressed in Charles Baudelaire's celebrated perspective on the determined child's quest for 'the soul of the toy' – the thing that gives a treasured object a special presence, a life of its own – and the child's need to take it apart and destroy it in the process. Entangled feelings of curiosity, fear, wonder, love and hatred can inform each act of iconoclasm.

Artworks – whether abstract or figurative – are often personified when wilful, unlawful damage occurs: the work is 'assaulted' or 'attacked'. Anthropomorphism, the association of inanimate objects with human bodies, is a longstanding reflex or habituation, understandable and most often unconsciously felt.[14] Again, the author or viewer understands that such objects are not alive, but

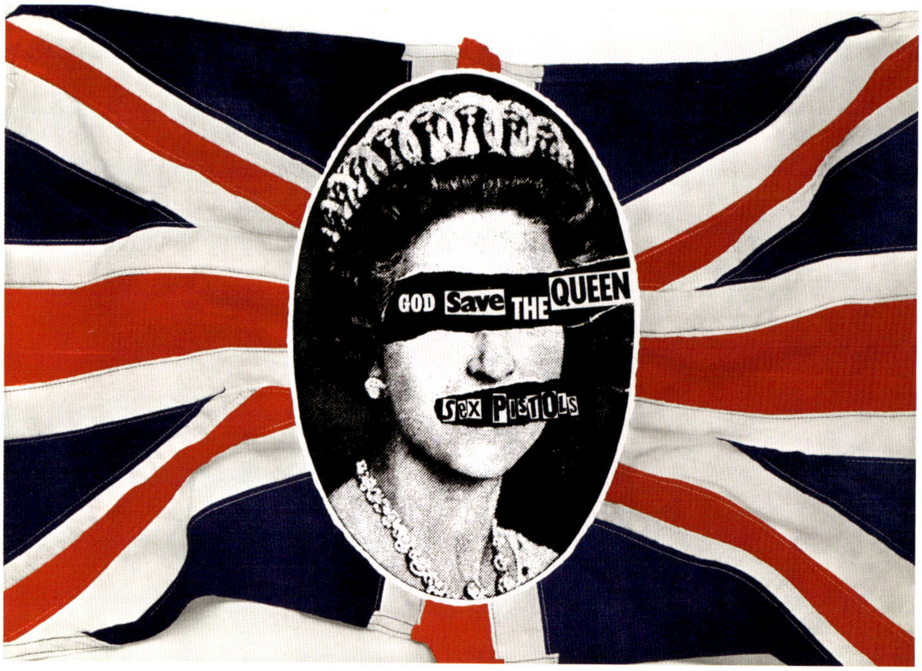

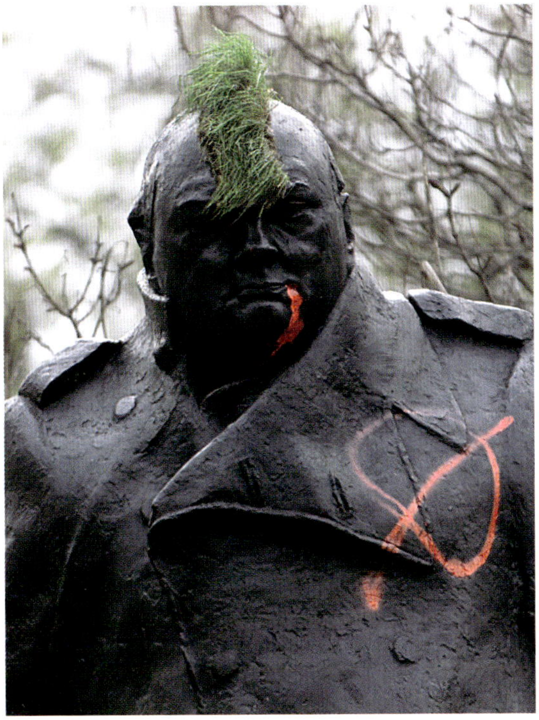

nevertheless refers to them as if they were. When works of art are reused for other purposes they are often described as being cannibalised or, when groups of artworks are subjected to widespread destruction, the action may be compared to a cull or even a holocaust; when the group is shipped away, it is a diaspora.[15] Motivations for individual actions against art often involve personification, as in the case of László Szilvassy's outrage at Reg Butler's 'reduction' of *The Unknown Political Prisoner* to 'scrap metal' (ill.100).[16] By contrast, when Mary Richardson damaged *The Rokeby Venus* as a form of protest against the imprisonment of Emmeline Pankhurst (ill.96), she emphasised the fact that she was striking an inanimate representation in order to save the living Pankhurst from being tortured in prison.[17]

In many cases art objects have been subjected to the same forms of physical punishment as people: in England and throughout sixteenth- and seventeenth-century Europe, acts of systematic abuse and degradation such as mutilation, the severing of heads and hands, dismemberment, burial and immersion in water were applied to human and sculptural bodies.[18] Two frequently cited dramatic examples of the destruction of personified art objects include the Boxley Rood and the Cheapside Cross (ill.7). A rood, a crucifix with a sculpture of Christ located in the chancel and elevated on a wooden beam, was the most important large-scale sculptural focal point of any parish church in the Middle Ages. In 1538, in the wake of the injunction against the abuse of images, the rood from the Cistercian house of Boxley in Kent, a sculpture of Christ made of paper, cloth and wood with movable parts (eyes, lower lip and arms), was denounced for being a puppet manipulated by 'engines'. It was taken down and publicly broken by Bishop Hilsey at the pulpit of Paul's Cross in London; he gave it to 'the rude people and boyes' who 'brake the said image in peeces, so that they left not one peece whole'.[19] In 1643 the Cheapside Cross was actually placed under arrest and punished, eventually to be dismantled.[20] Each of these acts of destruction generated fiercely divided reactions of desperate loss or bullish triumph from different groups who felt either affection for and attachment to the objects, or fear, distrust and hatred of them.

In the present survey, 'image breaking' is shorthand for any action that substantially changes an art object's physical integrity. The power of an image can be broken in many ways, from barely noticeable damage or markings to complete obliteration. The significance of image breaking also varies. In each case it is a transformation of some form of power – an implication of degradation or desecration, or a positive sign signalling transition or transformation, or at times a bit of both. Long before the Reformation

5
Jamie Reid (b.1947)
God Save the Queen 1977
Printed poster

6
Statue of Winston Churchill by Ivor Roberts-Jones, Parliament Square, London, defaced on 1 May 2000

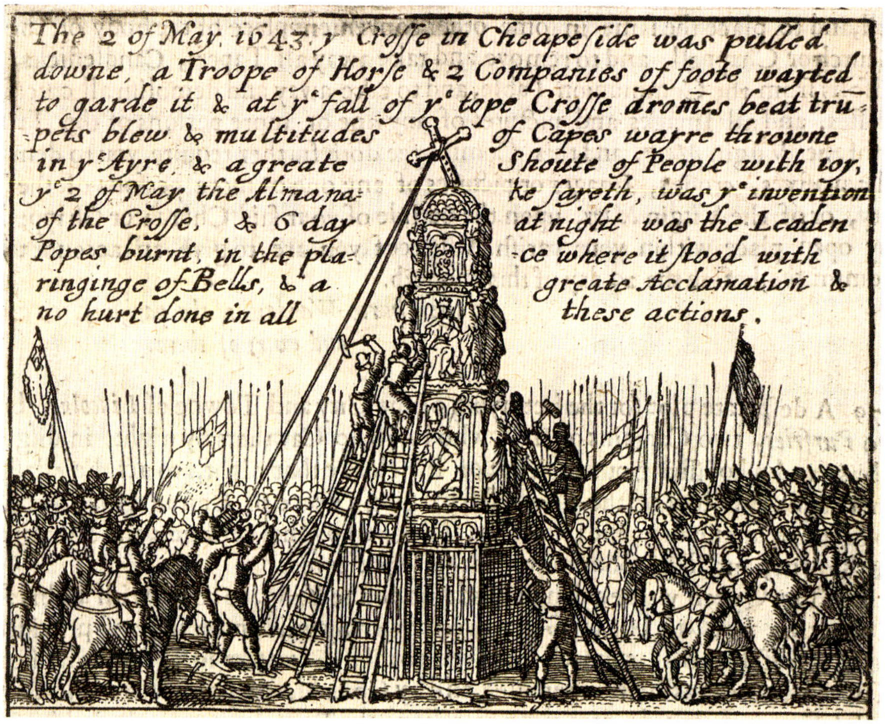

in Britain, many practices involved changing the form and function of symbolic objects, including high-status artefacts such as crosses that were crumpled (as with the Folded Cross from the Staffordshire Hoard from c.650–700) and stall plates that were broken in two, and more common objects such as coins and pilgrim badges that were bent.[21] Breaking medieval seals destroyed their authenticating power after the owner's death.[22] Damaging symbolic objects could (and still can) signify the ending of an associated person's status, power, or the end of their life, or often it was simply a way of ridding someone of something that was no longer powerful or useful, or legal, in its original form. All such forms of breaking changed the original meaning of the object.[23] In some instances certain forms of official iconoclasm, such as the policies imposed under the Dissolution, demanded that specific actions and their results be documented and described: iconoclasm was administered in order to identify, sort and value materials in the salvage operation as part of the calculation of the total value of each dissolved monastery.[24]

The works included in this survey display visible signs of iconoclasm, from scratching, whitewashing and erasing to recycling and toppling. Certain forms of iconoclasm are invisible – removing and hiding, burying and covering, or other forms of reversible change – and, since they do not mark the object with permanent visible or material effects, are difficult to study and display.[25] Much of the material that survived the Scottish Reformation may have been hidden, including the Fetternear Banner from 1520, the only medieval religious banner to survive in Scotland, resplendent with images of the bleeding body of Christ and the signs of the Passion. Made

7
Probably W. Hollar (1607–77)
The pulling down of the cross in Cheapside, London
Engraving from John Vicars, *True Information of the Beginning and Cause of all our troubles*, 1648–9
The British Library

for the Confraternity of the Holy Blood based in St Giles Collegiate Chapel in Edinburgh (now St Giles Cathedral), it was never completed and was hidden when the edicts of the Reformation came into force.[26] Many other religious objects and images survived in this way.

The remains of actions such as burial, burning and dismantling are also often invisible when evidence of the action is erased through conservation or when the completion of the action leaves either unidentifiable fragments or no material remains whatsoever.[27] This survey explores burning in the context of more recent works. The burial of precious symbolic things, broken or intact, is a longstanding practice:[28] the Folded Cross from the Staffordshire Hoard may have been buried either by non-Christians, intending to disempower the objects in the hoard or the ruler who owned them, or by Christians wishing to honour someone or something.[29] Burial inside a church or churchyard – within a wall or under the ground – or within any sacred site is an action that can signify rescue, reuse or both; it is often impossible to confirm which. It may seem likely that the Whittlesford fragments were walled up in order to save or protect them but, like the Winchester fragments, they also may have been reused as building material.[30]

Iconoclasm in Britain did not start with the Reformation; forms of image breaking have always accompanied image making. Iconoclastic policies related to longstanding debates about the place of religious images in devotional practice and the appropriate use of the wealth of the Church. The biblical commandment against idolatry in Exodus 20:4–5, one of many biblical references to idolatry, prohibits the making and worshipping of images: 'Thou shalt not make to thyself a graven thing nor the likeness of any thing that is in heaven above, or in the earth beneath, nor of those things that are in the waters under the earth. Thou shalt not adore them, nor serve them [...].'[31] Theologians from Gregory the Great to Bernard of Clairvaux, as indeed in our own time, addressed the dangers of images as idols, and emphasised the appropriate use of images – to venerate or worship the religious personage rather than his or her material representation.[32] By the later Middle Ages the precise nature of the relationship between the viewer and religious imagery was further contested because of the proliferation of devotional offerings, images and objects, and the 'overt materiality' of these objects.[33] Painted stone and wooden sculptures, reliquaries, textiles and other objects embellished with brightly coloured gemstones or gold drew attention to their materials. The profusion of opulent objects illuminated by candlelight gave them a spectacular presence that encouraged and intensified devotional experience for many viewers, but for heretical groups such as the Lollards and, later, during the Reformation, these artefacts were disturbing and became targets of derision.[34]

While the significance of the Lollards to the Reformation is debatable, they had an undoubted role in the longer history of iconoclasm in Britain.[35] Inspired by John Wycliffe in England in the fourteenth century, the movement proposed reforms to quash the problematic aspects of material devotion to images. Although there was no coordinated campaign to destroy all religious images, the Lollards wrote against their status as cultic objects and occasionally removed them, calling them 'dead images', 'dead stones and rotten sticks' and distancing them from the saints or holy figures they represented: 'When men give not alms to poor needy men, but to dead images ... they rob poor men of their due portion ... they rob Jesus Christ...'.[36] Lollard iconoclasm took the form of the physical removal of images, 'ritual disproof': testing their sacred powers, then destroying them.

Although some Lollard texts supported the simplest action, removal of the image or object, many recommended burning, beheading or dismembering as ways of disproving a statue's vivacity, manifested either in miraculous powers or human attributes.[37]

By referring to religious sculptures as 'dead images' the Lollards sought to exterminate them with words – and in some cases with deeds. By the later Middle Ages, certain representations of Christ, such as the Boxley Rood mentioned above, were animated, given movable arms, heads, eyes, lips and even the power of speech.[38] In the 1380s the first recorded Lollard iconoclast, the chaplain William Smith, faced trial when he and a colleague beheaded a statue of Saint Catherine to see whether it could prove its divine powers by bleeding; they then used the wood as firewood for cooking. Another case from before 1441 involved the Lollard Hugh Knight 'smoking a beard' on a statue of the Virgin in Newport chapel, Devon, by holding a flame close to its face and addressing it: 'Mable, ware thy berde'.[39] The trial, punishment and mockery of such sculptural images can be understood as cruel and humorous in its subversion, but both instances are responses to conflicting devotional attitudes and practices, whereby sculptures are either focal points for devotion, or regarded as animate, vulnerable and powerful bodies.[40] Such stories can be understood in relation to anxieties around the 'circulation of material goods, or what we might call the vivacity of objects'.[41] The consumption, presentation and display of costly material offerings to religious images and sculptures at altars and shrines conflicted with the Lollards' ideals of the Church redistributing wealth to the poor and with the prohibition of idolatry.[42]

By the 1530s the Reformation was advancing across the Continent and pressures for the systematic destruction of images were growing in England. The first treatise on the destruction of images published in England was Martin Bucer's *Treatise declaring and showing ... that pictures and other images ... are in no wise to be suffered in the temples or churches* of 1535 (translated from the German by William Marshall and sent to Thomas Cromwell). As James Simpson notes, Bucer called for images to be destroyed with force, not 'softly and so tenderly handled' because of any sympathy the iconoclast might feel for the representation they were striking, as if the sculptures had 'wit and reason': the destruction needed to 'work according to the dictates of Scripture: "we oughte to breke them, yea, and that all to powder that they might never be made whole agayne nor be restored into so wycked an abuse".'[43] It is thought that Bucer's treatise, and others like it, contributed to the injunctions that followed.

Once forms of iconoclasm became 'official' or state-sanctioned in the 1530s under Henry VIII and Thomas Cromwell, they had widespread physical consequences. Initially the complete destruction of all religious images was not the primary aim of the reformers; rather, the idea was to control problematic attitudes to objects. Injunctions of 1538 prohibited many common forms of devotion: 'wandering to pilgrimages, offering of money, candles or tapers to images or relics, or kissing or licking the same, saying over a number of beads, not understood or minded on'.[44] The Dissolution of the Monasteries resulted in the dismantling and destruction of monastic buildings and associated shrines. These were accompanied by injunctions banning references to the Pope and images of Thomas Becket, and requiring that all offices, antiphons, and prayers in Becket's name should be 'erased and put out of books'. Some of the results of these policies – fragments from monasteries and shrines as well as altered manuscripts – are included in the present survey.[45]

From 1550 the edicts and policies of Edward VI and Elizabeth I were much more severe and focused: religious images were to be 'defaced and destroyed'; such comprehensive culls of religious images dramatically changed religious experience inside church buildings.[46] (Mary Tudor's attempts to restore Catholicism, shrines and the inclusion of images during her brief reign failed.) The pre- Reformation experience of religious ritual was corporeal, involving all the senses but particularly smell, sight, hearing and touch. Not only were focal points of devotion taken away or changed altogether and replaced by words, but the full sensory experience was gone.[47] Eventually, steps and rails – non-representational spatial elements that elevated and divided – were also swept away under William Dowsing and the Puritans; funeral monuments were also attacked.[48] This was a break with all of the senses, a breaking of the bodily experience of belief.

The long history, or rather individual histories comprising specific moments of iconoclasm in Britain are neither neatly consistent nor continuous. As Simpson suggests, iconoclasm 'is driven by a set of paradoxes: it wants to reinstate true history by subtracting accretions; it attempts to reinstate true history by an act of violence that is always anti-historical; by that anti-historical act it activates a new historical tradition'.[49] Two significant issues for iconoclasm that relate to many of the works in this survey are that of the paradoxical status of images and art objects as dead matter personified, and the idea that images and art objects are valued for and understood through their materiality. Describing works of art as dead, emphasising their lifelessness or extending their state into the realm of the rotting corpse is often is fundamental to the thinking behind iconoclastic acts. But the denial of vitality only surfaces when there is also some degree of fear that the image could be alive or that it has a degree of power.[50] References to dead images, and to death itself, resound throughout this book, although the referents operate within vastly different frameworks and their purposes are many and varied – from the Lollards' condemnation of dead images, to the ritual dismembering of public monuments, to John Stezaker's interest in 'image death' (ills 123, 124).[51]

Materiality, or the material elements that make up an artefact and the attitudes towards them, plays an important role in the destruction of a piece, either by initiating a response to it or informing an iconoclastic strategy or method, regardless of value.[52] The Destruction in Art Symposium artists argued for destruction in opposition to consumption (ill.108). Destructive practices are conventional for artists now: cutting up, marking on, painting over, blocking out, burning, dismantling, unspooling, the practice of 'doing something to' or 'undoing' an image or object. The destroyed material may be transformed into something else, or the work may be understood to be 'improved', rectified or even, as the contemporary artist Kate Davis puts it, 'healed'. Artists responding to materials as matter make unlikely transformations: a film or a video can become a sculpture, idealised portraits transmogrify into decomposing bodies, and changes and additions or subtractions can inform new aesthetic relationships. At the heart of materiality there may be an interest in a toppling of the idol of consumption, of the fetishised commodity status of the object, but there is also an interest in unsettling preconceptions about materials and in generating new perceptual experiences and new meanings. The remains of iconoclasm survive as relics, objects with the capacity to unfold before the viewer visions of past, present and future moments in time, glimpses of the strange dynamics between people and between people and things, and as evidence of their violent breaking and perpetual remaking.[53]

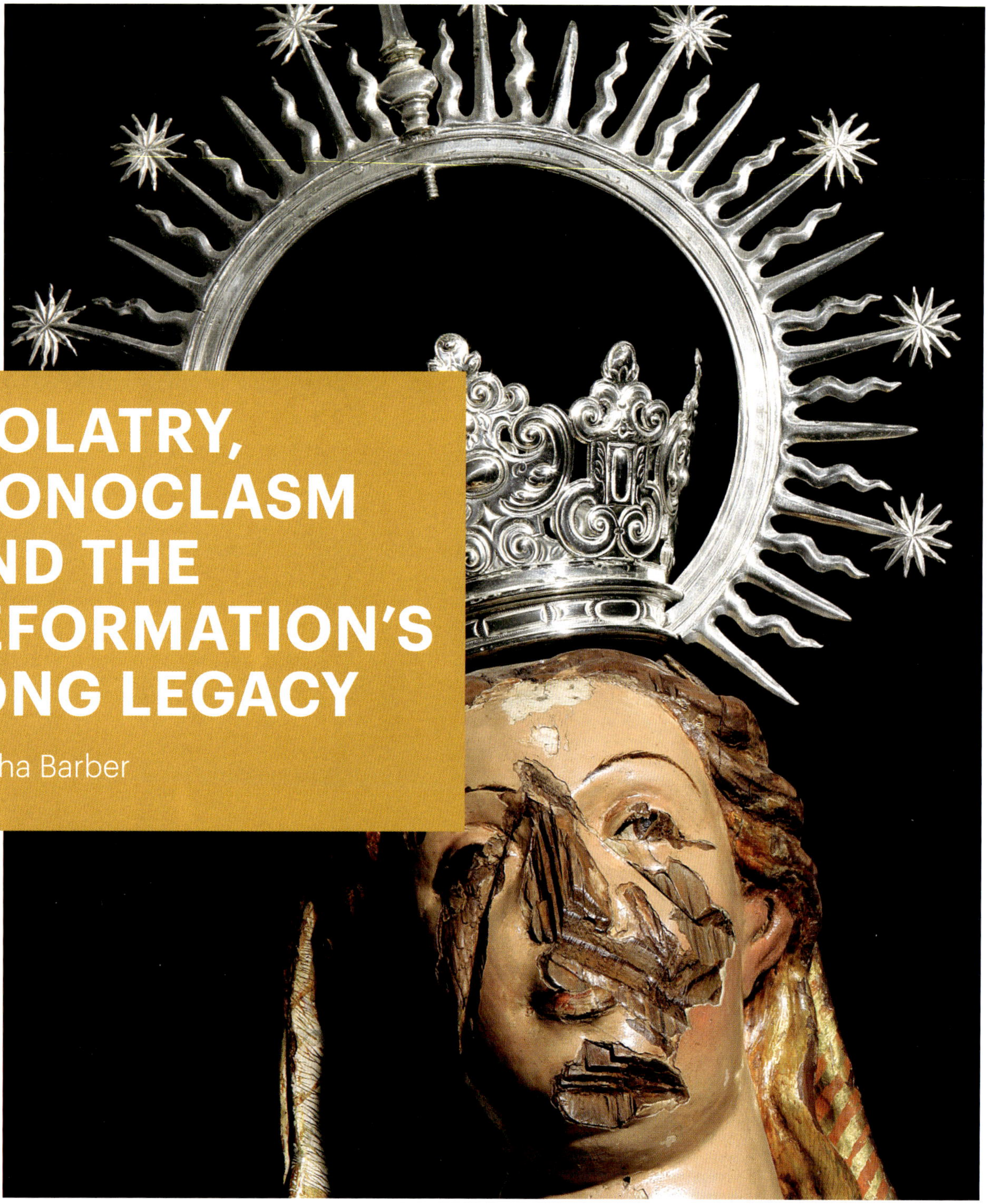

IDOLATRY, ICONOCLASM AND THE REFORMATION'S LONG LEGACY

Tabitha Barber

The Elizabethan *Homily Against Peril of Idolatry* 1563 forcefully underlined the inter-relationship between images and the abominable sin of idol-worship – the mistaken veneration of man-made images in place of the divine. 'Idolatry cannot possibly be separated from images', it stated. The two were cleaved together, 'as an unseperable accident, or as a shadow followeth the body, when the sun shineth'. As idolatry was to be 'abhorred and avoided', it continued, 'so are images (which cannot be long without idolatry) to be put away and destroyed'.[1] Iconoclasm therefore presupposed idolatry; and the notion that images were idolatrous was a strong motivating force for iconoclasts. As images enticed, lured and seduced people into false worship, so their power had to be neutralised and their sway and hold over the weak and credulous prevented.[2]

Elimination of the sin of idolatry was the goal of sixteenth- and seventeenth-century religious reformers. The Reformation made it 'the deadliest of sins'.[3] Strategies for eradicating, minimising and avoiding it not only characterised the Church of England's approach to images, but a terrible fear of idolatry became ingrained in the English, and British, consciousness. A deep-rooted anxiety about images, a suspicion of them and a need to justify their use and possession was an attitude that extended into subsequent centuries. While the Reformation and Puritan period of systematic, ideological religious iconoclasm is the concern of one third of this present survey, the cultural inheritance of that century – a particular sense of what it was to be Protestant, an accepted, almost visceral anti-Catholicism and a belief that idolatry was a 'Popish' sin – had a resonance that continued well beyond that time. Reformation tracts on the dangers of idolatry were read, the sophisticated, complex arguments both for and against images were used to inform fresh debates, and Reformation settlements on images – those that were allowed or proscribed – became the standard against which fresh disputes were judged. In the nineteenth century it was a fear that the Reformation was being undone that was at the forefront of the furious attacks on ritual revival. The spectre of idolatry was also applied to spheres beyond religion. Religious rhetoric was appropriated to make attacks on political figures more charged (false idols could be political as well as religious); and sensual abandonment to any thing of beauty, an unchecked response to its immoral allure, could be cast as a sinful transgression. That hundreds of years beyond the Reformation people's attitudes to images were still being shaped by the fear of idolatry shows, as Margaret Aston has remarked, 'how effectively reformers had done their work'.[4]

While iconoclasm can be seen as the natural conclusion to idolatry, the Protestant need to eradicate this sin did not necessarily result in a complete denial of the image. As Tara Hamling and Richard Williams have made clear, the Reformation period saw creative attempts to produce imagery that had been safely 're-formed'.[5] It was the wide range and difference of opinion concerning images that inflamed debate. Whilst radical iconophobes were virulently hostile to all images, and promoted instead the superiority of the word and the truth of the written scriptures, those with more tolerant views held that issues of site, use and the role of the viewer were important factors in ascertaining risk. The Elizabethan *Homily* was aimed against images in churches, while those in civic or private spaces, divorced from the context of worship and thus divested of power, were deemed to pose little or no danger.

Even within churches some argued that historical narratives had an educative role. Divergent opinion thus stoked controversy, and continued to do so well into the second half of the seventeenth century and beyond. Arguments over the correct use of images remained current and heated, and prompted action to be taken against them. Images continued to be contested, attacked (physically and verbally), removed or avoided altogether. In 1681, for example, the clergy and churchwardens at All Hallows-by-the-Tower were accused of 'suffering the graven image of St Michael to stand and remain undestroyed over the Communion Table, to the great danger of Introducing Idolatry and Superstitious worship'. Edmund Sherman, the leading churchwarden, removed the 'great, carved, gilded image ... with great spreading wings', dismantled it and burnt it in the vestry, and a war of words, in pamphlet form, unfolded.[6] In 1758 a similar controversy erupted at St Margaret's, Westminster, over the installation of a stained-glass window depicting the Crucifixion. Branded superstitious by detractors, it was argued that it contravened Edward VI's 1549 'Act for the abolishing and putting away of divers Books and Images', the major principles of which had been accepted in the 1662 Act of Uniformity and which continued to set the parameters for defining what was permissible and what could tend to superstition and idolatry until the middle of the nineteenth century.[7] A tract in defence of the St Margaret's window, *The Ornament of Churches Considered* 1761, used the language and reasoning of the Elizabethan *Homily* (which said 'the process of a story' was not as dangerous as 'one dumb image ... standing by itself') to set out a positive case for historical narratives.[8] Reformation settlements on images thus provided the framework to judge new ones; and new arguments for images were conceived as a continuation of the intellectual debates of the past.

Arguments for religious paintings as art, rather than symbols of religion, had been made since the sixteenth century. Their placement in neutral, secular surroundings minimised the risk of idolatry; and an associated argument held that it was not the image that was at fault, but the eye of the beholder that created an idol. Clare Haynes has shown how by the eighteenth century the seemingly incompatible roles of religious paintings – symbols of idolatry or works of art – were rationalised by art theorists by championing people's ability to judge properly. Jonathan Richardson thought it the 'glory of the Reformation' that men had been able to 'resume their rights as rational creatures'; and Horace Walpole thought that 'in the enlightened liberty of an English picture gallery' the individual's rational, Protestant 'strength of reasoning' was able to divorce the idolatrous 'fable' of the picture from an admiration of the artist's skill.[9]

The association between art and idolatrous sin was difficult to dislodge, however. Art's aesthetic power to transport and sensually overwhelm, thus throwing the spectator into the role of helpless idolator, is vividly evoked in Charles Kingsley's novel *Alton Locke* 1850. On a visit to Dulwich Picture Gallery, Kingsley's character at first hesitates to enter as the 'narrow dullness' of his puritan inheritance has taught him that pictures, 'above all foreign ones', were 'vile Popish and Pagan vanities'. To visit a picture gallery was in itself an act of moral, sinful trespass. Inside, confronted by Guido Reni's *St Sebastian*, he stands transfixed, transported and moved to tears by the emotional power of the painting. Looking back on the incident, he has learnt to understand, he says, 'how the idolatry of painted saints could arise in minds even of the most educated', but it is rational discipline, 'the strength of Englishmen', that controls people and pulls them back.[10]

The above passage demonstrates how deeply embedded the notion of idolatry as a Roman Catholic sin had become. Since the sixteenth century a pronounced anti-Catholicism had characterised denouncements and criticisms of images. Images were at fault for being 'popish' and for encouraging 'popery'. For Sherman, the All Hallows St Michael was 'an abominable badge of superstition' and superstition itself 'of kin to Popery'. The window at St Margaret's was 'downright Popery, if not blasphemy', and in 1773 Bishop Terrick rejected (or avoided) paintings for St Paul's Cathedral on the grounds that it would be opening the doors to popery.[11] In 1826 Benjamin West's *The Angels Announcing to the Shepherds the Birth of Our Saviour*, installed only nine years previously, was removed from St Marylebone Parish Church for being too 'popish'.[12] Its conspicuousness, size (17ft), emotional drama and transparency (it was painted on 'transparent' canvas, and was illuminated) gave it too much of an inappropriately Catholic presence. The fear of 'popery', or the fear of being tainted by popery, thus continued to colour assessments of religious images in places of worship. That Benjamin West's religious paintings could happily be exhibited at the Royal Academy, and function as altarpieces in several churches and chapels but be rejected from and removed from others, is expressive of a remaining confusion and unease with images, which some still viewed as idols.

Anti-Catholicism, it has been argued, was not just a national prejudice and a cultural tradition but an ideology that promoted national cohesion.[13] Violent acts of iconoclasm aimed against Roman Catholic chapels, which occurred in 1644, 1688, 1745–6 and the Gordon Riots of 1780, had a xenophobic dimension – not only did the chapels symbolise a sinful religion, but a threat to the Protestant nation. George Bower's design for the official medal struck to commemorate the destruction of London's Roman Catholic chapels in 1688 (ill.8) shows rejoicing around a great bonfire of popish emblems in Lincoln's Inn Fields, with the Franciscan chapel in ruins behind. The iconoclastic rage against the chapel is officially celebrated as a symbolic national purging. The frenzy of the 1780 attack on the Bavarian chapel in Warwick Street saw the destruction of Andrea Casali's altarpiece, and an eyewitness described the savage destruction of the Sardinian chapel. Everything that could be found – altar fittings, pews, pictures, mass books, vestments – were 'pulled all to pieces and burnt before the door'.[14] As in 1644 (see p.79), the ritualised burning before the chapel doors of the offensive imagery stripped out from their interiors was a feature of all these attacks.

The dreadful fear of idolatry was given renewed and dramatic currency in Victorian England with the revival of Catholicism in 1829. Catholic emancipation and the 1850 'Papal Aggression' (the re-establishment of the Catholic hierarchy in England) placed Roman Catholicism, and the dangers it posed to the purity of the Protestant nation, at the forefront of people's minds. The simultaneous emergence of Anglo-Catholic ritualism within the Church of England, with its emphasis on pre-Reformation ceremony and

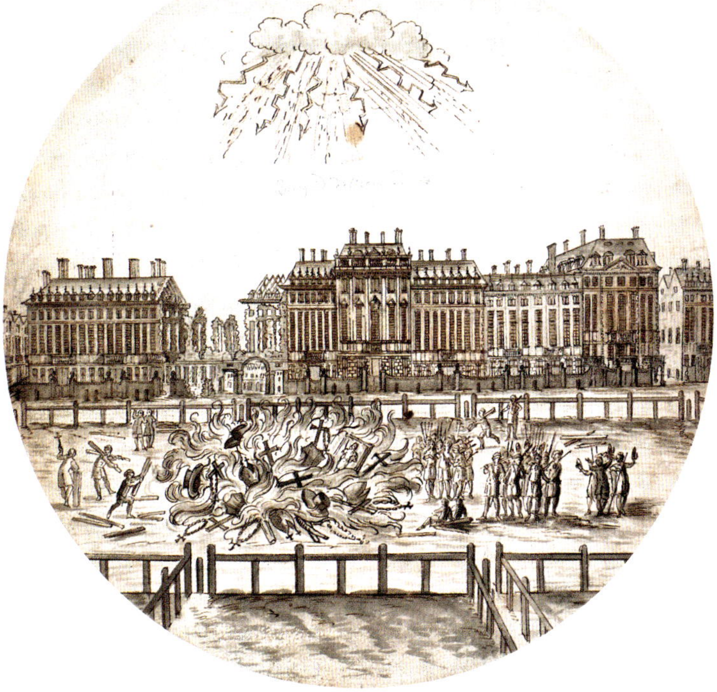

8
George Bower (d.1690)
Design for the medal struck to commemorate the destruction of the Roman Catholic chapels, 1689
The Pepys Library, Magdalene College, Cambridge

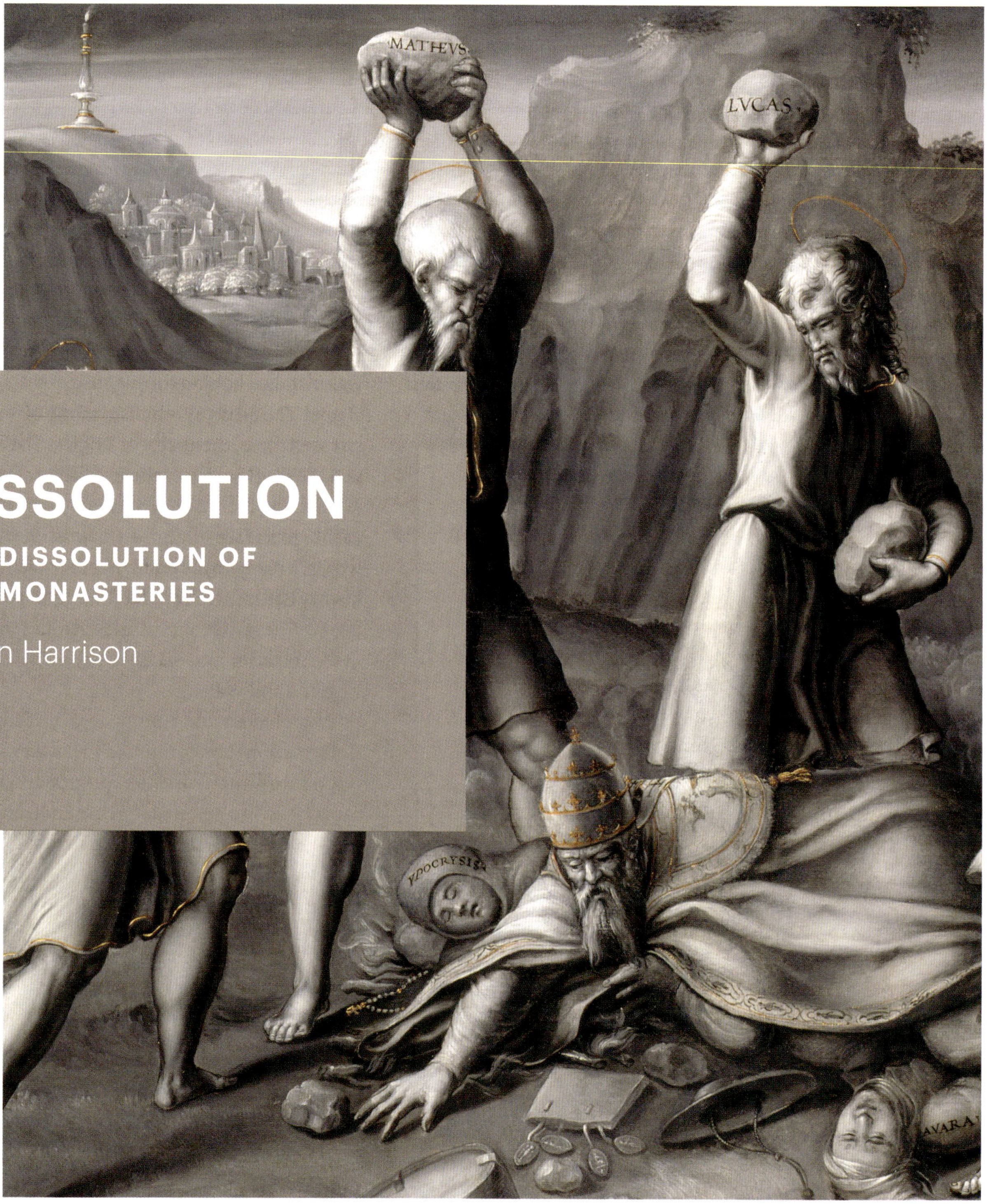

1

DISSOLUTION

THE DISSOLUTION OF THE MONASTERIES

Susan Harrison

characterised denouncements and criticisms of images. Images were at fault for being 'popish' and for encouraging 'popery'. For Sherman, the All Hallows St Michael was 'an abominable badge of superstition' and superstition itself 'of kin to Popery'. The window at St Margaret's was 'downright Popery, if not blasphemy', and in 1773 Bishop Terrick rejected (or avoided) paintings for St Paul's Cathedral on the grounds that it would be opening the doors to popery.[11] In 1826 Benjamin West's *The Angels Announcing to the Shepherds the Birth of Our Saviour*, installed only nine years previously, was removed from St Marylebone Parish Church for being too 'popish'.[12] Its conspicuousness, size (17ft), emotional drama and transparency (it was painted on 'transparent' canvas, and was illuminated) gave it too much of an inappropriately Catholic presence. The fear of 'popery', or the fear of being tainted by popery, thus continued to colour assessments of religious images in places of worship. That Benjamin West's religious paintings could happily be exhibited at the Royal Academy, and function as altarpieces in several churches and chapels but be rejected from and removed from others, is expressive of a remaining confusion and unease with images, which some still viewed as idols.

Anti-Catholicism, it has been argued, was not just a national prejudice and a cultural tradition but an ideology that promoted national cohesion.[13] Violent acts of iconoclasm aimed against Roman Catholic chapels, which occurred in 1644, 1688, 1745–6 and the Gordon Riots of 1780, had a xenophobic dimension – not only did the chapels symbolise a sinful religion, but a threat to the Protestant nation. George Bower's design for the official medal struck to commemorate the destruction of London's Roman Catholic chapels in 1688 (ill.8) shows rejoicing around a great bonfire of popish emblems in Lincoln's Inn Fields, with the Franciscan chapel in ruins behind. The iconoclastic rage against the chapel is officially celebrated as a symbolic national purging. The frenzy of the 1780 attack on the Bavarian chapel in Warwick Street saw the destruction of Andrea Casali's altarpiece, and an eyewitness described the savage destruction of the Sardinian chapel. Everything that could be found – altar fittings, pews, pictures, mass books, vestments – were 'pulled all to pieces and burnt before the door'.[14] As in 1644 (see p.79), the ritualised burning before the chapel doors of the offensive imagery stripped out from their interiors was a feature of all these attacks.

The dreadful fear of idolatry was given renewed and dramatic currency in Victorian England with the revival of Catholicism in 1829. Catholic emancipation and the 1850 'Papal Aggression' (the re-establishment of the Catholic hierarchy in England) placed Roman Catholicism, and the dangers it posed to the purity of the Protestant nation, at the forefront of people's minds. The simultaneous emergence of Anglo-Catholic ritualism within the Church of England, with its emphasis on pre-Reformation ceremony and

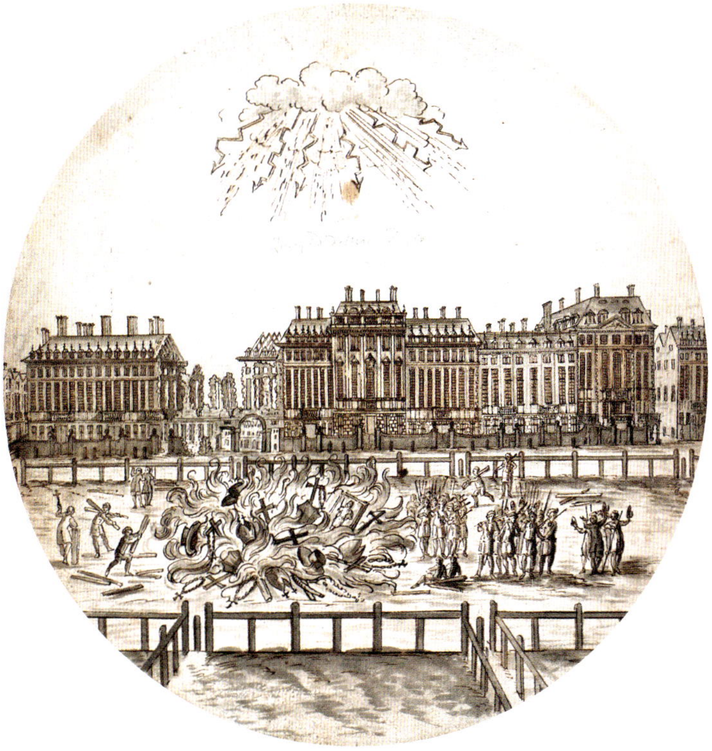

8
George Bower (d.1690)
Design for the medal struck to commemorate the destruction of the Roman Catholic chapels, 1689
The Pepys Library, Magdalene College, Cambridge

ornament and its new churches such as St Paul's, Knightsbridge and St Barnabas, Pimlico, decorated with paintings, statues on reredoses, rood screens and stone altars, as if the Reformation had never happened, was a vivid demonstration to detractors that the Reformation's legacy was in danger and being undone. Just as Laudian ceremonial and 'innovations' had inflamed rail riots and iconoclastic attacks in the 1640s (see p.76), so the nineteenth-century violent ritualism riots and legal challenges to Anglo-Catholic ornament were stimulated by a need to purify the Church and rid it of a re-infiltration of idolatrous practice.[15] As in the 1640s, the definition of superstitious images was not confined to representational statues and paintings but encompassed vestments, candles, crosses and crucifixes. Roman 'toys' and tapers before shrines were mocked; and elaborate ceremonial itself was attacked through persistent interruption of its performance. Violent ritualism riots at St George-in-the-East saw service disrupted with constant shouting, scraping of feet, hissing, and even fireworks. On 4 February *The Eastern Times* reported that, after the clergy had filed out, 'a cry arose from the centre of the Church – "Let us smash the altar!"'.[16] In 1877 the anti-Ritualist J.C. Ryle, later Bishop of Liverpool, urgently advocated the people of Britain to 'flee from idolatry'. 'I believe that idolatry is near us, all around us and in the midst of us, to a very fearful extent', he wrote, 'The Second Commandment, in one word, is in danger. "The plague is begun"'.[17]

The appropriation of the rhetoric of idolatry to lend a larger, darker meaning to criticism was a useful stratagem. By casting targets as false religious idols their condemnation became more charged. In 1850 John Everett Millais' *Christ in the House of His Parents* was metaphorically pulled to pieces in the press. Although the criticisms of it were aesthetic, the language deployed – as well being 'the lowest depths of what is mean, odious, repulsive and revolting' (Dickens), it was heretical, a work of pictorial blasphemy and an 'Art-idol' – suggested that the real criticism was aimed at its overtones of Catholicism and inclusion of ritualist symbolism.[18] The religious rhetoric made the picture more scandalous. In 1649 John Milton had applied idolatry to the realm of politics, noting that people were prone 'to a civil kind of Idolatry in Idolizing their Kings', and was amazed at how people were ready to 'fall flat' in adoration of Charles I (see p.81).[19] Similarly, in 1802 two satirical prints attacked the proposal to erect a statue to William Pitt by presenting his image as a brazen idol set up for the people to worship. In *John Bull and his favourite Statue of Bronze!!* (ill.9), John Bull, the personification of England, kneels before the statue, cap in hand, in an act of mock adoration. 'O Wonderful Man! – how I revere thy sublime resemblance', he exclaims, 'I feel so enraptured. – O that fine brass countenance how it shines with conscious integrity!' *The Brazen Image erected on a Pedestal wrought by Himself* (ill.10) presents Pitt standing on a pedestal commemorating his new taxes. 'There's a Monument of Integrity', his political opponents remark, 'Nebuchadnazzars Brazen Image was nothing to it, Nor his people half so Idolatrous'. By paralleling Pitt's statue with the biblical king's golden idol, the print attacks the audacious notion of Pitt as a fit object of public commemoration and places his admirers in the role of sinful idolaters.

The deliberate association between secular hero-worship and religious idolatry was also made by Thomas Carlyle. In his 1840 lecture series 'On Heroes, Hero-Worship and the Heroic in History' he used the arguments of religious reformers to make a clear distinction between true and false

9
John Bull and his favourite Statue of Bronze!! 1802
Hand-coloured etching
35.6 × 25.1
Trustees of the British Museum, London

10
The Brazen Image Erected on a Pedestal Wrought by Himself, 1802
Hand-coloured etching
41.1 × 25.3
Trustees of the British Museum, London

idols,[20] a theme he returned to in his 1850 tract *Hudson's Statue*. Prompted by the proposal to erect a statue to the York railway financier George Hudson, which was never realised as Hudson's finances and reputation unravelled in 1849, Carlyle hit out at the modern-day idol-worship of men of short-lived and dubious reputation. By raising Hudson to the status of hero, people were making a god of him, he was the 'English Vishnu', or an aesthetic icon, the '*new* Apollo Belvidere'. Carlyle objected to the current 'statue-mania' and misplaced reverence of men of mediocrity, the 'extraordinary population of Brazen and other Images which at present dominate marketplaces of towns, and solicit worship from the English people'. Such 'irreverence' was akin to a national sin. 'I will with pious joy … reduce [them] to the state of broken metal again', he says, 'As warming pans, as cheap brass-candlesticks, men will get good of this metal; as devotionary Images in such form, evil only'. 'These are not heroes, gods, or demigods', he continues, 'and it is a horrible idolatry … to set them up as such'.[21] Carlyle's imagined iconoclasm was a biting verbal attack on false idols, or statues of doubtful aesthetic merit commemorating individuals of spurious worth. It was also a criticism of people's failure to judge properly.

Reformation and Puritan reformers understood the power that images possessed and the dangers that were posed to people in thrall to them. In order to eradicate idolatry, iconoclastic breaking was accompanied by a need for destruction, for as long as even a vestige remained, the memory of what had been could linger.[22] The Elizabethan *Homily* had called for images in churches to be 'put away and destroyed' and parliamentary legislation of the 1640s advocated 'utter demolition'. For Sir Robert

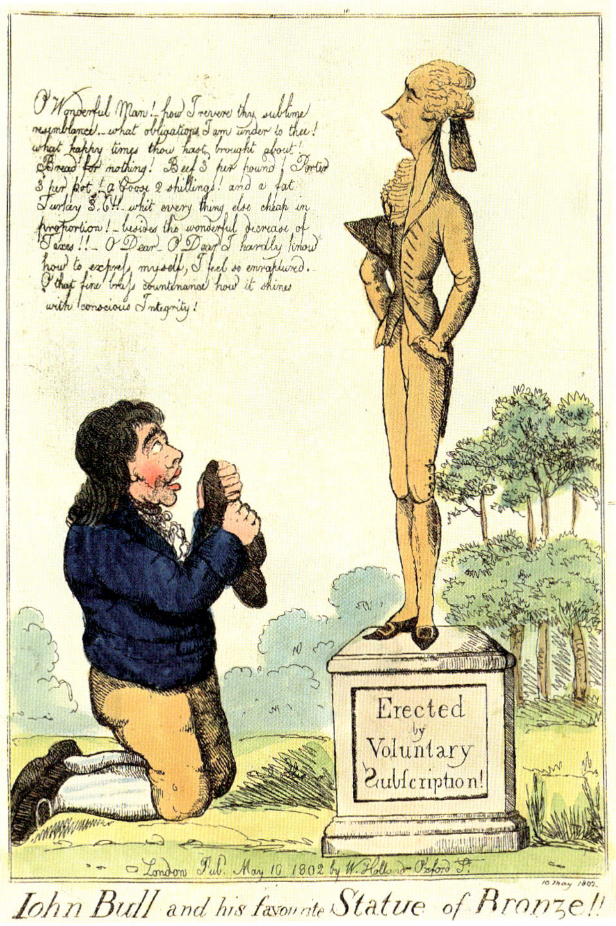

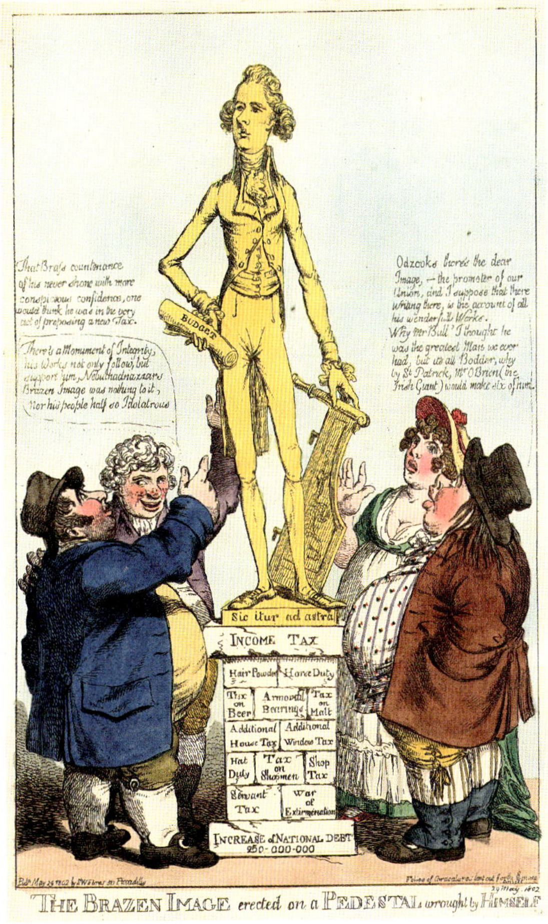

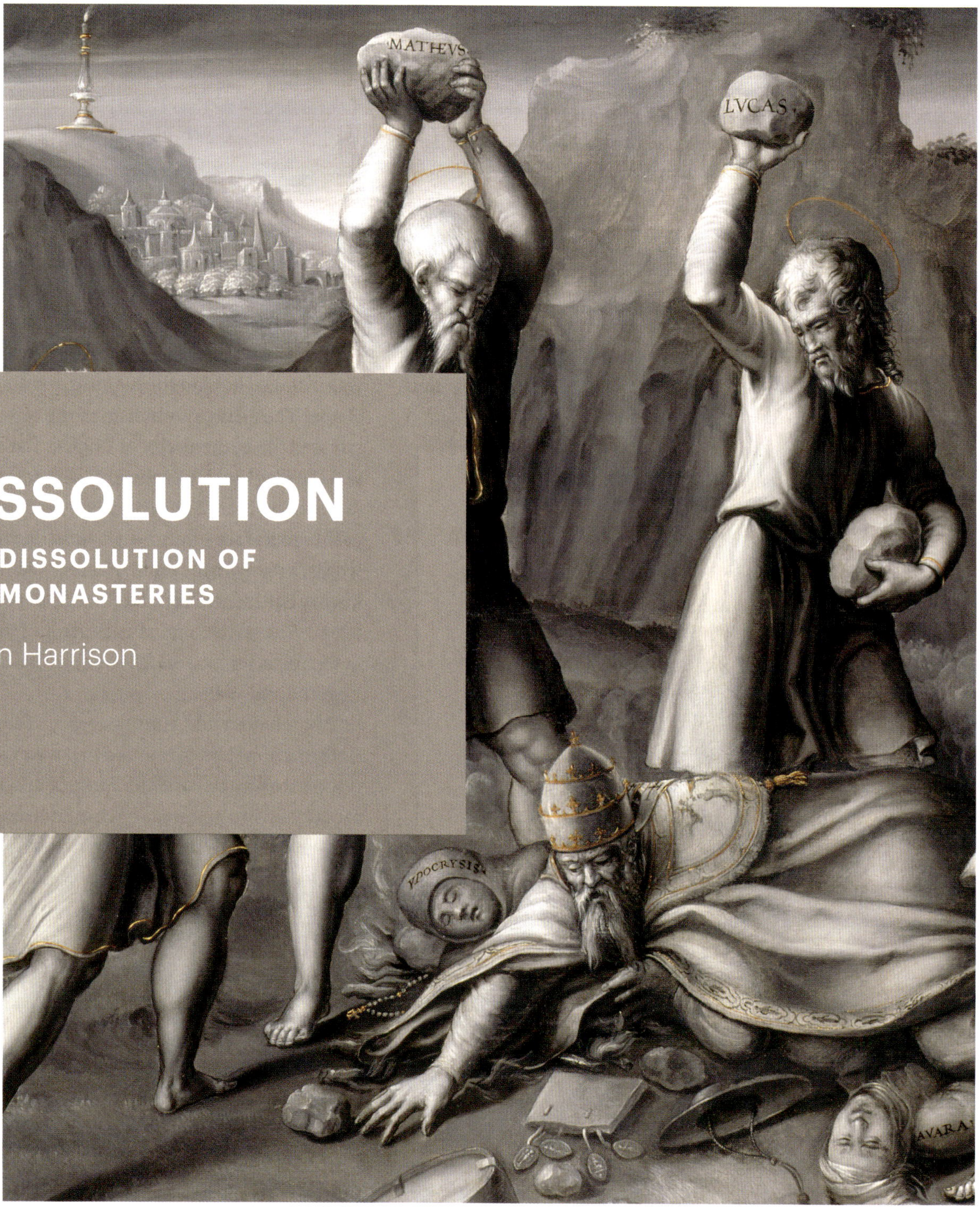

1 DISSOLUTION

THE DISSOLUTION OF THE MONASTERIES

Susan Harrison

From austere, principled beginnings in the twelfth century, the main monastic orders in Britain rose to establish an unparalleled power base controlling extensive areas of income-producing land with a network of contacts across Europe. The monasteries were establishments upholding the Catholic faith, answerable to the Pope and interacting with many levels of society, from courtiers to labourers. During the Middle Ages many monasteries also played pivotal social roles, acting as secular and spiritual overlords.[1] The heads of thirty important abbeys and priories were members of the House of Lords.[2] Collectively these establishments were pilgrimage sites, guesthouses and centres of learning, acting as estate managers, judiciary and commissioners on behalf of the Crown, collectors and producers of books and, significantly, patrons of art and architecture. Some orders remained true to their early principals but many developed magnificent buildings, complete with fine decoration and furnishings.

Many of these monasteries and priories are now in ruins, forced into that state by the Dissolution of the Monasteries (1536–40) and subsequent quarrying and neglect until the twentieth century, when sites were protected by legislation.[3] Programmes of clearance of centuries of over-burden and consolidation of the ruins by His Majesty's Office of Works[4] were set up following the end of the First World War.[5] In order to gain a more complete sense of how the medieval monasteries appeared and functioned we must seek the records of the liturgy, charters, inventories, accounts and excavation records, and thus establish the process of their destruction and the significance of the Dissolution of the Monasteries.

The reform of the English Church following the break from Rome established Henry VIII as 'the only head, sovereign lord, protector and defender'. A panel painting owned by Henry VIII, *A Protestant Allegory* by Girolamo da Treviso (ill.23), acts as a piece of anti-papal propaganda. The Evangelists hurl stones onto the fallen figure of a pope, who lies surrounded by symbols of the Catholic church and two figures representing avarice and hypocrisy. The violence of their action represents the zeal of the Protestant Reformation. Reform of the Church was overseen by Thomas Cromwell, the king's chief minister. The census of Church property and revenues, the *valor ecclesiasticus* of 1535, was swiftly followed by the Visitation of the Monasteries. This commenced in the summer of the same year, ostensibly to examine the monasteries' moral character. Their libraries were searched for evidence of opposition to the declaration of faith in the Act of Supremacy.[6] The census enabled effective taxation of Church property, whilst the visitation gave evidence of 'sordid corruption and vice' leading to the Act for the Suppression of the Lesser Monasteries in March 1536.[7] No single Act of Parliament directly dissolved the larger monasteries, but rather a series of acts ultimately led to the dissolution of all the monasteries in England and Wales.[8]

Opposition to the suppression of the monasteries first broke out in Lincolnshire in 1536. This was followed by a greater rebellion, the Pilgrimage of Grace, led by landowners and aided by the heads of some of the larger abbeys which still remained. The Abbot of Jervaulx, the former Abbot of Fountains Abbey and the Prior of Bridlington Priory were accused of complicity in the uprising and were executed as traitors.[9] When suspicion of complicity in the rebellion was cast on Abbot Pyle of Furness Abbey, he surprised the commissioners by offering to surrender the Abbey in return for a pension. They readily accepted and on 9 April 1537 Furness became the first of the great abbeys to be suppressed. By early July the buildings were being demolished, even though monks were still in residence.[10] Pressed by the commissioners, other abbots followed suit.

Jervaulx Abbey, which fell by the attainder of its abbot for treason, exemplifies the process of suppression. Jervaulx was initially visited by Cromwell's representatives Layton and Legh in 1536. Its suppression was under way by May 1537, when the Duke of Norfolk wrote to the king offering his assistance, especially 'because the neighbouring country is populous and the houses greatly beloved of the people, and also well stored with cattle and other things that will not come all to light so well if I were absent.' By the end of May Jervaulx Abbey was controlled by commissioners Lawson, Bowys, Blythman and auditor Anthony Rouse. It is clear that the recovery of assets was a major driving force. In June the plate and seal were sent to Cromwell and at the beginning of August work had begun to smelt the lead into fothers (half-ton ingots). The huge amount of lead (almost four hundred fothers[11]) took until mid-November to process, by which time the weather had turned and they could not be transported until spring.[12]

'By various means, by statute, by legal process, and by simple deed of gift, the monastic lands became vested in the king, to be at his absolute disposal.'[13] The circumstances that led to the Dissolution of the Monasteries paved the way for iconoclastic acts which resulted in the physical and deliberate destruction of both status and symbols of the Catholic Church in England and Wales. It is unlikely that the labourers tasked with realising the assets of each institution thought precisely in these terms, and indeed may have had qualms about destroying shrines and icons. Local sympathies were recognised as an issue and mitigated by attendance in person by commissioners,[14] or by bringing in a new workforce from a different area.[15] The local economy was significantly disrupted: tenants were evicted or answerable to new landlords and alms were no longer distributed.

The deliberate dismantling of an abbey should be seen more as a salvage operation, to extract maximum value for the king and subsequent owners of the site and ensure that the main buildings, especially the church, could never serve their original purpose again. Treatment varied at the hands of different people. John Freeman reported 'that the King's Commysion commaundeth me to pull downe to the grounde all the walls of the Churches, Stepulls, cloysters, fraterys, dorters, chapter housys, with all other howsys, savying them that be necessary for a farmer'.[16] By contrast, John London reported to Cromwell in 1538: 'I pulled down no Howse so thoroughly at noon of the Fryers butt so defacyd them as they shud nott lightly be made Fryerys agen.'[17] At Jervaulx, because the abbot had been accused of treason, the Abbey church was completely levelled.[18]

Once a site had been surrendered it was immediately defaced, the community dispossessed and movable items sold; only then did the business of salvage and realising the full potential of the assets begin, whilst at the same time protecting those assets against looting. Sir John Williams, the Royal Treasurer, received money, jewels, plate, copes, vestments and other ornaments and goods which came from the surrender and dissolution of abbeys, monasteries, priories and colleges. He also lists 'foundry Juelles and plate wch came by occafion of the defacing and takinge downe of fhrynes and vther vayne and fayned thinges called Reliques and vther fupfluous plate founde ... made for the advydinge thabufe of Idolatrye'.[19]

The evidence presented through the 1920s clearance records at Rievaulx Abbey (ill.12) supports this chain of events. The surviving inventory, compiled shortly after its acquisition by the Duke

12
Glimpse of the ruins of Rievaulx Abbey from the Terrace, Helmsley, North Yorkshire

of Rutland in early spring 1539,[20] details a site spoiled primarily with the 'falling of the steple'[21] but in which a quantity of the furniture remains, including some shrines and altars and the roof lead. There is no mention of books, plate or vestments because they had already been removed. The audit identifies saleable material and lists the king's property, including that already conveyed away by William Blythman.[22] Sir John Williams does not include Rievaulx's monastic treasures in his account.[23] Significantly, in the Duke of Rutland's inventory there is no mention of the shrine to the uncanonised, locally celebrated Saint William, the founding Abbot of Rievaulx, in the west wall of the Chapter House. Yet clearance work of the 1920s revealed that the shrine had been spoiled, the Agnus Dei decorated

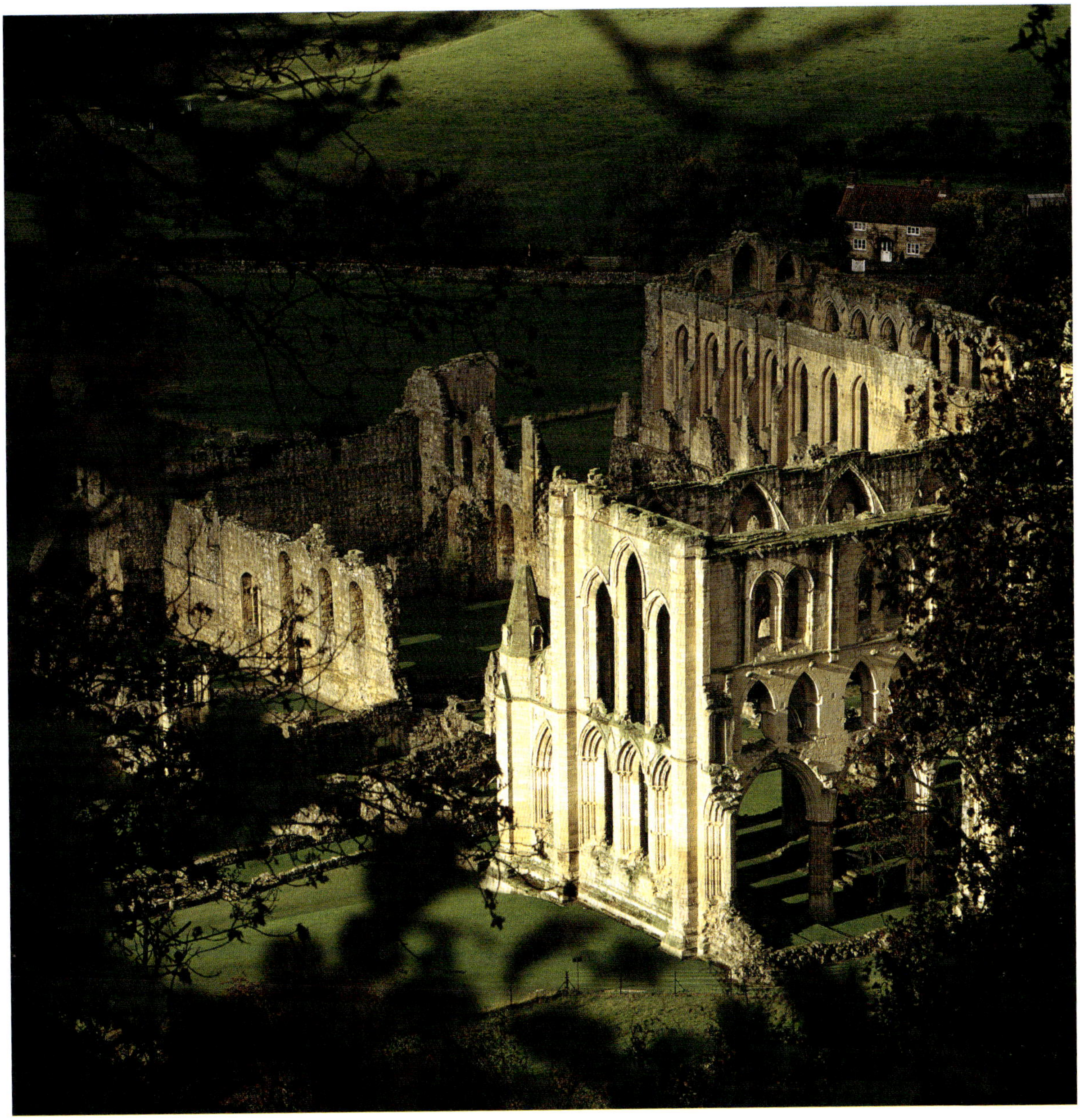

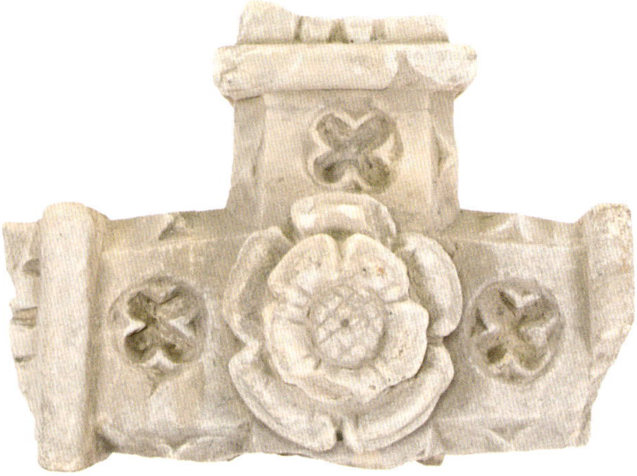

keystone[24] cast out into the cloister walk along with benching inscribed 'SCS WILLMUS ABBAS'.[25] This suggests that it was despoiled at an early opportunity, perhaps in the same tranche of work as the dismantling of the steeple and the screens, when statues and tables were removed for safekeeping on site.[26]

The elegant gable cross[27] from the Galilee Porch at Rievaulx may have been erected as a finishing touch to fifteenth-century church modernisation work (ill.13).[28] It was found in debris above the medieval floor level, indicating that it was part of a destruction layer. It is tempting to see the spoliation of the cross as part of the primary symbolic destruction of the site, being an obvious symbolic target, although any destruction in this area may have impeded the main entrance into the heart of the abbey. The cross has been heavily damaged, with one arm missing and the terminals of the others all broken. The boss is a five-petalled rose in relief, with sunken quatrefoils on the face of each arm decorated with small cusps. The rose is symbolic of the Blessed Virgin Mary[29] but may also

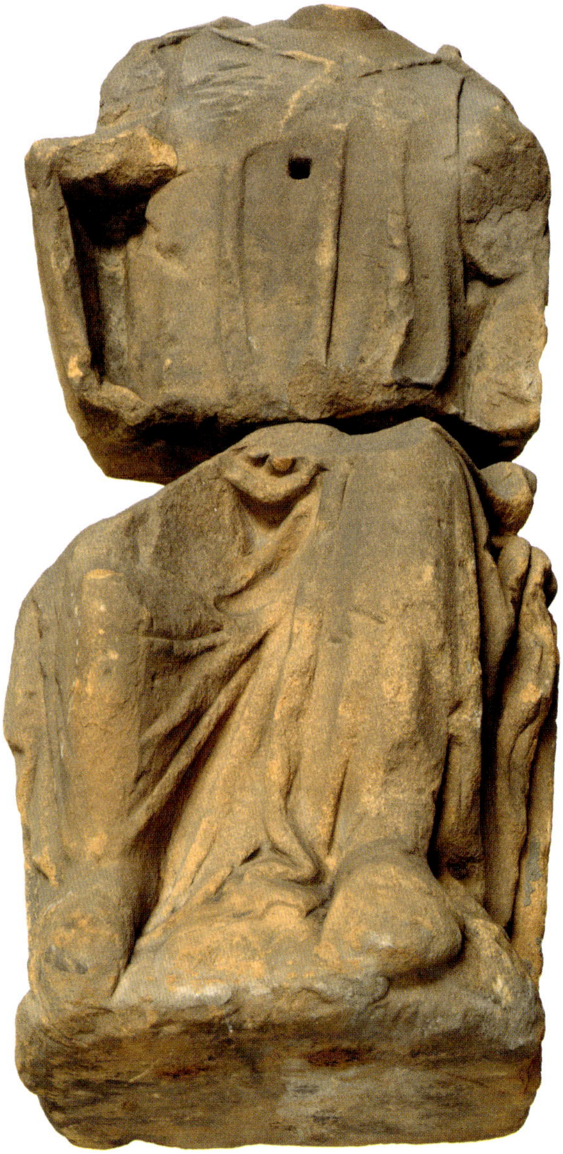

13
Finial cross from the Galilee Porch,
Rievaulx Abbey 15th century
Stone
28 × 38.5 × 19.5
English Heritage, Rievaulx Abbey

14
Enthroned figure from Gisborough Priory
1300–1350
Stone
Legs 65 × 45 × 35; torso 53 × 50
English Heritage, Gisborough Priory

be seen as a Yorkshire rose in support of the royal House of York. The leaders of a Cistercian monastery would certainly have been politically aware, so such dual symbolism is entirely plausible.

The west front of a church was an obvious place to strike an iconoclastic blow. At Gisborough Priory the loose architectural stone and statuary of the ex situ assemblage suggest that it was one of the most elaborate west fronts ever built in England.[30] Gisborough church had suffered a catastrophic fire in 1289 and was largely rebuilt.[31] It is most likely that the life-sized enthroned statue,[32] either a saint or even Christ in Majesty, originated from the west front and was part of a figural sequence (ill.14). This seated male figure has a cloak fastened over full-length robes; he originally held a book across his body, supported by the left arm on his lap, while his right arm was raised, bent at the elbow. The book was attached to the sculpture by a metal fitting into the socket in the centre of the chest.

Most strikingly, this sculpture bears evidence of its spoliation: it is broken in two, with axe marks on the right shoulder (made while removing the book, which may have been metal) and around the neck (made while destroying the head). Neither the head nor the right arm remains. It is plausible that the damaged sculpture was later pulled from its plinth and that this occurred at the dissolution of Gisborough Priory in 1540. Similar evidence from Fountains Abbey can be seen with the likely pulling down of the Virgin and Child statue from the west front,[33] found below in the Galilee Porch in 1854.[34]

Almost thirty components of the fifteenth-century Rievaulx Abbey pulpitum screen have so far been identified (ill.15).[35] This originally divided the presbytery from the crossing and was spiritually symbolic, being the entry point into the inner sanctum. It is stylistically close to the Kings Screen at York Minster, although its workmanship is of lower quality. The screen would have had a lower order of large statue niches with crocketted gables, interspersed with blind panelling, flanked by crocketted standards and ribbing on the niche head interiors. The upper order of niches was finely

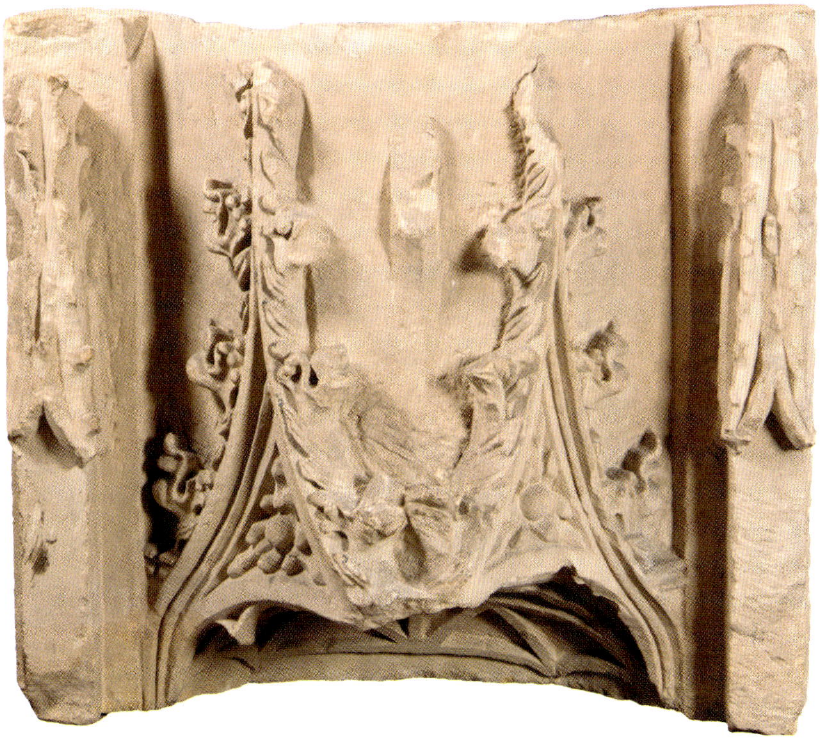

15
Niche canopy from the pulpitum screen, Rievaulx Abbey 15th century
Stone
69 × 58 × 40
English Heritage, Rievaulx Abbey

carved, with extensive undercutting, and was originally painted. This was topped by crenelations above small niche heads with architectural details matching the lower order. These niches may have held small statues.[36] Some sections of the Rievaulx pulpitum screen would have been eminently saleable. These were excavated near the north-west door of the nave, having been placed there ready for onward transport but never retrieved after the collapse of the nave walls after the removal of the roof.

Many members of the dispossessed religious orders were pensioned off and a number found new roles as chaplains and priests. There was continued solidarity demonstrated by various communities, including those at Rievaulx Abbey, who bequeathed gifts to former brethren.[37] At Roche Abbey, Abbot Henry Cundal was granted an annual pension of £33, as well as his books, a quarter of the abbey's plate, cattle and household items. The other monks each received half a year's allowance and every servant of the abbey was given half a year's wages.[38] In this way some books from the monastic libraries survived the Dissolution, alongside those requisitioned for the Royal Library, while others were saved by monks or sold into private hands.[39] The former monks of Monk Bretton Priory listed 148 books saved from their priory in 1558, of which the prior purchased thirty-one at his own expense.[40] The monks of Roche Abbey were less successful in saving their books, only six having apparently survived.[41] According to an account written by Michael Sherbrooke in 1591, service books at Roche Abbey were taken and reused as cart covers, their material value exceeding their functional purpose.[42] Groups of book fittings recovered from site clearance excavations add credence to this account, with sets of studs found discarded at locations where books may have been pulled apart.[43] A late Saxon-type book clasp was also found at Roche Abbey, cast as a simple openwork sexfoil one-piece strap-end with fittings for a leather strap and a catch (ill.16).[44] It is an unusual survival and indicates that books older than the foundation of the abbey were kept in the library until the Dissolution.

Another fitting from Roche Abbey may also have decorated a book (ill.17).[45] It is a fine roundel plaque of thin copper alloy, with a scene of the Annunciation in relief, and may be compared to carved stone Annunciation scenes from Fountains Abbey (ill.20) and Rievaulx.[46] On the left the Virgin Mary stands behind a lectern, the archangel Gabriel kneels on the right, facing the Virgin, and a central vase of lilies separates the two. The plaque is damaged and incomplete. The Virgin's face is slightly indented, probably due to damage during use or post-deposition; the missing portions suggest that it may originally have been stitched to leather or cloth and deliberately torn off and discarded.

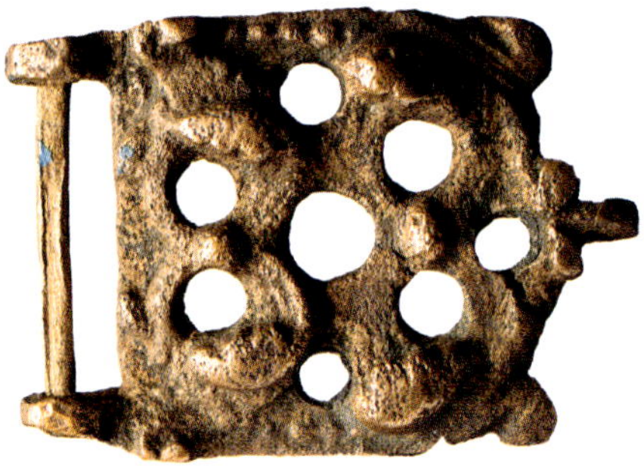

16
Book clasp early 12th century
Copper alloy
2.6 × 3.8 × 4
English Heritage, Roche Abbey

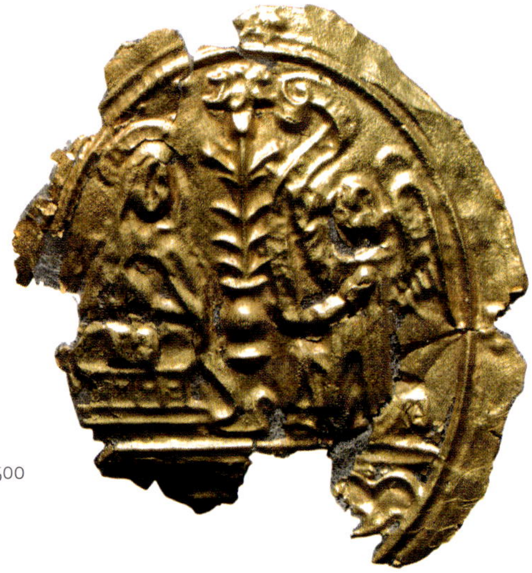

17
Plaque, possibly a book fitting *c.*1500
Copper alloy
3.3 × 3
English Heritage, Roche Abbey

Documents kept in the monastic libraries and muniment rooms were also pillaged. Indeed, John Bale, a friend of Henry VIII's chaplain and librarian John Leland, complained in the 1550s that 'in turnynge over of the superstycyouse monasteryes so lytle respecte was had to their lybraryes ... and ... it was to be wished that the profitable corne had not so unadvisedly and ungodly perished with the unprofytabe chaffe'.[47] Documents defined and proved ownership and authority and included accounts, charters and letters; many of these bore seals to verify their authenticity, and lead papal seals were recovered from both Fountains Abbey and Roche Abbey. The nineteenth-century scholar John Richard Walbran[48] found a papal seal of Innocent III in rubbish outside the Abbot's House at Fountains Abbey, one of at least nine recovered during subsequent excavations on the site, several having been found in drainage channels. Archaeological investigation in 2011 on one of the collapsed Infirmary drainage tunnels at Fountains Abbey revealed that these were Dissolution deposits.[49]

A discarded seal of Pope Innocent IV, torn from its parchment, was recovered from the river at Roche Abbey (ill.19).[50] The obverse, as on all papal bulls, depicts Saint Peter and Saint Paul surmounted by an inscription giving their abbreviated names. The reverse is inscribed 'INNOCENTUS PAPA IIII', dating it to 1243–54 – an indication of the longevity

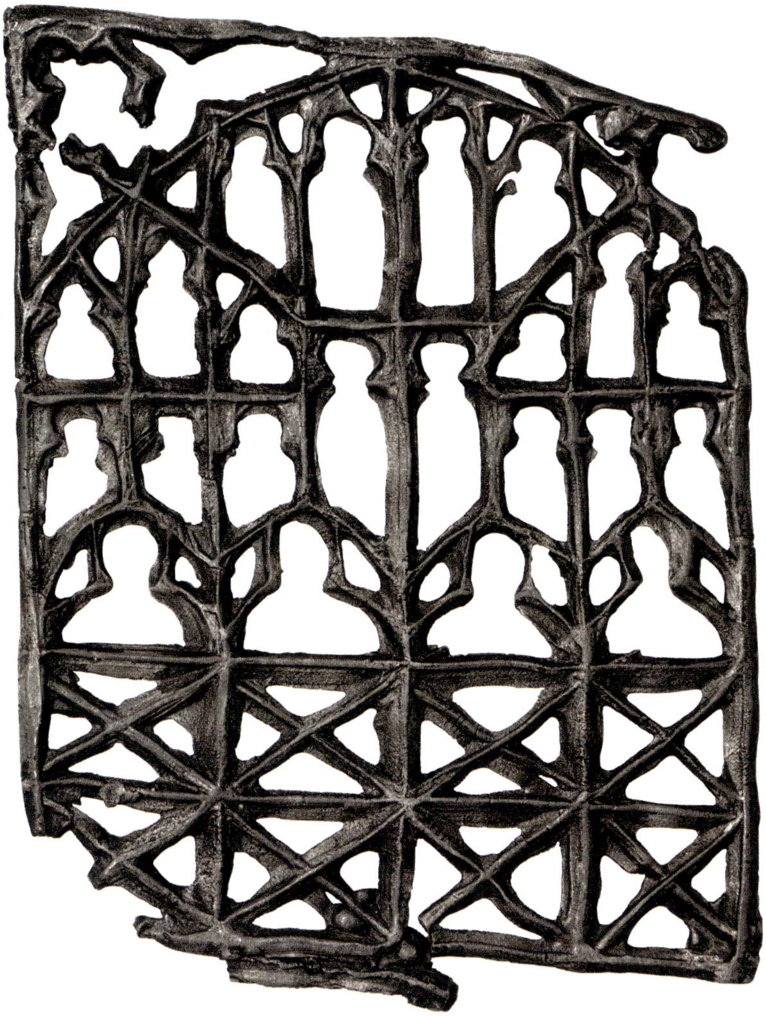

18
Window ventilator panel from
Rievaulx Abbey 14th century
Lead
9.8 × 7.8
English Heritage, Rievaulx Abbey

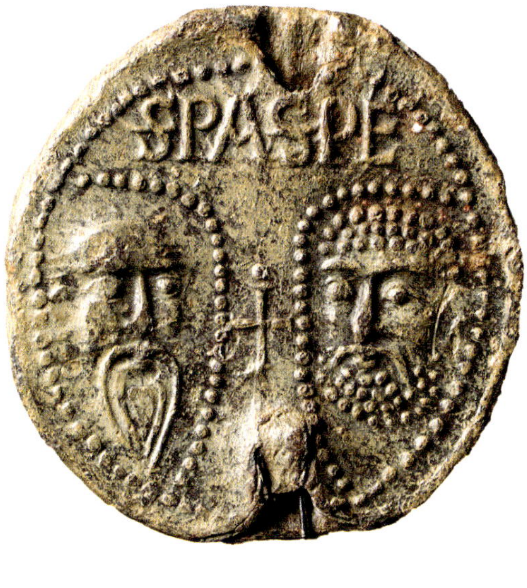

19
Papal bulla of Pope Innocent IV
from Roche Abbey 1243–54
Lead
3.6 × 3.6 × 0.4
English Heritage, Roche Abbey

of these documents. The unvarying iconography of the papal seal from the eleventh century onwards could be viewed as proof of the continuity of the Church, the damage wrought on them emblematic of the attacks on the Roman Church in the sixteenth century.

From the windows of both Rievaulx and Fountains Abbeys came the remarkable survival of small lead ventilator panels, cast in moulds in the style of window tracery (ill.18).[51] These were probably stripped out of the windows and discarded. It is likely that tracery was also removed as salvage operations turned towards the architectural stone. In the southern chapels of the church at Fountains, Walbran observed that 'large quantities of stones had been hewn and dressed here, as was proved by the large accumulation of fragments and chippings found upon the surface of the floor'.[52] Similar evidence was revealed in the cloisters at Thornton Abbey.[53] During site excavation (1949–53), small decorative capitals and slender tracery from the cloister arcade were found in a deep layer of stone chippings. The pieces were too small for economic re-use so they were discarded while larger architectural pieces were refashioned into usable, saleable building blocks.

The large Annunciation panel from Fountains Abbey (ill.20)[54] and its parallel still in situ at Rievaulx Abbey[55] shows the fate of many panels and friezes at the Dissolution. In both scenes the Virgin stands to the right, by a lectern bearing an open book. There is a central vase of lilies, to the left of which stands the archangel Gabriel, with a scroll supported by the Holy Spirit in the form of a dove. The scroll bears the legend 'ave m[a]ria [gratia] plena d[omi]n[u]s tecu[m]'. God is depicted in the clouds. Both panels seem to have been simply defaced by the beheading of the Virgin; in both cases, further damage may be of a later date.

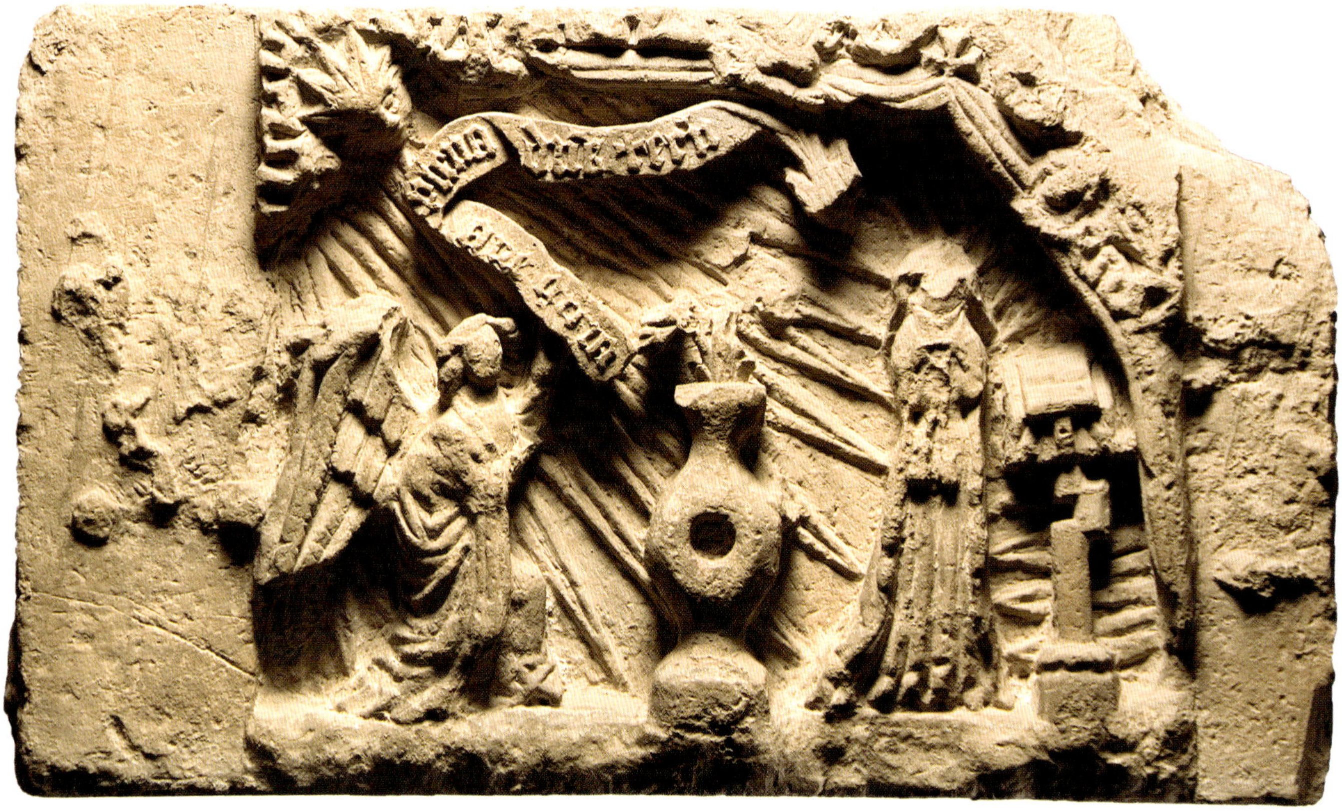

Archaeological evidence suggests that monastic graves were robbed in the immediate post-Dissolution period. This was not a sanctioned activity, neither was it consistently carried out. In the Chapter House at Jervaulx Abbey five stone coffins were disturbed,[56] while at Rievaulx Abbey a photograph taken in the Chapter House in the 1920s shows a disarticulated human skeleton probably removed from the central grave and re-laid in the space previously occupied by a supporting pillar.[57] Not all graves were targeted, as demonstrated by the discovery in 2010 of an intact abbatial burial in the centre of the presbytery at Furness Abbey, complete with a crozier and ring.[58]

At Fountains Abbey John Richard Walbran reported the 'ransacked' grave of Brother John of Ripon, who died c.1504, 'the bones being found in a disturbed position'.[59] The cover was extensively damaged and, according to Gilyard-Beer and Coppack, reset and repaired with plaster, an arrangement which could only have occurred 'after the dissolution of the abbey on 26 November 1539, and before the abandonment of plans to make Fountains a cathedral of the New Foundation the following summer'.[60] Many memorial brasses on monastic grave covers were deliberately removed; in some cases only pins remain. Two brass letters found at Fountains Abbey, an 'S' and an 'M' (ills 21, 22), were each cast as a single piece and are slightly worn from use; both exhibit damage likely to have been caused when they were removed from their setting during the Dissolution. Several fragmentary lengths of tomb inscription also survive from Fountains Abbey, including a strip reading: '...Ani + millesimo + tr ...' ('in the year 13...'), the words separated by eight-petalled flowers and the background decorated with cross-hatching. The strip is in remarkably good condition, having escaped the

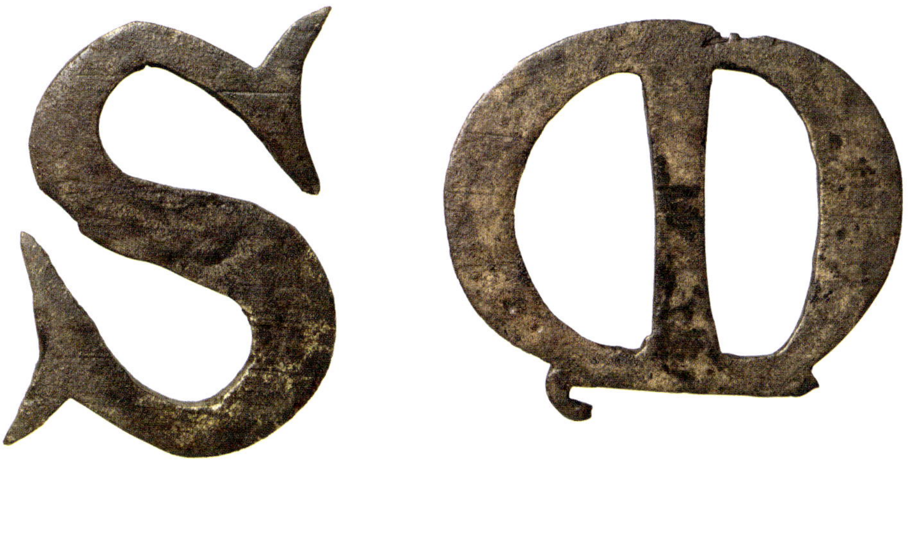

20
Annunciation panel late 15th century
Limestone
66 x 111 x 20
English Heritage, Fountains Abbey

21, 22
Letters from tomb inscriptions
13th century
Copper alloy
Letter 'S': 4.0 × 2.9; letter 'M': 5.1 × 4.4
English Heritage, Fountains Abbey

fate of others, either subjected to intense heat – possibly from lead furnaces – or otherwise discarded.[61] The fact that these fragments remain in the archaeological record is perhaps indicative of the haphazard nature of the retrieval of some valuable items. In other cases, similar pieces were removed, such as copper alloy inscriptions fitted to the Annunciation panel and Abbot John Burton's rebus panel[62] at Rievaulx Abbey. Similarly, both enthroned figures from Rievaulx Abbey and Gisborough Priory have had metal fittings removed.

Lead was identified as a valuable asset early on and was removed from the roofs, windows and architectural fittings and smelted to form fothers. These solid, canoe-shaped ingots were stamped on the upper surface with a crowned rose to signify Crown property. Four fothers were found during site clearance at Rievaulx Abbey, where they had been placed by the west door, ready for transport, when the building shell collapsed over them.[63] Deeply buried under rubble, it must have been deemed uneconomic to recover so few – a very small proportion of the overall lead recovered.[64]

Fuel used to fire the furnaces to smelt the lead may have included wooden furnishings from within the abbey, even books and coal.[65] At Fountains Abbey, according to Walbran,

> its spoliation had been conducted with no ordinary wantonness or avarice. The stalls, screens, and other wooden fittings, had, apparently, been used ... to make fires for melting the lead of the roofs; for here and there were found, within the walls, heaps of ashes, nay in the nave, part of the furnace where the operation had been conducted.[66]

Walbran also noted that the acoustic jars found in situ under the choir stalls were 'also partially filled with charcoal. These ashes have, no doubt, been cast here from the adjacent furnace where the lead stripped from the church had been evidently melted into a marketable shape at the time of the dissolution'.[67] The Dissolution account of Roche Abbey by Michael Sherbrooke in 1591 parallels this sequence of events, noting that 'those who cast the lead into fodders [fothers] plucked up all the seats in the choir where the monks sat when they said service. These seats were like the seats in minsters; they were burned and the lead melted, although there was plenty of wood nearby'.[68] Fairbank reports on the nineteenth-century excavations in the church at Roche Abbey that a cavity filled with lead ashes, the site of the furnace used for melting the lead of the roof, was discovered in the centre of the nave.[69]

Within just a few years the religious foundations had been thoroughly stripped, with the deliberate intention of effecting a physical and institutional break with the past.[70] The Act of 1539,[71] sometimes called the Second Dissolution Act, did not transfer to the Crown the property of a single abbey: its purpose was 'to legalise retroactively such surrenders as had taken place, and prospectively all that might yet occur'.[72] The few institutions that emerged relatively unscathed from this period, such as cathedrals and colleges, have evolved over more than four centuries, including post-Dissolution iconoclasm during the Reformation, so that many now bear little evidence of their medieval character. Similarly, later attacks on some monastic sites may have resulted in their further damage. Nevertheless, original accounts and archaeological evidence reveal many of the actions undertaken by the iconoclasts who served their king and masters in the Dissolution of the Monasteries.

23
Girolamao da Treviso
(active c.1497–1544)
A Protestant Allegory c.1538–44
Oil paint on panel
68 × 84
The Royal Collection Trust, London

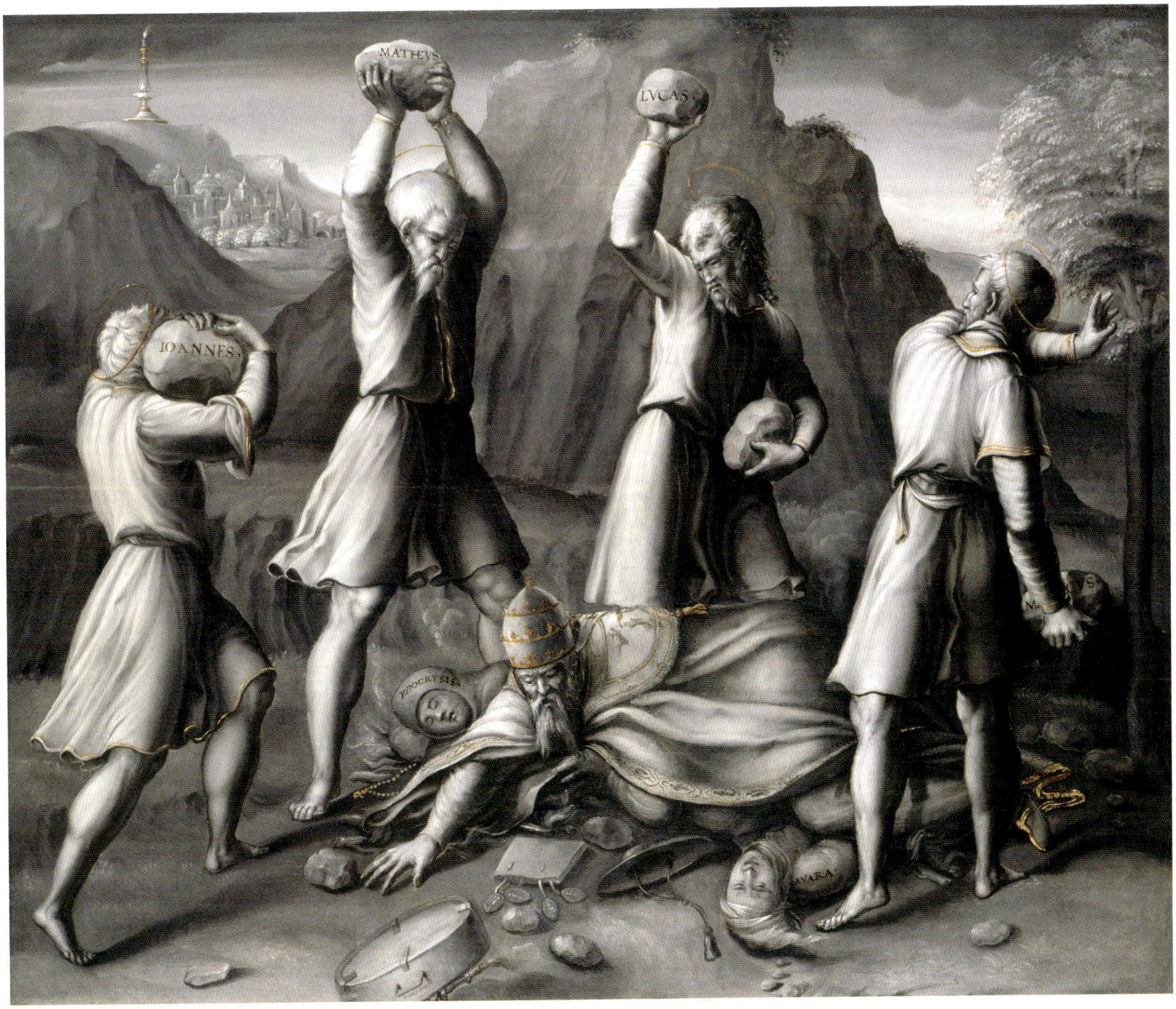

Christ in Majesty

24
Christ in Majesty *c.*1260–90
Stone
69.6 × 43.3 × 29.2
English Heritage, Rievaulx Abbey

Fortunately not all the spoliation at Rievaulx Abbey was as heavy-handed as at some other sites. The Christ in Majesty statue[73] bears fewer scars than the enthroned figure from Gisborough Priory, although it was similarly displaced rather than defaced in situ. This was not the case with many other pieces, such as the carved Christ in Majesty from the gatehouse of Kirkham Priory, of which part of the head and the upper right arm were simply smashed off. The crisply carved sculpture of the Rievaulx piece is complete except for the upper right arm, the left hand and the head and it retains traces of original pigment. The figure's full-length robes are tied at the waist with a broad band of loosely folded cloth in the style of the Christ in the Judgement Porch at Lincoln Cathedral. An overgarment is gathered over the left shoulder and drapes in deep hollows over the left arm. The flat back and angled seat suggest that the piece was designed for a high, shallow niche.

The fragmentary right arm is raised; directly below this, on the right knee, are two square sectioned holes, apparently original, slightly offset from each other to take a metal attachment such as a staff or scroll. The fitting has been removed, possibly at the same time as the right arm and the head. The left hand may also have borne an attribute such as a book resting on the left knee; the area of broken stone and damage to the upper left knee support this theory. The breaks to the sculpture are clean and the sculpture is in a good state of preservation, which suggests that it was an internal statue. However its dating of 1260–90 in relation to other known features and building campaigns at Rievaulx Abbey is anachronistic: it may have been a reused icon positioned on the tympanum of the fifteenth-century pulpitum screen, or possibly formed part of a tomb structure.[74]

The Christ in Majesty was excavated in the Abbot's lodging and may be one of the 'imagys & tables gyldyd that cam out of the church and the portal karvyd' listed in the 1539 inventory.[75] No doubt the 'imagys' or sculptures were initially taken in their complete, undamaged state to the Abbot's Lodging, since sculptures that had been damaged would have had value only as building stone. The figure of Christ may have been defaced afterwards, probably because of its iconic status, while others were removed and sold.[76] No traces of the broken sections were recovered or noted during the site excavation.

The heads of few iconic sculptures from monastic sites have been recognised or recovered, whereas secular decorative and animal heads survive in large quantities. This suggests that the iconic heads were not merely damaged but largely destroyed during the Dissolution of the Monasteries. SH

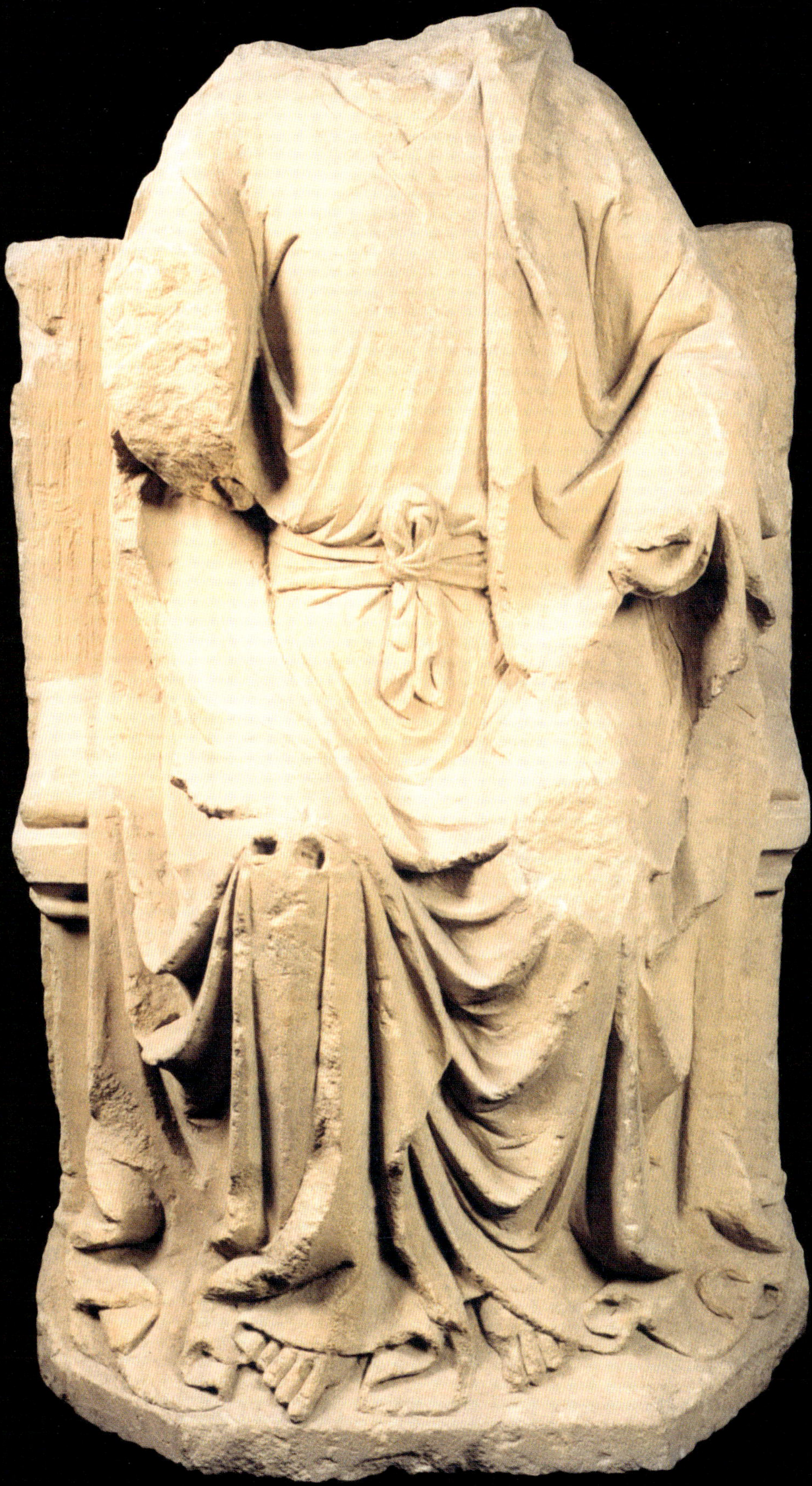

Window glass

Window glass was recovered from many monastic sites during excavation, some sites, such as Fountains Abbey[77] and Furness Abbey, producing no more than a handful of fragments. However, at Rievaulx Abbey thousands of broken fragments were discovered, ranging in date from the entire monastic occupation; few complete glass quarries were recovered. John London reported to Thomas Cromwell the extent of the damage inflicted to glass in some monasteries: 'I defacyd the church wyndoes and the sellys of the dorter as I dydd in every place saving in Bedford and Aylisbury where were few byars.'[78]

At Rievaulx Abbey the inventory of 1539 lists the grades of glass of the whole church:

> The glasse to be sortyd into iij partes
> On the fairest to be sorted
> The second sort to be sold
> The iij sort to be taken out of the lede
> and the lede molten[79]

The list continues with the iron window bars and nails to be saved and sorted. Walbran discovered a scrap heap at Fountains Abbey containing 'some fragments of stained glass of the early English period, which had been forced with its leadwork and iron stanchions from a window above'.[80]

Of the thousands of fragments of glass excavated from Rievaulx Abbey only a relative handful are figurative, architectural or have lettering. One such fragment has part of a crowned letter 'J' from a border, possibly from the scene of a saint (ill.25).[81] It is difficult to distinguish wanton from accidental damage in glass, but glass with iconographic significance was no doubt deliberately targeted. One such is the finely painted angel glass from Furness Abbey (ill.26), found discarded and broken by the guesthouse just north of the abbey church.[82] Jasmine Allen describes the piece in detail, dating it to the last quarter of the fifteenth century (c.1475–1500) and suggesting that it was originally part of a tracery light or a canopy.[83]

The majority of fragments from Rievaulx are painted with grisaille decoration. This glass was of the lowest grade and by the time of the Dissolution was old and had no monetary value. Glass of the third grade may be further indicated by the discovery of crumpled lead nets[84] from Rievaulx Abbey (ill.27): not all, it seems, went it into the furnaces. Window lead was worth less than the pure lead used for the roofs, since it required more processing and refining. At Thorney Abbey part-melted lead was found,[85] while among finds from Fountains Abbey is a section of lead net from a mother and child roundel: although all the glass has been removed, the figures are still discernible from the lead outline (ill.28).[86] The best glass from Fountains Abbey was taken to York in 1540 to be sold in panels; the poorest became *cullet* (waste glass).[87] SH

27
Lead window came from
Rievaulx Abbey
Date and dimensions unknown

28
Lead window came from
Fountains Abbey date unknown
10 × 10.2

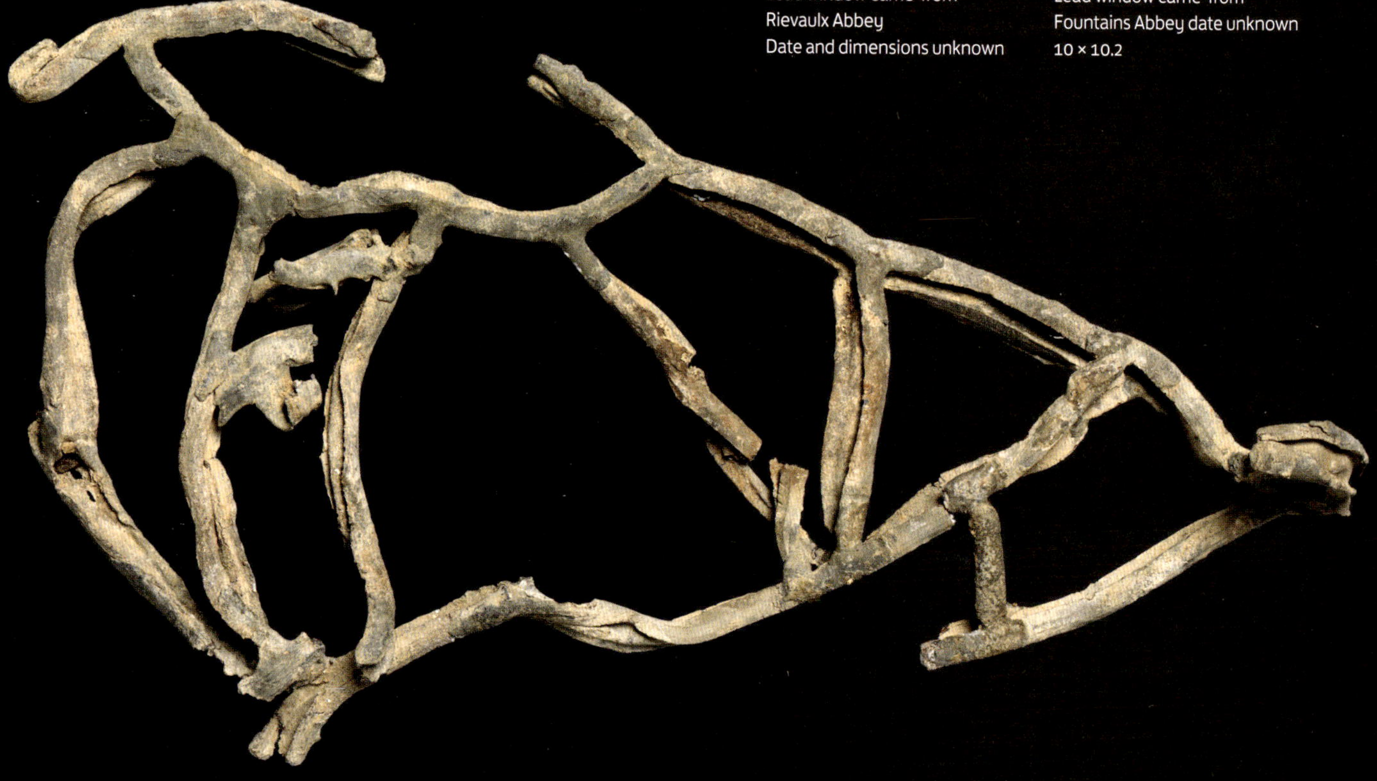

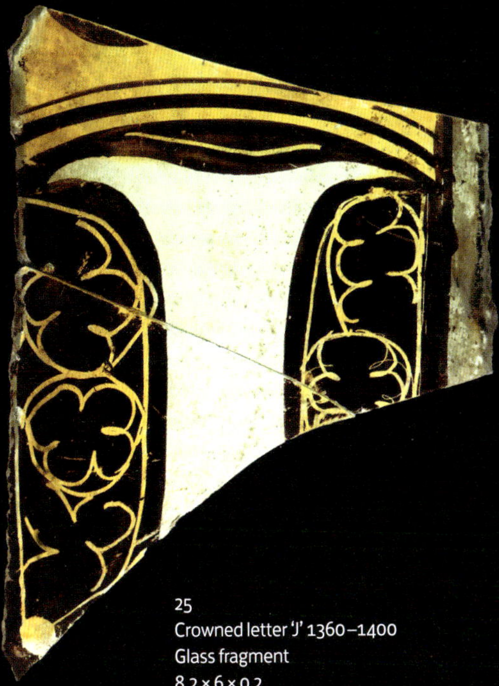

25
Crowned letter 'J' 1360–1400
Glass fragment
8.2 × 6 × 0.2
English Heritage, Rievaulx Abbey

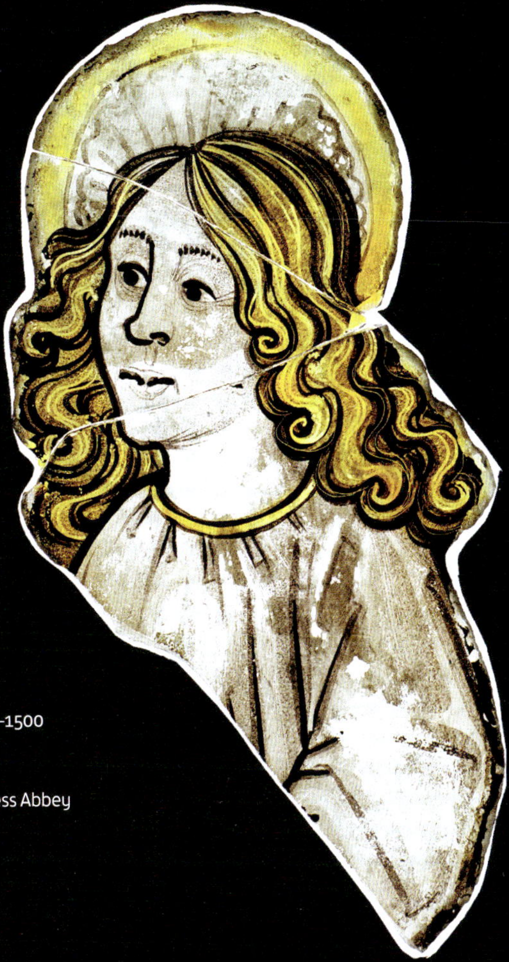

26
Head of an angel 1475–1500
Glass fragment
14 × 10
English Heritage, Furness Abbey

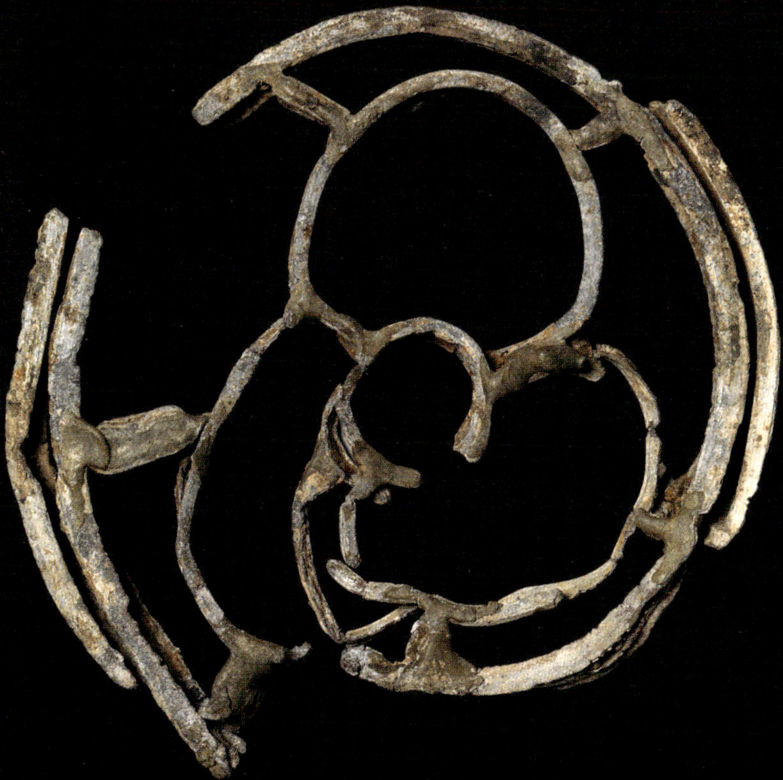

29
Shattered fragments of glass
from Rievaulx Abbey

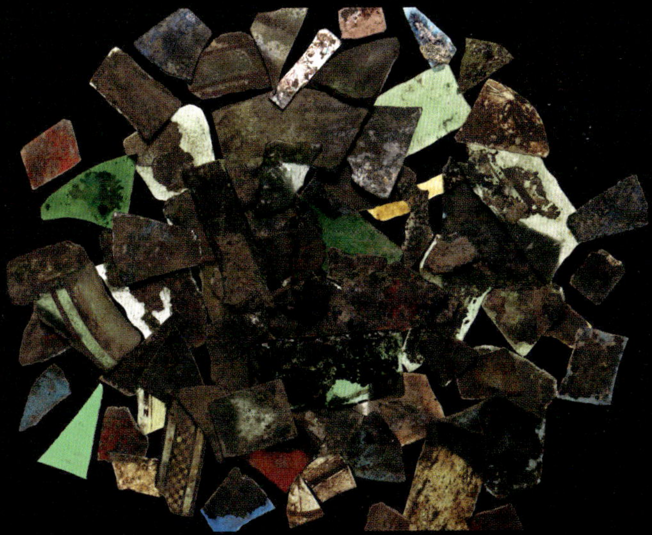

Shrines, pilgrimage and the cult of Becket

The shrine of Thomas Becket (d. 1170) at Canterbury Cathedral was the most important pilgrimage site in England before it was demolished in 1538.[88] Although little evidence survives to confirm its precise design and appearance, the shrine would have been visually resplendent, probably consisting of a gold-plated casket resting on an ornate stone base with niches, with a wooden cover that could be raised and lowered to protect the casket. (Ill.31 gives an idea of how a medieval shrine would have appeared.)[89] Over the centuries, the shrine accrued a spectacular array of precious objects ranging from candles to jewels and other valuable objects left by pilgrims as votive offerings.[90] Located in the Trinity Chapel at the east end of Canterbury Cathedral, the shrine stood on a platform with three steps framed by a rectangular band of pink marble pavement that still survives; as John Crook observes, 'the wear marks left by the feet of pilgrims, perhaps kneeling on the bottom step, are apparent'.[91] These ghostly impressions in the tiles, worn by three hundred years of kneeling pilgrims, are the only material remains of the shrine, along with two small fragments of rose-coloured marble (ill.30).[92] It has been suggested that the two fragments – a fragment of a foliate capital, and part of a base or a capital – survive from the stone shrine base and were made from the same type of rose-coloured marble from the Phillipeville area in southern Belgium as that used in the Trinity Chapel.[93] Paul Binski considers the fragments' pink rose marble colour to be a symbol of Becket's blood and martyrdom.[94]

Like many small, undocumented remains from iconoclastic acts, the provenance of these fragments cannot be completely confirmed. However, if they are indeed the only fragments to survive the demolition of the shrine, they represent not just any ordinary shrine, but an archetypal one. Writing after the bones of Thomas Becket were translated into a new shrine in 1220, the historian Matthew Paris described the new *theca* or receptacle as made 'of the finest refined gold and most precious stones' (*de auro obrizo purissimo et gemmis pretiosissimis*).[95] After the relics' translation, many other local saints were also enshrined or given new shrines, and it is thought that the form of the high shrine may have emerged as a result of Becket's newly designed shrine.[96]

Over the centuries, the shrine remained a sacred destination for pilgrims, but for Henry VIII and Thomas Cromwell it became a threat and a target: as an individual, Becket was a rebel who defied royal authority; as the site of a cult, the shrine represented an ostentatious display of material wealth. On 8 September 1538 it was dismantled and 26 wagonloads of

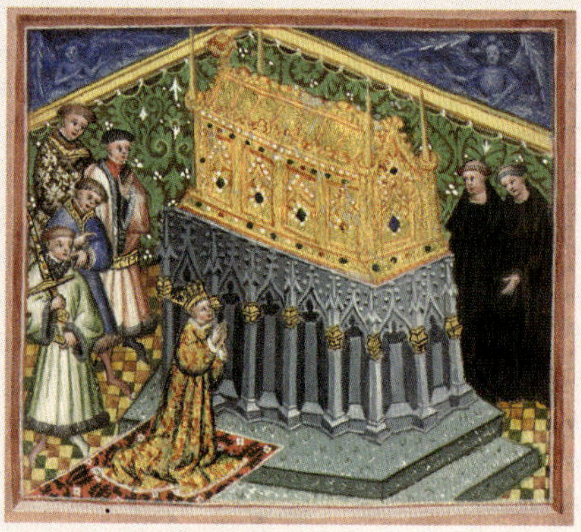

31
Bury St Edmunds
Henry VI kneeling before
the shrine of St Edmund
From John Lydgate, *Lives of Saints Edmund and Fremund*, 1434–39
Harley 2278, f.4*v*
British Library

silver and gold offerings were taken away.[97] Most likely, Henry VIII witnessed the destruction of the shrine, but rumours (originating in Rome) proliferated about the king subjecting Becket's bones to a mock trial and burning them.[98] Meanwhile, propagandists such as John Bale (1495–1563) reversed the roles of victor and vanquished in Becket's hagiography: in a play performed for Henry VIII, Bale deconstructed Becket's status as a saint, one of many gestures that exacerbated the eradication of cult and image.[99]

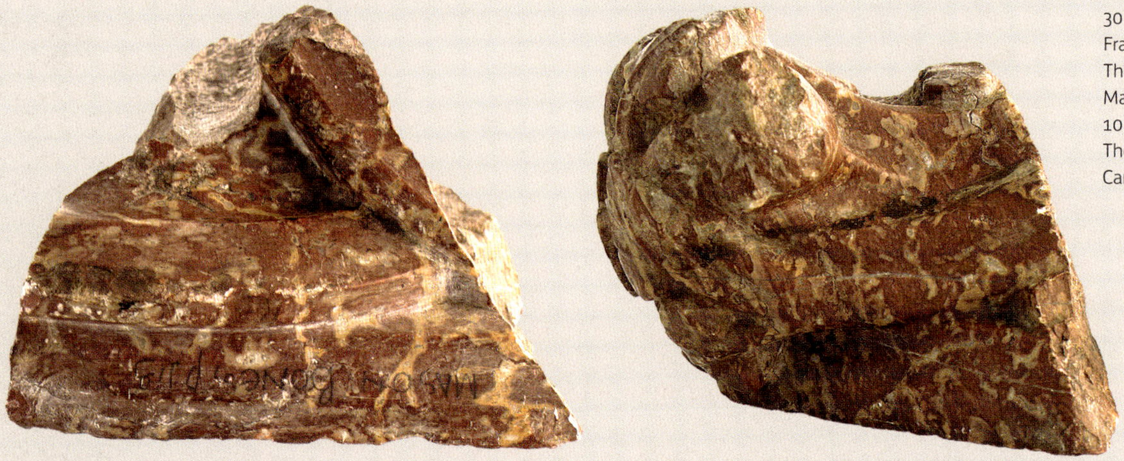

30
Fragments from the shrine of
Thomas Becket, probably before 1220
Marble
10 × 12.8 × 12.5; 7.5 × 16.5 × 12.6
The Dean and Chapter of
Canterbury Cathedral

The demolition of the shrine was necessary to abolish the cult of Thomas Becket, but iconoclastic orders extended far beyond Canterbury Cathedral. Throughout England, all evidence of saints' cults were under threat, and pilgrimage sites and shrines swiftly faced the same fate. Of all the saints, only Becket was singled out in Henry VIII's injunctions and edicts against images, however: to thoroughly extinguish the saint's memory in individual minds, images of and prayers to Becket were to be taken out of churches and private devotional books.

On 9 June 1535 a royal proclamation had been issued to 'utterly' abolish, eradicate and erase all references to the Pope and papal authority in 'mass-books and all other books used in churches'.[100] By November 1538 royal orders demanded the destruction of all images of Becket and that all offices, antiphons and prayers in his name should be 'erased and put out of books'.[101] As one of the few forms of private image ownership available to increasing numbers of lay people, Books of Hours and other forms of private devotional literature were consulted in public, but practically the objects could not be policed. Individuals responded to these orders in different ways. Many completely complied with the erasure of appropriate images or text, cutting out, crossing out, blotting, scraping the vellum and smoothing it down, but others did not; some only deleted prayers to Becket, leaving the images.[102] The two manuscripts shown here present two forms of this image destruction; in one (ill.32) only the prayer to Becket, not the image, is cut out, and in the other (ill.33) both image and prayer are scraped off. (The prayer was reinstated at a later date.)[103]

Since 1538 antiquarians and historians have maintained a steady interest in the whereabouts of Becket's bones and in reconstructions of the shrine.[104] In 1975 the Cathedral Archivist William Urry wrote: 'Matter cannot be destroyed and somewhere at Canterbury, however shattered, both structures [tomb and shrine base] must still exist in a dispersed form. The gold, silver and gems were carried off in 1538, but the stone must have remained.'[105] Urry believed that several fragments may have been part of the shrine or related to it, reused in parts of nearby walls and roads or discovered in the Cathedral precinct, including these two fragments. Like many historians, he wanted to reconstruct the shrine's original form in order to restore a vision of its magnificence in the face of its loss, and belief in the survival of fragments was part of this vision. SB

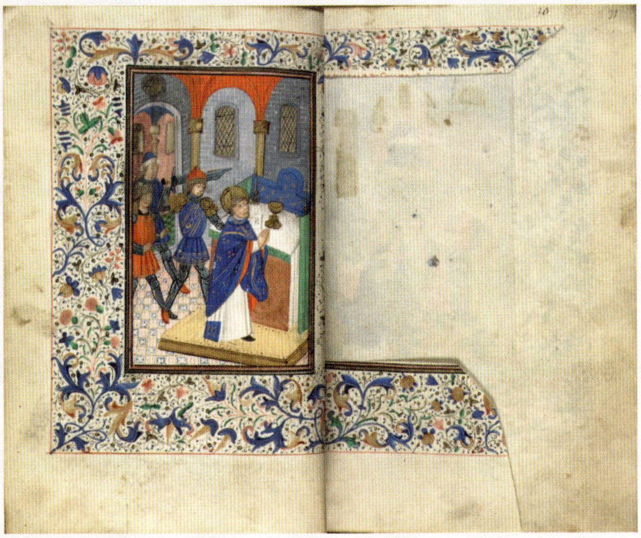

32
South Netherlands
Book of Hours 1450–75
21.5 × 15
Open at the martyrdom of Thomas Becket, with the suffrage of Becket cut out
Harley 2985, ff 29*v*–30
British Library

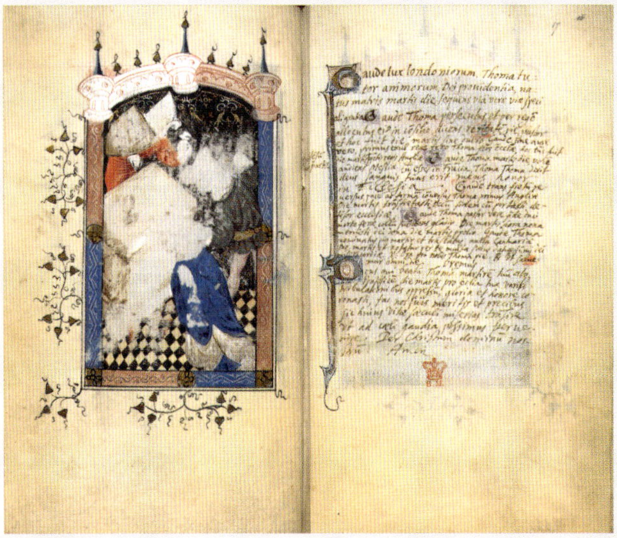

33
South Netherlands (Bruges)
Book of Hours c.1390–1400
19.5 × 12
Open at the martyrdom of Thomas Becket with the image of Becket erased
Sloane 2683, ff.16*v*–17
British Library

2

REFORMATION

Richard Williams

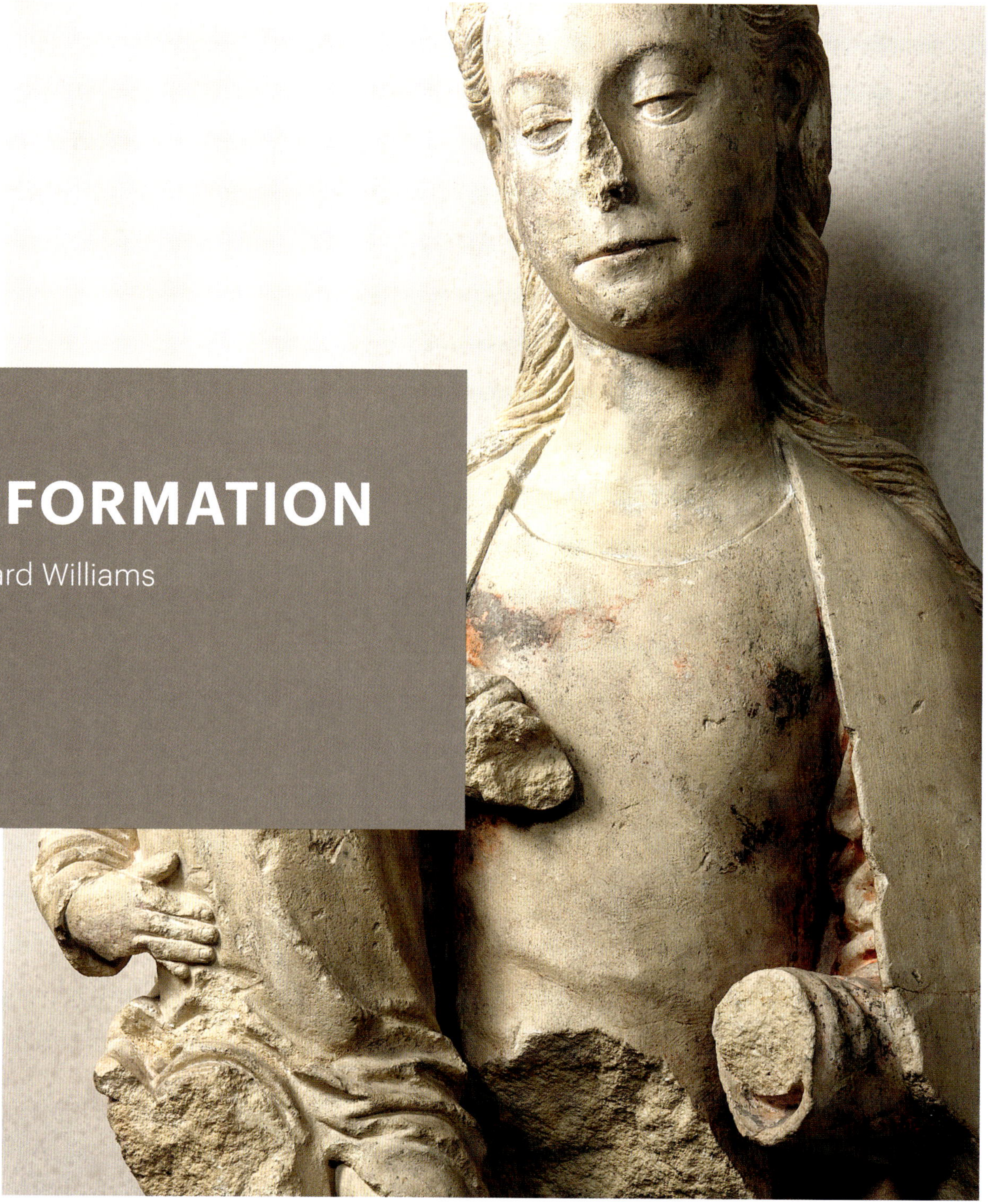

During the Reformation England experienced iconoclasm on an astonishing and unprecedented scale. This largely state-sponsored destruction affected every community across the country, as parish churches, chapels and cathedrals were stripped of their religious images. Centuries-worth of medieval art, whether painted, carved, illuminated, embroidered, cast in metal, stained in glass or fashioned in any other medium, was wiped from England's cultural history. However, just as the nature of iconoclasm itself has undergone a re-evaluation in more recent years, so too has the English Reformation and the destruction it caused. What earlier historians had angrily dismissed as mere acts of philistine vandalism is now increasingly recognised as a phenomenon of much greater diversity and meaning that can provoke relevant questions for our own time.

The issue of religious images had been central to the Protestant Reformation from its inception. From Martin Luther onwards, Protestant reformers made it their mission to rid the Church of what they saw as corruption and superstition that the medieval popes had allowed to prosper, and to return to the 'True Religion' of the Early Church established by Christ. Sculptures, paintings and other religious images in churches had been infected with this superstition, they argued. Although the official teaching of the Church had been that praise offered to a religious image reverted to its prototype, Luther and others claimed that, in practice, the behaviour of people towards images indicated that too many were confusing or conflating the two and so worshipping the wooden sculptures and painted panels themselves.[1]

It is certainly true that images were far more than mere decoration. Altarpieces could symbolise and instruct the laity in the doctrines that underlay the liturgy of the Church, wall paintings could instruct and commit to memory the stories of the saints, and other images served to stimulate individual devotion and prayer. Communities could form personal relationships with specific local images, often sculpted figures, by carrying them in procession, dressing them with garlands of flowers on saints' days, and petitioning them for spiritual or material help. Pleas might be made to the image of a 'helper saint' known to cure particular ailments or afford protection during pregnancy, for instance. In thanks for prayers being answered, candles might be lit and precious items of clothing or jewellery might be bequeathed to a specific sculpture in a will. Images reputed to be miracle-working could even be the object of a pilgrimage, although this was very rare. To Protestant critics, however, praying to images, making offerings, kneeling before them and kissing them was the very definition of the terrible sin of idolatry.[2]

To avoid sin and return to the pure religion of the Early Church, Protestants looked to the Bible. Since the Bible was the unmediated Word of God, only those practices and beliefs that could be verified within its pages could constitute 'True Religion'. Therefore, when evaluating the legitimacy of images in churches reformers looked to the Ten Commandments and other biblical texts. An English version of the Second Commandment appears on a triptych of texts painted in the reign of Edward VI or Elizabeth I for a church in Suffolk (ill.34), reading:

> Thou shalt not make to thyself any graven image nor the likeness of anything that is in heaven above, or in the earth beneath ... thou shalt not bow down to them, nor worship them for the Lord thy God am a jealous God, and visit the sins of the fathers upon the children, unto the third and fourth generation of them that hate me ...

In spite of its uncompromising language, opinion was divided within the Protestant movement as to the extent of this prohibition of images. The more moderate Protestant position, exemplified by Luther, tended to emphasise the part of the commandment that forbade the worshipping of such images, believing their legitimate, instructional use to be an issue of individual conscience. In contrast, the radical Protestant position held a more fundamentalist understanding of the commandment as an unequivocal condemnation of all religious images in church, requiring their total destruction. It was the latter, radically iconoclastic interpretation that came to be advocated by most Protestant leaders of the Reformation period.

This lack of uniformity was reflected in attitudes towards images in sixteenth-century England. Most historians no longer characterise the English Reformation as a single event but as an on-going *process* of reform, beginning with Henry VIII and continuing as far as the Civil War and Puritan reaction of the seventeenth century.[3] These were turbulent years of dramatic religious change that many must have found bewildering. Despite the break with the Pope and the Roman Catholic Church, Henry VIII cannot be called a Protestant. As Supreme Head of the Church of England he permitted religious reform but only up to a point. For example, it remained heresy punishable by burning even to question the central doctrine of the

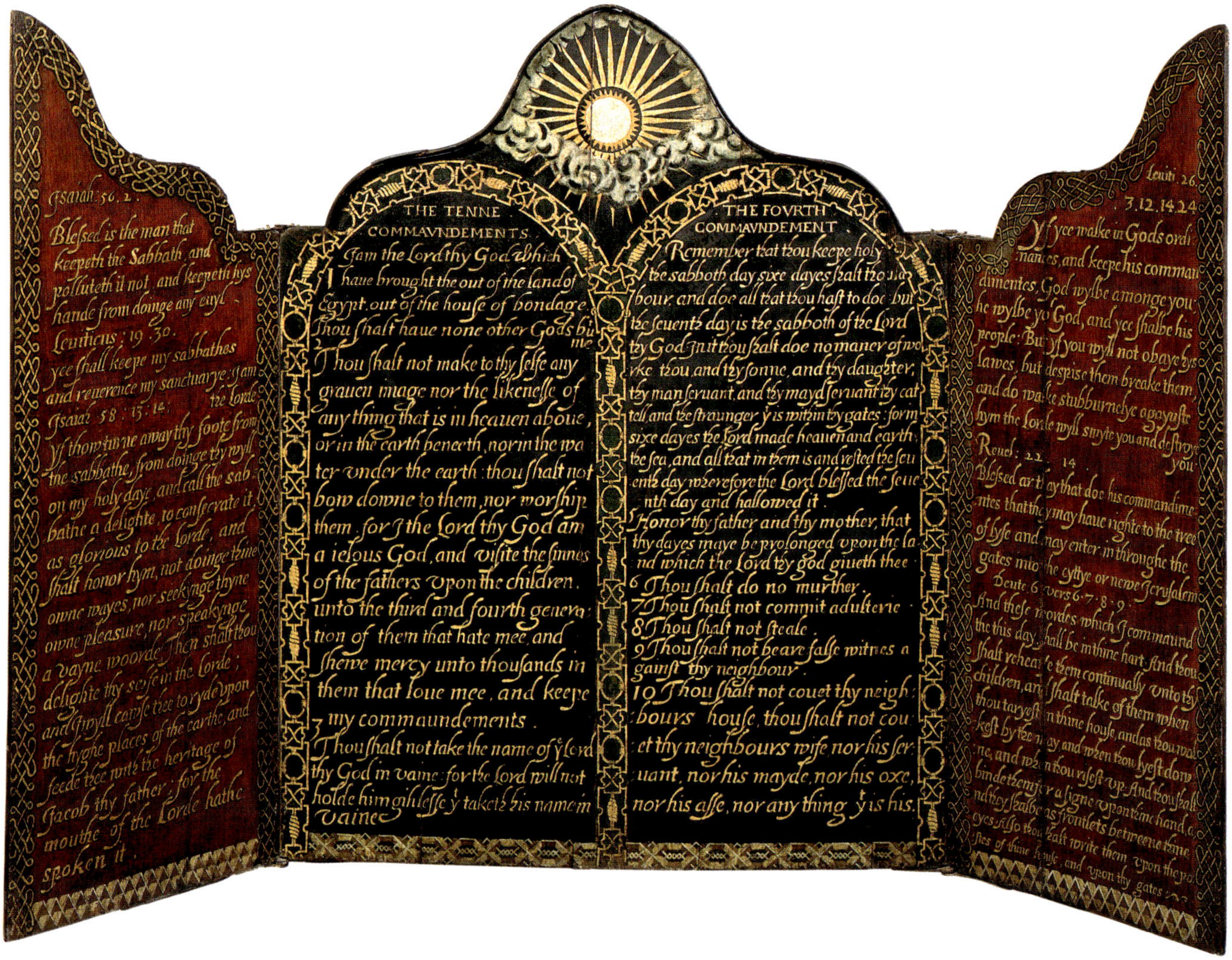

Catholic mass throughout the whole of Henry's reign. Although he ransacked the monasteries and pilgrimage sites, his new laws and regulations governing images in parish churches and other places of worship had remained unclear. Church images were still permitted, provided they were not 'abused'. Some cases of 'abuse' related to lighting candles before images or making pilgrimages to them. However, the confusion lay in the failure to offer a precise legal definition of the word 'abused' in this context, so that disputes broke out within local communities in various part of the country as to whether a given image was legitimate.[4]

After Henry's death in 1547 the ambiguous legal position of ecclesiastical imagery persisted in the first year of the reign of Edward VI until finally, in February 1548, the ruling Privy Council issued an order for the removal of 'all' images from the churches. It was this order, reflecting the lurch in religious policy to radical Protestantism, that began the more systematic iconoclasm that reduced the churches and cathedrals of England to the largely plain and empty interiors that we see today. This decisive moment is commemorated in a painting made some years later, for an Elizabethan patron (ill.36). It depicts Henry VIII pointing from his deathbed to the young Edward, who crushes the Pope underfoot, while above the Privy Councillors sitting in session are figures wielding pikes and axes, enacting the regime's policy of iconoclasm.[5]

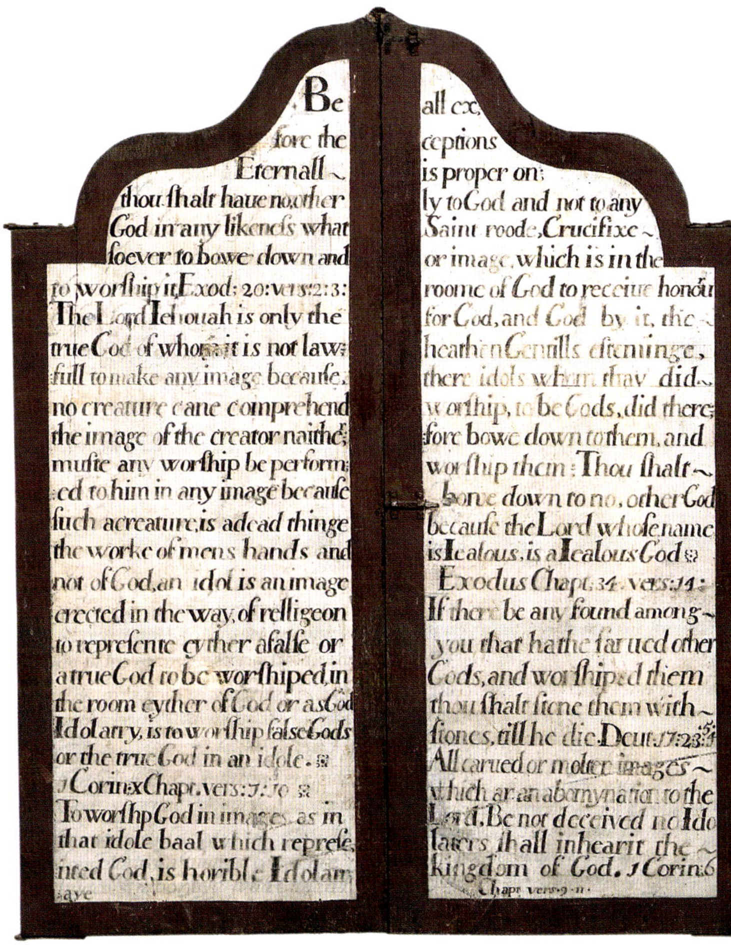

34
Triptych painted with the Ten Commandments
16th century
Oil paint on panel
125 × 201 (open)
Preston St Mary Church, Suffolk

35
Triptych painted with the arms of Elizabeth I (shown closed, displaying painted text sermonising against images and idolatry)
16th century
Oil paint on panel
117 × 990 (closed)
Preston St Mary Church, Suffolk

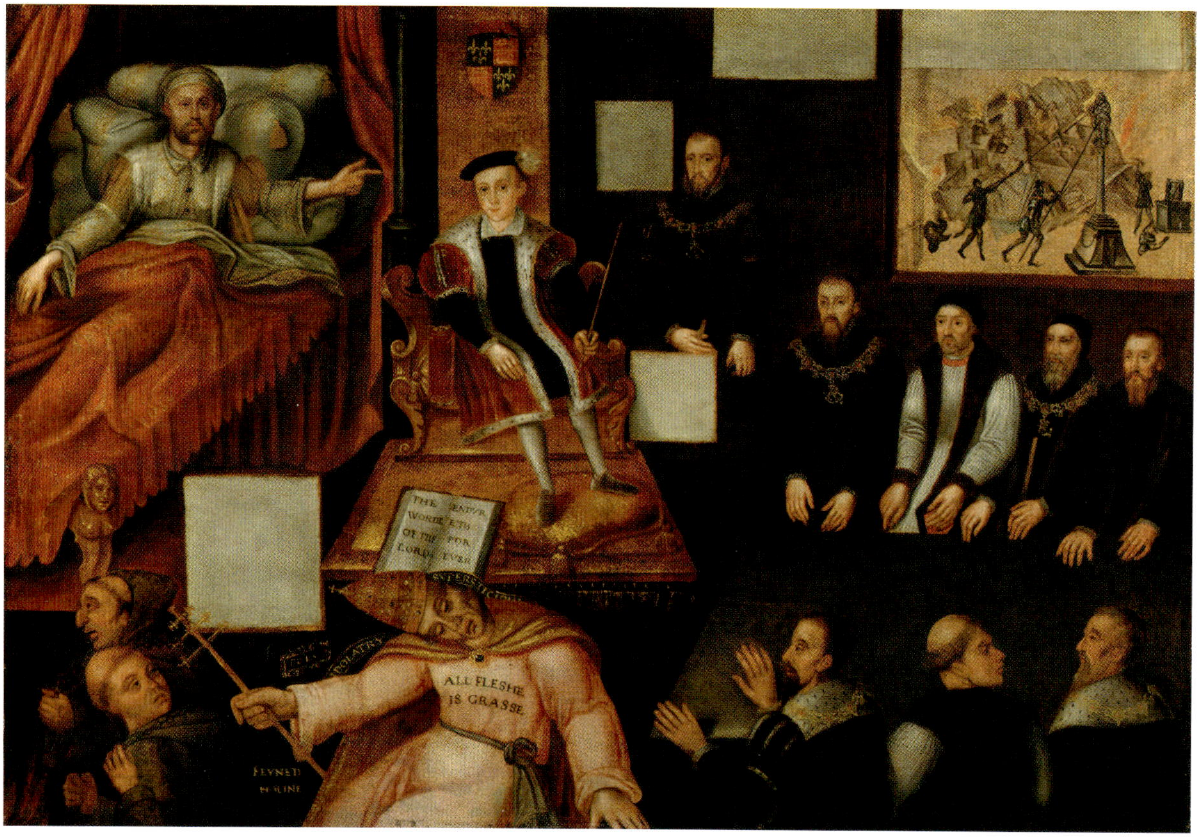

Following Edward's premature death, Mary I (r. 1553–8) sought to reinstate as much ecclesiastical imagery as was practicable, as part of England's return to the Roman Catholic Church. This complete reversal in religious policy was short-lived as, following her five-year reign, Elizabeth I (r. 1558–1603) reverted to the path of Protestant reform. Yet religious images still remained highly controversial, since Elizabeth's government was divided according to the radical and the moderate Protestant positions on the issue. Although the queen's own moderate stance was evident in maintaining a silver crucifix in the Chapel Royal, her more radical bishops won the right to resume the policy of iconoclasm begun by Edward VI's regime across the public churches and cathedrals.[6]

The shifting religious and political context of Tudor England provides a crucial corrective to many of the common preconceptions that endure about the nature of iconoclasm. It has often been automatically assumed to be an act of great violence carried out in a frenzy of hatred, whether by a crazed individual or an out-of-control mob. However, most of the destruction of church images in sixteenth-century England was not the result of a spontaneous act, nor even one necessarily done out of any ideological conviction on the part of the perpetrator. The Reformation was something enforced from above. Historians disagree over the extent to which reform was imposed on a reluctant or even hostile population, or else embraced by a willing population hungry for change, but there is

36
Unknown artist
King Edward VI and the Pope c.1570
Oil paint on panel
62.2 × 90.8
National Portrait Gallery, London

no question that it was aggressively enforced in obedience to the legal directives of the authorities.[7]

Although there were periodic uncontrolled outbreaks of iconoclasm by rampaging crowds like those observed in other parts of Northern Europe, the vast bulk of imagery removed from the parish churches of England was dismantled in an organised and systematic fashion directed by the authorities. In fact the process was effectively carried out on a professional basis, since churchwardens' account books from parishes across the country document the hiring of named individuals with payments made to them for dismantling church screens, taking down sculptures and whitewashing over religious paintings. Although the end result was no different, being the destruction of church images, it is appropriate to differentiate the actions – sometimes reluctant actions – of form-filling local officials obediently following the dictat of government, from what Eamon Duffy has called 'true iconoclasm, expressing deeply held religious conviction'.[8]

Difficulties of this nature in assessing the phenomenon of image-breaking were addressed in a major exhibition held in Karlsruhe in 2002, which coined the term 'iconoclash' to refer to the ambiguities in action and motive that arise when images are in dispute.[9] Whereas the term 'iconoclasm' has more often come to describe a deliberate act of destruction inspired by a clear-cut ideological motivation, 'iconoclash' would encompass that Tudor image-breaker who might only have been following orders with reluctance or even resentment. Furthermore, the notion of 'iconoclash' throws into doubt not only intentions but the very nature of the destructive acts themselves. For example, the well-meaning interventions of an incompetent conservator can result in just as much damage as an ideologue armed with a blunt instrument. Research conducted for the present survey has discovered that the most catastrophic damage inflicted on the painted figures of saints from Gressenhall church in Norfolk (ill.51) came not from the actions of Protestant Reformers, who made 'thin vigorous scratches through the faces only', but from 'inappropriate cleaning techniques' undertaken probably in the early 1970s.[10] This no doubt well-intentioned individual effectively scrubbed the otherwise intact saints from their wooden screen, thereby doing a far more thorough and efficient job than the iconoclasts of the English Reformation.

In order to understand damage done to images it thus becomes crucial to try to determine when the damage took place. Without supporting evidence it is often impossible to judge under which Tudor regime a scratch or blow was inflicted. Furthermore, the destruction did not cease in the sixteenth century. In spite of the repeated efforts by successive Tudor governments, it is clear that a considerable quantity of imagery remained in the fixtures, fittings and windows of churches in England. What survived was subject to yet another wave of iconoclasm in the seventeenth century, during the Civil War and the Commonwealth.[11] More meticulous in approach, this campaign of destruction sometimes re-targeted objects already attacked by Tudor iconoclasm. The consequent problems of dating the damage done to an image are even further complicated by abuses committed in later centuries. In the eighteenth century neglect sometimes combined with indifference, as in the fate of some of the medieval windows at Great Malvern Priory. Two shocked antiquarians castigated local schoolboys, 'whose recreation consisted in throwing stones at the numerous windows, all full (as we have observed) of the finest stained glass'.[12] Even by the time of the Victorians' enthusiastic Gothic Revival the destruction did not cease, as medieval churches deemed to be not quite medieval enough were subject to 'improvements'. In our own time, the botched attempts at cleaning and restoration mentioned above indicate that the damage and destruction of English church images is far from over.

Failure to recognise the importance of situating each act of iconoclasm in its specific context runs the serious risk of historical anachronism and cultural misrepresentation. It was this that led to certain nineteenth- and twentieth-century historians condemning iconoclasts of the Protestant Reformation as 'philistines'. Accusing them of failing to uphold nineteenth-century aesthetic values and appreciation of art seems misplaced. The notion of 'art' depends on a body of aesthetic theory that values an object as a personal expression of creativity by an 'artist' of exceptional talent. This notion did not exist in sixteenth-century England.[13] By contrast, the early items in the present survey were practical objects, usually with a religious function, made by workshops of anonymous craftsmen. The attitudes of nineteenth-century critics came from looking back at history through the prism of their own time, in particular their disgust at the French Revolution that had indeed witnessed iconoclasm by crowds bent on anarchy.[14]

More recent research into iconoclasm has come from a broad range of different academic disciplines from religious history, art history, archaeology, anthropology and other perspectives. Although some of this has attempted to find a pervasive psychological impulse, most have recognised that in terms of motivation there are so many unbridgeable disparities of politics, culture, religion, gender, class and so forth that 'there can be no useful meta-history of iconoclasm', as one recent survey of the issue succinctly put it.[15]

Shifting from attempts to write universal histories of iconoclasm to investigating the motivations of specific individuals responsible is, however, replete with pitfalls of its own. Protestant theologians who advocated iconoclasm published their justifications in the vast numbers of lengthy books on the subject printed in the sixteenth century. These ranged widely, from the strict interpretation of biblical texts, to a desire to save the common people from the temptations to idolatry that images posed, to a whole range of more practical matters such as the cost of images being money better spent in relieving the poor. Some, such as Luther's former colleague Karlstadt, offered highly personal insights, including his anger against images coming in part from the humiliation he felt when recalling his naïve attachment and love for them in his youth.[16] However, the realm of intention is difficult if not impossible to infiltrate. Individuals, then as now, can attempt to rationalise their actions after the event, or offer multiple, conflicting reasons as justification. Highly personal motives too shameful to admit publicly might remain hidden beneath the surface, from feelings of resentment or jealousy to a primitive pleasure and satisfaction in breaking and shattering.[17]

If the personal motivations of Protestant iconoclasts remain ambiguous or unknowable, an alternative approach is to look at iconoclasm as a strategy, or what Bruno Latour has called a 'resource'.[18] This more general approach could gain an understanding of what results or practical effects image-breakers might hope to achieve through their actions. For example, not all iconoclasm seeks the complete annihilation of the image. Other strategies can come into play, such as defacing the object and leaving the remnants as ostentatiously conspicuous as possible in order to make a particular point. Even comparisons with present-day acts of iconoclasm

37
The Great Screen at Winchester Cathedral, *c.*1470–80, with 19th-century sculpted figures replacing those destroyed at the Reformation (restoration completed 1899)

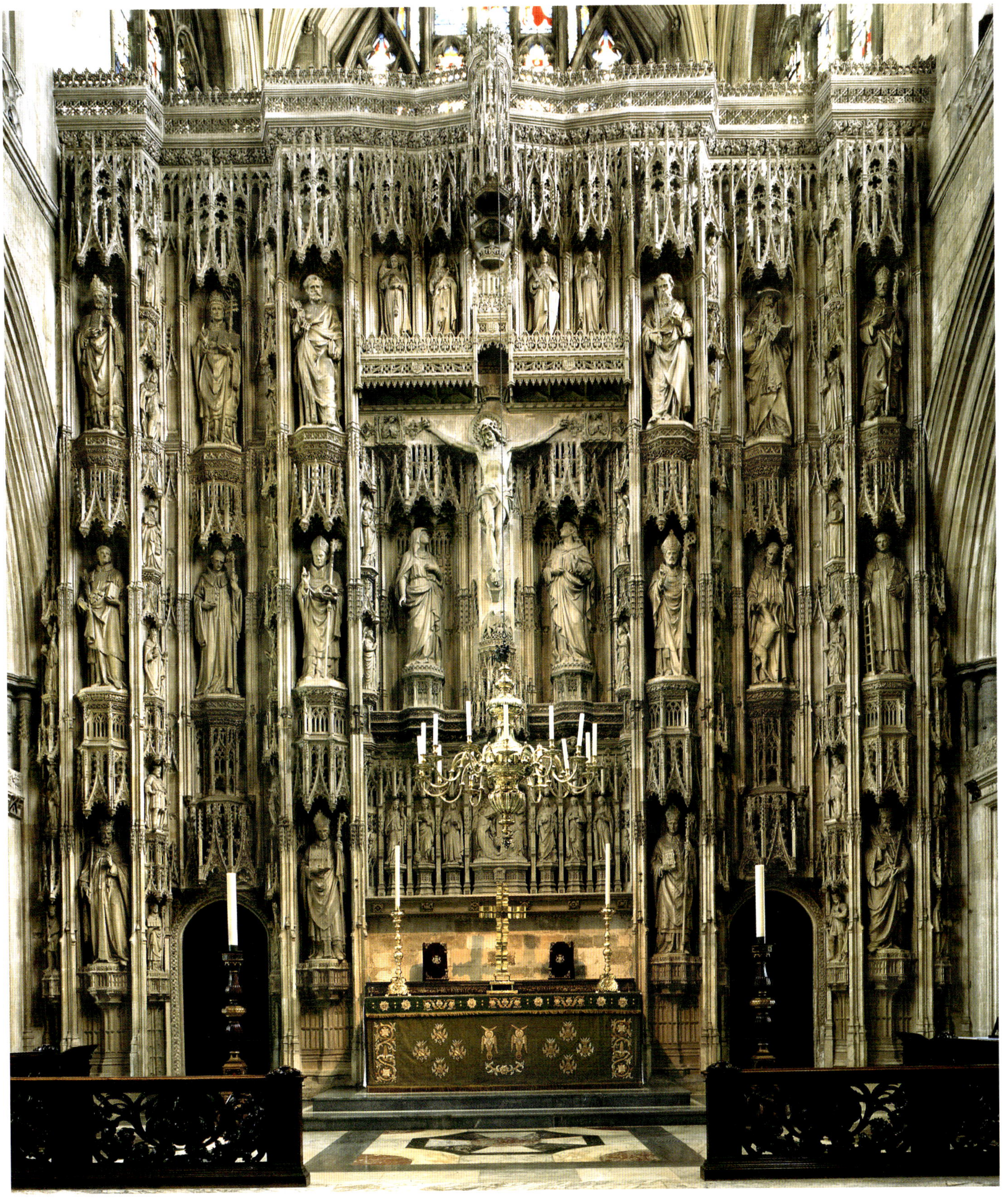

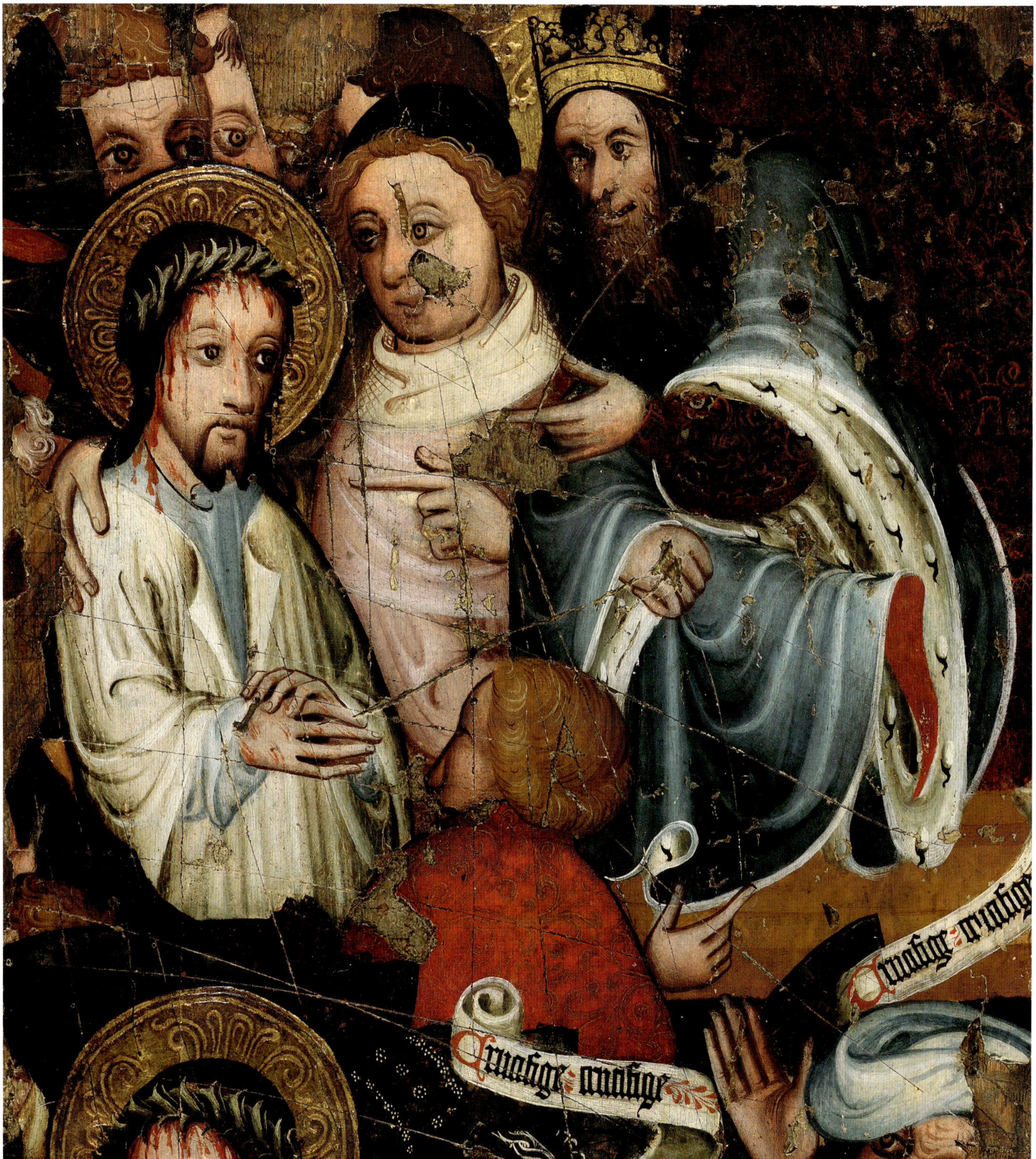
Crucifige crucifige

However, the handling of these sculptures might have had more to do with practical recycling than vindictive anger. Most of the bodies of the figures were sawn up and reused as building blocks, some parts used as hard core, but the heads, being of no further use, were discarded. The chips to the noses and other parts of the faces do not resemble the deep and quite deliberate gouging out of the eyes from stone heads found in examples from other sites where a directed attack has unmistakably taken place. Even a casual disregard for religious sculptures cannot automatically be connected to a deep ideological commitment since, as Phillip Lindley has pointed out, schemes of sculptures had been cannibalised or utterly destroyed in English churches and cathedrals throughout the medieval period. This had usually been done to make way for new structures or rebuilding. Indeed, would the fragments of the twelfth-century sculptural scheme at Lincoln Cathedral, which was destroyed to make way for a large window in the thirteenth century, have looked so different from the fragments that survive at Winchester?[21]

The dismantling and recycling of images and other objects, as opposed to their utter obliteration, took place across the parish churches of England especially during Henry VIII's reign and the early years of Edward VI's. Costly chalices were sold to local parishioners to be used as wine goblets on the dinner table, just as other liturgical vessels were refashioned into elaborate salt cellars, like the Stonyhurst Salt (ill.43).[22] Made from fragments of Catholic reliquaries and pre-Reformation church plate, originally its rubies and garnets would have symbolised the blood of Christ. It has been suggested that viewers were supposed to recognise their provenance.[23]

Paintings too could be subjected to a similar treatment. Two early fifteenth-century fragments of panel painting possibly fall into this category (ill.42).

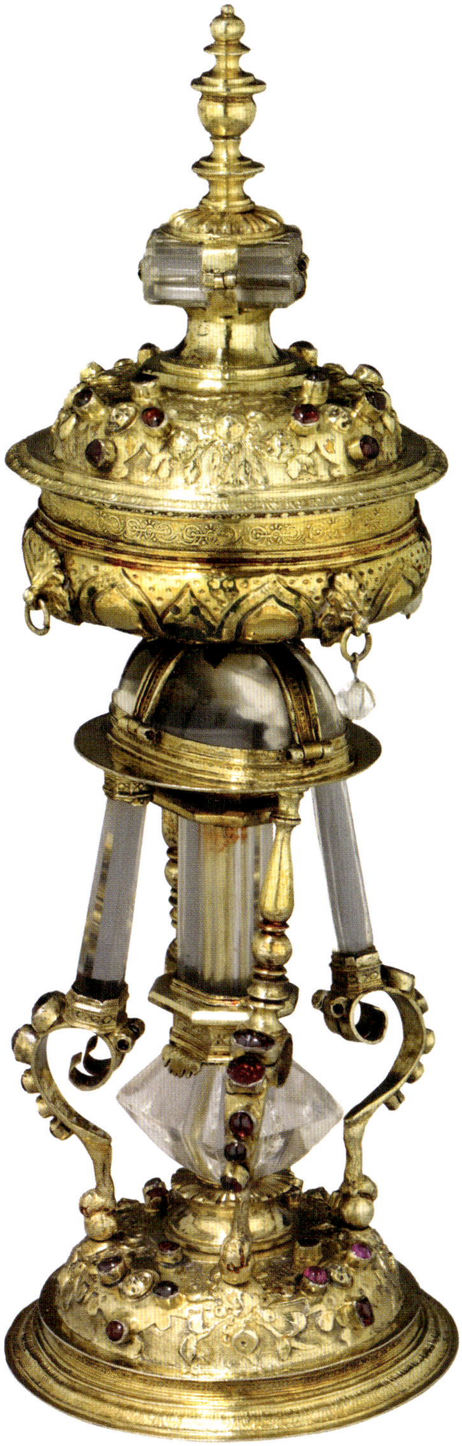

42
British School
Christ before Pilate c.1400–25
Tempera on panel
33 × 29.5
Fitzwilliam Museum, Cambridge

43
The Stonyhurst Salt 1577–8
Silver-gilt, rock crystal and gemstones
26.3 × 9.4
The Trustees of the British Museum, London

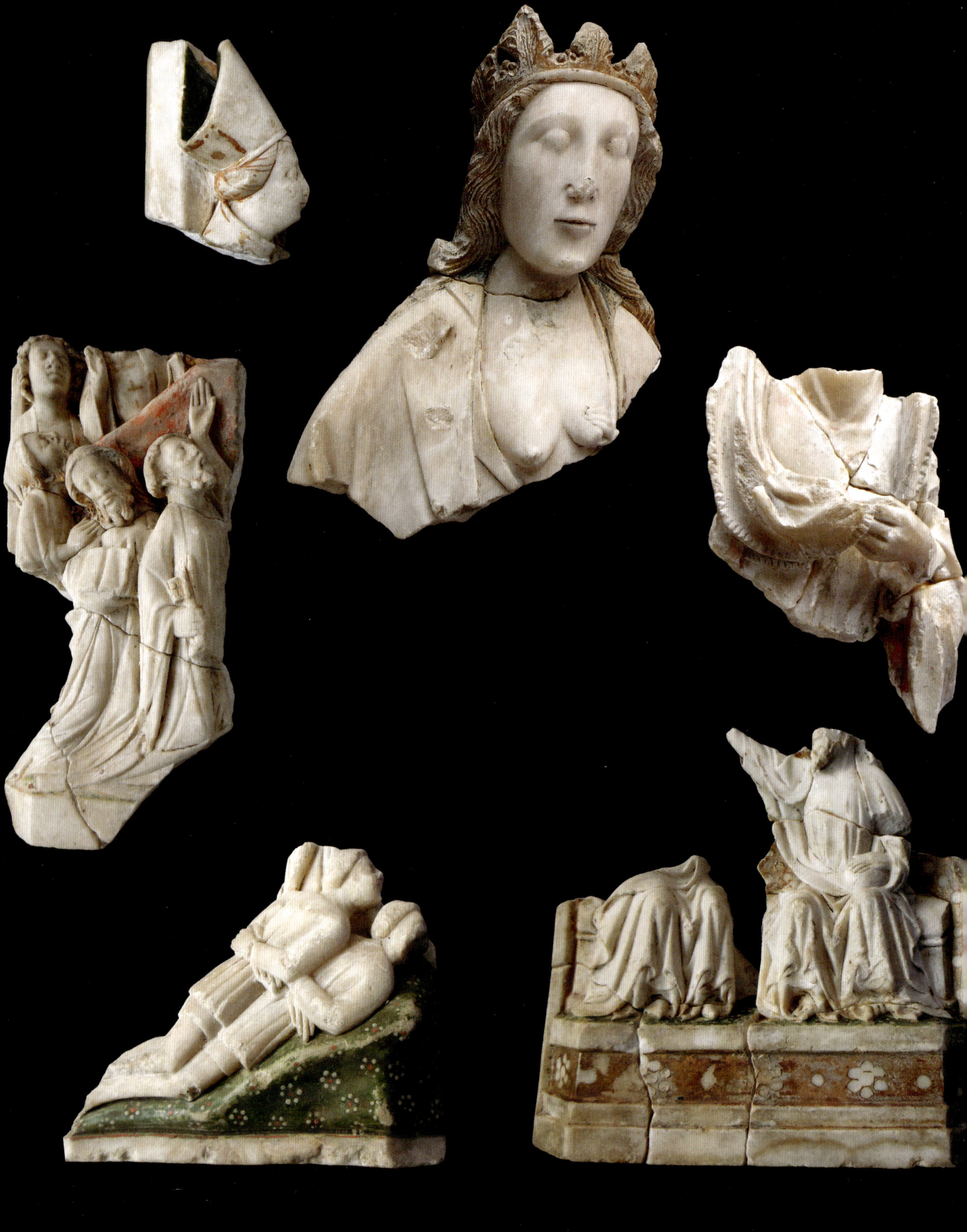

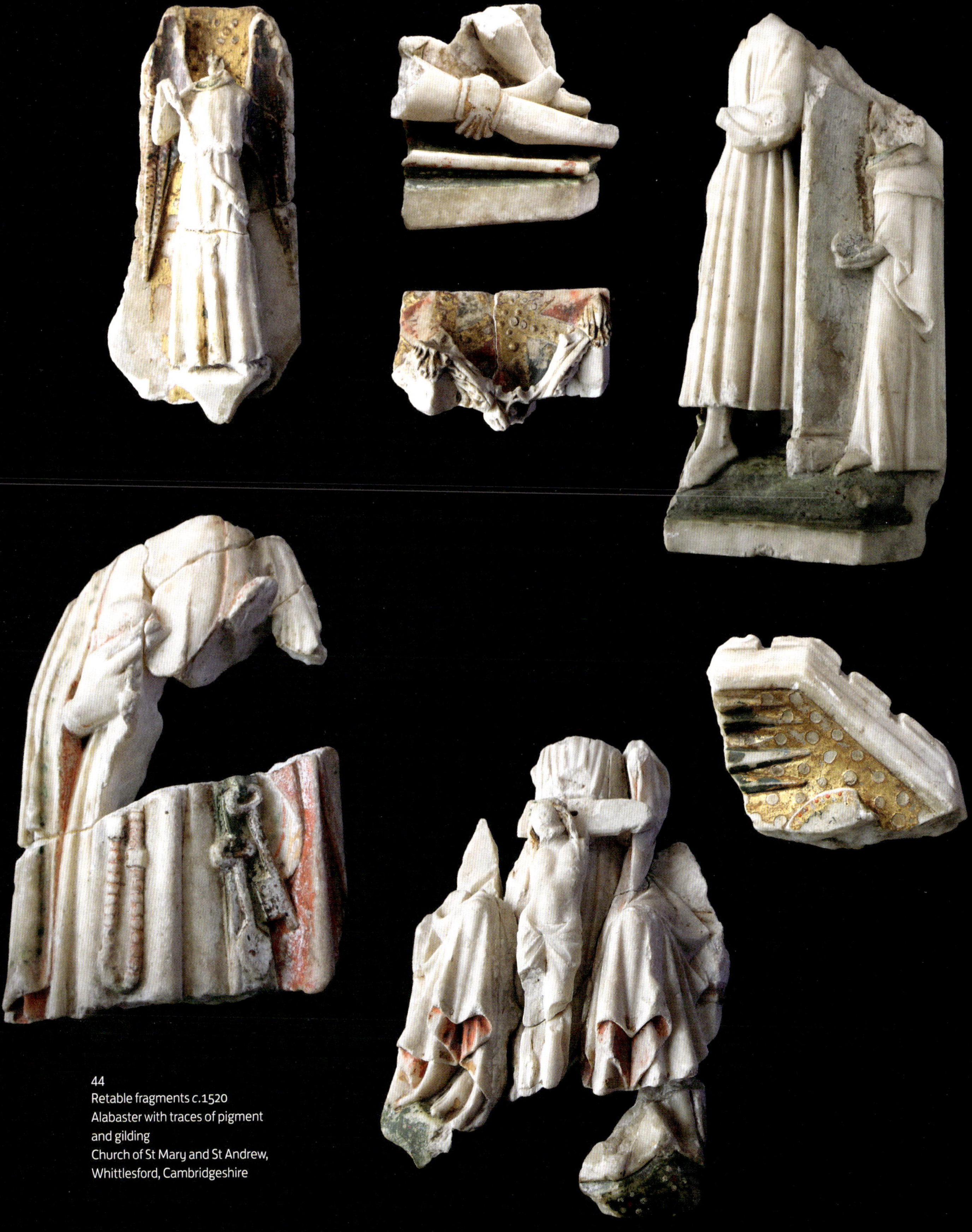

44
Retable fragments c.1520
Alabaster with traces of pigment
and gilding
Church of St Mary and St Andrew,
Whittlesford, Cambridgeshire

The panel representing Christ taken before Pilate has been sawn along the bottom edge where it has chopped off the top of Christ's head from the scene below.[24] Yet this particular mutilation might have been a by-product of cutting the whole work into equal-size pieces, since another fragment, depicting Christ carrying the Cross, is of matching dimensions. Wooden panels could be reused as table tops, cupboard doors and a host of other functions. Officially, however, such objects were supposed to be defaced before sale so as to prevent a return to their former use. This might account for the network of cuts and scratch marks inscribed across both panels. If so, this would certainly follow the letter of the law if not its spirit, given that the figure of Christ with his gold halo has received minimal damage compared to other, less significant areas of the painting.

Destruction

Iconoclasm that seeks the total destruction of the image can be understood as an idealistic strategy of purification.[25] Characterised by a rigid fundamentalism, it presents itself as a vital mission to re-educate hearts and minds by obliterating the entire corrupt ideology of which the image is a symptom and replacing it with purity and truth. Despite the fundamentalism of its terms, this phenomenon is not at all restricted to religious conflict but just as evident in, for instance, the Cultural Revolution of Communism.

It was probably as part of this process that the alabaster reliefs from Whittlesford Church in Cambridgeshire were shattered into small pieces (ill.44). The rich seam of alabaster stone in Nottinghamshire had allowed a large-scale production of these religious sculptures, particularly in the century before the Reformation.[26] Perhaps originally forming an altarpiece of plaques carved in low relief and set into wooden housings, these examples were not stripped down for recycling but were put beyond any further use. A more definitive erasure was possible when consigning wooden sculpture to the fire. Large figures of Christ on the cross, the Virgin Mary and St John the Evangelist, usually carved in wood, were once found in virtually every parish church in England on top of the rood screen (the wooden screen separating the chancel from the nave, named after the 'rood' or cross it displayed). The regimes of Edward VI and Elizabeth I ordered the dismantling of these screens and the destruction of their sculpted groups.[27] It is little surprise then that, except for a handful of meagre fragments, not a trace remains of these figurative works or indeed of any other examples of medieval wooden sculpture. Of English origin and dating from the eve of the Reformation, a wooden Christ figure found in 1952 in the derelict Great Hall of Fiddleford Manor, Dorset, is thus an exceptionally rare survival (ill.45).

The total obliteration of an image is a strategy aimed at the collective memory. A profound cultural shift can hardly be achieved efficiently if the population is surrounded by objects and symbols of the old order – whether these were the religious images in English churches that embodied the beliefs and practices of the pre-Reformation Church, or indeed temples and artefacts of traditional religion and culture that have been subject to the same strategy in modern Tibet.[28] The reason given in Edward VI's legislation to 'utterly extinct and destroy' images was 'so that there remain no memory of the same in walls, glass-windows and elsewhere'.[29] In implementing this strategy, the Elizabethan Bishop of Winchester even objected to the empty niches in the Great Screen of his cathedral, wanting them 'filled up and the places made plain'[30] to destroy the memory of the sculptures having ever existed.

In this strategy of iconoclasm the image comes to stand symbolically for so much more than it represents visually. Church images had disappeared in the reign of Edward VI, reappeared in the reign of Mary I and then disappeared again under Elizabeth I. Their presence or absence had become a very public barometer of religious conflict and a marker of which political faction had come to power. In addition to empty churches with whitewashed walls, the Royal Supremacy of Edward and Elizabeth was made manifest by painting the royal arms directly over religious paintings on the church wall or even in a triptych that copied the format of an altarpiece (see ill.35). The political associations of church images only intensified in Elizabethan England in reaction to Catholic plots against the queen and foreign threats such as the Spanish Armada. Rescuing a church image from destruction in the hope of reinstating it once Catholicism was re-established had become a hope denoting potential treasonous intent, given that it required the overthrow of the queen and her entire government.[31]

The aim to obliterate images has been connected by Bruno Latour to a fantasy to rid the world of mediators and access truth directly.[32] Praying before the Fiddleford Christ (ill.45), for example, was to communicate with Christ through the mediation of an image. This was 'horrible idolatry', according to the sermonising passages based on biblical text painted on the exterior wings of the triptych of the royal arms (ill.35), since it was giving worship that was 'proper only to God and not to any Saint, rood, Crucifix or image…'. Since unmediated access to God was believed to come through reading His Word, what could be a better replacement for corrupt images than the incorruptible text of the Bible? In many cases this was a direct substitution, with religious paintings being whitewashed over and repainted with passages from scripture in clear

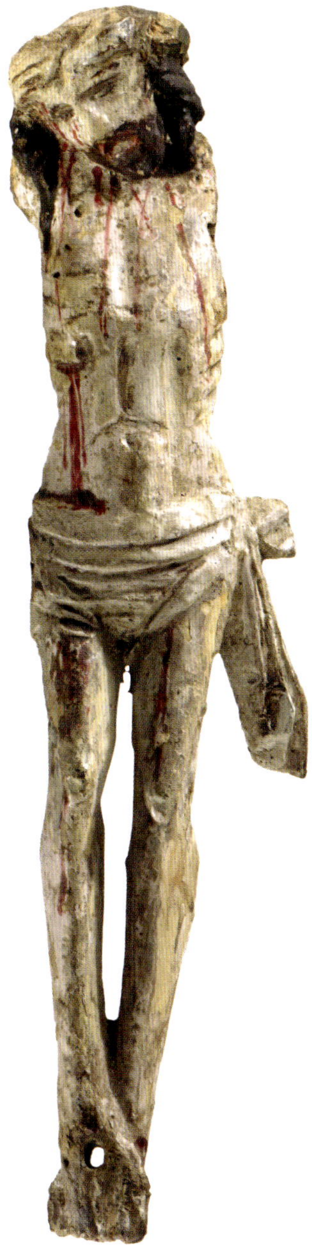

45
Figure of Christ 1475–1525
Wood with traces of pigment
16.5 × 4.1 × 2.5
The Trustees of the British Museum, London

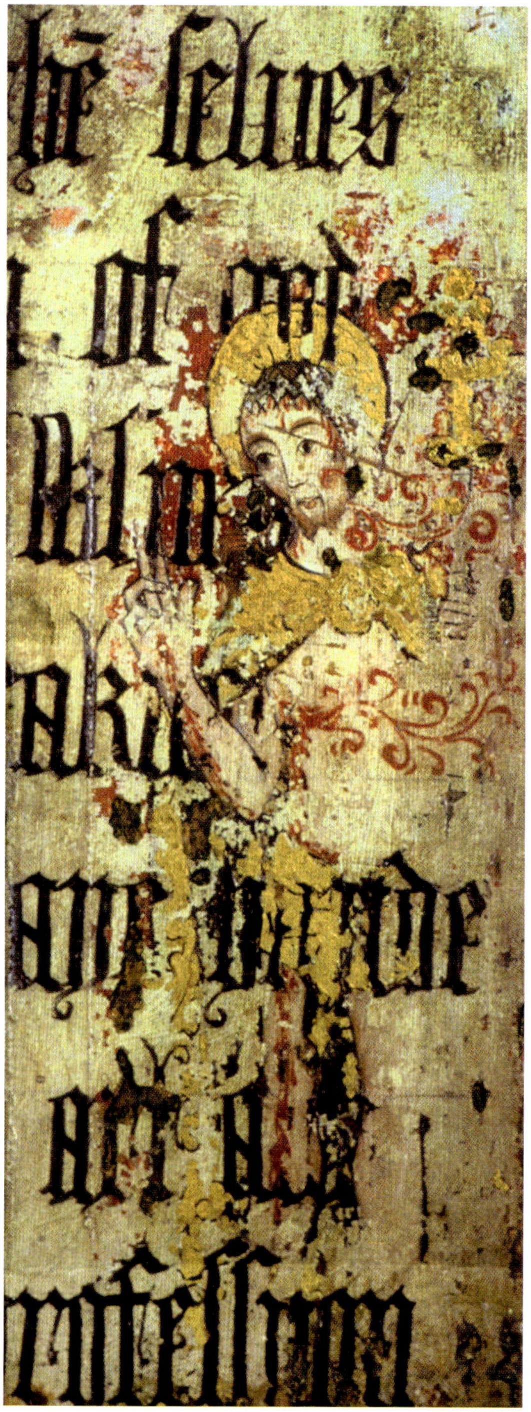

black letters. The panel from the former priory at Binham in Norfolk illustrates this procedure (ill.46). Coming from the lower register of the rood screen (comparable to the section of the screen from Gressenhall, ill.51), the original religious figures were effaced with quotations from Cranmer's Great Bible of 1539. Over the centuries, however, the layer of whitewash has worn and the late medieval painting of the Resurrected Christ has started to re-emerge and effectively rise again.[33]

Defacement

Although the visibility of Christ on the Binham Priory screen is the result of a failed attempt at obliteration, the saints on the screen from St Mary's Church in Gressenhall, Norfolk, seem to have been left visible quite deliberately (ill.51). Bearing in mind that the original iconoclastic attack was restricted to scratches and cuts to the figures (and not the scrubbing out by the modern conservator), enough of the painted saints would have remained visible to identify them; this task was made even clearer for the first three, whose names remain perfectly legible on the labels beneath each one. We are intended to *see* their absence. Unlike the attempt to wipe images and what they represent from the cultural memory, defacement is a strategy of iconoclasm that seeks to impress itself on that memory as an enduring symbol.

The same treatment was meted out to the painted panel of the Crucifixion preserved at Norwich Cathedral (ill.47). This rare survival, dating from the final decades of the fourteenth century, was probably one section of a larger altarpiece. With its elaborate raised *pastiglia* ornament on the gold background, it would have been a costly commission. The wealthy patrons are most likely the man and woman who

46
Section of a painted rood screen showing *Christ as the Man of Sorrows*, *c.*1500, later whitewashed and overpainted with Biblical text, *c.*1540–53
Oil paint on panel
80 × 24
Priory Church of St Mary and the Holy Cross, Binham, South Norfolk

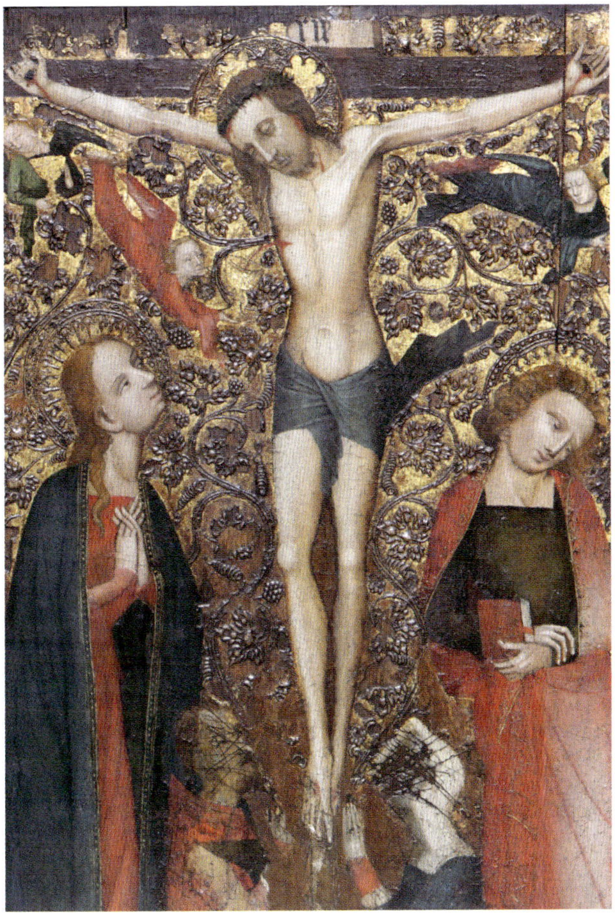

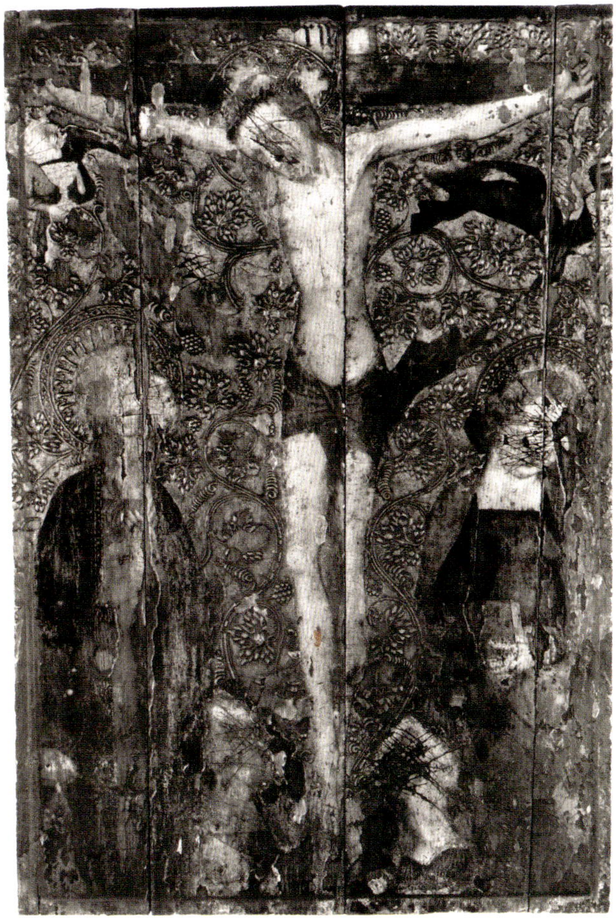

appear praying at the foot of the cross as traditional 'donor portraits'. But their act of piety met with the opprobrium of an iconoclast who scratched out their faces. However, similar scratch marks applied to the faces of the religious figures above, which can be seen on a photograph taken of the panel in the early 1950s (ill.48), are no longer visible on account of the restoration undertaken at that time. Lack of time or money might account for the patchy extent of this restoration. Indeed, it is difficult to imagine professional restorers today thinking that such a scheme of overpainting would be appropriate.[34]

47
British School
The Crucifixion c.1380–1400
Oil paint and mixed media on panel
71 × 50 × 4.5
The Dean and Chapter of
Norwich Cathedral

48
Pre-conservation photo, taken in the early 1950s, of *The Crucifixion* (ill.47)
Department of Conservation and Technology, The Courtauld Institute of Art, London

Scratches to the face, particularly blotting out the eyes, in examples like these are representative of the ways in which iconoclasts have sought to deface figurative images. In 1977, when a portrait painted by Rubens on display in Düsseldorf had acid thrown at it, the face and eyes of the figure were the target. The eyes in particular can create a sense of communication between the figure represented and the viewer, which in turn can evoke a powerful sense of presence.[35] Protestant reformers, like many other iconoclasts, assumed naïve belief in those venerating images. Rather than praying through the image to the transcendent prototype, the Reformers accused them of worshipping (idolising) lumps of stone and painted panels. The more realistic the image the greater danger it was believed to pose. Applying colour to a statue, for example, was one way in which an image could be brought to life and, as with most medieval sculpture, the figures in the Winchester screen and the alabaster reliefs from Whittlesford were originally brightly painted. The limestone sculpture of the Dead Christ found at Mercers' Hall in London was coloured too, and was also designed to evoke an emotional response in the viewer through other realistic details such as the thorn that punctures the Saviour's eyebrow (see ill.49).[36] Breaking such objects apart and scratching out the eyes severed the connection with the viewer and exposed images as lifeless and powerless 'stocks and stones'.[37]

Iconoclastic attacks to faces and eyes occur so frequently across the world and throughout history that Professor David Freedberg believed that a sense of presence in images is hardwired into the psyche of the human species as a whole, which accounts for the exceptional power of images and the related urge to commit iconoclasm. According to Freedberg, 'We fear the image which appears to be alive, because it cannot be so; and so people may evince their fear, or demonstrate mastery over the consequences of elision, by breaking or mutilating the image…'.[38] Although anecdotal evidence might lend credence to Freedberg's theory, subsequent research has called it seriously into question. Scholars working in anthropology and across other disciplines have found that the imputation of presence is not a property peculiar to images. All manner of non-figurative and non-representational objects can be thought to embody the presence of an ancestor or of the divine. A sense of presence in images is far more culturally contingent and confused. Confused in that it is far more common than we care to admit to hold entirely incompatible beliefs at the same time. We can relate to and even interact with an image whilst at the same time being fully aware that it is an inanimate object. Thus for many, Freedberg's theory seems too dogmatic, not allowing for the ambiguities and inconsistencies of human behaviour, particularly if it were to apply universally.[39]

The supposed inability to differentiate between image and referent was more often a polemical construct used by one religious group against another. At the time of the Reformation, Catholic defenders of images turned this accusation back upon their Protestant critics. They pointed to the behaviour of Protestant iconoclasts towards the images they attacked, especially the figurative sculptures which they would, for example, decapitate, or chop off the hands, burn on a pyre or even hang by the neck. These were, of course, punishments imposed upon criminals by the justice system. Moreover, there are accounts of iconoclasts attacking images of Christ in a ritualistic way that mimicked the roles of the soldiers who mocked and beat Christ as re-enacted in Passion plays.[40] Whether a conscious ploy to ridicule and parody or an unconscious reaction to the power of images, there is undoubtedly a dilemma or paradox facing all iconoclasts: are images to be destroyed because they are powerless, empty and worthless, or because they pose a threat, are dangerous and thus powerful?

If certain strategies adopted by iconoclasts in sixteenth-century England can be recognised in use in our own time, so too responses of Tudor defenders of images can have contemporary resonance. For example, in 1567 the silver crucifix Queen Elizabeth I retained in her Chapel Royal was thrown to the floor by a 'certain youth' during the service and stamped underfoot.[41] In many respects the episode reads like modern newspaper reports of lone individuals entering public galleries or museums to attack a work of art, such as the young man in 1975 who attacked Rembrandt's *Nightwatch* at the Rijksmuseum in Amsterdam. In response, the museum's Director of Public Relations is reported to have said: 'The assailant and his motives are wholly uninteresting to us; for one cannot apply normal criteria to the motivations of someone who is mentally disturbed.'[42] Similarly, the response of Queen Elizabeth was to question the assailant's sanity. To do so meant he could be released without further charge and, more conveniently for her, without the religious controversy and debate that her radical Protestant subjects were so keen to air. Could this make us look again at the way attacks on art in galleries are rationalised and marginalised? This has been a standard response by museums over the years, and for the very good reason that so often the individuals charged do indeed turn out to be suffering from a mental illness. But might this not also be the convenient means adopted by Queen Elizabeth I for shutting down unwelcome public debate?

Acts of iconoclasm are shaped by the ideology and culture of their time. The precise motivations of those responsible, so far as they are knowable, can differ radically yet, as we have seen, similarities are noticeable in their deployment of image-breaking as a strategic tool. Furthermore, the history of iconoclasm in Tudor England, and the way it is written ought to alert us to the fact that our responses to iconoclasts are equally shaped by the ideology and culture of our own time, whether that response is of disgust or admiration.

The Dead Christ

The spectacular discovery of the late medieval figure of the Dead Christ was made in 1954 during an excavation of the chapel of the Mercers' Company on Cheapside in the City of London. The sculpture emerged from beneath rubble left from the bombing of London during the Second World War. It was immediately recognised as one of the most important surviving examples of religious sculpture produced in England before the Reformation.

Carved from a single block of limestone on a life-sized scale, the Dead Christ was clearly the work of a sculptor of considerable talent. However, rather than being English in style, the Mercers' Christ compares most closely with late Gothic stone sculpture produced in the north-eastern Netherlands. In particular, a stone Entombed Christ in Utrecht Cathedral, datable to 1521, is remarkably similar. Both represent the body with a high degree of naturalism, including the convincing musculature and raised veins on the legs. They also feature the illusionistic attention to detail so closely associated with Netherlandish art. For example, the rickety bier or stretcher on which the body of the Mercers' Christ is laid closely resembles those commonly used in medieval Europe to carry the dead to church for the Office of the Dead. A more subtle illusionistic device is featured on the inscription running along the right side of the base, where a drop of blood has been carved between two of the words as though it has dripped from the right hand that originally rested above it. These comparisons help date the Mercers' sculpture of Christ to about 1500–20, and ascribe it to a sculptor who probably trained in the Netherlands but was working in England on account of the use of Chilmark stone from Salisbury.[43]

Although it emerged from beneath the floor of the Mercers' chapel, there is no mention of the sculpture in the company records. It was, therefore, more likely to have been commissioned by a benefactor connected with the site when it was the hospital church of St Thomas of Acon. The Mercers' Company purchased the church to serve as its chapel in 1541 as part of the Dissolution of the Monasteries. In addition to uncertainty as to the patron, the original position and function of the sculpture within the church also remains unknown, whether created as part of a funeral monument in a chantry chapel or intended as a devotional piece.[44] However, what the archives do make unequivocally clear, is that the Mercers' Company very promptly complied with the iconoclastic injunctions of the radically Protestant regime of Edward VI. In 1547–8 the Mercers recorded 'takyng dowen of the image[s] in the church…'.[45]

Whether it was at this juncture that the sculpture of Christ was reduced to its ruined state is not known, but the damage is so serious as to suggest a deliberate attack. The whole right arm and parts of the left are missing; sections of the legs and feet are also gone, and a portion of the top of the head, along with the Crown of Thorns, is lost. What makes this unlikely to be anything other than the result of Protestant iconoclasm is that the sculpture of Christ in Utrecht was damaged in almost exactly the same way. The extent and positioning of the breaks parallel each other so closely that the same motivation might have been the cause of the damage in both instances. One hypothesis is that the wounds received by Christ at the crucifixion were targeted, the reason being that the Cult of the Five Wounds (to hands, feet and side) had been one of the most popular subjects of devotion in the pre-Reformation Church.[46]

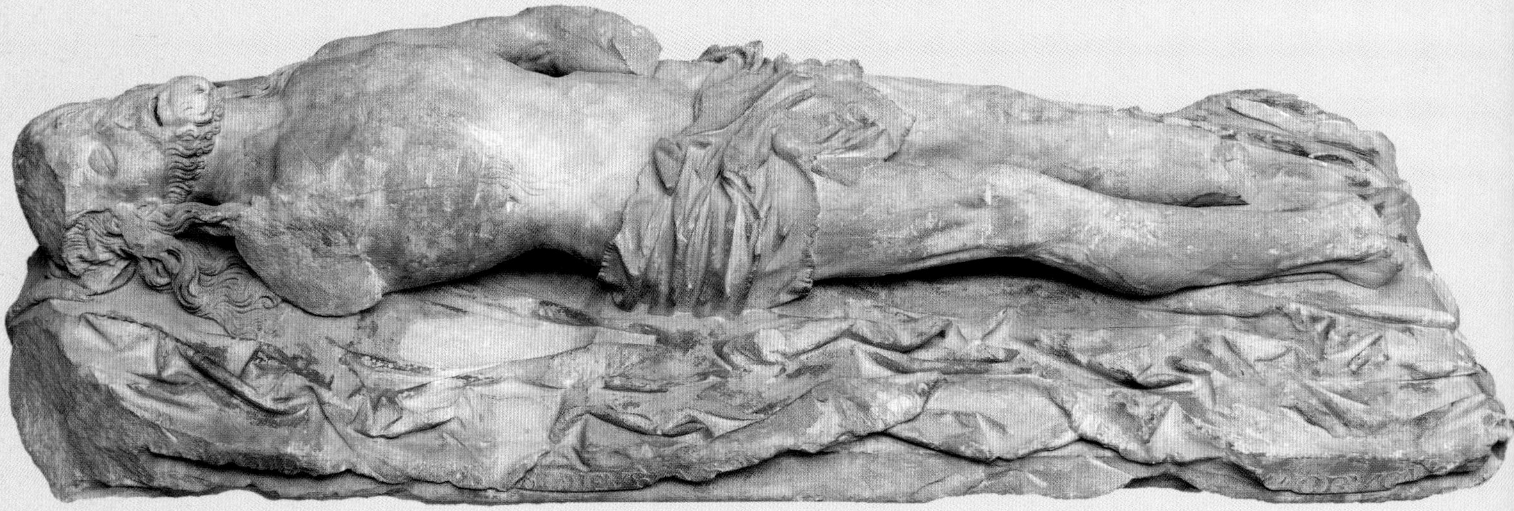

Prayers were said and masses dedicated to the wounds in the hope of spiritual help and protection. The symbol of the Five Wounds, arranged like a heraldic shield, had been inscribed into the fixtures and fittings of churches across England and had even been adopted as the emblem of the rebels who rose up against Henry VIII's religious reforms in the 'Pilgrimage of Grace'.[47] The many associations with the pre-Reformation Church made the Cult of the Wounds anathema to Reformers, who attacked its symbolism wherever they found it.

Although smashing off the hands and feet of the Mercers' Christ removed four of the wounds, the side wound, whose access to Christ's heart had made it the holiest and most powerful, can still be seen, with carved streams of blood flowing from it. Nevertheless, its survival could be no more than expediency since its position on the central block of the torso would have required considerable heavy work to remove. Other impact marks, such as the 'X' incised into the upper right chest, only add to the difficulties of interpretation.[48] Whether or not the wounds were a particular target, this sculpture of Christ embodies the more general cult of images that Protestants sought to abolish. It conforms to late medieval conventions of devotional imagery that aimed to affect the viewer emotionally, heightened by the pathos of the eyes not fully shut, the open mouth, the limbs stiffened by rigor mortis and the thorns that pierce the eyebrows.[49] Experiencing the Passion of Christ as if an eyewitness would have been enhanced by the original application of naturalistic colour of the flesh tones, blue veins, red blood flowing from the side wound, and white teeth.[50] Relating so personally to an image, as though Christ were present, was condemned by Protestants as idolatry.

Even the biblical quotations inscribed along the edges of the cloth would have been objectionable, for rather than being a clear expression of the Word of God in English these included a Latin text used in the Catholic Psalter (Philippians 2:8) and recited as part of the liturgy of the Roman Catholic Church.[51]

The act of burying the statue is another intriguing feature. It could have been the most practical way of disposing of such a heavy object, but it could also be another instance of Protestants treating church images in a ritualistic and even anthropomorphic fashion of punishment and burial of the body.[52] Yet it is also possible that the broken Christ was buried by those who sought its preservation by concealing it beneath the church floor.

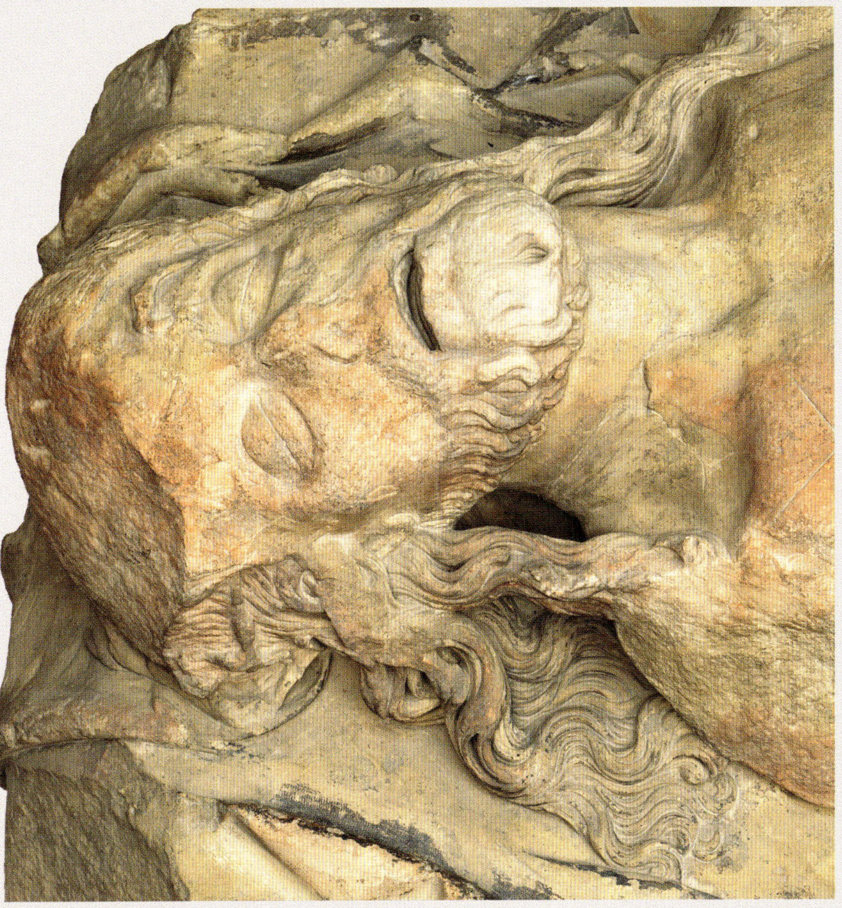

49
The Dead Christ *c.*1500–20
Limestone
197 × 68.6
The Mercers' Company, London

There are several instances of sculptures, both fully intact and badly damaged, being hidden beneath paving stones or holed up within the walls of English parish churches.[53] Whatever the intention, this act served to protect the sculpture, even from such catastrophic events as the Great Fire of London and the Blitz, and ensured its survival for four hundred years.
RW

The Great Screen of Winchester Cathedral

The ruination of the Great Screen of Winchester Cathedral lays bare the magnitude of the decimation of English medieval sculpture wrought by the Reformation. Erected as a reredos behind the high altar in the mid-fifteenth century, the sophistication and superb craftsmanship of its carved ornamented niches can be appreciated today but not the statues within them, which are all late nineteenth-century replacements (ill.37). The niches indicate that the screen originally displayed eighteen life-sized and thirty-four smaller figures, which were probably supplemented by additional sculptures of intermediate size that survive as fragments.[54] The replication of such losses across the country means that even a destruction rate of over 90% of English medieval sculpture may, in Phillip Lindley's words, 'be optimistic'.[55]

Of the life-sized figures in the Winchester screen, only some of the heads (ill.41) and a solitary gloved hand remain (ill.39). What survive of the smaller figures are headless. Other fragments, including the Virgin and Child (ill.50) and God the Father (ill.38) might have come from elsewhere in the cathedral but most probably were part of the screen. The likely date for the whole scheme of figurative sculpture is about 1470–80, suggesting that the patron was Bishop Waynflete.[56]

The figure of the Virgin and God the Father in particular demonstrate the virtuoso handling of naturalistic detail characteristic of late fifteenth-century Netherlandish sculpture, which was the dominant influence in England at the time (see ill.49).[57] The crumpled fabric of Mary's bodice (ill.50), for instance, contrasts with the taughtly drawn cloak across her shoulders. The furrowed brow and downcast eyes of God the Father (ill.38) convey sadness or resignation which, since the figure was most likely shown holding his dead Son in his arms, would have been wholly appropriate. The illusionistic details of the bejewelled lower section of God's triple tiara, with its ornamental hanging ribbons, must have been enhanced by the addition of metalwork inserted into the upper section of the sculpted crown.[58] Gilding was applied to some of the figures, now only detected as residual flecks, and numerous samples of pigment confirm that all of the figures were brightly coloured. The brilliant red of Mary's bodice is most clearly visible but tiny flakes of other colours have been discovered, including flesh tones at the wrist.[59] The overall effect of polychrome figures inhabiting the entire screen must have been very striking, as though the Host of Heaven had descended to earth to stand before the viewer.

The destruction of the screen began with the arrival of Henry VIII's commissioners on 21 September 1538. As part of the suppression of pilgrimages Winchester Cathedral was targeted for its shrine of Saint Swithun, but the commissioners did not fail to notice the Great Screen as well. What caught their eye was the altar and the section of the screen above it that displayed a large image of Christ Crucified, all of which was ornamented with silver, gold and precious gems. Knowing very well their master's priorities, they set about dismantling the altar. The destruction was no spontaneous act by a popular movement of the disaffected but the highly organised operation of high-ranking officials, including Thomas Wriothesley, Earl of Southampton, who was personal secretary to Thomas Cromwell, the Bishop of Winchester's chancellor, the mayor and others. It is not known, however, whether this group went on to oversee the removal of the stone sculptures from the screen at this point.[60] The figures could have been left in place since the law under Henry VIII only required the removal of images that were shown to be 'abused' (see p.51). The sculptures were not specifically connected with pilgrimage and so, in spite of the lack of legal clarity, could have remained legitimate. It might, therefore, have been under Edward VI's regime that the wholesale destruction was carried out in accordance with its programme of Protestant iconoclasm. Certainly, anything left by the time of Bishop Horne in the reign of Queen Elizabeth I would have been subject to his purge of images which included the demand, in 1571, to fill up the niches of the Winchester Great Screen.[61]

Many of the statues were sawn into three equal-sized sections, with heads and hands removed to create a more streamlined and hence more practical piece of masonry for reuse (see p.59). This systematic and pragmatic process serves as a reminder that not every act of iconoclasm is mindless. Whatever the precise strategy, however, the result is still one of devastation. Many of the surviving fragments at Winchester were only recovered in the nineteenth century. The broken head of God the Father, for example, was discovered in 1885 in the stonework around a doorway between the north transept and the nave.[62] Indeed, the process of recovery might not have finished even now if yet more heads, bodies and other fragments remain embedded in the fabric of the cathedral. RW

50
The Virgin and Child late 15th century
Limestone with traces of
pigment and gilding
48 × 38 × 20
Dean and Chapter of Winchester Cathedral

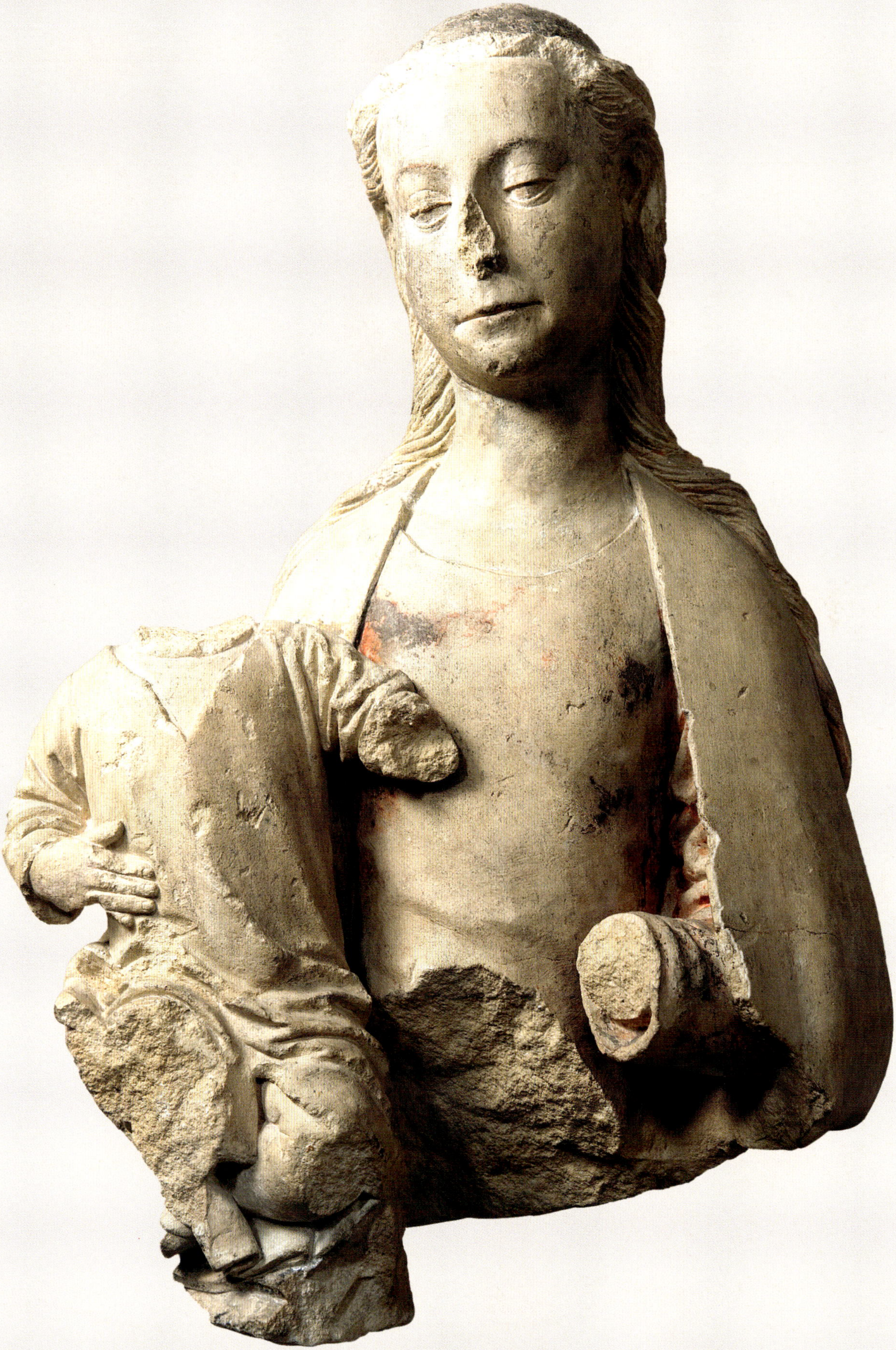

The painted screen at St Mary's, Gressenhall

The painted section of a wooden screen from St Mary's Church in Gressenhall, Norfolk, makes starkly apparent how a once glittering world of richness and piety was brought to a brutal end by the Reformation. Its original paintwork and applied gold and silver leaf remind us how medieval churches had been ablaze with bright colour that to our eyes can appear gaudy and quite alien. A late fifteenth-century date is suggested by its very close resemblance to the screen at another Norfolk church, St Catherine's, Ludham, which is dated 1493.[63]

Such screens dominated almost every parish church in the country by the fifteenth century, principally in the form of rood screens. Named after the 'rood' or cross that was placed on top, these separated the holy space of the chancel, reserved for the priest to celebrate mass at the high altar, from the nave or body of the church where the laity would congregate.[64] The Gressenhall fragment is a part of the lower register or dado of the screen, above which an open framework allowed an uninterrupted view of the altar, and above that stood the rood loft which supported the monumental sculptural group of the Crucified Christ flanked by the Virgin Mary and John the Evangelist. It is known that Gressenhall also had a 'parclose screen' marking the entrance to a side chapel, and it is quite possible that the surviving fragment actually came from this. Whatever its precise location within the church, it is clear that its unpainted left edge is where it abutted the stone wall, whereas the right edge is painted and has a slot for hinges, indicating that the screen had a central door (an unusual feature for East Anglian screens). To the right of this door another section of screen matching the surviving fragment would once have stood but this has been lost.[65]

The role of rood screens in separating chancel from nave not only carried religious symbolism but also held more practical significance. The chancel area to the east of the screen was the responsibility of the rector, whereas the nave to the west, together with the screen itself, was the responsibility of the laity of the parish. This means that rood screens were commissioned and funded by the local parishioners themselves, and that it was they rather than the institution of the Church that determined its scheme of religious imagery. The choice of iconography thus provides a snapshot of the devotional lives of ordinary laymen and women in pre-Reformation England. Some elements of the imagery followed established convention and did not vary, such as the sculpted

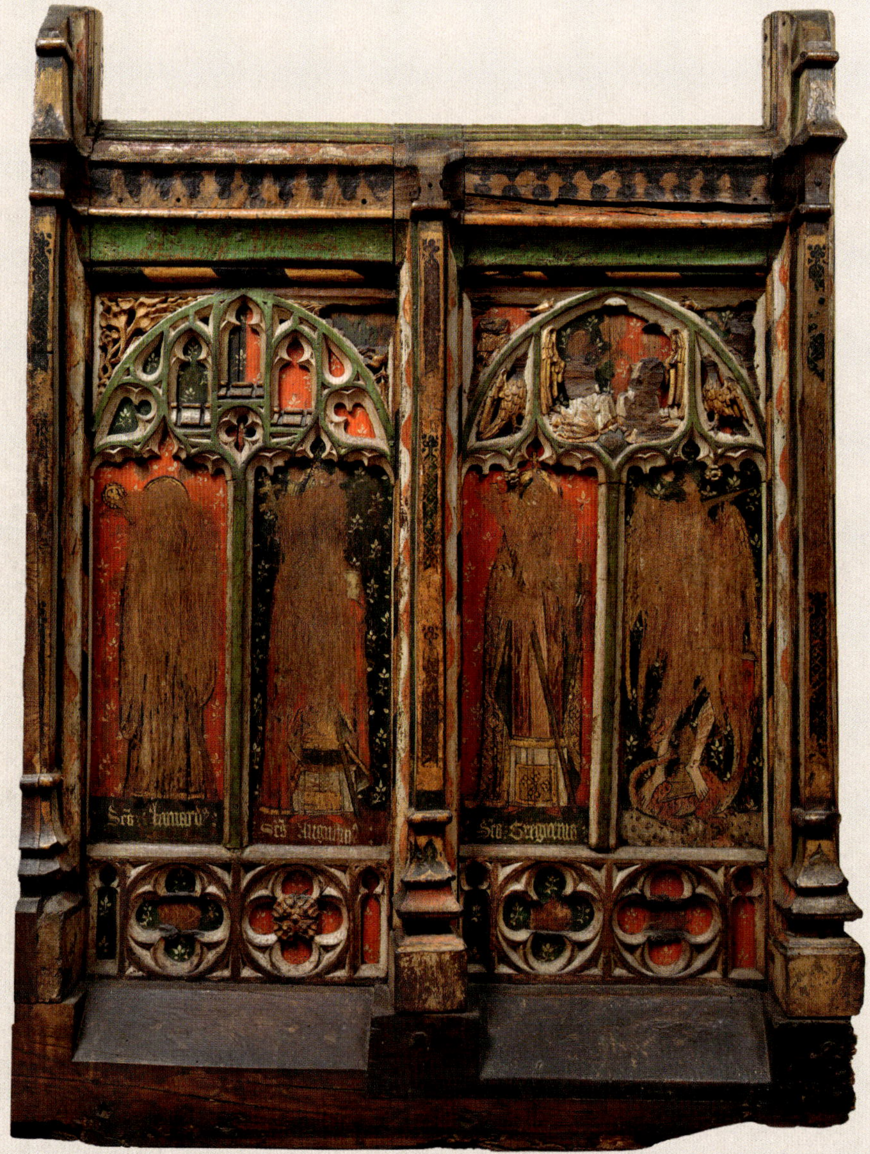

51
Section of painted screen
late 15th century
Oil paint and gilding on carved oak panel
152.5 × 116.8 × 24.2 cm
Church of St Mary, Gressenhall, Norfolk

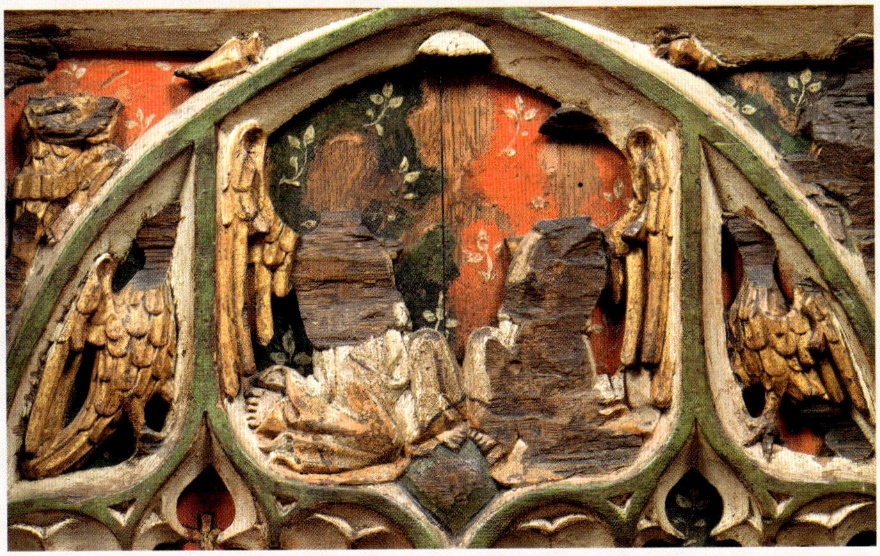

crucifixion group on top of the screen, and when the backing to this was painted, the scene was invariably the 'Doom' or Last Judgement. However, the dado section and sometimes the front of the rood loft were painted with saints that often did reflect local connections and personal preferences.[66]

The choice of saints represented on the Gressenhall fragment was rather traditional. From left to right are the standing figures of Saint Leonard, Saint Augustine, Saint Gregory and Saint Michael Archangel. The ghostly shadow of the wings, raised sword and devil at the feet of Saint Michael emerge like features in a photographic negative. The other three retain their identifying labels. Saints Augustine and Gregory came from one of several popular sequences of saints, such as the twelve Apostles, whereas in this instance they represent two of the Four Latin Doctors of the Church.[67] The other two, Saints Jerome and Ambrose, were included on the lost right-hand section of the screen. More unusually, in fact unprecedented among surviving screens in Norfolk, is the inclusion of what were originally two angels adoring the Eucharist, carved into the apex of the arch above the two saints on the right (see detail). The gold wings of the angels still survive but the rest of their kneeling bodies has been hacked off, together with the chalice they held up, presenting the consecrated Mass wafer. Just the top of this wafer has managed to stay attached, and very close examination reveals the tips of the letters making the 'ihs' monogram of the name of Christ that was inscribed upon it. The golden eagles to either side of the angels are missing their heads, and another pair of angels above them has been almost completely obliterated, save for details such as the ends of the incense burners they were swinging in front of them.[68]

The consecrated Host that miraculously transformed into the body of Christ became the subject of intense devotion, and this provides a strong clue as to one of the benefactors of the screen. Among the religious guilds or religious confraternities that met and worshipped at Gressenhall church was the Guild of Corpus Christi. Groups of layfolk such as these could pool their resources when contributing to the cost of an expensive item such as a rood screen. They could also expect to influence its imagery so that it reflected their interests and priorities. However, it was rarely ever just one group or one individual who financed a rood screen, but a corporate effort that could include the entire community; even poorer parishioners might make a modest contribution.[69]

All this meant that rood screens embodied the pride, aspirations and faith of that community. They heavily invested precious resources and hopes for salvation into this major act of patronage that became a focal point of religious life. In some instances, however, this was to be short-lived, as several rood screens had barely been finished when the first impact of the Reformation was felt. In Henry VIII's reign it was often a selective censorship that was required, so that figures such as Saint Gregory (a pope) or Saint Jerome (a cardinal) were scratched from rood screens since they symbolised the Pope's authority, whereas other saints were allowed to remain. However, the hard-line Protestant regimes of Edward VI and later Elizabeth I specifically targeted rood screens, knowing what a blow this would strike against England's traditional Catholic faith.[70] Rood lofts were taken down and the sculpted figures burnt. The lower section of the screen could remain in place but the imagery was whitewashed over and, as at Binham (ill.46), painted over with biblical texts. As has been pointed out, the most severe damage to the painted saints on the Gressenhall screen was perpetrated by the incompetent efforts of a 1970s restorer (see p.53). However the attempt to strip away the angels adoring the Eucharist was undoubtedly a reformer's attempt to strike out a theology and an entire belief system from the religious and cultural life of England. For those not inspired by the new spirit of Protestant reform it is hard to imagine how far-reaching and traumatic this turn of events must have been. RW

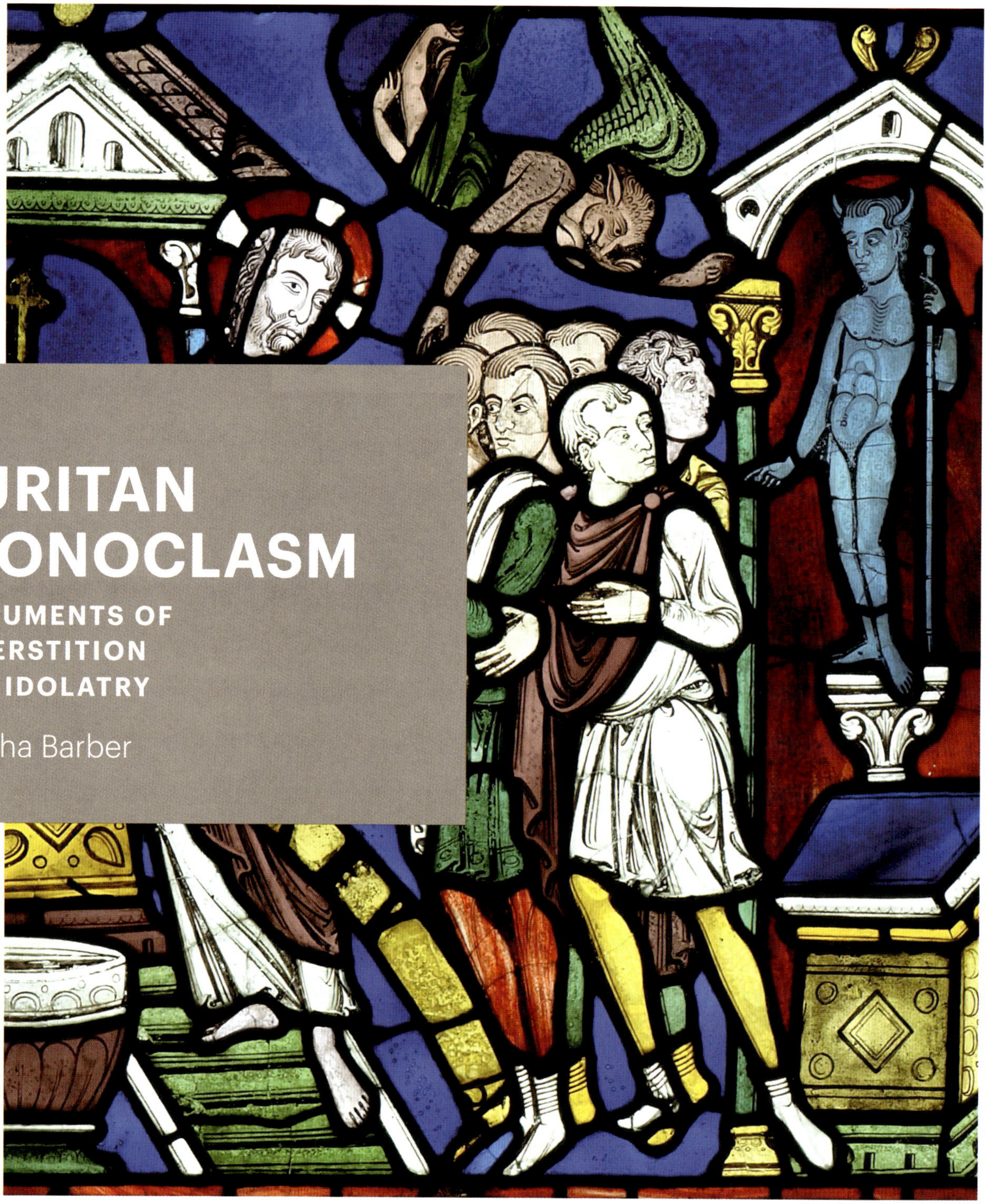

3 PURITAN ICONOCLASM

MONUMENTS OF SUPERSTITION AND IDOLATRY

Tabitha Barber

The violence and thoroughness of 1640s Puritan iconoclasm in England is the stuff of popular legend. Not only were cathedrals desecrated and religious imagery in parish churches defaced and destroyed, but Puritan killjoys extended their remit to exercise a moral iconoclasm, banning stage-plays and maypoles and even popular festivals such as Easter and Christmas. Oliver Cromwell himself is said to have personally undertaken acts of destruction. At Peterborough Cathedral in 1643 he heroically scaled a ladder to beat down from the west window an image of a crucifix too high for others to have dared.[1]

In fact, there is little evidence for Cromwell the iconoclast of popular legend and the Peterborough incident is most likely propaganda.[2] Civil War iconoclasm was accompanied by a sophisticated written narrative that manipulated and exaggerated events, and which remains to distort and deceive even today. In an age of greater literacy, partisan newsbooks, spirited personal accounts, sermons and satirical tracts became weapons in the war against images. The vigorous polemic and loaded symbolism they employed made acts of destruction more powerful than events themselves had been. Parliamentary propaganda even harnessed the military successes of its troops to the pious acts of destruction of soldiers.[3] Biblical precedent was cited to demonstrate that the current turmoil of war was God's vengeance against an idolatrous people, and that iconoclasm was necessary to cleanse the country of sin. The violence of war itself was presented as an essential passage towards the country's spiritual regeneration. Royalists, on the other hand, painted parliamentary Puritans as profane desecrators not only of cathedrals but of the traditional hierarchy of society and the sanctity of monarchy. Cromwell, 'so perfect a hater of Images', was belittled, his only 'military' victories being his iconoclastic battles with stained-glass windows and monumental effigies in churches.[4]

Rather than an uncontrolled, rampant vandalism, recent studies of both iconoclasm and individual iconoclasts of the Civil War years have highlighted the Puritan campaign against images as one that was focused, systematic and highly administered.[5] Parliament took the lead role as iconoclast. Iconoclasm was officially sanctioned and its parameters enshrined in legislation, the aim being to complete, finally and decisively, what the Reformation had begun. Parliamentary ordinances of 1643 and 1644 ordered not only the removal of images, but their 'utter demolishing'. 'Scandalous' representations of the Trinity, Virgin Mary and other saints were proscribed, but so too were fixed altars, altar rails, crucifixes and candles on communion tables. Superstitious inscriptions were also banned, as were plain crosses, not just those in churches and churchyards but also ones in public, secular spaces. Not only was it figurative imagery that was under attack but the physical, visual symbols of a 'popish' and erroneous form of worship. In 1644 the list of things forbidden was expanded to encompass symbolic representations, organs, angels, images on church plate and vestments.[6] This radicalisation of the agenda was the hallmark of 1640s iconoclasm. As war progressed and the Puritan minority gained power, what constituted a 'monument of superstition and idolatry' was redefined and iconoclasm, an extreme position (not all Puritans were iconoclasts), became official policy. Parliament's intention to purge the nation of idolatrous sin was made in emphatic language, and its ordinances provided the templates for the iconoclastic actions of zealous individuals such as William Dowsing in East Anglia and Richard Culmer in Canterbury.

that received sustained attention during the 1640s, not just recently installed painted schemes of the 1620s and 30s but earlier, medieval windows that had survived previous reformations. Stained glass had been specifically mentioned in the 1547 injunctions against images, but Elizabethan rulings in 1559 and 1560 had restricted its breaking.[20] In part this was practical – glass was expensive to replace – but because of their height and therefore distance from the viewer, images in windows were regarded as less dangerous than others.[21] In 1573 Anthony Gilby had complained that images that remained in windows were a lingering aspect of popery that deformed England,[22] and in the 1640s their eradication became one of the chief objectives. While high churchmen argued the case for figurative glass as a beautiful enhancement that inspired devotion (ill.64), for those with more radical beliefs stained or painted glass was offensive just by nature of its colour. The coloured light refracted through the windows of Henrietta Maria's Roman Catholic chapel at Somerset House was said to pollute the space, and several objectors made the symbolic point that dark, false idols in windows hindered people from seeing and reading with clarity the written scriptures. The godly John Bruen pulled down the 'painted puppets, and popish idols' from the windows of his family chapel in Tarvin church as they had been 'so thicke, and darke' and had obscured 'the brightnesse of the Gospell'.[23] Following acts of eradication, windows were reglazed with 'clear' or 'white' glass, the colour of truth and purity. Bills deliberately describe it as such and in July 1644 the parliamentary newsbook *Mercurius Britanicus* made the point more powerfully, designating the clear glass that replaced the painted windows in the Chapel Royal at Whitehall Palace as good and 'Protestant'.[24] Rather than the indiscriminate smashing of entire window schemes, precise, targeted attack against specific images within them seems to have been a widely employed strategy. There is evidence that this was the case at Canterbury Cathedral (pp 86–87) and in Oxford (pp 90–91) and it was also Dowsing's approach. In some cases, heads only were removed and bodies allowed to remain.[25] As well as this being a financially pragmatic policy, Dowsing would have viewed his uncompromising yet forensic iconoclasm (leaving behind what had not been proscribed) as the enactment of Parliament's brief.

The orderly, controlled iconoclasm undertaken by officials is in stark contrast to the narratives of profanity and desecration committed in cathedrals by parliamentary soldiers that were published in the royalist newsletter *Mercurius Rusticus*. Harley's cleansing of Westminster Abbey was thorough but

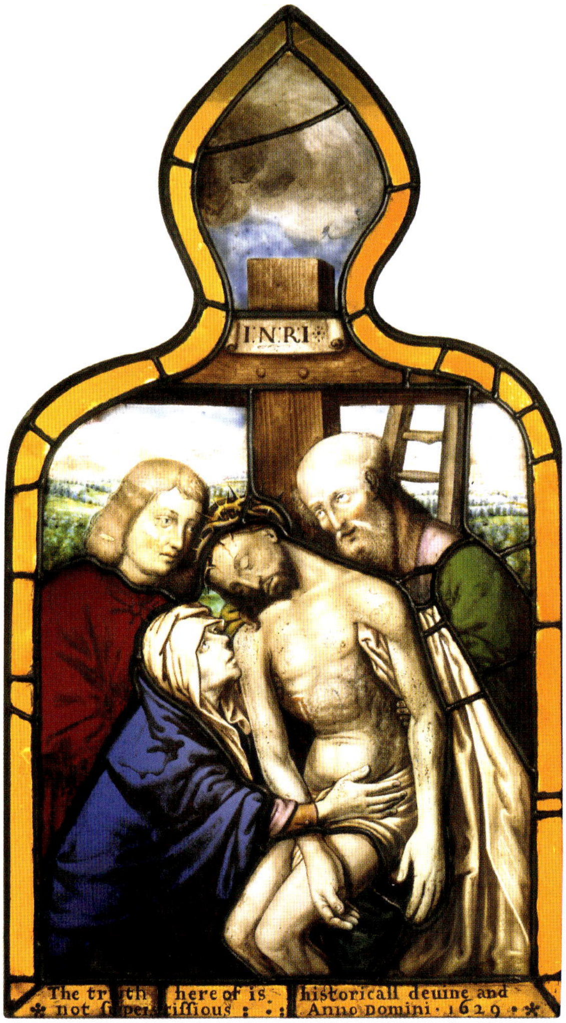

52
Abraham van Linge (active 1623–42)
The Deposition, 1629
Painted and stained glass
81.3 × 41.9
Victoria and Albert Museum, London

controlled, whereas the actions of soldiers quartered there was a 'horrible abuse', their actions more awful as the Abbey was where monarchs were crowned. They burnt the altar rails, pawned the organ pipes at local ale-houses, raucously played hare and hounds dressed in surplices, sat around the communion table eating, drinking and smoking tobacco, but most abominable of all, they 'did their easements of nature, and laid their Excrements about the Altar'.[26] *Mercurius Rusticus* was written by the royalist Bruno Ryves and his exaggerated, provocative conveying of events was aimed at stimulating fury and outrage against the sacrilegious, anti-monarchical rebels. Violent vandalism of cathedrals by troops certainly took place.[27] The physical evidence of the comprehensive and brutal stripping of Peterborough Cathedral is still apparent today. Puritans cast cathedrals as dens of idleness, evil and depravity and the iconoclasm of soldiers as a godly duty. As symbols of Laudianism and episcopal corruption, ornately decked inside and with, in Milton's famous description of ceremonial worship, 'all the gaudy allurements of a whore',[28] they were justified targets for iconoclasm. The actions against altars, deliberate mocking of the wearing of surplices and symbolic burning of the Book of Common Prayer on public bonfires, occurred in most cathedral cities. But the heavily symbolic actions with which the soldiers are credited in the pages of *Mercurius Rusticus* must in most cases be propagandist rhetoric. While the arras hangings at Canterbury Cathedral were most probably attacked, as stated, in 1642, it is debatable whether the soldiers proclaimed 'Here is Christ' while deliberately stabbing and disembowelling the depicted figure.[29] At Winchester, as well as supposedly attacking Le Sueur's statue of the king (ill.52) the troops are also said to have violated the ancient tomb chests in the Presbytery, but the narrative of events leaves us wondering where truth and embroidery, to make events more shocking, conjoin. The 'Monsters of men to whom nothing is holy, nothing is sacred' turned the bones now scattered over the Pavement, including those of Edward the Confessor, into 'passive Instruments', hurling them at the stained-glass windows to break images otherwise too high to reach.[30]

While satire and iconoclastic polemic were utilised to galvanise and inflame opinion, and rival newsbooks such as *Mercurius Rusticus* and *Mercurius Britanicus* sought to manage and control the agenda through aggressive propaganda, acts of iconoclasm themselves could be publicly stage-managed for maximum impact. The method and manner of breaking, and the disposal of the remains of what had been broken, were ritualised and iconoclasm transformed into events of public ceremony and spectacle. During the violent cleansing of the Queen's Roman Catholic chapel at Somerset House in 1644, pictures and statues were attacked with halberds and hammers. A statue of the Virgin and Child was hurled to the floor and the faces kicked and smashed with clubs. In his destruction of Rubens' great altarpiece *The Crucifixion*, Sir John Clotworthy defaced its most offensive imagery first, before moving on to total demolition. He viciously struck the crucifix, slashed the Virgin's face and then, thrusting his halberd 'under the feet of the crucified Christ, he ripped the painting to bits'. The remains were later tossed into the Thames.[31] This eyewitness account is partisan but indicates that the chapel's painted and sculpted figurative imagery underwent some form of symbolic, focused and furious punishment. Following the ransacking, the destruction not being quite complete, service books and other 'popish trinkets' were massed on to a great bonfire outside the chapel. Just as crosses, books, vestments and other ornaments were paraded

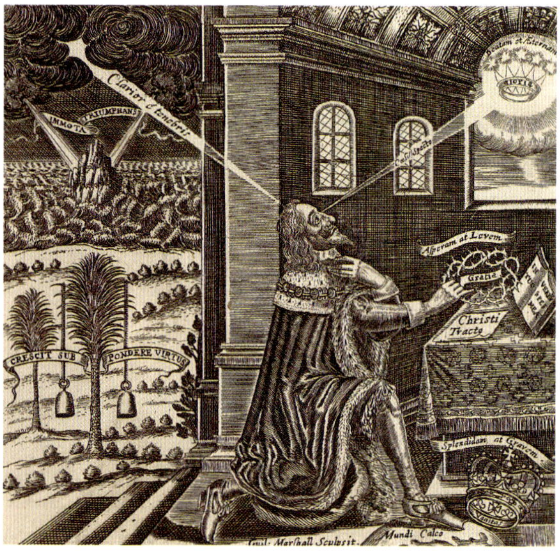

53
William Marshall (active 1617–48)
Engraved frontispiece to
Eikon Basilike 1649
The Trustees of the British Museum

through the streets and burned at the market crosses of cathedral cities, so 'popish trash' confiscated from recusant households was similarly treated, and publicly burned in ritualised, staged ceremonies.

Ceremonial punishment, ritualised obliteration, anti-Catholic rhetoric and the utilisation of satire, propaganda and impassioned polemic to attack and defend images come together in one of the most 'iconic' instances of Puritan iconoclasm, the demolition of London's Cheapside Cross.[32] One of the Eleanor Crosses erected in the thirteenth century, but much rebuilt and renovated over the centuries, the cross occupied an important site in the City and was a focal point for City processions. In 1643 it rose in three tiers to nearly 11m, was surmounted by a gilded cross and was decorated with statues of the Virgin Mary, saints, bishops and kings. It had long been contested, attacked, vandalised and repaired. While regarded by some as a familiar and decent ornament to the City, for Puritan radicals it was a 'huge great papisticall image' that lured passers-by into idolatrous sin. People committed 'spiritual fornication' before it,[33] it was argued, and an attack against it in January 1642, in which limbs and noses were wrenched off its idols, was applauded.[34] In a substantial trading of words in pamphlet form the cross was tried, found guilty and condemned to death. In satires it became animate, imagined its destruction (its statues started trembling), made a last will and testament and was given an elaborate funeral.[35] For Parliament the cross became a potent target for eradication, which was finally achieved in May 1643. Its demolition was a public spectacle, accompanied by trumpets, drums, guns and bell ringing (see ill.7), which was followed by a great public bonfire on its former site onto which were cast its lead and gilded statues. They were melted, according to John Vicars, 'to make bullets yet further to bang and beat down the living idols or idolators of Rome'. While Cheapside Cross had been a mere idol of stone, its staged downfall and the deliberate linking of its demise with the current war and need to purify the nation of sin was calculated propaganda. Its site remained charged, with symbolic burnings of offensive and popish items, at the hands of the public hangman, taking place there.

By the action of his execution in 1649 Charles I, in whose person the temporal and spiritual had been combined, was transformed from earthly monarch to martyred icon. He was presented as such in *Eikon Basilike*, the textual image of the king that was available to buy within days of his beheading. The emblematic frontispiece (ill.53) shows him kneeling in prayer, connected to his heavenly crown by a brilliant ray of divine light. In *Eikonoklastes*, 1649, Parliament's commissioned riposte, Milton set out to break with the virulence of his arguments and the truth and power of his words the false image of the King that *Eikon Basilike* promoted.[36] While the engraving 'would Martyr him and Saint him to befoole the people', he argued, and the book 'would have the people come and worship him' as if it were his shrine, adoration of the king was in fact a mistaken idolatry. He likened his demolition of the king's image to the godly iconoclastic actions of the Byzantine emperors and argued that the king's execution had been justified because, as with all superstitious images, there was a compelling need to break them 'to peeces'.[37]

Just as Parliament had beheaded the king to purify the nation, however, so the restored Stuart regime felt compelled to eradicate the book that had given that act validation. In 1660 copies of *Eikonoklastes* were rounded up and publicly burned by the public hangman. To re-emphasise Charles I as sainted martyr, in 1662 *Basilika* (ill.54) was printed – a collected volume of the king's works including *Eikon Basilike* together with a history of his trial. A copy was seized on board a ship bound for Portugal and a thorough expurgation and correction of it demanded by the Catholic Portuguese inquisitors.[38] Black inked lines have been systematically scored through offensive words. References to Charles I as 'martyr', as 'sacred', as 'Defender of the Faith' and 'Head of the Church' have been deleted, and savage pen strokes cross through the king's meditations on death as well as his final prayer. While the text offers one interpretation of Charles I and the Church of England, its scoring through and partial censorship suggests that another reading, not just of the king's reign but of the English Protestant Reformation itself, is possible.[39]

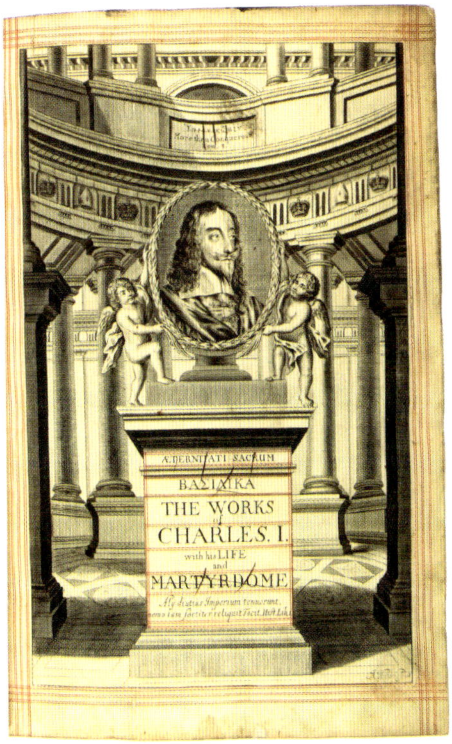

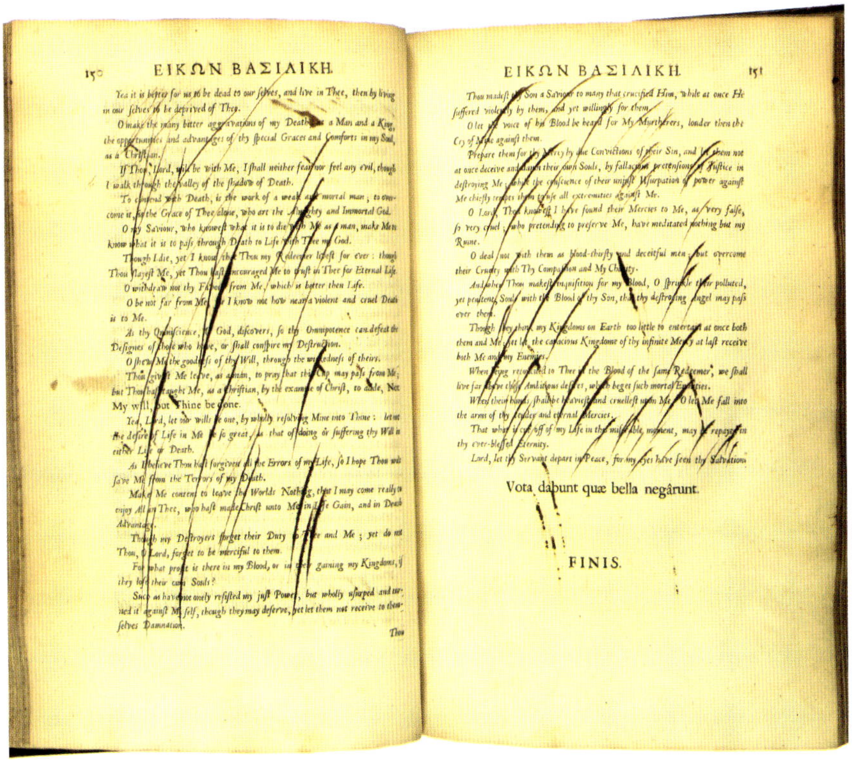

54
Basilika: The Works of King Charles the Martyr, 1662

Printed book, expurgated by the Portuguese Inquisition, MS 322
36.8 × 25 × 8.5
Trustees of Lambeth Palace Library

Image and text at Little Gidding

The domestic religious community at Little Gidding, Huntingdonshire, established by Nicholas Ferrar in 1625 and made up of members of his extended family, became known in the 1630s for its production of religious concordances (scriptural harmonies), which combined text with printed images. Elaborately and painstakingly produced by cutting and pasting verses of the Gospels into a reordered, continuous Life of Christ,[40] in which text was cleverly combined with cut images, for some these concordances were beautiful aids in the worship of God but to others they were popish and idolatrous abominations. The king possessed, and greatly valued, a particularly lavish example, made especially for him, and Archbishop Laud also owned one; but for Puritan radicals the Little Gidding community itself was akin to a nunnery in a popish land beyond the seas.[41]

In fact, the Little Gidding community lived a life of carefully regulated religious discipline according to the scriptures. As well as making the concordances (an act of godly industry), the harmonised gospels played an important part in the daily hours of communal worship. Nicholas Ferrar directed their production in the Concordance Room, which on its green walls had godly text: 'Prosper Thou, O Lord, the work of our hands'. With scissors and knives, Ferrar's nieces cut, sliced and expertly spliced together and pasted down not just complete textual verses, but sometimes individual sentences and words. Text was combined either with whole prints, or sections of prints, or carefully excised details – figures, flowers, symbols – that were carefully placed near appropriate words. The words themselves sometimes overlap the prints. The role of the images was thus not incidental. They were integral to the books, in which word and image became mutually supportive.[42]

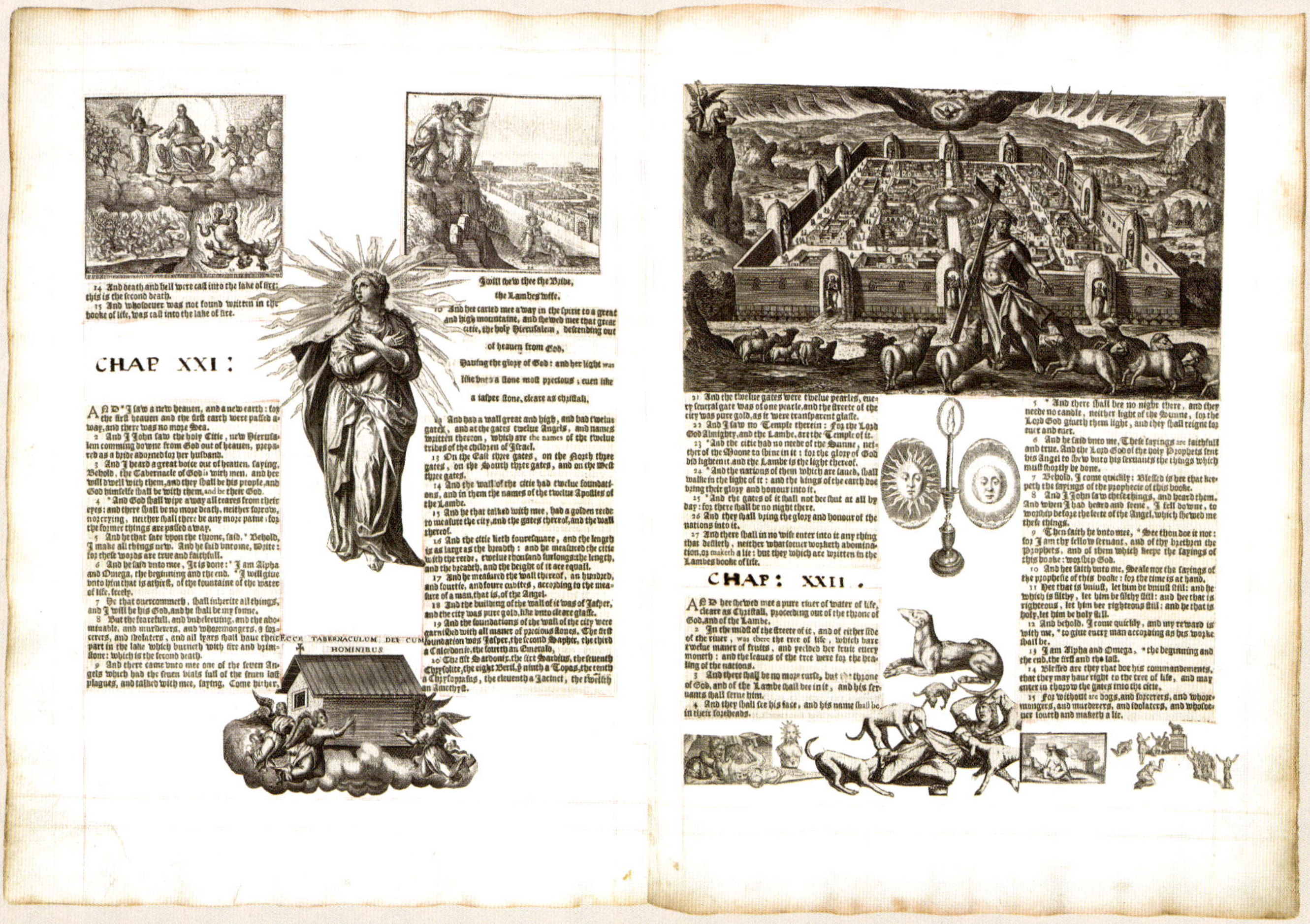

55
Little Gidding Harmony
Acta Apostolorum Elegantis Monochromatis Delineata c.1635–40
Pasted book
47.3 × 72.5 × 17 (open)
The British Library

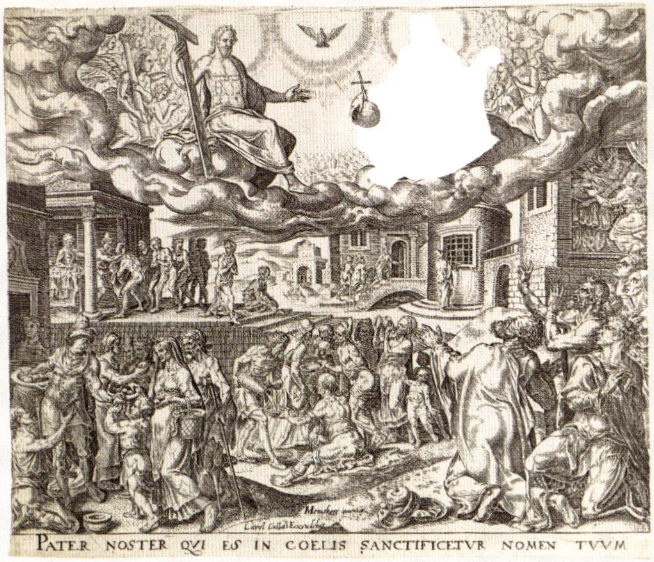

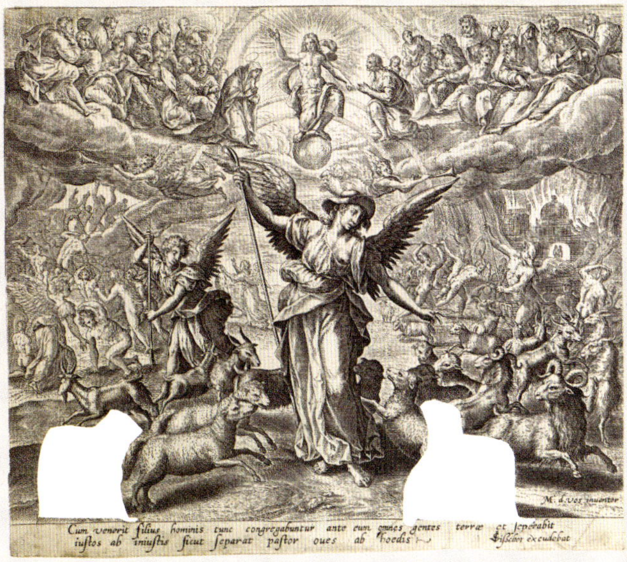

56
After Maarten van Heemskerck (1498–1574)
Plate from the late 16th-century Lord's Prayer series (Ferrar print no.122)
Engraving on paper (with excision)
The Master and Fellows of Magdalene College, Cambridge

57
After Maerten de Vos (1532–1603)
The Last Judgement, *c*.1580. (Ferrar print no.123)
Engraving on paper (with excision)
The Master and Fellows of Magdalene College, Cambridge

On the title pages of several of the concordances the images are explained as 'Sundry Pictures expressing either the Facts themselves Or their Types & Figures Or Other Matters appertaining thereunto'; and on some pages ink inscriptions appear instructing people to use the images in conjunction with the words, which together fully illuminate the meaning. The *Acts of the Apostles and the Book of Revelation* (ill.55) has been described, after the king's concordance, as visually the most impressive of the Little Gidding concordances.[43] The precise clipping from an assortment of prints and the practice of elaborately scattering images across the page are evident, as is the use of images to literally illustrate the word. Bottom left, accompanying the Book of Revelation 22:15, 'for without are dogs and sorcerers, and whore-mongerers, and murderers, and idolators, and whosoe-ever loveth and maketh a lie', are literal visual renderings: a female figure being set upon by dogs, scenes of sorcery and murder, and tiny figures worshipping the golden calf.

The Little Gidding stock of prints from which clippings were taken was collected by Nicholas Ferrar, both while he had been travelling on the Continent and later.[44] For the most part they were sixteenth-century religious prints, many of them from Antwerp. The use of Catholic prints to illustrate the English Bible became a hugely controversial issue in the 1630s.[45] Their placement there was seen as a sure way of luring people into popery, superstition and idolatry. At his trial in 1644, Archbishop Laud's possession and use of such prints was used as proof of his sin. His chamber had been searched and inventoried, and illustrated Catholic devotional works highlighted.[46] Little Gidding's extensive use of prints, therefore, which were used not just as mere illustration but as essential tools that worked alongside scriptural text, and their 'indulgence of the visual' in the famous concordance made for the king, would have been regarded by some as contentious and controversial.[47]

In the pool of surviving prints from Little Gidding's Concordance Room, now at Magdalene College, Cambridge, prints survive sometimes in duplicate and triplicate, and many have been excised. Sheep, for example, have been clipped out of a scene of the Last Judgement for use elswhere (ill.57); others illustrate members of the community acting as their own censors. Images of God the Father, prohibited by the Second Commandment, have been systematically removed from the sky, as shown here in a print published in Antwerp by Philips Galle (after Maarten van Heemskerck) (ill.56). In several instances in the concordances, God the Father has been pasted over by innocuous pieces of sky or cloud, or replaced by the IHS monogram to represent Jesus Christ.

The aggressive action of cutting the scriptures does not seem to have been regarded by the community as in any way a transgression. For them, their defacement and dismembering with knives and scissors, and reordering and pasting together again, was a pious act of creation.[48] TB

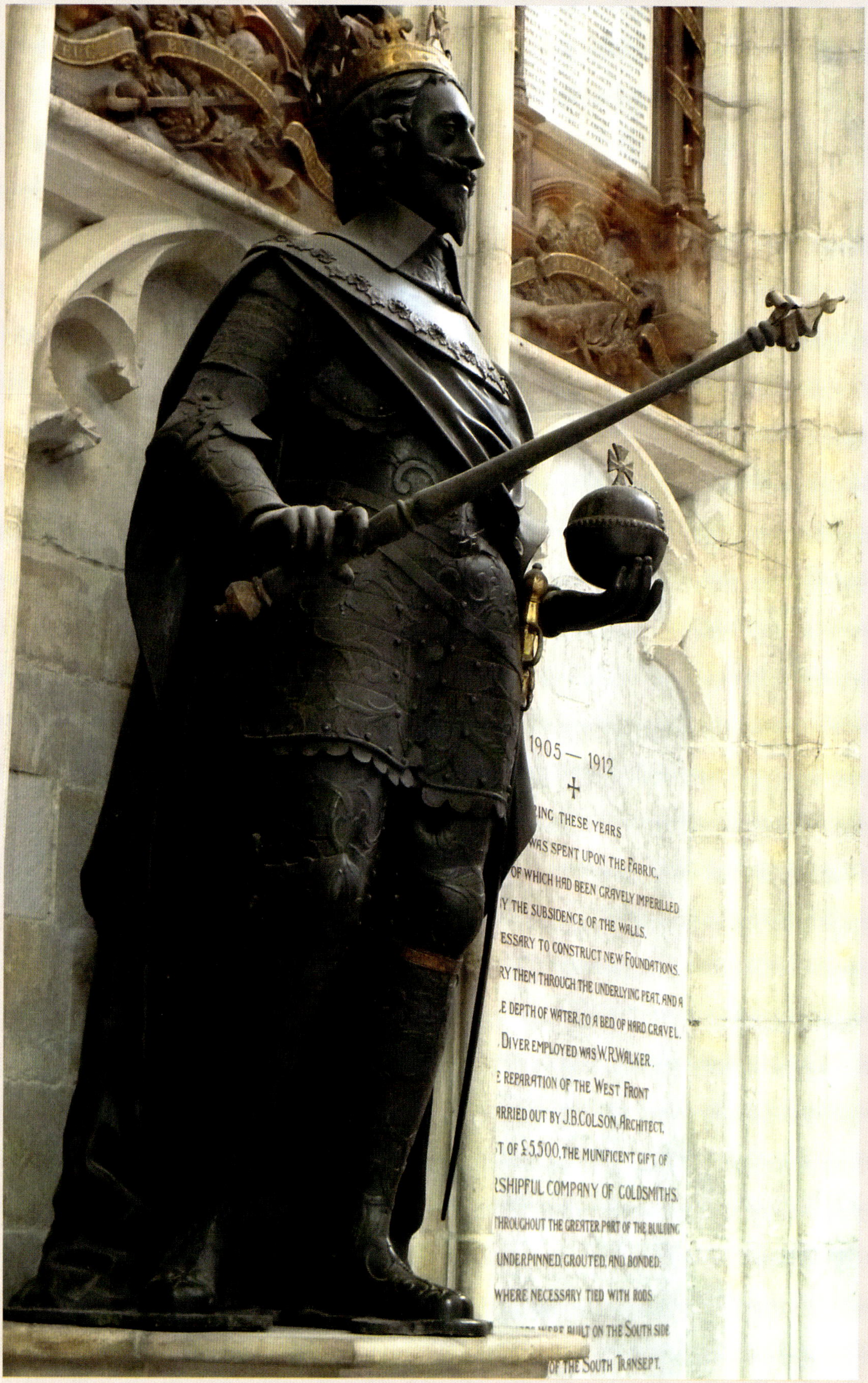
1905 — 1912
THESE YEARS
WAS SPENT UPON THE FABRIC,
OF WHICH HAD BEEN GRAVELY IMPERILLED
THE SUBSIDENCE OF THE WALLS.
TO CONSTRUCT NEW FOUNDATIONS
THEM THROUGH THE UNDERLYING PEAT, AND A
DEPTH OF WATER, TO A BED OF HARD GRAVEL.
DIVER EMPLOYED WAS W.R.WALKER.
REPARATION OF THE WEST FRONT
OUT BY J.B.COLSON, ARCHITECT,
OF £5,500, THE MUNIFICENT GIFT OF
COMPANY OF GOLDSMITHS.
THROUGHOUT THE GREATER PART OF THE BUILDING
UNDERPINNED, GROUTED, AND BONDED:
WHERE NECESSARY TIED WITH RODS.
BUILT ON THE SOUTH SIDE
OF THE SOUTH TRANSEPT.

Charles I and symbols of the Stuart regime

Accounts of the destructive rampages of parliamentary soldiers that appeared in the royalist newsletter *Mercurius Rusticus* pointedly lingered on the symbolic violation of images of the king. On 18 August 1642, for example, the royalist Sir Richard Minshull's house, Bourton House, Buckinghamshire was plundered and a stirring narration of events was published. 'The first thing on which they expresse their rage is the King's Picture', it says, 'which with their swords they most traitorously pierce through in divers places: and not content to wound him in that representation ... they whet their tongues against their Sovereigne, using Traiterous and scornfull language against Him'. If this physically violent and verbal assault is what they do to a mere 'shadow' (his portrait), the author asks, what would they do to the actual king?[49]

Anti-Stuart feeling was an important dimension to the iconoclasm of parliamentary troops, on which royalist propaganda capitalised in their exaggerated and carefully crafted reports. The conflation of the sacrilegious desecration of cathedrals and religious images with the violation of images of the king, a sacred power, is deliberately stressed in the reported abuse of Hubert Le Sueur's statues of Charles I and James I in Winchester Cathedral. A gift of the king and installed in 1639, the two full-length bronze sculptures occupied places of prominence in niches on Inigo Jones' new choir screen. Their conspicuous presence, stressing the concept of sacred kingship, would have been a powerful provocation.[50] The attack occurred as part of the frenzied spoliation of the cathedral following the taking of Winchester by Sir William Waller's troops in December 1642, although the action against the statues appears to have been undertaken with a focused deliberation. The 'Atheisticall Rebells' broke Charles I's sword and the cross on top of the orb, and 'hacked and hewed' his crown. As well as being 'indignities to the Representation of his Royall Person', the breaking was also aimed at the 'Emblems of his Sacred Power' and likened to the symbolic attacks on the Emperor Theodosius I by the citizens of Antioch in their violation of statues of him in 387 AD.[51] In fact, the statue today shows no indication of targeted attack, although a musket-ball hole is still visible on his left leg (ill.58). How it came about – a soldier taking direct aim or evidence of indiscriminate mayhem – is not known. With an eye to their monetary value, the two statues were taken from the cathedral and sold to a royalist, Benjamin Newland, in Portsmouth for £10. Newland hid them by burying them on the Isle of Wight until 1660, when they were sold back to the cathedral for £100.[52]

After the execution of the king in 1649, legislation against images was broadened to encompass Stuart symbols: the image of Charles I was now one that, like religious images that signified a particular ideology, had to be eradicated.[53] The order was given for the defacement and destruction of Stuart arms, inscriptions and statues in churches and public spaces in a deliberate annihilation of reminders of the old regime. The Council of State went to particular lengths to ensure the destruction of certain high-profile public statues of the Stuart monarchs. Not only was their destruction ordered, but the manner in which it was to be carried out was specified. Those of James I and Charles I on the west front of St Paul's Cathedral were to be 'thrown down and broken to pieces' and the inscriptions under them deleted; and, in a symbolic re-enactment of the execution of the actual king, his statue at the Royal Exchange 'was to be demolished by having its head taken off'. The sceptre was also to be taken out of his hand, the inscription 'Exit tyrannus Regum ultimus, anno primo restitutae libertatis Angliae 1648' added, and it was to be achieved 'by Saturday next'.[54] (In 1659, with the Restoration imminent, the inscription was symbolically eradicated with black paint and the action quickly celebrated in print in *An Exit to the Exit Tyrannus*.) Le Sueur's famous equestrian statue of the king was also hunted down. Located in the possession of John Rivett, a brazier, in 1655, he was ordered 'to break ye said statue in pieces to ye end That nothing might Remaine in memorie of his said Majestie'.[55] Rivett in fact hid it by burying it and falsely produced scraps of bronze to prove he had done as instructed.[56]

While painted, stone and bronze images of Charles I had stood as substitutes for the man himself, and were acted against accordingly, the ultimate act of iconoclasm was of course the execution of the king himself (see pp 80–81). But as new regimes are inaugurated, the idols of outgoing ones inevitably fall and just as Stuart symbols were obliterated by Parliament, acts of vengeance against images of Cromwell were meted out after the Restoration in 1660. In June 1660 Cromwell's wooden funeral effigy was hung by the neck from one of the windows of Whitehall Palace;[57] and on 30 January 1661 (the anniversary of the execution of Charles I) his actual body was exhumed, posthumously hanged at Tyburn and his head displayed on a pole above Westminster Hall as an object of revulsion, not veneration. TB

58
Hubert Le Sueur (*c*.1580 – after 1658)
Charles I 1638–9
Bronze. A musket-ball hole is visible above the left knee
190 × 80 × 120 (including mace)
The Dean and Chapter of Winchester Cathedral

Richard Culmer and the glass of Canterbury Cathedral

In 1644, in *Cathedrall newes from Canterbury*, the iconoclast Richard Culmer described with relish and in detail the cleansing of the cathedral that took place in December 1643. Unlike the iconoclasm by parliamentary soldiers that had taken place the year before, his was an orderly reformation, he said, officially commissioned by the city authorities to execute Parliament's ordinance against images. He rebutted royalist claims that the 1642 ransacking had been a fight 'with God himself'. It had been a fight against the cathedral idols, he said, such as altars, altar rails, 'greasie' service books, surplices, organs and tempting images, which had been hewed and 'slasht' to pieces. Such action was

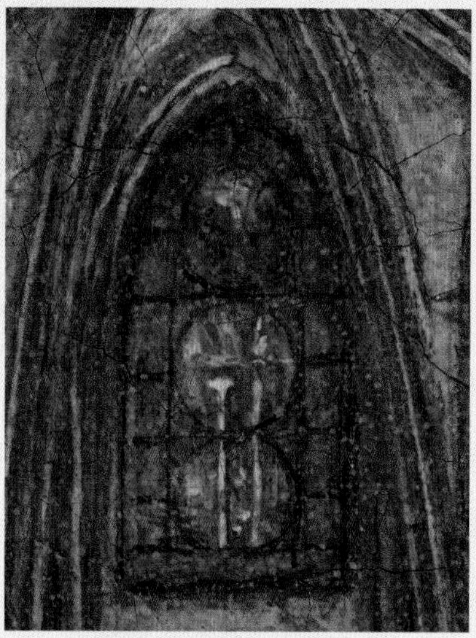

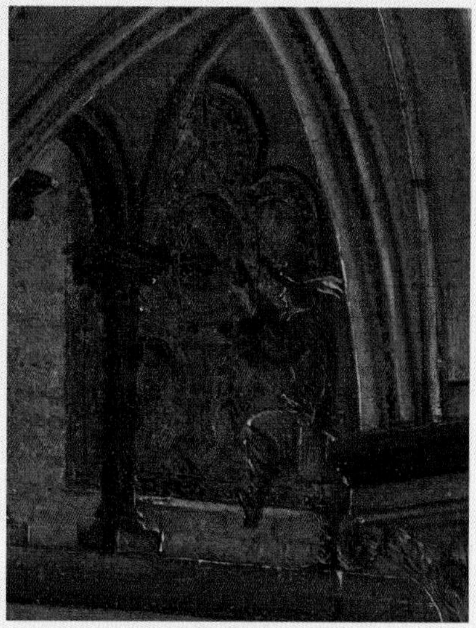

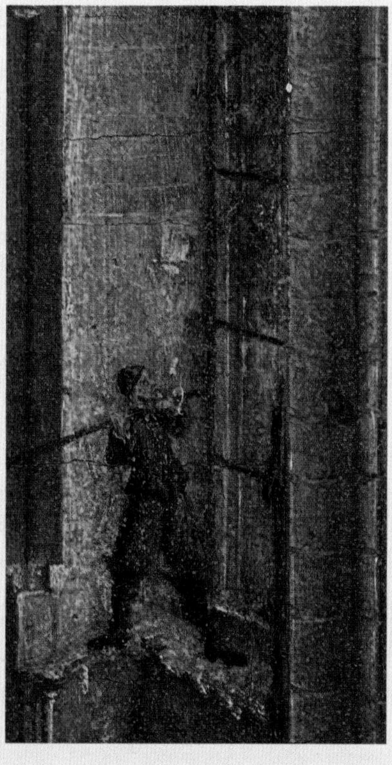

necessary as the cathedral was in a corrupt and rotten condition. When Culmer and his fellow commissioners arrived to begin their systematic purging, 'they knew not where to begin', he says; 'the Images and Pictures were so numerous, as if that Superstitious Cathedrall had beene built for no other end, but to be a stable for Idolls'.[58]

Canterbury Cathedral's ancient glass windows were its glory and the cathedral authorities had been worried that the 'spoiling' of them was the city corporation's design.[59] They were right to have been anxious, for as well as attacking sculptural representations of Christ, the apostles and bishops (that fell on their heads and broke their necks) and the praying hands of tomb effigies, it was idols in glass that preoccupied the iconoclasts. Culmer's first action was against the great east window but his biggest prize was 'the great Idolatrous window', or Royal Window, in the north west transept. Images of God the Father, Christ, a large crucifix, the apostles and seven depictions of the Virgin Mary were beaten down; so, too, was the image of Thomas Becket, the 'prime Cathedrall Saint-Arch-Bishop'. Culmer personally climbed 'neer 60. steps high' and 'with a whole pike in his hand' rattled down 'proud Beckets glassy bones'. That particular act of iconoclasm had been an 'honour', said Culmer, and the window, having been so comprehensively superstitious, was now the most defaced in the cathedral.[60]

Culmer's description of himself high up a ladder wielding a pike is vividly brought to life in Thomas Johnson's painting of the interior of Canterbury Cathedral showing iconoclasts at work (ill.59). Johnson was familiar with the cathedral (he had produced elevation drawings of it for William Dugdale's *Monasticon* 1655) and his detailed depiction of the stripped, bare interior and its architecture (even the wear on the stone

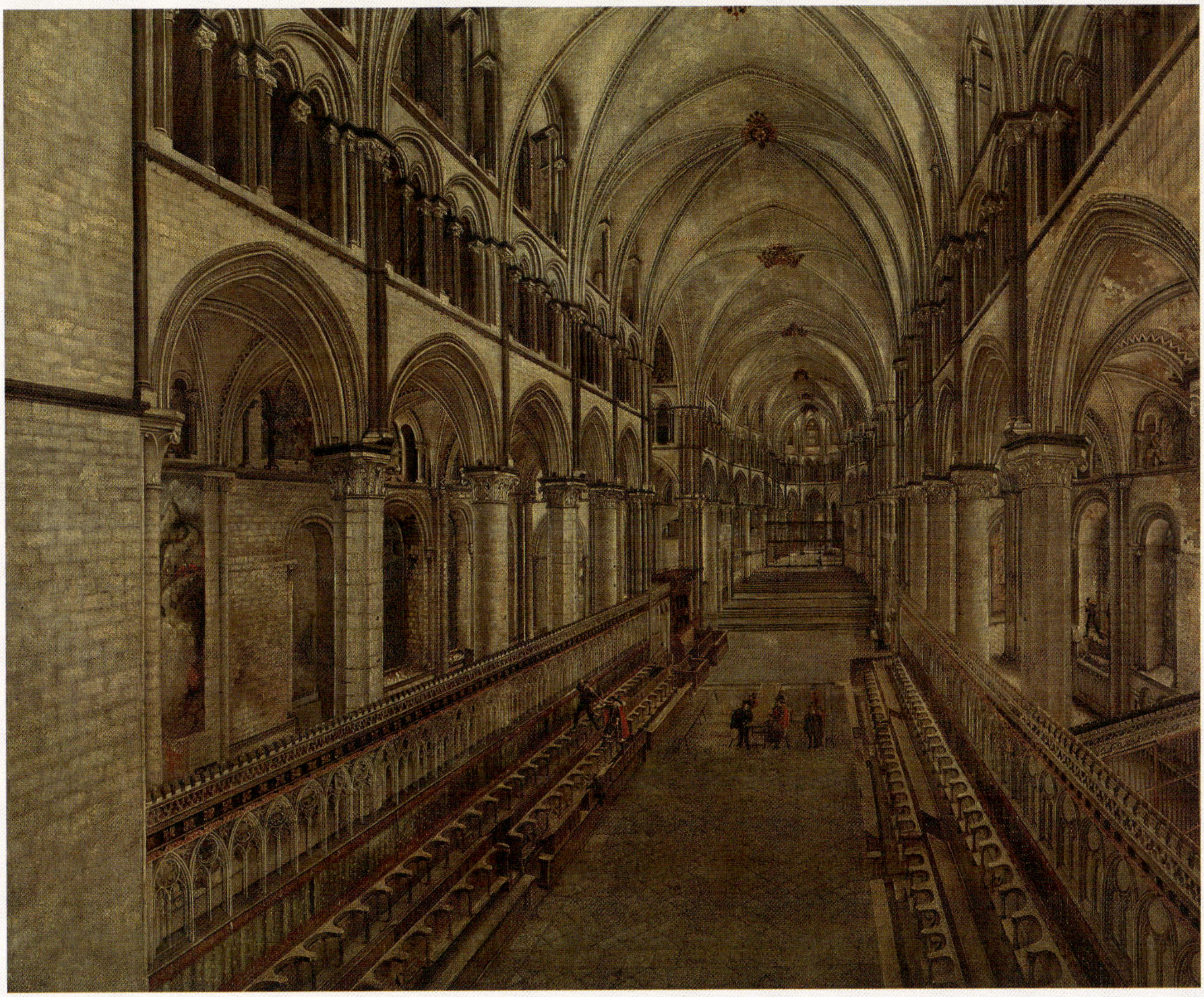

59
Thomas Johnson (active 1634–76)
Canterbury Cathedral Choir, 1657
Oil paint on canvas
83.5 × 95
Private collection
(Details: 59a–c)

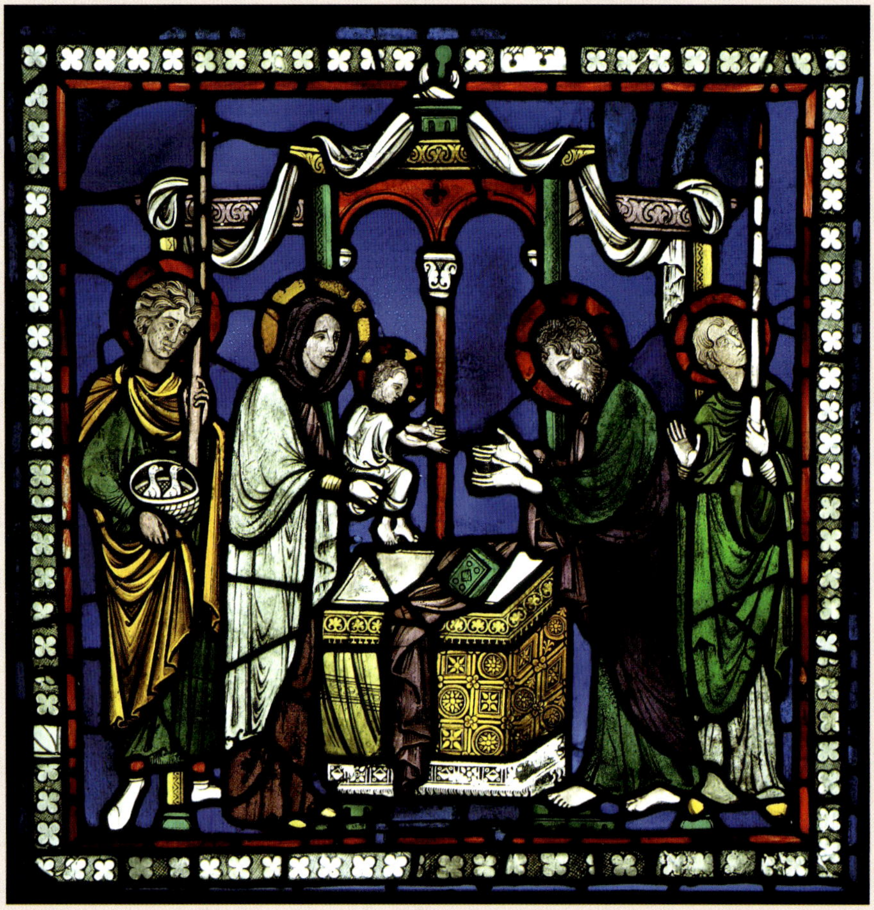

60, 61
The Presentation in the Temple and *Christ Leading the Gentiles from Pagan Gods* c.1180
Stained glass
69.5 × 70 × 0.7
The Dean and Chapter of Canterbury Cathedral

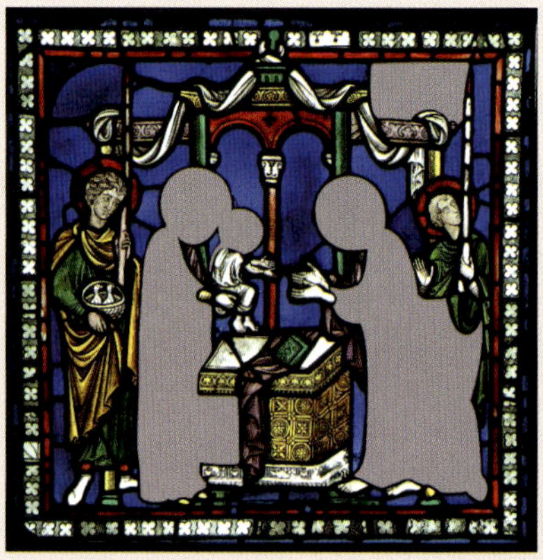

62, 63
Diagrams indicating where losses to the stained glass were most likely sustained

steps) is astonishingly accurate.[61] So too is his minute observation of the windows themselves. On the right-hand side of the painting, the north choir aisle windows (from where the panels illustrated here are from) correctly show square-framed compositions alternating with circular ones. Close inspection reveals iconoclasts about their destructive task. As well as the figures in the main body of the choir, including one on top of the stalls with a raised pickaxe (ill.59 – see centre left of the painting), another can be seen on the left-hand side, at work on a window in the south choir aisle (ill.59a). Light comes in through the gaps he has created and the sill is littered with coloured shards. Iconoclasts are also in action at windows in the north and south choir galleries, and another beats out glass high up in the north transept clerestory.

Accounts of Canterbury Cathedral's plunder during the Civil War are dramatic and post-Restoration assessments of the damage, and bills for repair, show that the destruction had indeed been far-reaching. Throughout 1660 and 1661 supplies of glass and lead were urgently needed for the repair of the windows.[62] Given the quantity of surviving medieval glass in the cathedral today, it has been proposed that Culmer exaggerated his heroic despoiling, although Spraggon points to records that show that more than thirteen chests containing 3,913ft of glass were stored away by glaziers, to be restored in 1660–1.[63] An assessment of Johnson's evidence, Culmer's own written account of his actions, and the glass panels themselves (what within them is original, and what is restoration) suggest that the breaking entailed the elimination of whole panels but also, as occurred with official iconoclasm elsewhere in the country, the precise targeting of specific images within others.

The Presentation of Christ in the Temple (ill.60) and *Christ Leading the Gentiles away from Pagan Gods* (ill.61) are two panels from the famous medieval typological windows commissioned by the Benedictine monks of Christ Church following a fire in 1174.[64] Both show evidence of precise attack. In the first, the figures of the Virgin and St Simeon are restorations, as is the head of Christ; in the second, the cross on the altar, the figure of Christ and the pagan deity's altar frontal are replacements. The history of the restoration of the cathedral's glazing is a complicated and badly documented one. Glass was being restored, moved and replaced from the 1660s, and in the early nineteenth century a systematic restoration campaign began which

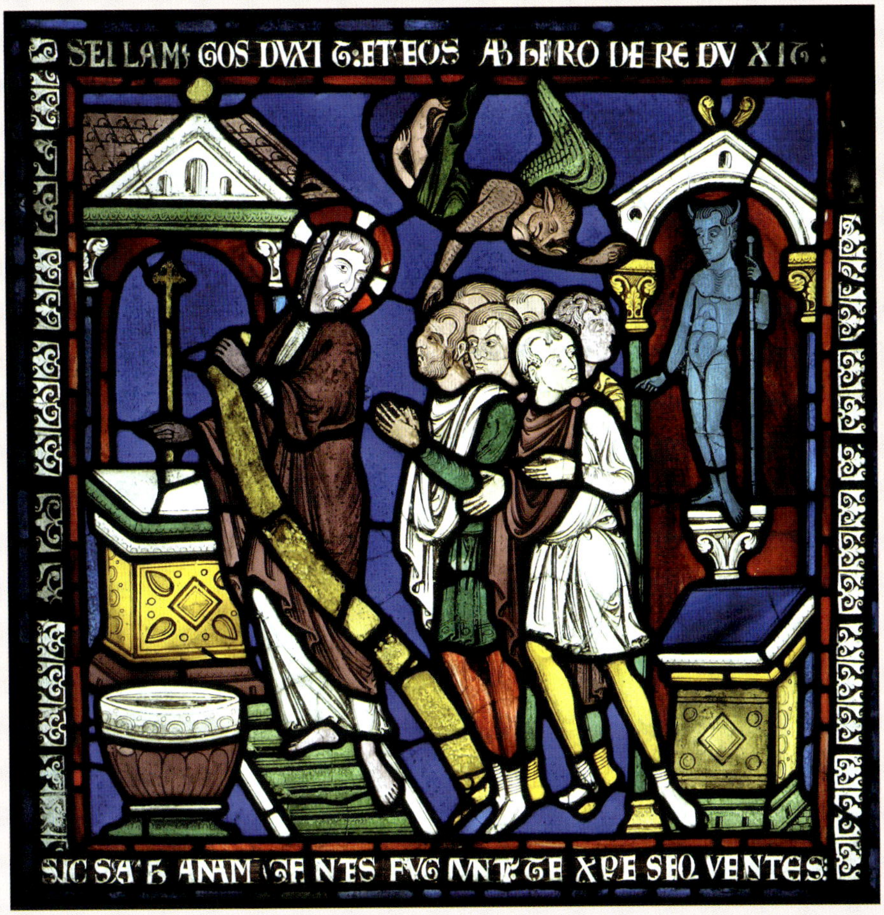

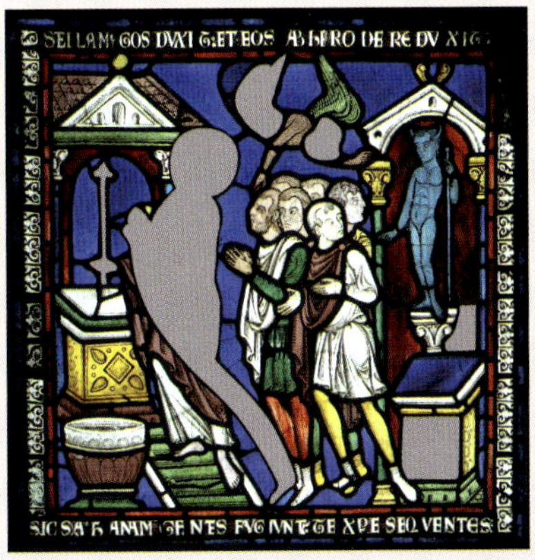

continued until 1952 and which was at times aggressive. Old glass was cut, repainted and reused for different parts of the cathedral and original panels were removed and replaced with modern replicas. Losses have also occurred for more mundane reasons, from pieces falling out due to the technical weakness of the glass or lead (before the First World War the sills of the north choir gallery were thickly covered with glass fragments) to firing at pigeons.[65] In his painting, Johnson shows both complete elimination of windows and what appears to be damage as the result of precise targeting. Entire panels are being smashed in the south choir aisle, and today there is no surviving medieval glass in that area. He also shows very precise damage done to the east window of the clerestory. High up, in the centre of the picture at the very far east end, a window with three vertical roundels is shown (ill.59b). The two lower roundels are void but the top one has a distinctive pattern of loss. The original roundel, now in the Richmond Museum, Virginia, shows that its later restoration corresponds exactly to this pattern.[66]

The subject of the roundel is the Last Judgement and it is the image of God the Father that has been removed. Culmer's description of the action against the windows clearly states that it was a defacement of specific images within them. 'Severell pictures of God the Father, of Crucifixes and men praying to Crucifixes, and to the Virgin Marie', were targeted. He took as his guide for breaking William Somner's *The Antiquities of Canterbury* 1640, which described the scenes in the windows. The book was 'a card and compasse to sail by, in that Cathedrall Ocean of Images' and by it 'many a Popish picture was discovered, and demolished'.[67] The destruction of the windows was vigorously opposed (the doors of the cathedral had to be locked so the iconoclasts could continue uninterrupted) and Culmer's 1644 description of events provoked anger as it reduced, it was argued, the extremities of what had occurred. Culmer had addressed his *Cathedrall newes* to Parliament, and proving to them that he had strictly enforced the 1643 ordinance and its list of what was proscribed would have been important. The evidence within the two panels illustrated here, however, where the symbolism of what has been lost is striking, suggests that the official iconoclasm of Canterbury Cathedral's windows was indeed specific and precisely targeted against offensive images and idols.

TB

The painted glass of Christ Church, Oxford

In 1998 over nine thousand fragments of painted glass were discovered in a coal bunker under Tom Quad at Christ Church College, Oxford. The pieces – parts of vivid green landscape backgrounds, expanses of sky, fractured faces, architecture and heraldry – were subsequently identified as survivors from the ambitious glazing programme commissioned for the college chapel in the 1630s by the dean, Brian Duppa.[68] Undertaken chiefly by Abraham van Linge, who with his kinsmen Bernard was responsible for most of the new glazing schemes in Oxford college chapels in the 1620s and 1630s, the windows were probably made and installed over a stretch of nine years, between 1631 and 1640.[69] There were nineteen in all and, to judge from the surviving (although much altered) window, *Jonah before Nineveh*, through their size, bold treatment of biblical narrative and the brilliance of their translucent enamel colour, collectively they must have presented a striking visual spectacle. Just over ten years later, however, the windows were removed and destroyed. On 2 June 1651 the new dean, John Owen (chaplain to Oliver Cromwell and preacher to the Council of State) ordered that 'all Pictures representing god, good or bad Angells or Saints shall be forthwith taken downe out of our Church windowes, and shall be disposed for the mending of the Glasse that is out of repaire in any part of the Colledg'.[70] This practical utilisation of the smashed fragments of proscribed images for the repair of others does not seem to have occurred. Instead, as the windows were laid out on the ground, Canon Henry Wilkinson, fearing that otherwise they would be preserved, 'with violent zeal … furiously stampt upon many parts of it, and utterly defaced them'.[71]

The fate of the windows reflects the changing political and religious climate of Oxford. By 1640 Laudian ceremonial worship and rich ornamentation characterised many college chapels. Whereas Laudian furnishings and imagery had largely been purged from most parish churches by the early 1640s, their persistence in royalist Oxford, where Laud had been chancellor and which the king had made his wartime headquarters, provoked considerable hostility.[72] The bitterness of political and religious division is evident in a poem that defends the Christ Church windows. Not only did the chapel at Christ Church serve the college, it was also the city's cathedral and the king's Chapel Royal, and as such was prominent, visible and a topic of debate. 'A poem in defence of the decent ornaments of Christ Church, Oxon, occasioned by a Banbury brother, who called them Idolatries', most likely written in the 1640s, appeared in a royalist and high church miscellany of university verse, *Parnassus Biceps* 1656. The anonymous author defends the cathedral's ornament – its windows, organ music, marble pavement, tapers and fragrant cedarwood – from the profaning tongue of Puritan criticism.[73] Its windows are singled out for particular praise. They are aids in devotion, he says, and their splendour conjures the majesty of the Divine.

Church windows were praised in several other poems of the period. Those at Fairford, Gloucestershire, dismissed by Puritans as 'brittle superfluity', heightened devotion; and for George Herbert painted histories in church windows were akin to preaching, which the sun glowing through them animated and made glorious and transcendent.[74]

In *The Deposition* 1629 (ill.52), a painted and stained-glass panel made for the private chapel at Hampton Court, Herefordshire, Abraham van Linge found it necessary to include a written qualification: 'The truth here of is historicall devine and / not superstissious'. The image cannot be construed as controversial, it argues, as it is based on the scriptures. The need to justify the presence and manage the use of images became particularly acute in Oxford following the surrender of the city in 1646. Even in 1641 the prevailing mood against images had meant that instead of being installed, van Linge's just-completed glazing scheme for University College chapel was hidden away for safety.[75] Of post-1647 Oxford John Aubrey exclaimed 'Down went Dagon … now no religion is to be found', noting the disappearance from windows of crucifixes and 'canonised saints'; and in 1651–2 Lodewijck Huygens noticed that faces of Jesus and the apostles in chapel windows had been blacked out.[76] What this suggests is a partial, focused

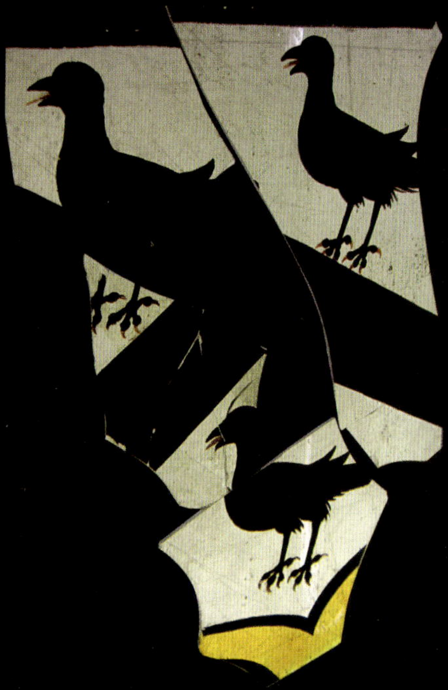

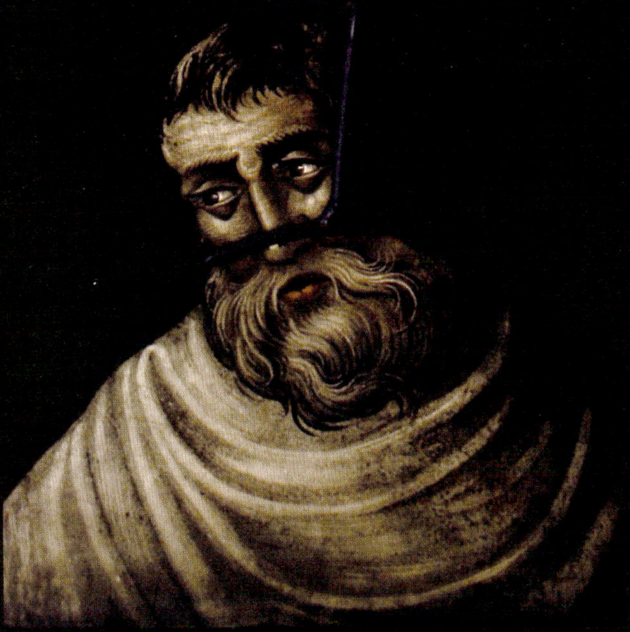

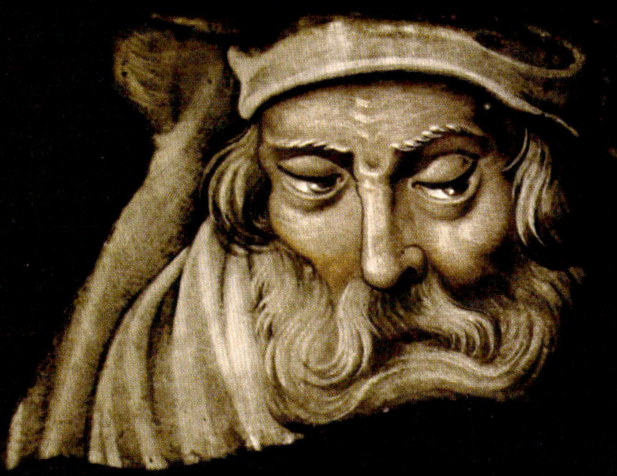

elimination of proscribed imagery, not wholesale destruction.

There is little evidence for any systematic drive to cleanse the university of superstitious imagery in 1646.[77] Instead, reform was left in the hands of the masters and fellows of individual colleges. But in 1651 iconoclastic reform seems to have been enforced on Oxford, perhaps tied to new legislation against Stuart symbols and enacted as a punishment against the former royalist stronghold. University College's reaction was to order a new lock for the storehouse containing its new glass.[78] The Oxford antiquarian Anthony Wood recorded 'the defacing of all tokens of Monarchy' as well as 'postures of Prophets, Apostles and Saints painted in College Chappels'. Christ Church was a great loser for 'Scripture History in Glass', he says, although his account of events at the cathedral is confused. He also claimed that the so-branded 'anti-christian, diabolical, and popish' glass was broken, and then removed for safety, in around 1648;[79] yet it was still there in 1651 for its figures to be ordered out by the dean, and for Canon Wilkinson to stamp on it. Recent examination of the surviving Jonah window has shown that the glass outlining the image of Jonah himself is late seventeenth century and technically corresponds to the work of the glass painter William Price who was working at the cathedral in 1696.[80] It is perhaps evidence that partial reformation – the removal of proscribed figures – did indeed take place, and that decades later restoration took place of what was salvageable from the van Linge scheme. The fragments of glass in the coal bunker are all from three identifiable subject windows, *Sodom and Gomorrah*, *Christ disputing with the Doctors* and *Christ's entry into Jerusalem*, but in the nineteenth century they fell victim a second time, to the aesthetic iconoclasts of the Gothic Revival. TB

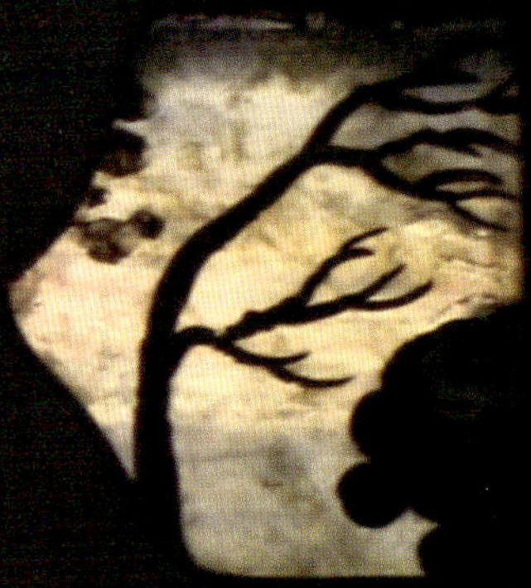

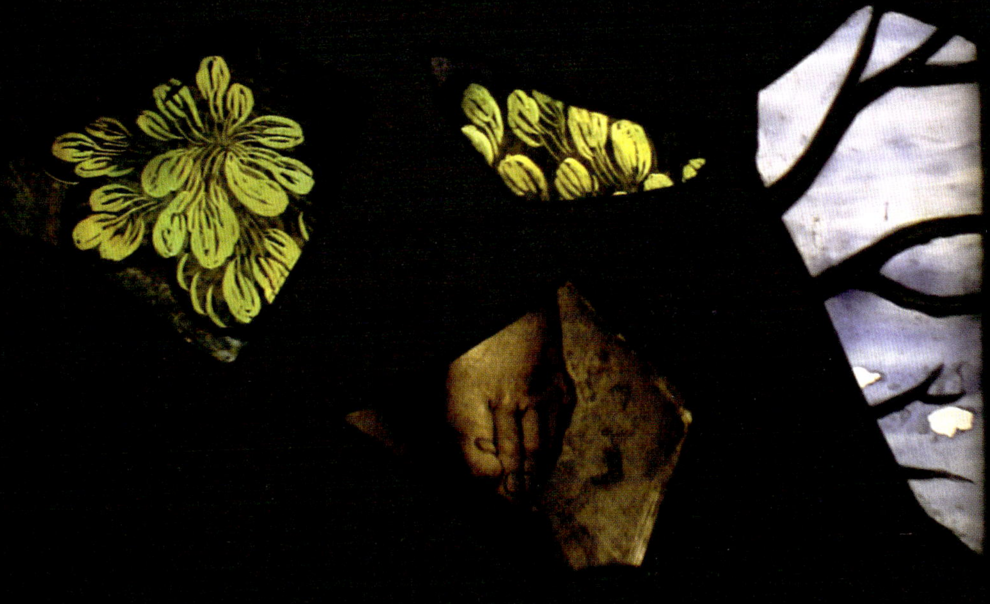

64
Abraham van Linge (active 1623–42)
Painted glass fragments 1630s
The Dean and Chapter of Christ Church Cathedral, Oxford

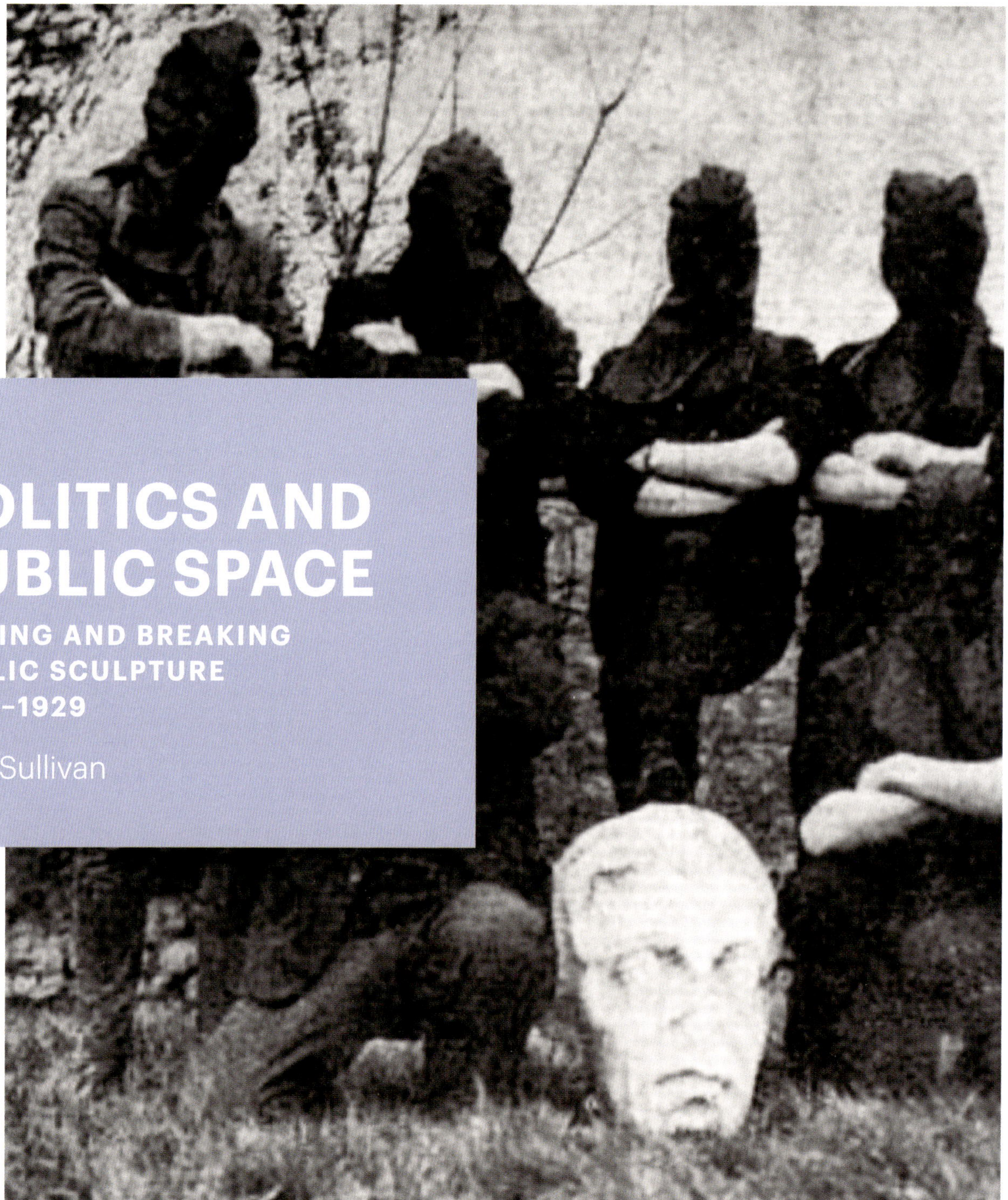

4 POLITICS AND PUBLIC SPACE

MAKING AND BREAKING PUBLIC SCULPTURE 1688–1929

M.G. Sullivan

Colonel Hayford came into Hedlam's Coffee house on the Sandhill, and there said that he had given orders to pull down the statue on the Sandhill, and he continued there until after it had been pulled down; and then, two of his soldiers came to him into the said coffee-house, and told him they had pulled it down, and so he took money out of his pockets and gave it the soldiers
(Witness statement concerning the successful attack on the statue of James II, Newcastle, 1689)

When word of what they were about was brought to my father, he exclaimed, with a smile upon his face, 'The cramps are leaded, and they may pull to doomsday'
(Peter Cunningham, witness to the failed attack on a statue of William Pitt installed by his father, London, 1831)

On the night of 11 May 1689 a crowd gathered near the brass equestrian statue of James II on the Sandhill in Newcastle. The statue, depicting the king mastering a rearing horse, had been erected the previous year by the corporation, led by a fiercely loyal mayor, Henry Brabant. Soon after, the town opened its gates to the forces of William, Prince of Orange, then supplanting the Stuart monarch, and it was the Williamite soldiers who led the crowd this May night. A Captain Killigrew, acting on the orders of Colonel Hayford, gave a speech on a stage (usually reserved for the sale of quack medicines), in which he gestured towards the statue announcing: 'our lives, liberties and properties were taken away, and all by that picture.' Several witnesses record Killigrew throwing money into the crowd, before a soldier mounted the pedestal and attacked the statue with a sword, 'endeavouring to break off the stirropps and spurrs'. Afterwards another soldier placed a rope around the neck of the statue and it was pulled from its horse. Once on the ground, the statue was beaten with stones by a crowd. According to a later source, the statue was dragged to the Quay and thrown into the Tyne.[1]

This remarkably well-documented episode was planned in advance. A witness recorded officers speaking about the event several days previously. Like many attacks on public statuary in this period, the iconoclasm was ritualised – in this case comprising an incendiary speech, a symbolic destruction and a watery ending. All these elements clearly show the stage-managed inversion of the symbolism of the statue. It was erected by Tory royalists on a divided city council to demonstrate their loyalty to James II, and torn down by soldiers who fought for the Protestant William III and were similarly showing their loyalty. The speech accompanying the iconoclasm no doubt mirrors the speeches at its erection. The unseating of the rider from his horse inverts the iconography of the military ruler mastering the horse and state. The watery ending mirrors the public humiliations of a custom known as 'riding the stang', which was carried out on the Sandhill in this period, whereby a transgressor (often a military one) rode a wooden horse in public before being dumped in a ditch. The trade in symbols did not end there. The head of the king's statue seems to have been removed (it was later in the possession of a York bell-founder, who described it as a 'relic'). The horse, however, was melted down and transformed into a set of bells for the (Protestant) church of All Saints.[2]

This was the first major iconoclasm of the period following the Glorious Revolution, but it was not the last. In Ireland, where the Protestant succession was most divisive, iconoclasm and public statuary were constant bedfellows. In London there were many reports of attacks on statues, worrying enough to lead to the Public Statues Bill of 1854 enforcing the maintenance of statues in public places.

The story of iconoclasm and public statuary in Britain and Ireland between 1688 and 1929 evokes many lines of enquiry. Attacks on public statues are frequent symbols of struggle between political groups: Orangemen versus Jacobites in Newcastle and Ireland, Reformist Whigs versus Tories in the attack on William Pitt's statue in Hanover Square at the time of Great Reform Act. Historical geographers have examined the erection and destruction of public statuary in Ireland as a key to struggles over public space and political territory. One could also study the attacks through their ritual and symbolism, intimately connected to customary forms of expressing disdain for individuals who transgress community norms (best demonstrated in E.P. Thompson's work on 'rough musicking'). Other possible explanatory frameworks might be the development of the British state, the debate over idolatry in the age of reason, the policing of public space, the culture of public mourning, heroism and masculinity.[3]

We should not, however, lose sight of the art-historical story that can be seen to unfold in this period of erection and toppling. Studies of these works of art tend, naturally, to focus on the commissioning of the works and their destruction, often leaving the artwork as a symbolic counter exchanged between rival groups. Equally, though, there is a third agency involved – the creator and the artwork. One can see this period not simply as one of varied fortunes for works of art, but as a period in which the context of iconoclasm in public spaces began to influence the production of the works themselves. Whether through the use of ornament, railings, pedestals or advanced cramping systems, artists can be seen to adapt and respond to the opportunities and challenges faced in producing art for contested public spaces.

William Larson's statue of James II in Newcastle was created at a good time for statuary. Five other statues of the monarch were erected in England, Scotland and Ireland between 1670 and 1688 (three of which still survive). William Larson came from a family of sculptors originally based in The Hague, Holland. His father was in London by the 1650s and in 1660 left his tools, moulds and other equipment to William, who continued the business in Pall Mall Fields.[4] Although we know relatively little about Larson today, he was clearly an artist of some standing, to judge from the top price of £800 that was agreed with the Corporation of Newcastle for the statue in April 1686. Larson issued his proposal and the council contracted, stipulating that it was to be a statue of 'His Majesty King James the Second in good Cannon Brass in moderne Habitt on a capering horse as large as that of his late majesty King Charles the First at Charing Cross on a pedestall of black or white marble of equall height and magnitude to the said figure'.[5] There is no doubt that this was a grand gesture. The prints of the work (in the British Museum) show the king in mastery, with the full suit of armour (rather than the 'moderne habitt' stipulated above) and the rich carvings of military trophies around the pedestal pressing home the impression of a military ruler triumphing over his enemies. The statue was also a grand work of art – the technical feat of balancing a large statue on two shafts of brass representing the horse's legs was not attempted by any of Larson's contemporaries.

A model which may have been made in preparation for this work (ill.65) is inscribed 'Baxter taught, Wyck drew, Larson embost and cast it tow'. This is thought to be a reference to Nicholas Baxter Esq. of the Great Horses to James II, and the horse-painter Jan Wyck, both of whom could supply specialist knowledge of how to depict a horse 'capering'. If this model is of James II (and it has been argued that it represents Charles II, although no equestrian commission to that monarch is known by Larson) it shows him in his 'moderne habit' as originally intended. What is certain is that Sir Christopher Wren, Surveyor-General, was asked to approve the finished work, and Larson himself was to oversee the freight to Newcastle and the erection of the great work.

Easily overlooked in the contract is the stipulation that Larson was to 'rayle the same with Iron and pave the same in like manner as that at Charing Cross now is'. This protective measure, sensible in hindsight, perhaps hints at the fact that the commission of this grand statement was extremely controversial within Newcastle and the local government. The Mayor, Sir Henry Brabant, who proposed the statue, was losing seats within the corporation to a faction led by Sir William Blackett. The proposal of the statue seems to have been a provocative test of the loyalty of the Blackett faction. Brabant did not scruple to bring his conclusions to King James himself in a petition of 1686, writing that Brabant and his loyal friends had proposed the statue, but:

> it was strongly opposed by the other partie, who refused at first signing an order for it, and some of them ... did not stick to say the erecting the said statue looked like Popery; so your Majesty may judge what service you may expect from such men ... however, the Mayor by threatening to send hither the names of such as refused it, he obtained at last their consent for the said statue, more out of fear than love.[6]

But the railings did not save the statue in May 1689. The destruction led to a set of witness depositions to the Mayor of Newcastle twelve days later, which were damning of the behaviour of the troops. Private letters reporting the conduct of the soldiers were circulated in London. The corporation made no official complaint, however, and the witness statements were sent to none other than Sir William Blackett (and remained unopened and unpublished until 1847). Whitehall promised to vindicate Heyford's actions, saying – in contravention of the evidence – that they thought it 'hard that those who are innocent should bear the reproach of what appears to be only done by the common people, who are sometimes apt to make escapes in what they think is service to a cause they are affected with'. They then added, in what appears to be a sly joke: 'The seizing of horses is usually entrusted to the deputy lieutenants and the justices.'[7]

If not an officially sponsored iconoclasm, the destruction of the statue of James II was certainly

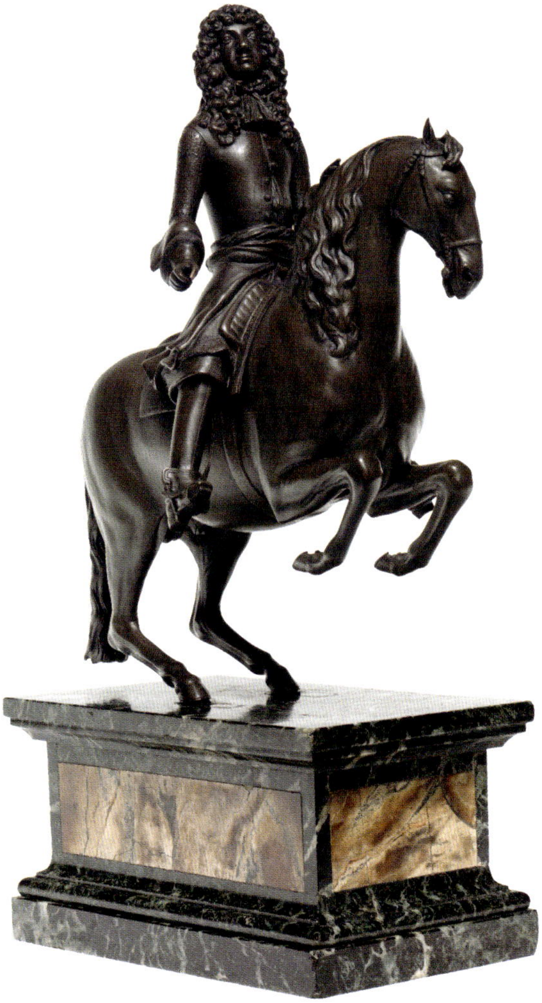

65
After William Larson (d.1692)
Equestrian statuette of King James II
*c.*1686
Bronze
64 × 40 × 22.5
National Gallery of Ireland, Dublin

excused by the Williamite government. The statue building of James II's reign was not immediately followed by a similar wave commemorating William's rule. A statue on the line of kings at the Royal Exchange in 1695 was the only contemporary effigy of William in England (although after his death many statues were raised to William, as an abiding symbol of British 'liberty').[8] The one great exception, and the most controversial, was the statue by Grinling Gibbons to William III on College Green, Dublin. This much-attacked and ill-fated work became one of the most divisive symbols of Anglo-Irish government (see pp 102–105).

It is perhaps not surprising – given the fate of the statues of James II in Newcastle and William III in Dublin – that the Hanoverian monarchs trod carefully in the field of public statues. It is one of the curiosities of eighteenth-century royal statues that they are frequently commissioned by individuals or groups as private gestures of loyalty, and erected in semi-public or private spaces.[9] One of the most prominent families in the production of royal monuments to Hanoverians was the Nost, or Van Nost, family. Initially arriving in England from Mechelen in the Southern Netherlands to work with Gibbons and Arnold Quellin, John Nost I made a good career carving monuments and casting garden statues before his death in 1710. His cousin, John Nost II, continued as the workshop master, and it was he who set the family up as purveyors of royal statues. Approached by the Dublin Corporation in 1717, John Nost II supplied an exceptional bronze statue of George I, to be sited on Essex Bridge, Dublin (now in the Barber Institute, Birmingham). The figure was original, although the horse was cast from moulds which Nost took from King Charles I's horse at Charing Cross (by Le Sueur). Indeed, one of the skills which Nost and his fellow Netherlandish immigrants brought to London was a remarkable facility in metal-casting. Following the Dublin commission, Nost made several lead copies from his moulds for private courtiers – Lord Cobham placed his equestrian statue of George I at Stowe, Buckinghamshire (still in situ), another was at Hackwood Park in Hampshire, Richard Grosvenor placed his in Grosvenor Square in London, and the Duke of Chandos placed his at his country estate of Cannons in Middlesex.[10]

In around 1750 the third generation master sculptor, John Nost III (styling himself 'John Van Nost'), relocated the family workshop to Dublin, where the Protestant oligarchy found much use for his skills. In addition to repairing the statue of George I by his father (which was subject to attacks), he also made an equestrian statue of King George II for St Stephen's Green.[11] The horse, again, was made from the moulds his father took from Charles I's horse.

Van Nost's George II was no less provocative than the royal statues by Larson or Gibbons. The king appears in Roman armour, commanding his horse (and the state), his arm holding with a baton (giving law or giving military orders), and was placed in central Dublin by the City Corporation in gratitude for 'His Majesty's gracious administration'. In 1758 it was erected with full procession around the city, accompanied by the city musicians.

It appears, however, that much had been learned from the previous Dublin statues. The site chosen – St Stephen's Green – was then highly conspicuous, although not on a main thoroughfare and no path led to the monument. The base and pedestal were also carefully considered. Not only was the statue placed on a 20-ft-high pedestal, but the pedestal was set on a raised rusticated chamber with a balustrade. On each of the four corners were placed spiky and forbidding martial trophies. The setting and pedestal seem to have been an innovative way

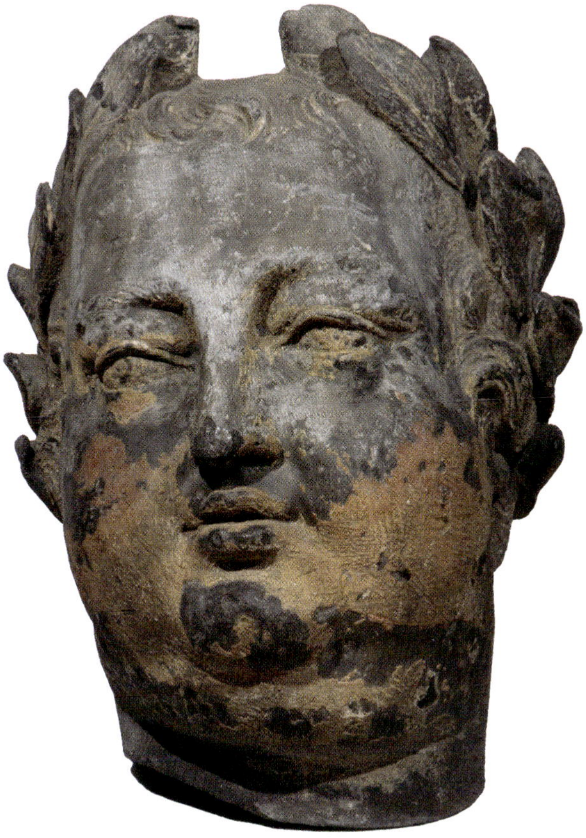

to display a divisive triumphal martial symbol in a way that is at once commanding, visible from great distances, and extremely difficult to dislodge. In his poem *The Beau Walk, in Stephen's Green*, Thomas Newburgh wrote:

> But lo! a Statue from afar salutes your Eyes,
> To which th'Inclosure all Access denies.[12]

It is a tribute to the tenacity of Dublin's metal thieves that some successful sorties were made to steal parts of the statue. 'Mid-night depredators', wrote a nineteenth-century author, were 'induced to make a trial of their skill in sawing off a leg or an arm for the value of the material'. On one occasion, 'one leg of the horse was cut off and a saw had nearly penetrated his neck when the watchman was alarmed by the noise and routed the depredators'.[13]

The specification of commanding space and resisting attack could be seen to reach its great neoclassical expression in the development of the single high column as a pedestal for a public memorial. Referring to the triumphal Roman columns of Hadrian and Trajan, the design found favour with many sculptors, architects and commissioners in the late eighteenth and early nineteenth centuries. The most recognisable example, of course, is the column in Trafalgar Square, London, to Admiral Nelson. The earliest example of the period, however, was constructed in Ireland in 1746–7, in the unlikely setting of Birr, County Offaly.

The column, 55ft high, was erected by Sir Lawrence Parsons to commemorate the recent victory of William, Duke of Cumberland, over the Jacobites at Culloden. Parsons, whose family had defended Birr against James II in 1690, was quick to plan the memorial. The *General Advertiser*, London, commended Parsons on 7 June 1746 for his scheme, the 'first public testimony of the gratitude we owe for his Royal Highness's eminent services'. Parsons was in the process of planning and building a modern Georgian town in which he transformed Birr into Parsonstown, a regular plan of avenues and villas. At its centre was the column, topped with a martial standing statue of Cumberland, one decisive foot forward, his body dressed in a Roman tunic and his pudgy head wreathed with laurels (ill.66).[14] The column was designed by architect Samuel Chearnley, a relative of Parsons, and the lead statue was the work of London-based sculptors Sir Henry Cheere and his brother John.

Cumberland was not a universally admired figure. Even in the relatively controlled atmosphere of Parsonstown there were voices of dissent for the commemoration. A local poet in the nineteenth century described how the statue 'still seemed to

66
Sir Henry and John Cheere
(1702–81, 1709–87)
Head of the Duke of Cumberland 1747
Lead
34 × 92 (circumference)
Courtesy of The Hunt Museum, Ireland

gloat on slaughter'. According to local legend, the statue was finally removed in March 1915 following the objection of Scottish soldiers based at the nearby Crinkhill barracks. Photographic evidence suggests, rather, that the statue was starting to lean dangerously to one side as a result of cracks in the lead (ill.67). A firm of Northamptonshire steeplejacks was employed to build a scaffold and bring down the statue. The complexity of the operation detailed in these photographs demonstrates that whatever feelings may have existed for Cumberland, it was always going to be a major project to get the statue down. Once down, however, there appears to have been no appetite to put the statue back again. In a chain of events that is not exactly clear, it was subsequently dismembered, with only two fragments surviving in museums today.[15]

In London Cheere was commissioned by Lieutenant-General Strode to execute an equestrian statue to Cumberland for Cavendish Square, in memory of his 'private kindness and public virtue', although in the nineteenth century it was removed for recasting and never put back. Nineteenth-century commentators, such as Charles Knight, commented that the statue was set up 'in disregard to the best feelings of human nature', and whilst men might disagree over the value of his service at Culloden, 'the horrors of the wanton cruelties that followed must be universal ... "The Butcher" was the title applied to him in his own day, and it is likely to outlive the statue which, in disregard to the best feelings of human nature, has been set up'.[16] Elsewhere, painted portraits of Cumberland have fared little better. A portrait after Reynolds (ill.68), lent by the National Portrait Gallery to Aberdeen in modern times, was found in a recent conservation report to be frequently marked with saliva.

The nineteenth-century attitudes to the statue of Cumberland were part of an increasingly common discourse about public sculpture, which held that statues in public spaces should not be erected by private groups or embody factional interests, but should express (or at least appear to express) a widely held admiration. In the wave of statue building that followed the Napoleonic Wars, and continued as an index to Britain's Empire and to civic and national pride, statues were increasingly erected through parliamentary vote and/or by public subscription. These mechanisms – in theory

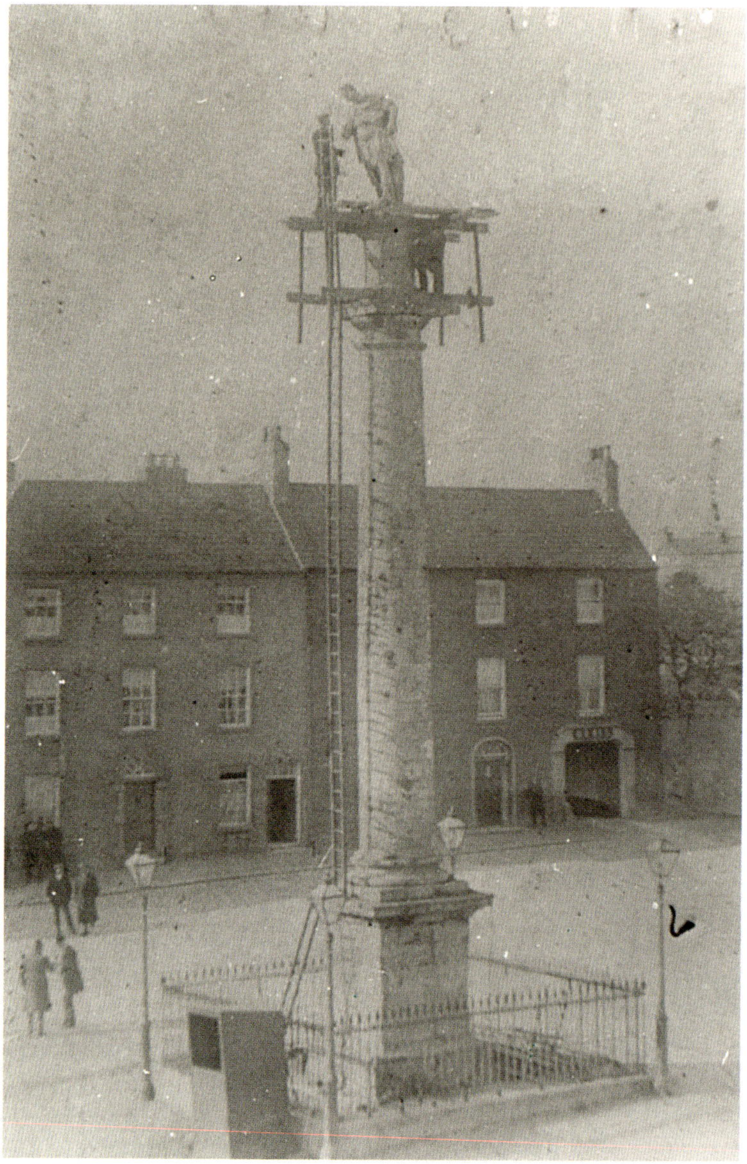

67
Sir Henry and John Cheere's statue of the Duke of Cumberland, Parsonstown, County Offaly, being taken down *c*.1915

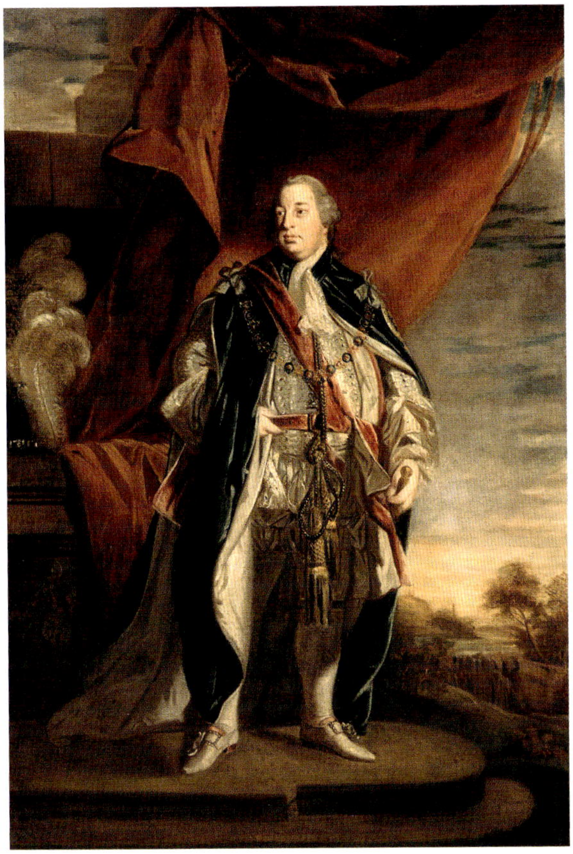

at least – safeguarded the notion that permanent commemoration expressed some kind of consensual admiration.[17]

At the same time, however, British industry gave statuary an increasing resistance to physical attack. Sculptors like Francis Chantrey and Richard Westmacott used new engineering to build their own powerful foundries and produce bronze statues of a quality, consistency and size that far excelled the technologies used by the previous generation. New, stronger tools made it possible for sculptors to work with denser materials, as in the case of Samuel Nixon, who carved the statue of William IV at Greenwich out of granite.[18]

68
After Sir Joshua Reynolds (1723–92)
William Augustus, Duke of Cumberland
c.1758–60
Oil paint on canvas
87.6 × 59.1
National Portrait Gallery, London

Engineering feats such as the columns on which Nelson and the Duke of York stood placed the figures far above the attentions of possible opponents. Although none of these figures seems to have been the target of any enmity, the new technologies meant that where iconoclastic intent existed it could be withstood. Chantrey's colossal statue to the Duke of Sutherland, carved from local Brora stone,[19] which has been a target of attacks by opponents who see Sutherland as the hated landowner of the Highland clearances, has withstood ferocious and repeated attacks.[20] Allan Cunningham, Francis Chantrey's foreman, sniffed at the attempts of the pro-reformist iconoclasts who tried to topple his master's statue of Pitt out of confidence that the leaded cramps placed the destruction of the statue beyond the means of most traditional iconoclasts (see pp 108–109).

But if modern statuary, through a combination of (theoretically) consensual commissioning and strong cramps, was increasingly impervious to attack, there was growing concern for the vulnerability of older statues. In 1854 the Public Statues Act responded to the theft of the sword from the statue of Charles I in Trafalgar Square with legislation that compelled authorities to maintain the statuary.[21] Another prominent example was John Nost II's equestrian statue of George I in Leicester Square, London. A private commission, it had been made for Cannons in Middlesex but was sold in 1748 and re-erected in Leicester Square. It was unveiled on the Prince of Wales's birthday in November that year at a ceremony attended by George II. It was carefully cushioned sculptural propaganda as George I was dead, George II had not commissioned the statue, and it stood on private land in London. Yet it was publicly accessible and in the nineteenth century, when this area became an increasingly bawdy part of town, the statue was subject to frequent indignities.[22] *The Builder* in 1851 recorded seeing 'a ragged urchin riding en croupe behind the stately effigy', mocking 'defunct royalty with grimace and antics'.[23] During the night of 16–17 October 1866 a number of practical jokers, assisted by the property-room artists of the Alhambra, embellished the statue with a dunce's cap, a broomstick and a rash of painted spots (ills 70, 71). The same year horse and rider parted company (ill.69), prompting the government to intervene through the new Towns and Gardens Act, which permitted the state to intervene to compel owners to maintain private property. The statue was beyond repair and was sold, presumably for scrap, in 1872. The legislation again increased the power of the state to police and protect public sculpture.[24]

What is notable about these episodes, however, is that they appear to have been entirely without any specific political agenda. *The Graphic* described the statue as a 'butt for practical jokers', including some 'systematic wags' who 'bedaubed it with whitewash'. Even in the House of Lords, where the matter was raised, some hilarity was recorded when the statue was described as 'with only one leg and that crooked, and with only one arm which was quite distorted'.[25] Although the maintenance of public space was clearly regarded as an issue, the attacks on this statue seem to have been intended, and accepted, as performative humour. There is a rich seam of this type of humorous symbolic inversion in attacks on public statues in Britain (especially in university towns). For example, the green turf mohican placed on the statue of Sir Winston Churchill in London's Parliament Square during protests in 2000 (see ill.6) has been widely indulged as a clever intervention (although swinging on the flags on the cenotaph was prosecuted as a serious offence).

In Ireland in the nineteenth and early twentieth century, against the backdrop of the struggles for independence, the statues of William III and the Hanoverians had lost none of their potency as potential targets for attack, as the 1836 bombing of Gibbons' statue proved (see pp 103–104). Once independence had been achieved in 1922 there was a steady removal of these symbols of the Union. Again, the destruction was carried out with as much symbolism as the original erection. Nost's martial statue of George II on St Stephen's Green was targeted with explosives on Armistice Day 1928, the same day that Gibbons's William III was bombed beyond repair. Unlike the Gibbons, however, it survived the bombing. It was finally destroyed in 1937, the day after the coronation of

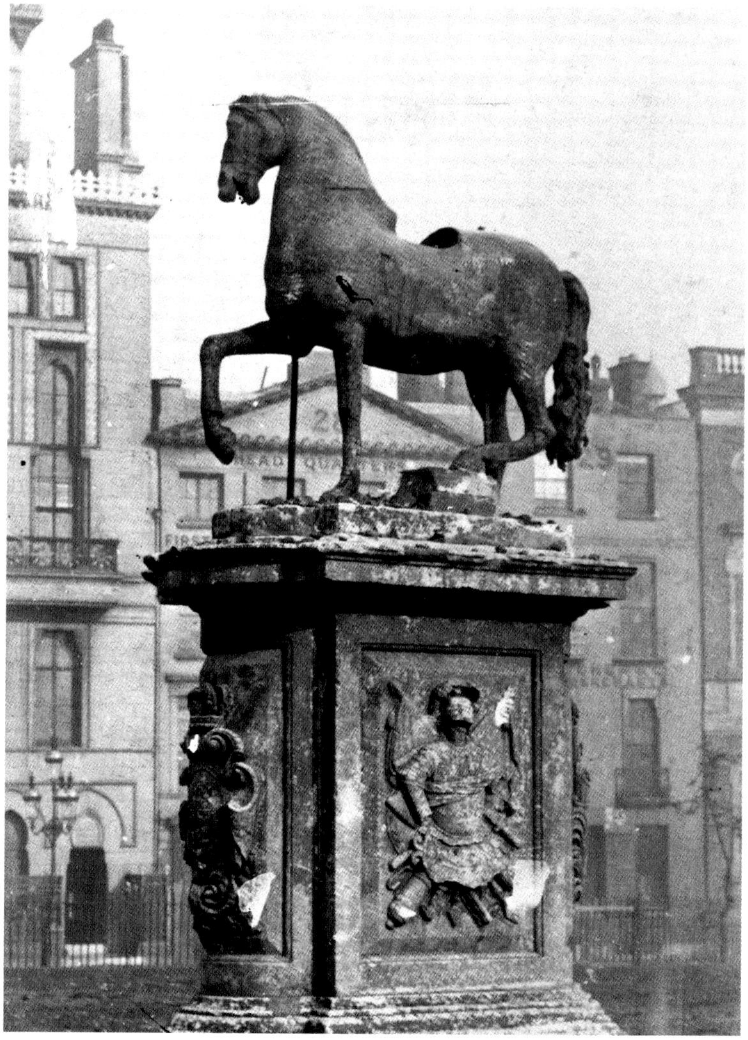

69
Photograph of John Van Nost's statue of George I in Leicester Square, London, *c.*1872
English Heritage

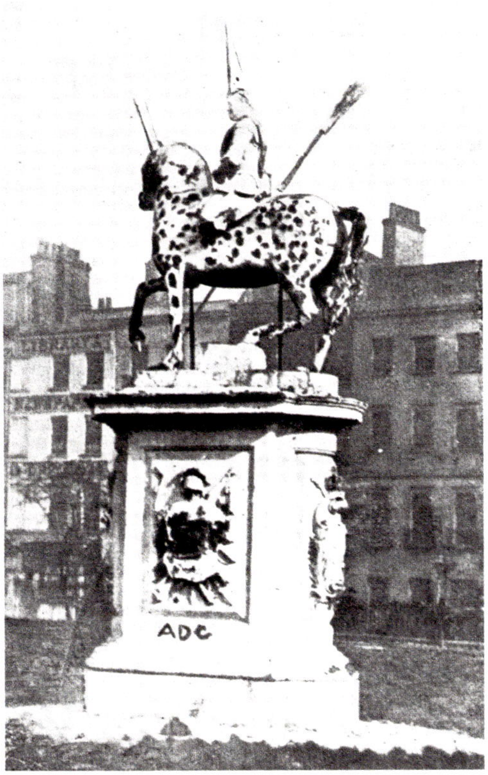

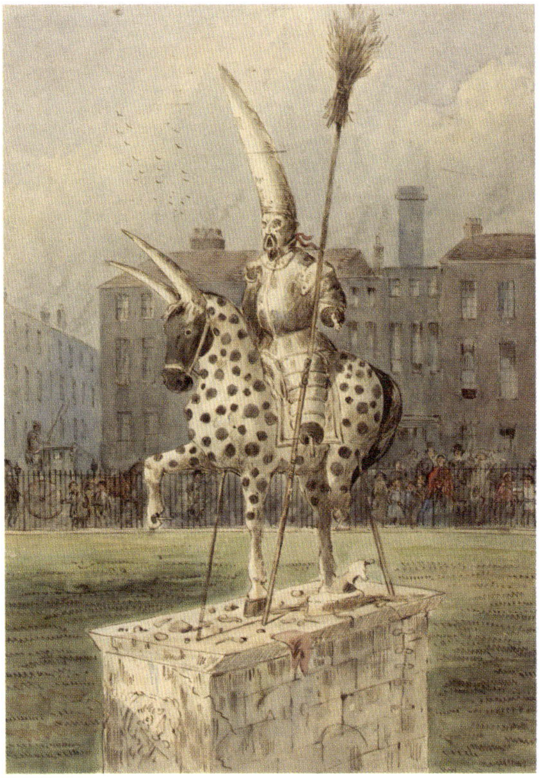

George VI, when three sacks of explosives were detonated beneath and around the statue, propelling it to the ground. One source suggests that the statue was subsequently melted down for bullets,[26] a transformation of the material that had earlier been adopted by iconoclasts in the former American colonies.

Public sculpture, one of the most distinctive art forms of the eighteenth and nineteenth centuries, has lost none of its power to act as a medium for the expression of conflict. The steady removal of Stalin's statues from former countries of the USSR, or the stage-managed toppling of Saddam Hussein's statue in Baghdad, all attest to the symbolic potency of destroying a statue of an ousted leader. In Britain debates over how far public statuary appropriately conveys the public will remain strong, and have inflected the debates over the future of the empty fourth plinth in Trafalgar Square and the suitability of raising public statues to Margaret Thatcher and Arthur 'Bomber' Harris. Similarly there is a continued debate over the extent to which sculpture can be permitted to be the target of political protest. That the making and breaking of these inanimate objects have inspired technological innovation and meditations on public will, as well as conveying insurrection, or the triumph of state over state, is no small tribute to the remarkable power of public sculpture.

70
Photograph, taken on the morning of 17 October 1866, documenting the overnight defacement of the statue of George I in Leicester Square, reprinted in *The Sketch*, 14 September 1898

71
Ernest Griset (1843–1907)
The Statue, 17 October 1866
Watercolour, pen and ink on paper
Victoria and Albert Museum, London

Grinling Gibbons' equestrian statue of William III, College Green, Dublin

For over two centuries an equestrian statue of King William III stood on a pedestal at the centre of College Green, Dublin. Although cast and carved by one of the most distinguished of British artists, Grinling Gibbons, it gained more attention as a visible touchstone of political division in Ireland. It was subject to celebration and attack in equal measure, finally succumbing to destruction in 1928.

The statue was erected during William III's lifetime, commissioned by a number of Dublin merchants and aldermen, to commemorate William III's victory over James II at the Battle of the Boyne on 1 July 1690. The burghers met with Grinling Gibbons in London and agreed to pay him £800 in instalments. Gibbons, who had carried out much carved work for both James II and William III, completed the statue in 1701.

The statue showed William III, laurels of victory around his head, in Roman armour, astride a horse. The composition drew upon the statue of Marcus Aurelius, Le Seueur's statue of Charles I in Trafalgar Square and Gibbons' own of Charles II at Windsor (although Gibbons did not reproduce the pose of the horse from his earlier work, suggesting that this is not simply a cast of the horse from the same mould with a different rider). Gibbons is not known to have carved William III's portrait, although he worked extensively at Hampton Court under William and Mary and presumably knew his subject. William III was not shown dramatically gesturing with his baton (as the later statue of George II on College Green) but the symbolism of a warrior coming in triumph, bringing law, was clear enough.[27] The carvings on the marble plaques for the pedestal showed (and still show) the intricate carving of still life for which Gibbons was famed (ill.73). They include military motifs, quiver, arrows and gloves, and appear to show all the virtuosity of Gibbon's other carving in marble and wood.

It was clear, though, from the date of its installation, 1 July 1701, that the statue was not simply an ornament or a memoir, but was intended as a symbol and constant reminder of Protestant victory over Irish Catholicism. The plaque, inscribed to the Mayor of Dublin, Mark Rainsford, and the sheriffs, celebrated William as the upholder of religion, the restorer of law and the guardian of liberty. The statue was the focus of ritual celebration every year on the anniversary of the Boyne and the birthday of William III, when it was bedecked with orange ribbons, sometimes painted white, sometimes with green ribbons underfoot. Every year processions would circle the statue three times, punctuated by an oration to William III, before volleys were fired by Grenadiers and a large party closed proceedings, with fireworks and bonfires.[28]

For others the statue was not a symbol of liberation from tyranny, but the opposite. It was the backdrop for retribution against Jacobites such as a porter who had proclaimed for the Pretender in Dublin, who was whipped in front of the statue in February 1716.[29] It was also disliked by Trinity College students, who claimed that the statue, like the king himself through his toleration of dissenters, had turned his back on them. Trinity students were often at the forefront of indignities heaped upon the statue in subsequent years. A combination of religious and political grievance resulted in the statue being frequently attacked.[30]

The press reported in 1710 that the statue needed to be repaired 'with zeal and

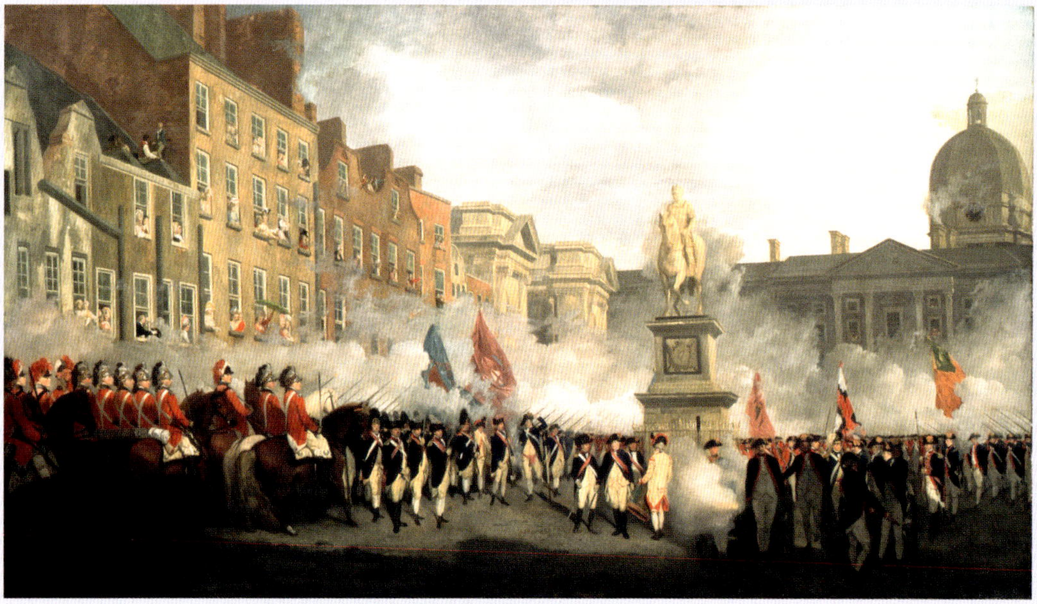

72
Francis Wheatley (1747–1801)
The Dublin Volunteers on College Green, 4th November 1779, 1779
Oil paint on canvas
221 × 364.5
National Gallery of Ireland, Dublin

73
Grinling Gibbons (1648–1721)
Fragment from the plinth of the equestrian statue of William III, 1701
Marble
100 × 80 × 10.8
Dublin City Council

care' following an attack in which the king's face was smeared with mud and his baton stolen.[31] The ensign, who revealed the culprits to be three students from Trinity College, thus pocketing a £150 reward, was subject to 'many hardships' subsequently.[32] The attack symbolically deprived the statue of its symbol of law – the baton – and thus deprived the object of the symbol of rule. This was a very effective means of overturning the symbolism. The punishment for such attacks was not trifling. The Trinity students were given a six-month jail sentence and a £1,000 fine, as well as a ritualistic humiliation of standing before the statue with a placard around their necks detailing their crime.[33] The crucial baton was replaced with a replica, and a solemn ceremony attended its restoration. Even the punishments did not deter attackers. In 1714 the Lords Justice offered a reward of £100 for information leading to the arrest of culprits who defaced the statue in November that year.[34] In February 1716 the London *News-Letter* reported that 'the statue of King William III has been assaulted, and one of the hand's broke; the horses ears knock'd off, and a thing like a Scaramouch set behind him, with other indignities, too scandalous to be mentioned; for which a reward of £10 is offer'd, to discover the actors and contrivors thereof.'[35]

In 1779 the statue became a rallying symbol for the Dublin Volunteer movement, whose members campaigned for greater devolved power for the Irish legislature. That year they gathered over a thousand men on College Green on William's birthday, to witness volleys fired over the statue (painted white), shown in a scene painted by the artist Francis Wheatley (ill.72).

According to J.T. Gilbert, the statue was 'frequently found decorated with green boughs, bedaubed with filth or dressed up with hay; it was also a common practice to set a straw figure astride that of the king'.[36] *The Times* recorded that in 1798 someone climbed the statue and attempted to cut off its head ('after working a considerable time he became alarmed, and desisted from the attempt'). In 1800 the sword and baton were once again stolen. In 1805, shortly after the statue had been decorated for the celebrations, a person ascended the pedestal and painted the statue black with 'a greasy substance'.[37]

In the 1820s legislation was introduced to stop the processions and the decorating of the horse.[38] This did not, however, stop the attacks. On the night of 11 April 1836, after two unsuccessful attempts, assailants made a hole in the horse, filled the cavity with a chemical explosive and lit a rope dampened with turpentine. The night-watchmen who

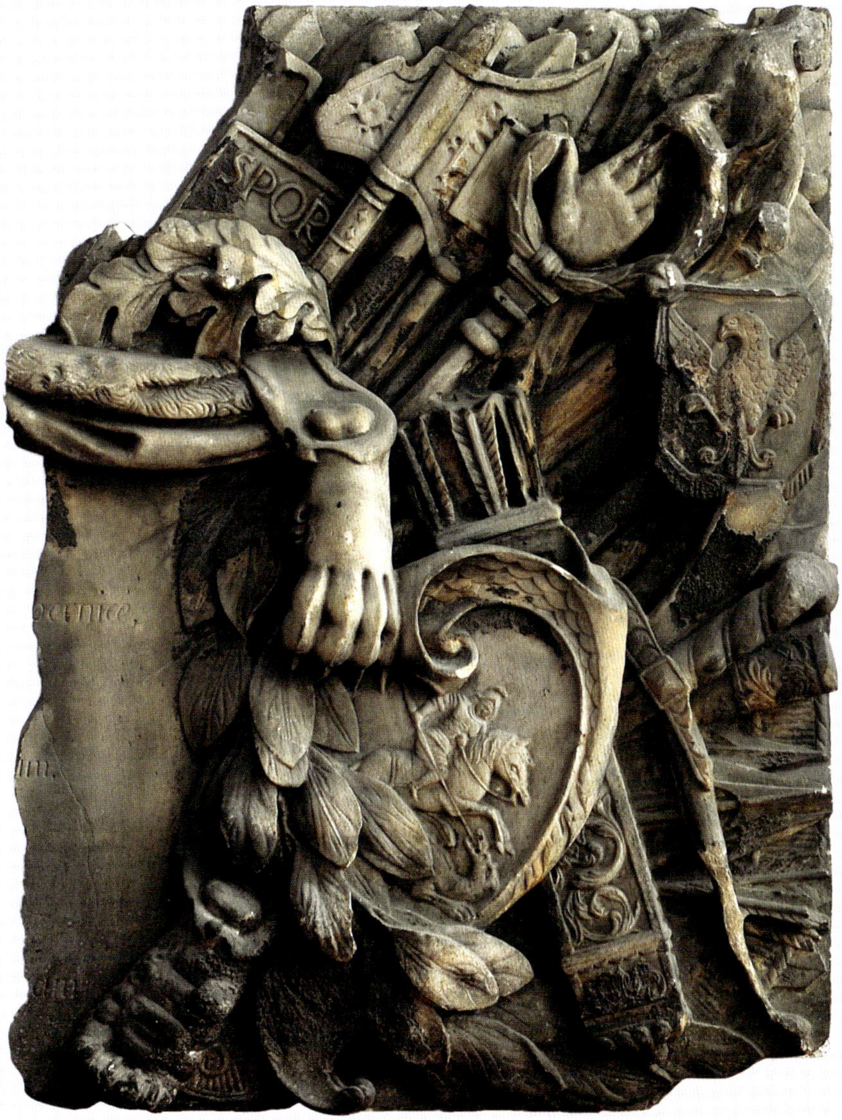

came across the burning fuse retired from the scene and an explosion 'as loud as a piece of artillery' propelled the 10-ft-high statue into the air. The figure was 'shockingly disfigured, and one of the arms and legs broken'.[39]

The attack baffled the reporter from *The Times* who could not see any peculiar political advantage to any party in Ireland at the time, especially as the Orangemen, who yearly decorated the statue, were in the process of disbanding and were (he considered) scarcely worth insulting. He recorded that Conservatives were blaming Radicals and Radicals were blaming the Orangemen. The reporter had felt that the statue was losing its status as an Orange symbol and was becoming simply a fine ornament to the city, attracting Catholics and Protestants alike as a focus for William's birthday celebrations.[40] The magistrates made little headway in finding the culprits, despite the Lord Lieutenant offering a £100 reward and the Dublin Corporation a further £200. Opinion, as ever, was divided on the statue. According to *The Times*, some of the crowd the day after the attack celebrated, made jokes, or said good riddance, whilst others mourned an outrage.[41]

The Ordnance made a review of the statue, along with an engineer, and less than three months after the bombing the *Dublin Mail* reported that:

> This being the anniversary of the Battle of the Boyne, at an early hour of the morning the scaffolding was taken from around the statue of College Green, and the memorial of one of our greatest Kings, the conqueror of this country, and the promoter of civil and religious liberty, was displayed in precisely the same way in which it appeared preparatory to the insulting outrage committed upon Protestant feeling by its recent blowing up.[42]

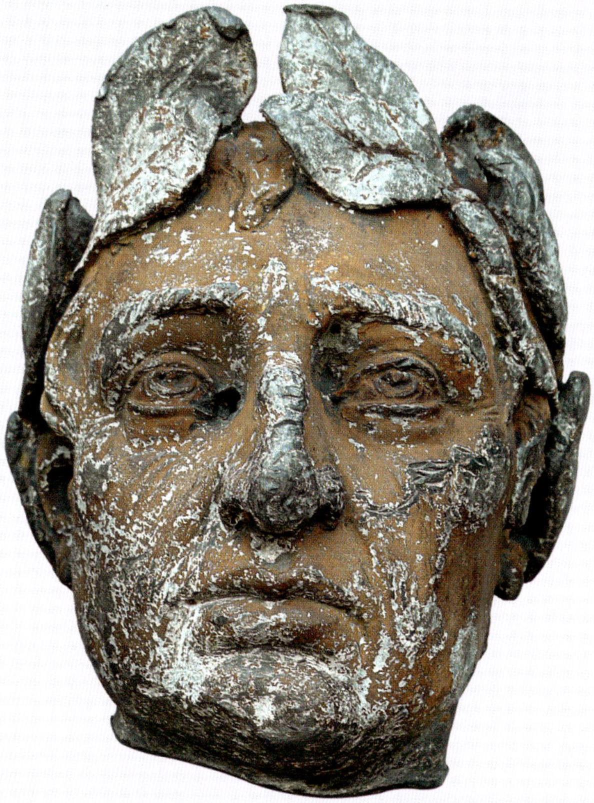

74
John Smyth (c.1773–1840)
Head of William III, 1836
(replacement of the 1701 original)
Lead
34 × 31 × 35 cm
Private collection

75
Photograph of the statue of William III on College Green, Dublin, in the 1870s
National Library of Ireland

The Corporation had employed John Smyth (son of the eminent Dublin sculptor Edward Smyth) to provide a new head, a new arm, and a new leg for the statue. Modelled on a 1754 bust of William III by John Van Nost, it is not clear how far the head corresponds to Gibbons' original.[43] Six years later the Catholic Mayor of Dublin, Daniel O'Connell, ordered that the statue be coated with a bronze paint – presumably the one still on this head (ill.74).

The statue limped on in its restored state but the attacks did not cease. The first was recorded just a few days after the unveiling of the restored statue in 1836, when an unknown assailant threw a 'flat stone and a bottle' at it.[44] In 1882 a crowd pelted it with stones.[45]

The advent of photography has provided a good record of the statue in its final decades (ill.75).[46] It must at this time have been a pale shadow of its original self, with a new head, several new truncheons, a new arm and leg. The horse seems to have lost its raised front leg, replaced by another that has drooped from its original erect right angle. In the early literature on Grinling Gibbons it was described as a 'poor thing' and listed as one of his minor works, a verdict that is surely a result of its history of iconoclasm rather than the skill of the sculptor.[47]

The final attack, when it came in 1928, was stage-managed for maximum impact. At five o'clock in the morning on Armistice Day, 11 November, two young men were seen to climb a ladder to the statue and place a quantity of explosive on the top of the pedestal. At the same time an attempt was made to bomb Nost's statue of George II on St Stephen's Green. The explosion could be heard more than 8 miles away. Initial reports suggested that the explosions had not succeeded, which was certainly true in the case of George II, but the statue of William III had been severely weakened and props were required to stop it falling into the street. On

30 November 1928 it was removed from its plinth for the last time and taken to a Dublin lumberyard.[48]

Its end, fittingly, was carried out symbolically. A statue of a conquering monarch, delivering law amidst martial trophies, was unseated by a warlike explosion, on a day devoted to celebrating peace. The statue had been erected as a memorial to a military achievement, a symbol of the ascendancy of a small group. This and its adoption as a high-profile focus for regular celebration made it a hated symbol for both Catholics and anti-Williamite Protestants, and a focus for a symbolic display of opposition. Despite the wishes of the London *Times* in the nineteenth century, the statue never transcended these factional disputes to become a symbol for the whole city.

As a work of art the statue provides an unusual case study for the art historian in that so little of what survives – or that was photographed in the late nineteenth century – is by Grinling Gibbons. An inspection in 1836 confirmed that the material of the statue, always thought to be brass, was lead.[49] Whatever its material, it is a tribute to the durability of Gibbons' work that it managed to survive two centuries of almost constant attack. MGS

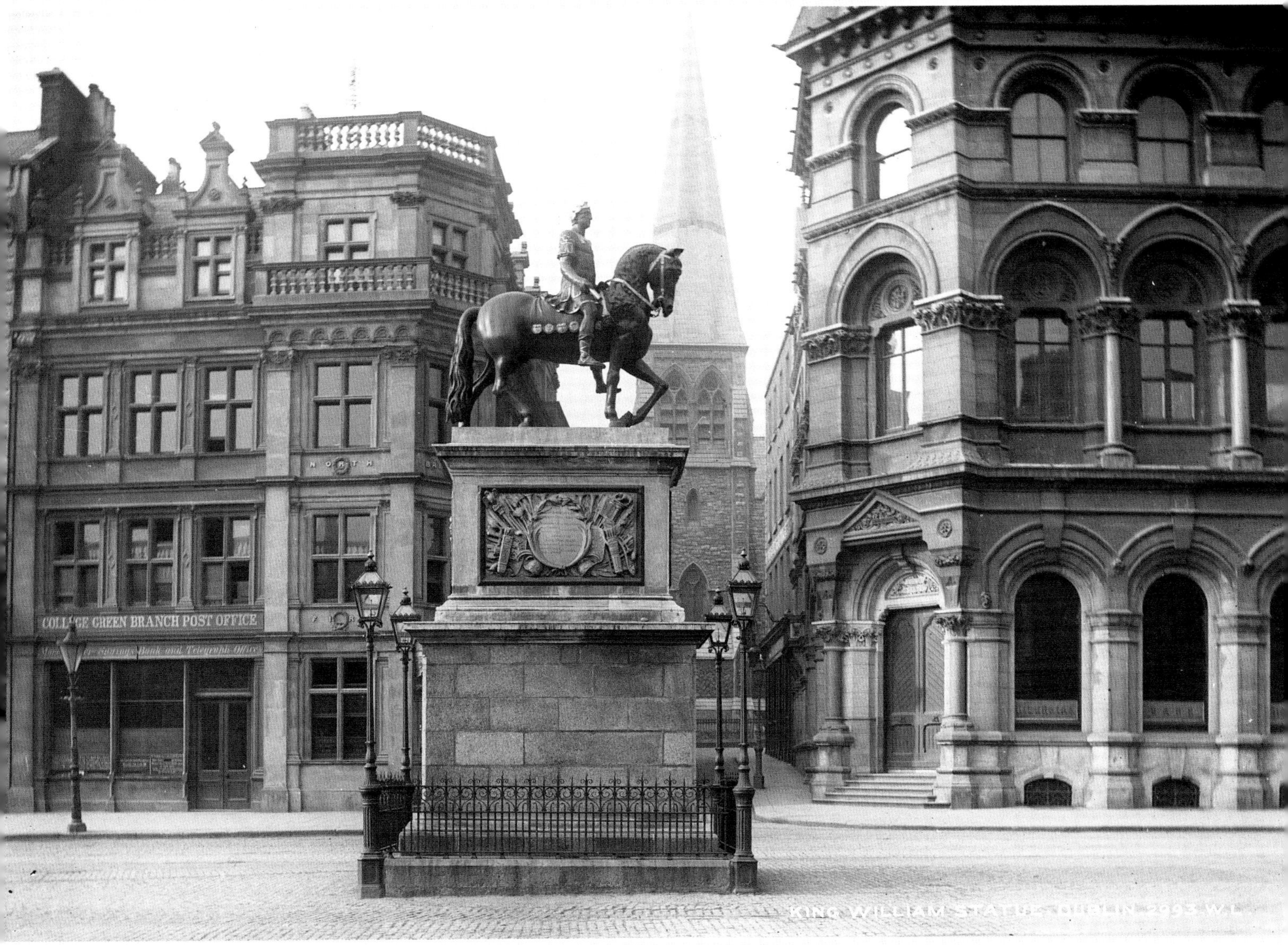

Joseph Wilton's equestrian statue of George III, Bowling Green, New York

In 1766 the General Assembly of the Colony of New York commissioned the prominent British sculptor Joseph Wilton to execute a likeness of George III to celebrate the repeal of the unpopular 1765 Stamp Act, which had imposed a direct tax on printed materials in the American colonies. Advantageously, Wilton was already at work on a lead statue of George III for Berkeley Square in London, commissioned by the king's sister Princess Amelia.[50] As far as can be determined, it seems the New York statue was to be a copy of the London version and was probably cast from the same mould.[51] When completed, the sculpture was shipped to America and erected at Bowling Green, adjoining Fort George at the southern tip of Manhattan. It depicted George III on horseback in classical attire, closely modelled on the well-established model for such works, the equestrian statue of Marcus Aurelius on the Capitoline Hill in Rome. One third larger than life, on an 18-ft-high pedestal, rendered in lead but 'richly Guilded to resemble Gold'[52] and weighing an estimated 4,000lb, the statue was an extraordinarily visible presence in the most prominent open space in the city. It was dedicated on 16 August 1770 – the king's birthday – in the presence of 'a very large number of the principal Inhabitants' with a toast to 'the king's Health and a long continuance of his reign, under a discharge of 32 pieces of Cannon'.[53] For its commissioners, the statue was evidently a clear statement of loyalty, which aimed to distinguish them from their increasingly unruly fellow colonists.[54]

However, against the backdrop of the increasingly fraught relationship between America and Britain in the run-up to the War of Independence, Wilton's statue soon attracted attention of the wrong kind. The erection of a tall fence around the pedestal was deemed necessary in 1771, followed by the passing of an anti-desecration law in 1773 to discourage further vandalism. The monument was finally toppled by George Washington's troops following a public reading of the Declaration of Independence on 9 July 1776, five days after its signing in Philadelphia. In a frenzy of patriotism, soldiers marched to nearby Bowling Green, slung ropes around the king's effigy and wrenched it violently from its base, causing it to shatter into a number of large pieces.[55] The head was carried away to a tavern near Fort Washington in northern Manhattan, but was rescued and subsequently shipped to Lord Townshend, whose infamous and much despised Townshend Acts – implementing new taxes on the colonies – had done so much to stir up revolutionary fervour. The head reached London safely and was seen in Townshend's house in Portman Square on 22 November 1777 by Thomas Hutchinson, former Governor of Massachusetts:

> Lady Townshend asked me if I had a mind to see an instance of American loyalty? and going to the sopha, uncovered a large gilt head, which at once appeared to be that of the King, which it seems the rebels at N. York, after the Declaration of Independence, cut off from the statue which had been erected there, and sent to Fort Washington, in order to fix it on a pole or pike: but by some means or other it was buried and after the surrender of the Fort, Montresor [British officer John Montresor] took it into his possession, and sent it to Lord T., which he rec'd last night. The nose is wounded and defaced, but the gilding remains fair; and as it was well executed, it retains a striking likeness.[56]

The bulk of the statue was shipped from New York to Norwalk, Connecticut from where it was conveyed by teams of oxen, under the supervision of Henry Chichester, to Litchfield, Connecticut, and the home of the colony's Governor, General Oliver Wolcott, recently returned from the Declaration signing ceremonies. Wolcott erected a shed in his orchard where he supervised a team, predominantly composed of local women, who melted the statue down and cast it into 42,088 bullets – meticulously counted and recorded in a surviving document – which were to be used against British troops.[57] While, as Wolcutt attested, such a scheme was primarily inspired by 'Lead then being Scarce and dear',[58] the irony of the process did not escape one Ebeneezer Hazard, who noted in a letter from New York to a Horatio Gates, written on 12 July 1776:

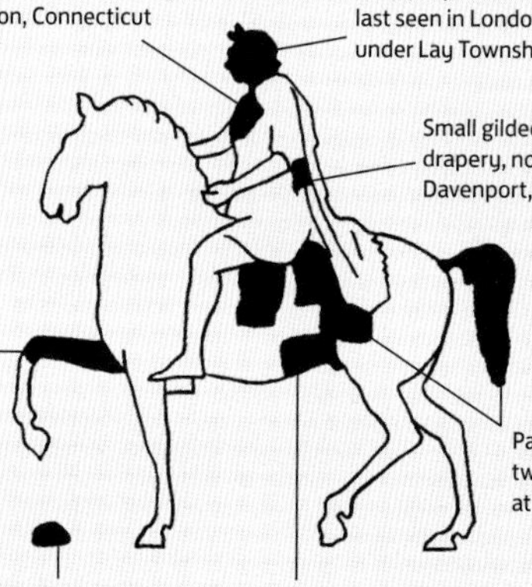

76
Diagram showing recovered pieces of the statue of George III
Courtesy of Robert Russell

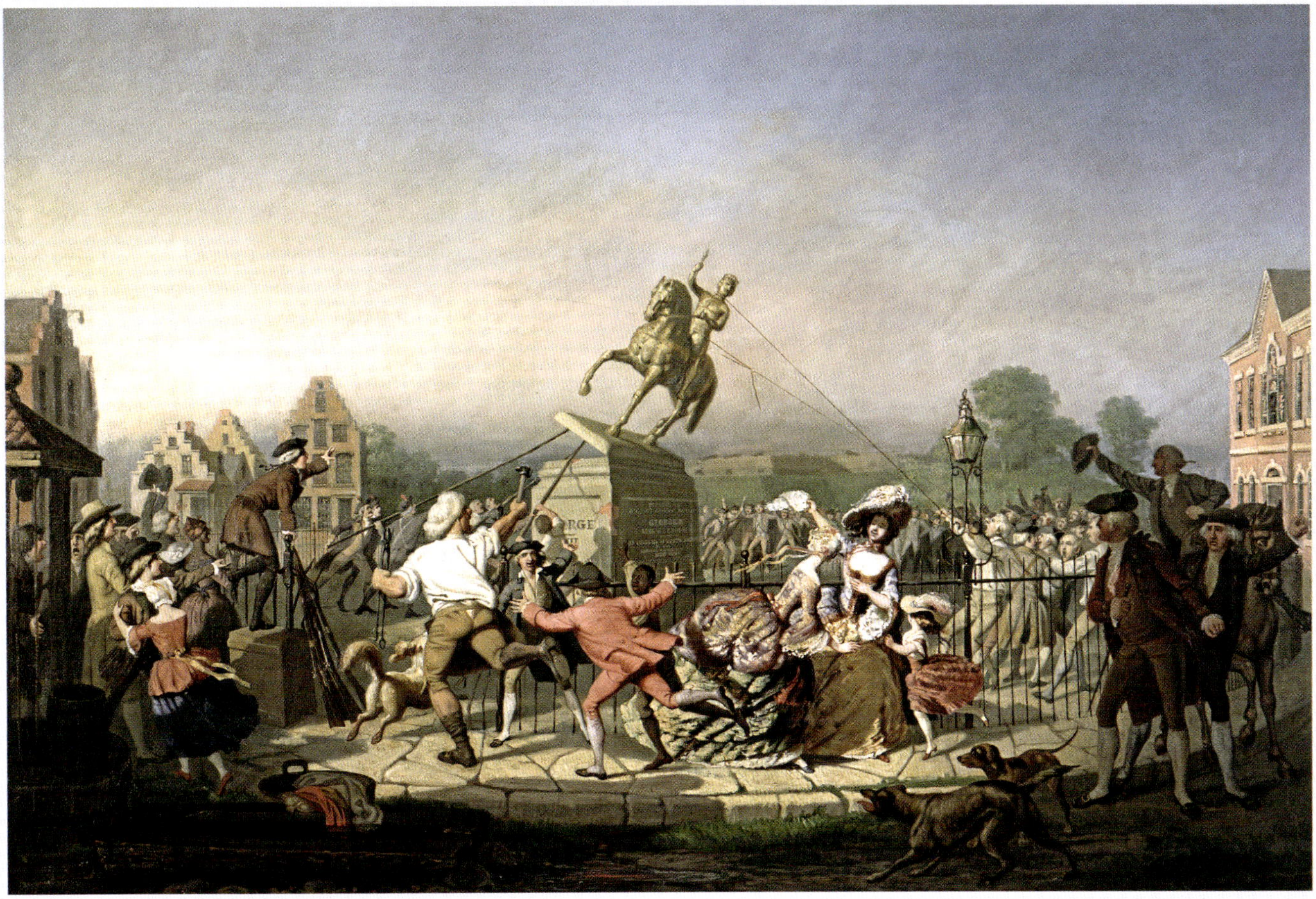

78
William Walcutt (1819–82)
Pulling Down the Statue of George III at Bowling Green, 1857
Oil paint on canvas
131.1× 197.2
Lafayette College, Pennsylvania

> The King of England's Arms have been burned in Philadelphia and his Statue here has been pulled down to make Musket Ball of, so that his Troops will probably have melted Majesty fired at them[59]

Yet, some simple mathematics suggest that 4,000lb of lead should have yielded almost twice as many bullets as those produced; subsequent discoveries reveal that parts of the statue escaped the melting-pot, buried for safe-keeping by local loyalists. Around 1822 a 75-lb piece of the saddle was dug up near a pond opposite the Clapp Raymond Tavern in Wilton, Connecticut, where Henry Chichester and his oxen had stopped overnight en route to Litchfield. Over the years various other fragments have been unearthed. The most significant find was in 1874, when some 200lb of tail, flank and saddle were ploughed up on an estate previously owned by known loyalist David Sloan.

In the years following the toppling of the statue, a number of prints and paintings portraying the event were produced. The first of these was rushed off the press – with numerous topographical inaccuracies and the curious omission of George III's horse – by Franz Xaver Habermann in Augsburg, Germany, in order to satisfy European hunger for cheap graphic accounts of events in America. Further depictions ensued, the most notable of which were paintings by Johannes Oertel and William Walcutt in 1852–3 and 1857 respectively. Though largely fictional imaginings, due to the paucity of useful descriptive documentation, they fed nineteenth-century interest in the formative years of the American Republic, inspired by the democratising revolutions that swept through much of Europe at this time. RK

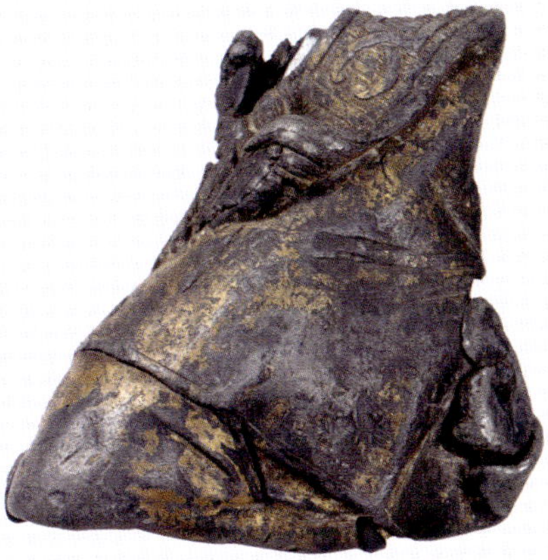

77
Joseph Wilton (1722–1803)
Fragment of the equestrian statue of George III, 1770–6
Lead
21.6 × 48.3 × 33
The New-York Historical Society

Sir Francis Chantrey's statue of William Pitt, Hanover Square, London

The colossal head below was once part of a full-size figure of William Pitt, made by Francis Chantrey and his workshop between 1825 and 1831.[60] It is a plaster cast taken from a clay model. Moulds were taken from this plaster model, into which molten bronze was poured. The final bronze statue was erected in Hanover Square in 1831, where it still stands today. Chantrey had built his own foundry, situated in Belgrave Place, Pimlico, and the signature on the finished statue proudly proclaims Chantrey the 'FOUNDER/SCULPTOR'.

The strength of Chantrey's workmanship was to be tested on the day of the erection of the bronze statue. Chantrey, along with his lifelong assistant, Allan Cunningham, oversaw the installation of the work. Allan Cunningham's son, Peter, was later to recall the events of the day:

> The statue was placed on its pedestal between seven and eight in the morning, and while the workmen were away at their breakfasts, a rope was thrown round the neck of the figure, and a vigorous attempt made by several sturdy Reformers to pull it down. When word of what they were about was brought to my father, he exclaimed, with a smile upon his face, 'The cramps are leaded, and they may pull to doomsday.'[61]

The cramps are the iron bolts fastening the statue to the pedestal. The attempt was soon abandoned. There seems little doubt that Chantrey, Cunningham and the patrons of the statue had been prepared for iconoclasts. The statue was commissioned in 1825, twenty years after the sitter's death, by a small group of elderly politicians who had served in the government when Pitt was Prime Minister. The group, who wished to pay homage to their former ally and paymaster, included Marquess Camden (Chancellor of Ireland under Pitt), Earl Spencer (Member of Parliament under Pitt) and Sir Charles Long (Member of Parliament and lifelong friend of Pitt). The group met Chantrey and agreed to pay the remarkable sum of £7,000, stipulating that the statue should be no less than 11ft high, that it should stand on a pedestal of Hagtor granite and that it should have 'an iron rail enclosing the whole'.[62] Clearly Cunningham and Chantrey also took care to ensure that the fixings were strong enough to withstand the attentions of a group of sturdy iconoclasts.

The Daily Examiner described the timing of the erection of the statue as 'rather oddly chosen'. Whether by reactionary design or coincidence, the statue was made and erected at a time in which Pitt's legacy had never been so widely vilified. The statue was erected during the progress of the Great Reform Bill, brought forward by the Whig Earl Grey to amend Britain's unrepresentative and corrupt electoral system. The surviving Pittites were opposed to reform, and the statue was held to be an anti-reforming gesture. The *Daily Examiner* made no bones about identifying Pitt and his followers as the architect of the current electoral crisis – he created a massive public debt, high taxation, and corruptly exercised his powers to create a class of supporters. Such a man, they wrote 'will find no difficulty in creating a number of admirers. William Pitt, in the estimation of courtiers, pensioners, contractors, boroughmongers, and all of those who desired

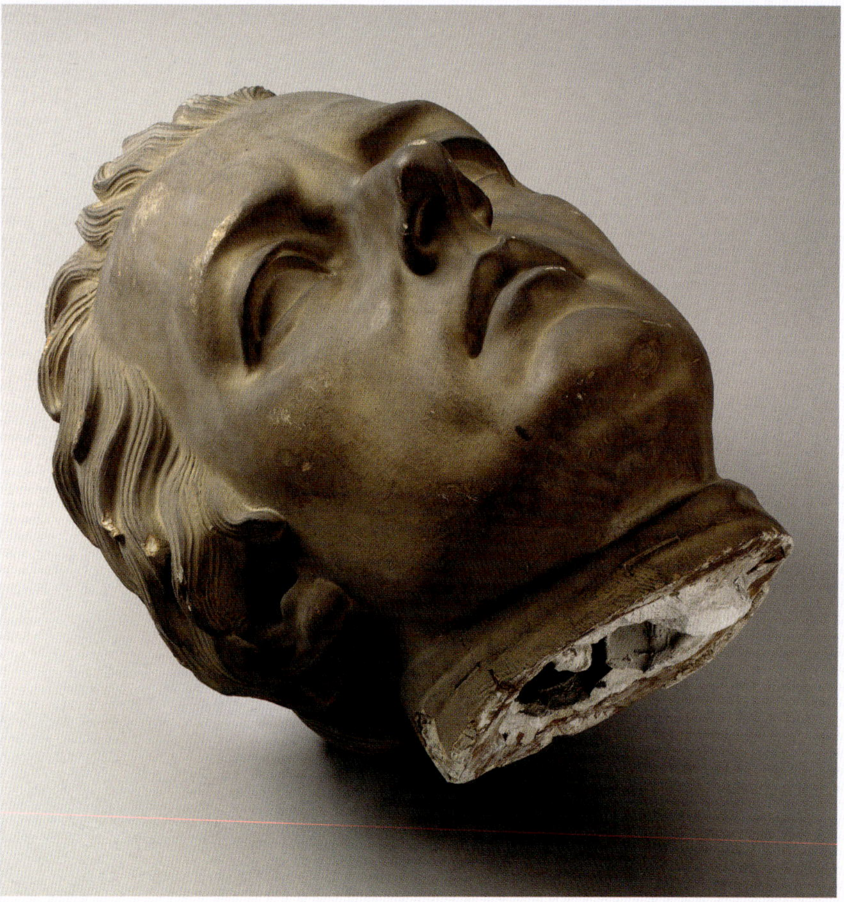

79
Sir Francis Leggatt Chantrey (1781–1841)
Plaster cast head of statue of the Rt Hon William Pitt 1831
Plaster
55 × 41 × 46
Ashmolean Museum, Oxford

to belong to this devouring legion, was the perfection of a minister, a man after their own hearts.'[63]

In the months after the attack on the statue in July 1831, the passage of the Reform Act was halted by the House of Lords, which refused to support the bill approved by the Commons. Earl Camden, one of the patrons of the statue, was among the Lords who opposed the bill. A wave of rioting followed across Britain, the prime minister resigned, and the Duke of Wellington attempted to hold firm during a financial and constitutional crisis that many feared or hoped would result in revolution. During May the *Morning Chronicle* published a poem to the statue of Pitt, beginning:

> Proud Statue of a Statesman! – in his time
> As great as any little soul can be;
> A most gigantic dwarf – a thing sublime,
> Yet insignificant exceedingly.
>
> I come to thee, O Statue! – lately set
> On high, to let this ancient truth be shown,
> That when a famished people bread would
>   get,
> The Tories always proffer them – a stone.

The poem describes Pitt as:

> The prince of peer-makers, who, scorning
>   detail,
> With Barons, earls, and Viscounts,
>   crammed the nation;
> Who wrote above his door – 'Lords
>   wholesale, retail',
> And – would that I could add – 'for
>   exportation'.

and imagines Pitt advising Grey on how to make many new peers to outvote the old, before the people decide it is time to make many fewer.[64]

Pitt's statue was clearly a divisive gesture at a divided time, and the attack needs to be read within the wider context of the politics of popular reform. It is perhaps notable, though, that Cunningham (and presumably Chantrey) regarded with pride their ability to produce a statue that was resistant to public attack. It is also notable that even those who wrote most damningly of the subject of the statue were also able to commend its pose, commanding air, placement, and the capturing of the 'acid' and 'uneasy' look of Pitt. The *Examiner* wrote:

> We confess that we do not like the raising of statues to second-rate men of any description, and least of all to second-rate Tory politicians; as a highly meritorious work of art, it may be as well perhaps, that this bronze figure should be allowed to remain upon its pedestal. It is from the accomplished hand of CHANTRY, whose good works will doubtless endure long after the effects of William Pitt's evil ones have ceased to operate injuriously on the general interests.

In 1842 the colossal plaster model was given by Chantrey's widow to the University of Oxford, along with around 170 other models by the artist. The statue of Pitt, because of its enormous size, was the most striking in the collection, and it was placed at the centre of the 'Chantrey Gallery' in the Ashmolean Museum, where it stood for half a century before being removed to basement storage.

It is a curious coda to this story that the plaster model – unlike its bronze counterpart – did not survive the attentions of iconoclasts. In 1939 the Keeper of the Museum, E.T. Leeds, was granted permission by the University to decapitate the statue and demolish the body. Leeds, who argued that the Chantrey collection was taking up room in the stores that could be used for an air-raid shelter, ordered the decapitation of forty-four Chantrey statues, the heads of which remain in the Ashmolean collection today.[65] MGS

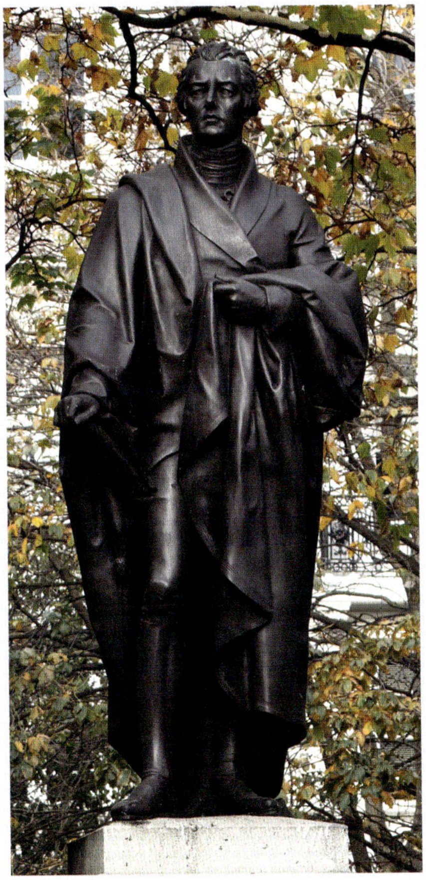

80
Sir Francis Chantrey's 1831 bronze statue of Rt Hon William Pitt, Hanover Square, London

Nelson's Pillar, Dublin

The foundation stone for a Dublin monument to commemorate Viscount Nelson was laid by the Lord Lieutenant, the Duke of Richmond and Lennox, on 15 February 1808, the anniversary of Nelson's victory at Cape St Vincent in 1797. Situated in the middle of Sackville Street (now O'Connell Street), the city's most fashionable residential and commercial thoroughfare, the Nelson Pillar was intended as a 'permanent proof of respect' for the recently deceased hero from the British Empire's second city, more than thirty years before London's corresponding memorial was commissioned.[66]

From the moment of its conception the monument seemed designed to inspire ill feeling. The foundation ceremony was a militaristic display of power, with members of the Dublin garrison lining the procession route to separate participants from the public.[67] The memorial itself was devised in a triumphalist Greek revival style which intentionally dominated its surroundings. The stark, blocky mass of the unadorned base drew opposition from local residents concerned about the curtailment of view and circulation, while the public subscription intended to fund the monument fell short, necessitating a substantial redesign. When the monument was finally completed in October 1809 – an occasion which attracted little attention from the press or public – a 13-ft-high effigy of Nelson, carved from Portland stone by local sculptor Thomas Kirk, stood in lonely splendour more than 120ft from the ground, atop a wholly disproportionate Doric column.[68]

As early as 1876, discussions regarding the modification or removal of the Pillar began. The declaration of the Irish Free State in 1922 intensified the debate as O'Connell Street – scene of the 1916 Easter Rising's final stand-off in the adjacent General Post Office – became an important geographical focal point in the creation of Ireland's post-colonial identity.[69] A range of alternative locations for the monument was proposed. Others suggested replacing the figure of Nelson with someone more culturally appropriate. Candidates included Wolfe Tone, Padraig Pearse, Saint Patrick or the Virgin Mary, the latter receiving little support from Thomas Bodkin, former director of the National Gallery of Ireland, who feared divine pique: 'I can't help thinking that she would not like to take charge of a column that was . . . erected to the memory of someone else'.[70]

Despite official moves to end Nelson's lofty reign over Dublin, the Pillar appears to have gradually transcended its political associations at ground level, inspiring a curious communal affection denied the nationalist icons Charles Stewart Parnell and Daniel O'Connell at either end of the street. It was a popular meeting place and viewing point, the terminus of the tram system and a landmark by which to orientate oneself, garnering over a dozen mentions in James Joyce's *Ulysses* (1904) and a robust public defence by W.B. Yeats.

As monuments to the British monarchy and military were removed or destroyed around him, Nelson remained steadfast, surviving the turbulence of 1916 with only a smattering of bullet holes to his lower lip. But at 1.32am on 8 March 1966 – the Golden Jubilee of the Easter Rising – Nelson's supremacy finally came to an end at the hands of a group believed to have been dissidents from the official IRA. As the *Irish Times* reported later that morning, 'the top of Nelson Pillar . . . was blown off by a tremendous explosion . . . and the Nelson statue and tons of rubble poured down into the roadway'.[71] The event was greeted with widespread approbation: 'gaiety and joie-de-vivre prevailed throughout O'Connell Street . . . and witticisms like "poor old Nelson" were

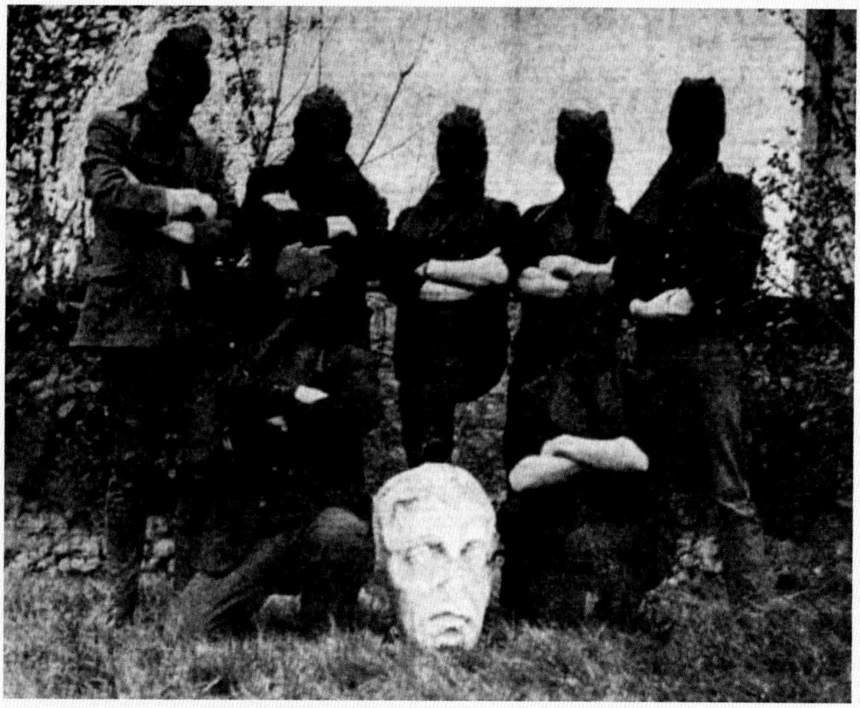

81
Nelson's head taken captive by students from the National College of Art, Dublin
First published in the *Evening Press*, March 1966

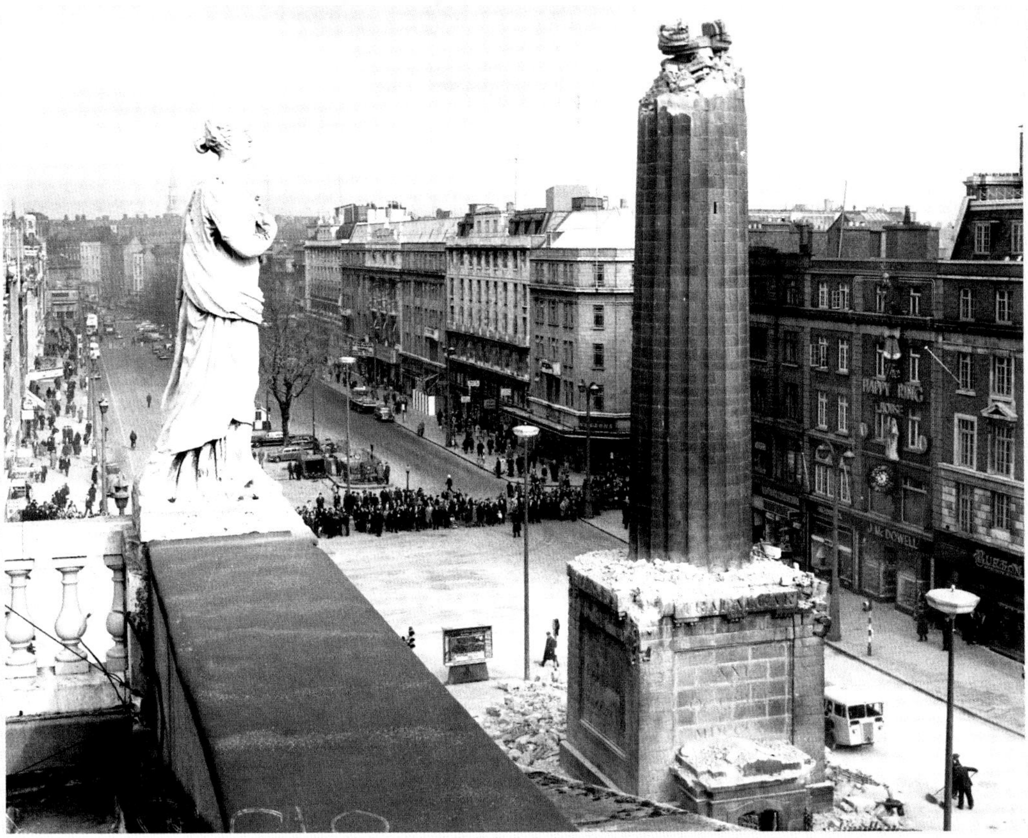

82
The remains of Nelson's Pillar, O'Connell Street, Dublin, March 1966

greeted with roars of laughter.' A senior police officer on guard at what quickly became known as 'The Stump' (ill.82) 'grinned broadly' and proclaimed it 'an absolutely expert job – not a window broken in the Post Office – – perfect!' The 'only mourner' was said to have been J.A. Culliton, the architect for Dublin City Defective and Dangerous Buildings Department, who deemed it 'tragic', while the brother of the present Lord Nelson hoped that 'there was nothing personal in it'. The prevailing mood was most accurately summed up by the Lord Mayor of Dublin Eugene Timmons: 'the destruction of such a landmark as Nelson Pillar evokes both emotional and sentimental reactions, but nevertheless it seems that there are a considerable number of people happy to see the end of the symbolism it represented'.[72]

The cultural potency of the monument and its destruction are well illustrated by the scramble for souvenirs that ensued. As rubble was cleared from the street by Dublin Corporation, pieces could be obtained from the Gardai on duty (as was the case with one of these fragments) or from enterprising local children who sold them for 2d or 3d an ounce, with no shortage of buyers. Recognisable fragments were highly sought after. Nelson's sword promptly disappeared, wrapped in the overcoat of a man seen walking swiftly from the scene.[73] Nelson's head was removed from the debris and taken to the City Council Depot, where it was placed in a locked store. Within days the City Manager, Mathew Macken, was inundated with letters from those looking to acquire the head as the ultimate trophy. Amongst the diverse group who registered an interest were Mrs Charles Nelson (widow of the late Lord Nelson), the authorities of Trinity College and celebrated Kerry strongman Buttie Sugrue.[74]

Such was the beginning of the colourful history of the statue's head over the summer of 1966. Sometime between 16 and 18 March, the City Council Depot was broken into and the head removed. The following week the sum of £2 was sent anonymously to the offices of the *Evening Press*, to be forwarded to Matthew Macken to cover the cost of damage from the break-in, carefully itemised down to six displaced screws. The next day an image appeared on the front page of the newspaper, with seven hooded figures gathered around Nelson's head in what appeared to be a surburban back garden (ill.81). They were later revealed to be students from the National College of Art. The head subsequently featured in a fashion shoot for city centre department store Boyers and appeared on stage with the musical group The Dubliners at the Gate Theatre. In mid-April the head was rented to Bennie Gray, a 21-year-old antiques dealer from London, who smuggled it through a customs post on the border and flew it out of Belfast airport. In September Gray arrived back in Dublin and drove triumphantly down O'Connell Street on top of a lorry with the much sought-after head beside him. As the lorry approached the former site of the Pillar, The Dubliners, who were riding alongside him, launched into *Nelson's Return*, a rewritten version of their hit *Nelson's Farewell* (one of three popular songs inspired by the blast). A Corporation official is then said to have emerged from the crowd to take possession of the head once again, which, after many years in Dublin Civic Museum, now presides over researchers in Dublin City Council Library. RK

Defaced coins

This remarkable collection of modified copper coins illustrates iconoclasm on a small-scale, intensely personal level. While some are scratchy and hastily wrought, others are highly crafted, with polished surfaces, carefully incised lettering and extra pieces of metal soldered on top of the original coin. The sheer physical effort required to smooth and carve these more worked examples speaks evocatively of anti-authoritarian zeal and passionately held beliefs.

Regrettably little is known about the authors of these protests-in-miniature, although given the similarities in script, it has been suggested that a number of the mid-nineteenth-century specimens are by the same hand. An 1849 coin (ill.83), poignantly inscribed 'The man who did this was born without a shirt', indicates that the author was on the lowest rung of society. Following the implementation of the new Poor Law in 1834 and the subsequent establishment of deterrent workhouses, poor relief was high on the popular political agenda in the 1840s. A further coin from 1845, possibly by the same hand, refers to an incident when Michael Gibbs, then Lord Mayor of London, was 'pelted with Rotten Eggs' by an angry mob. 'Gobble Gibbs', a wealthy fishmonger infamous for both his creative book-keeping and his stern judgements on vagrants, was the subject of many insulting popular ballads, one of which records this incident: 'He mounted his hack and from Walbrook was going / And the folks then at him rotten eggs began throwing'.[75] This probably refers to the attack mounted against Gibbs at the Lord Mayor's Show on 9 November 1845.

This particular member of the mob may also have been responsible for coins decrying George IV, William IV and Prince Albert. The defacement of an 1826 coin bearing George IV's head with the ironic and emphatically underlined epithet 'The Fine English Gentleman', qualified with the words 'Patron of Vice and Frivolity', evidently refers to George's well-known dissolute lifestyle. The denunciation of William IV as 'The Idiot King' may have been inspired by the Reform Crisis. After William refused to agree to the immediate creation of a large number of peers in order to force the electoral reform bill through parliament, widespread rioting ensued across the country. Mud was slung at William's carriage and he was publicly hissed. The condemnation of Prince Albert, in turn, may have been inspired by failures in the Crimean War (1835–56), for which he was held partly responsible.

Further coins reference specific political events, indicating a widespread engagement with current affairs, fostered by popular prints and broadsides. An elaborate modification of a George III coin, with a coffin and axe fused to one side and a swinging jackboot and female figure to the other (ill.84), may refer to the alleged affair between the Prime Minister, John Stuart, 3rd Earl of Bute (represented in a sustained campaign of graphic satire by a boot), and Augusta, Dowager Princess of Wales. The rumours regarding their liaison were almost certainly without basis and more accurately reflected dissatisfaction with Bute's leadership of the Seven Years War, which resulted in his resignation in 1763.

Several coins allude to taxes. A copper halfpenny minted in 1799 (ill.85) bears the addition of a noose around George III's neck and various symbols, including a tankard of beer, referencing increased levies. On its

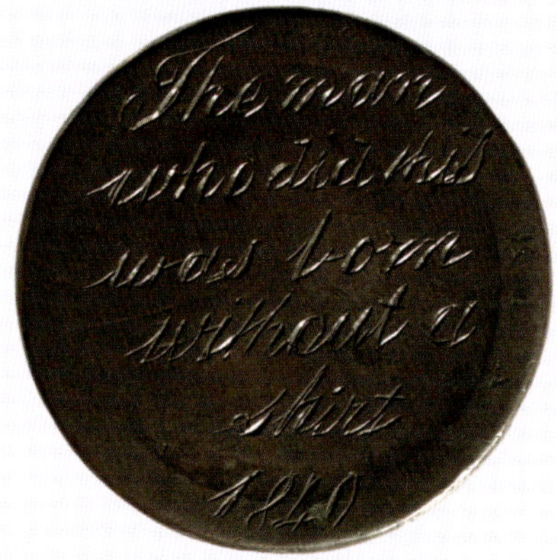

83
George III copper Cartwheel penny, inscribed 'The man who did this was born without a shirt 1849'
Timothy Millett Collection

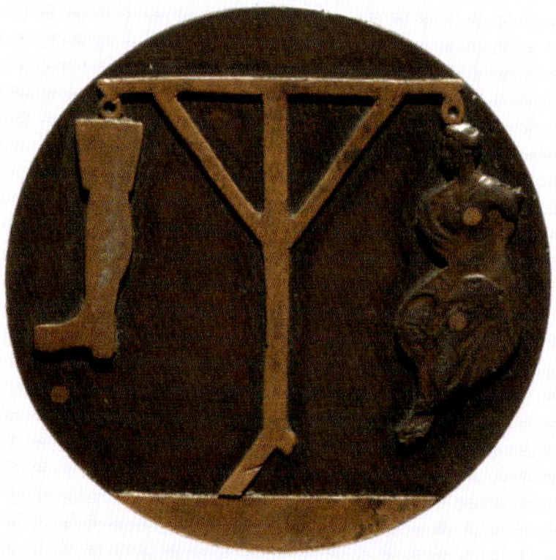

84
Modified George III copper halfpenny, date removed, with a swinging jackboot
Timothy Millett Collection

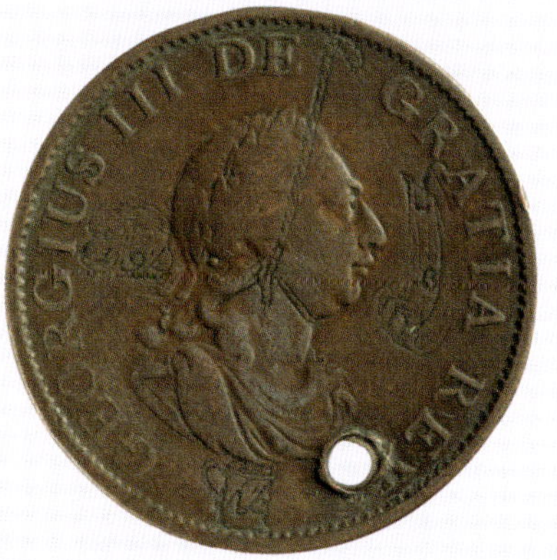

85
George III copper halfpenny, 1799, with an incised noose around the King's neck
Timothy Millett Collection

86
Victoria copper penny, 1841, showing the Queen smoking a pipe and inscribed 'I love shag'
Timothy Millett Collection

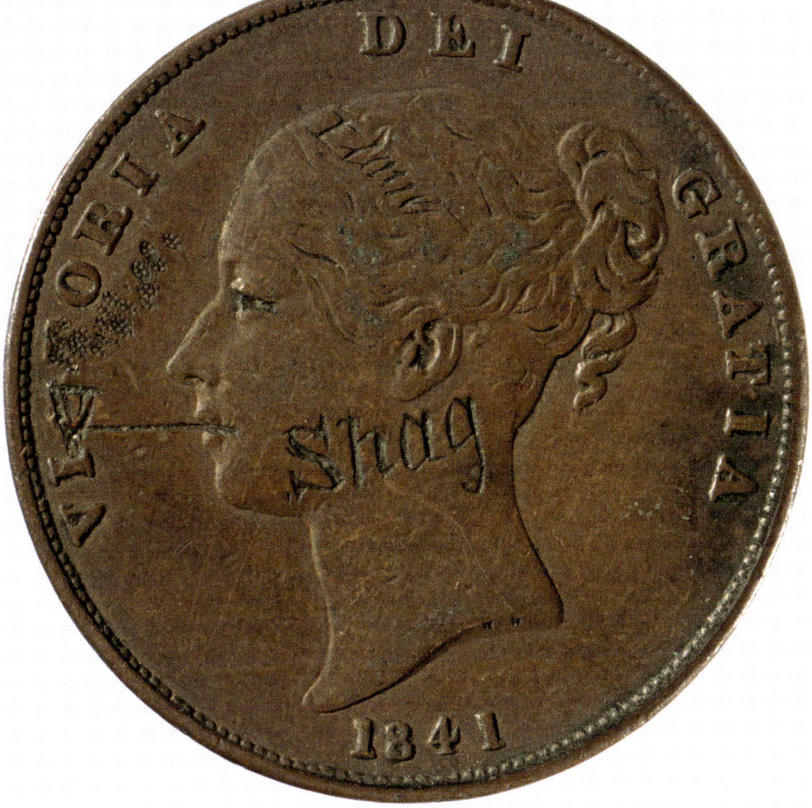

reverse, Britannia holds a skull in her hand above the lamentation 'Poor John Bull'. Another shows Prime minister William Pitt swinging from a scaffold with the inscription 'Pitts Deserts 1797' scratched around it and the exhortation 'No Triple Tax' on the other side, in reference to the introduction of Britain's first-ever income tax around this time. 'Down with the Rump 1747' probably refers to the snap general election that took place that year, while 'Down with the Catholics' may have been inspired by the Gordon Riots of 1780 against Catholic emancipation. One protester made economical use of a single coin to lament both the loss of the American colonies following the War of Independence – 'America lost and England Ruined by the OLD MUFF and his Whelps' – and encroaching industrialisation – 'Bad Luck to Machinery, Spinning Jenny and Peel'.

Other coins in the collection sound a humorous note. A young Queen Victoria, pictured in profile in 1841 has been augmented with a pipe and the inscription 'I love Shag' (ill.86). 'Shag' already enjoyed a double meaning by this time, indicating both a type of tobacco and copulation, perhaps in reference to the recent birth of her first two children within a year of each other.

While the authors of these many and various insults remain unknown, we are equally uncertain of the coins' precise purpose. The modification and counter-marking of coins for advertising, as love-tokens or in commemoration of births, marriages and deaths, was very common from the early eighteenth century onwards.[76] These examples may have been retained as personal tokens, to be carried in the owner's pocket. Alternatively, some of them may have re-entered circulation as a public signal of dissent. Mutilating copper coins, which were used by all sections of society, was an easy way in which to spread a message to a wide audience. While the modification of gold and silver currency was always closely monitored and legislated against, the defacing of copper coinage did not become illegal until 1853.[77] RK

5 SUFFRAGETTES

THE POLITICAL VALUE OF ICONOCLASTIC ACTS

Lena Mohamed

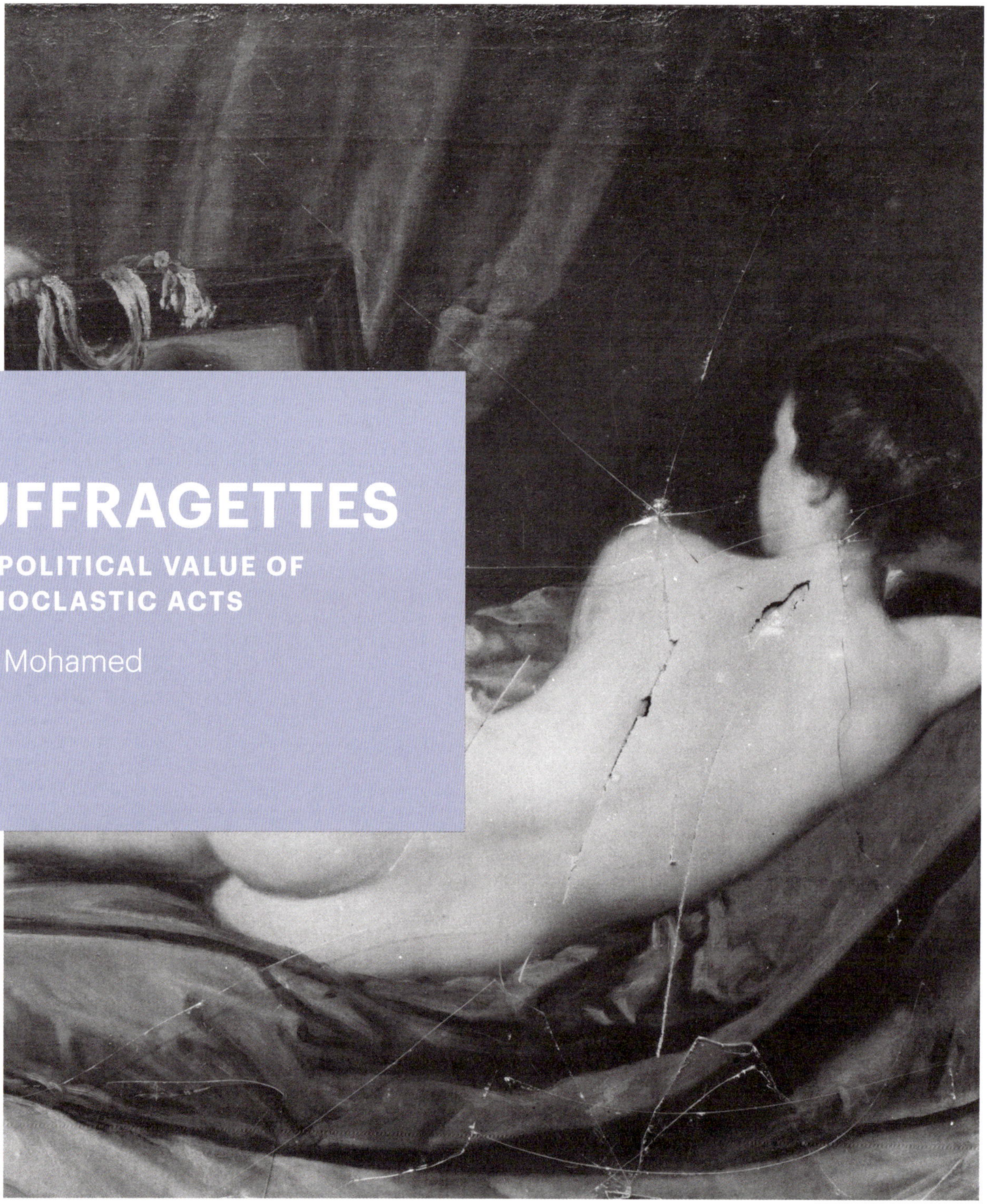

> This picture will have an added value and be of great historical interest, because it has been honoured by the attention of a militant [Suffragette].
> (*Annie Hunt*, 1914)[1]

The idea that members of the Women's Social and Political Union (WSPU), when attacking pieces of art, were not, as many publications reported, 'vandalising', but adding socio-political value to them, is an intriguing one. The act of image breaking to further their political cause to win women the right to vote was iconoclastic, and was part of their increasingly militant campaign. Furthermore, many Suffragettes, as they were often known,[2] acted to destroy both public and private property, including churches and the holiday homes of the parliamentary elite. They smashed windows and set fire to buildings, noting their targets with satisfaction within the pages of their newspaper, *The Suffragette*. By 1913 this action against property had infiltrated the interior spaces of galleries. The attacks provoked angry objections from press and public alike, resulting in the arrest of the women in question and the closure of museums and galleries, and forced the government to address the issue of votes for women.

The militancy of the Women's Social and Political Union was fundamental to its foundation. Established in 1903 by Emmeline Pankhurst and her daughters Christabel and Sylvia, the WSPU sought to highlight to the public women's lack of freedoms and to pressure the government into granting them suffrage. Unlike the National Union of Women's Suffrage Societies, the WSPU's slogan was 'deeds not words'. Protest marches and lobbying members of the Liberal government with banners as they exited their offices were tactics that spilled onto the streets and resulted in the women being declared a public nuisance. Window smashing was another strategy that garnered furious denunciation both from the press and from parallel suffrage organisations. Nonetheless, not wanting to make enemies of the people, Suffragette policy stressed that no harm would befall any member of the public in their campaign. In this context, the attack against artworks presents a particularly complex scenario. It involved attacks in public spaces (galleries), against property that belonged to the nation (and therefore every member of the public), and the damage was visible. Additionally, the majority of paintings attacked were representations of people – even if mainly mythological and religious figures. Nevertheless, their likeness to the human body was highlighted in the press and was enough to engage in the minds of the public a symbolic resemblance to attacks on real people.

Although it would have been possible for the Suffragettes to target artworks with elements representing the state (such as a painting of a government official), their gallery activities were driven by a notion of the painting as an object integral to the fabric of the museum as an authoritative space. On 12 February 1913 a conference of keepers of national museums was held at New Scotland Yard. The Chief Commissioner of Police had invited museum directors, having received information that the Victoria and Albert Museum may become a target for Suffragette action. The seriousness of the threat was such that the possibility of closing the galleries was considered (albeit summarily dismissed) and it was agreed that the institutions would act simultaneously to ensure a united front.[3] At the same time the directors were in close correspondence with government ministers,[4] who even debated the issue in Parliament.[5] This presents an interesting picture of the national museums' relationship with those in power and in a position to affect the changes for which the Suffragettes were lobbying, as well as with those who subjected the Suffragettes to poor treatment in prison cells, including force-feeding. Museums and galleries became highly charged public spaces echoing the power of the state, particularly since they received government funding.[6] As Suzanne MacLeod attests, they were seen by some as representations of 'civil society and encourage[d] notions of citizenship',[7] shaping a national identity that sought to align itself with the affluence of urbanisation and modernisation following the Industrial Revolution. This modernity extended beyond the elite classes, and brought with it a need to incorporate a wider public.[8] It was on this set of values that many Suffragettes based their cause – extending the democratisation of British society not only to the poorer populace, but also to women. Many museums and galleries operated 'free days' to encourage visitors otherwise unable to pay. It was on these days that most of the Suffragette actions occurred, utilising this democratisation of space to further their aims.

The focus of the iconoclastic act therefore involves not only the image, but also the gallery itself. As a site of protest, the space was potent. The shattering of glass, the shredding of canvas and the ensuing struggle were all elements that broke the stillness and austerity of the gallery space, which was representative of both the public (being open to all) and the state (through funding and management).

These Suffragette actions saw the convergence of image breaking and a symbolic defiance of authority; in other words, iconoclasm. While the desecration of an image is the most violent of the elements of iconoclasm, what is often overlooked is that ultimately, and not inadvertently, these Suffragette actions resulted in an action against their own bodies. On committing their damage to artworks their intention was to be subsequently arrested and imprisoned, at which point they would begin a hunger strike in protest at their treatment; this would result in them being force-fed, a torturous violation of their bodies that would in turn render them physically powerless. The dramatic consequences of their actions demonstrates how high the stakes were for the Suffragettes when committing their acts of iconoclasm.

Despite the significance of these protests to their contemporaries, it is interesting to consider how they are perceived today. The anger that they provoked, both from witnesses and the press who sensationally reported these 'outrages' as brutal assaults, contrasts with their invisibility now. This is upheld partly by impeccable restoration of the works of art themselves, and partly by the silence of the institutions as to this aspect of their works' history.[9] This makes Annie Hunt's declaration above all the more poignant: her certainty that her iconoclasm added value to the work is negated by a lack of acknowledgment of the action itself. Despite the fact that the scars are no longer visible, it is therefore important to recall these iconoclastic acts, not as vandalism against the nation but as vital contributions to the freedoms now perceived as inherent to British national identity.

One of the earliest Suffragette actions in a gallery occurred just before nine o'clock in the evening of 3 April 1913 at Manchester Art Gallery. Drawing inspiration from the window-smashing of their fellow campaigners, Annie Briggs (although later acquitted), Lillian Forrester and Evelyn Manesta proceeded to attack thirteen paintings in the room holding the permanent collection, including prized Pre-Raphaelite works, with the intention of shattering the glass in the frames. The cacophony brought many people, including guards, into the room, and led to the detention and eventual trial of the three women. This event is often dismissed as an act that had no lasting impact, its purpose simply to draw crowds and enable the women to announce their dedication to the cause and profess their allegiance to Emmeline Pankhurst, who was at that time in prison.

The fact that there was little damage to the works themselves seemingly relegates the actions in Manchester to arbitrary acts of vandalism rather than of iconoclasm. This is apparently confirmed by the diversity of subjects attacked – from landscapes and portraits of animals to religious scenes and idealised images of beauty – and the way in which the women moved around the room, opportunistically targeting whichever works they could reach.[10] However, if we consider each artwork in its entirety – canvas or panel, including frame – it is possible to regard an attack on any part of it as iconoclastic. The object comprises the image, but also the frame that enables its presentation in the gallery; thus each ensemble contributes to a space that is aligned with the power and authority of the state. The way in which this status is communicated to the viewer is also significant: the glass creates a clear barrier to place the artwork out of reach. Attacking this symbol of power was an iconoclastic gesture, albeit not destroying the icons of the paintings themselves.

The very act of targeting an icon, if not destroying it, was significant. Pre-Raphaelite works are celebrated for their representations of beautiful, idealised women and the overt sexualisation of the female body. Mythological characters, such as Edward Burne-Jones' *Sibylla Delphica* 1886 (ill.87), provided particular inspiration. Even George Frederic Watts' *May Prinsep: Prayer* 1867 (ill.88), depicting a girl apparently deep in religious

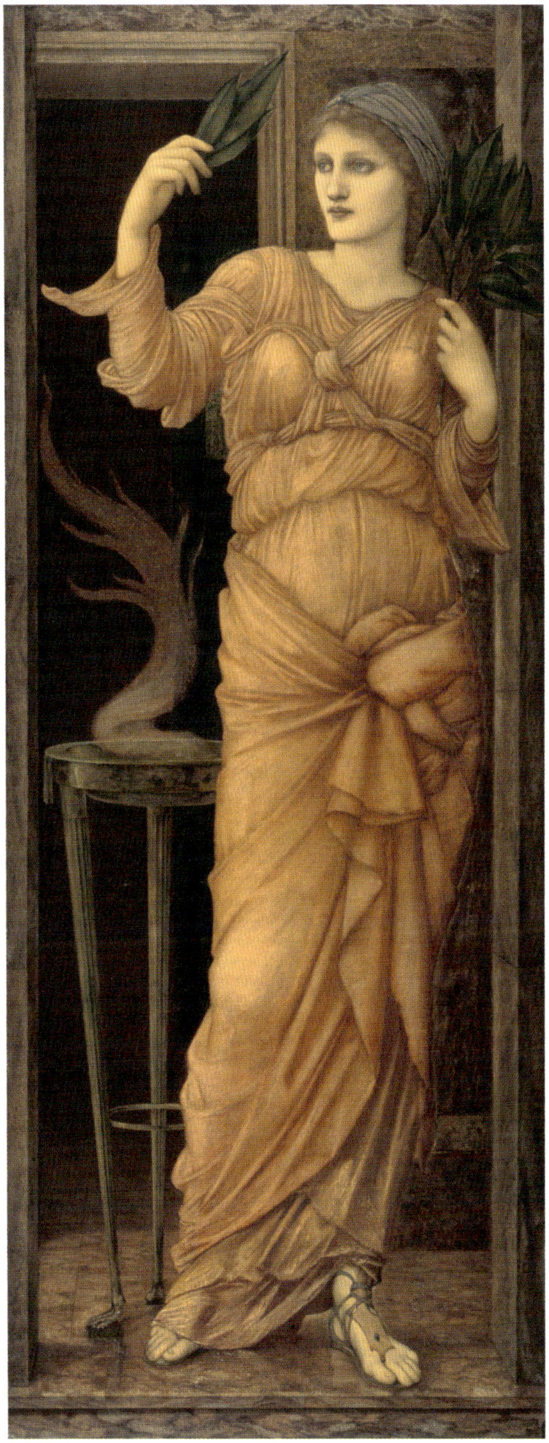

87
Sir Edward Coley Burne-Jones, Bt 1833–98
Sibylla Delphica c.1886
Oil paint on panel
152.8 × 60.3
Manchester City Galleries

devotion, displays her beauty, her averted eyes allowing the viewer to gaze on her uninterrupted. There was nothing arbitrary about these attacks: the Suffragettes thus targeted some of the most valuable works and familiar icons of beautiful women they could find.

Following the attack in Manchester, museums and galleries around the country were on high alert; indeed, board meeting minutes reveal that a total ban on women from some galleries was discussed. Although this did not happen, many institutions brought in plain-clothes policemen to keep a watchful eye,[11] while leaflets were distributed to museum warders bearing photographs and details of the offending women. The atmosphere of tension and apprehension that hung over art institutions as a result of the Suffragettes' iconoclastic protests is evidence of the impact of their actions. Ironically, their fight for greater freedom in this case resulted in increased restrictions for women as museums and galleries (in consultation with the police and the government) required them to leave muffs and umbrellas at the entrance.

Almost a year later was the notorious attack by Mary Richardson, referred to in the ensuing media frenzy as 'Slasher Mary', who used a meat chopper to cause serious damage to Diego Velázquez's *The Toilet of Venus (The Rokeby Venus)* at the National Gallery. The role of the iconoclast is significant here. While presented simply as an act of vandalism – then and now – in fact Richardson's protest was measured, premeditated, driven by socio-political concerns, and not without tortured self-doubt as to the need to destroy art works. At the time, BLAST, a journal produced by Wyndham Lewis as part of the Vorticist art movement, printed an open letter to the Suffragettes, pleading: 'stick to what you understand ... [and] leave works of art alone.' Quipping that they 'might some day destroy a good picture by accident',

88
Sir George Frederick Watts (1817–1904)
May Prinsep: Prayer 1867–87
Oil paint on canvas
102.6 × 69.6
Manchester City Galleries

89
Newspaper photograph of the aftermath of the suffragette attack at the Doré Gallery, London, 4 June 1914
Museum of London

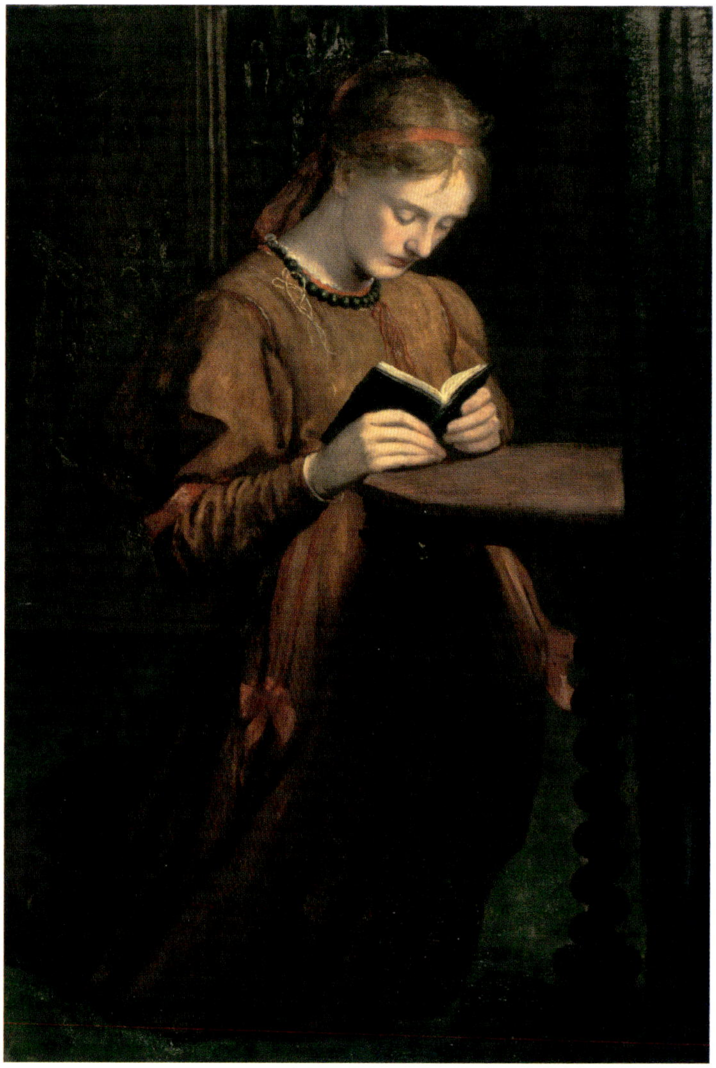

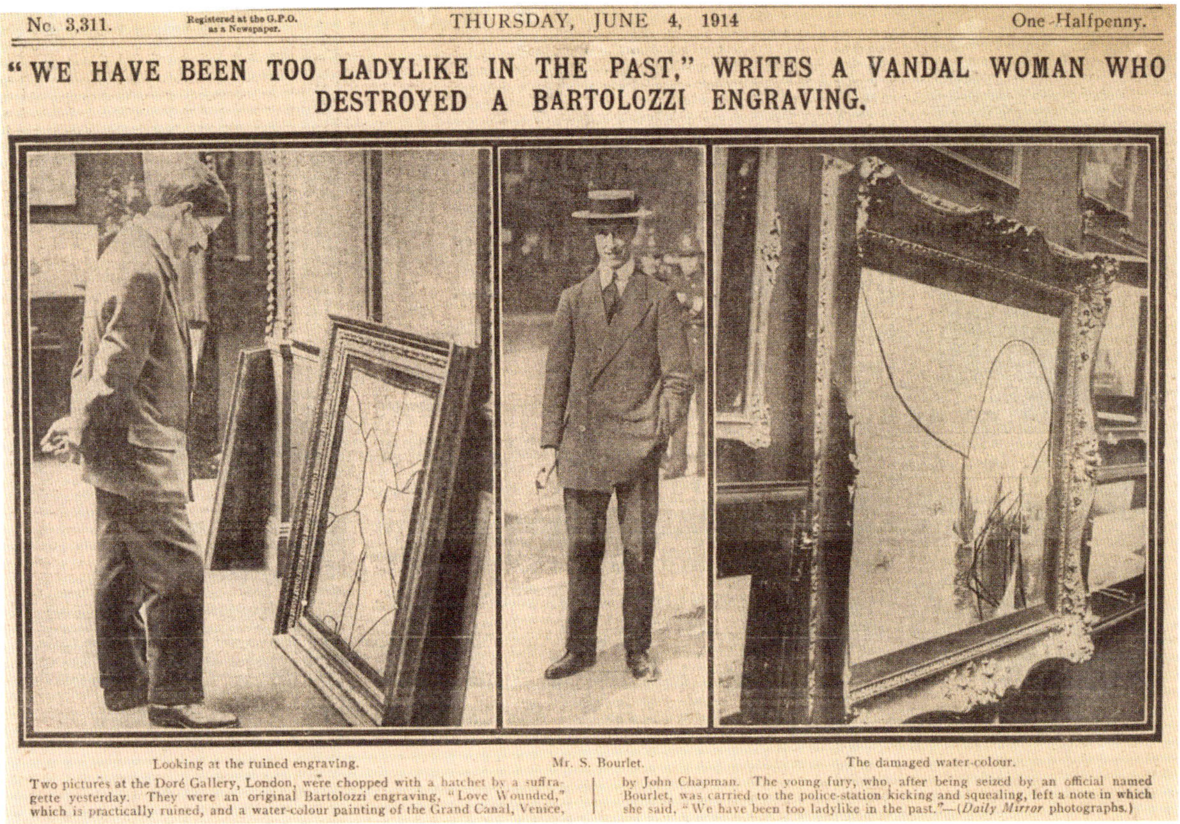

No. 3,311. Registered at the G.P.O. as a Newspaper. THURSDAY, JUNE 4, 1914 One Halfpenny.

"WE HAVE BEEN TOO LADYLIKE IN THE PAST," WRITES A VANDAL WOMAN WHO DESTROYED A BARTOLOZZI ENGRAVING.

Looking at the ruined engraving. Mr. S. Bourlet. The damaged water-colour.

Two pictures at the Doré Gallery, London, were chopped with a hatchet by a suffragette yesterday. They were an original Bartolozzi engraving, "Love Wounded," which is practically ruined, and a water-colour painting of the Grand Canal, Venice, by John Chapman. The young fury, who, after being seized by an official named Bourlet, was carried to the police-station kicking and squealing, left a note in which she said, "We have been too ladylike in the past."—(*Daily Mirror* photographs.)

the letter represents the condescension shown to these women, even by those who supported their cause and claimed to admire their 'energy'.[12] To suggest a lack of understanding of their subjects or imply that their attacks were merely arbitrary is to question the intellectual merit of their cause and the sincerity of their actions. Many Suffragettes in fact studied at art schools and were familiar with the artists and paintings they were targeting. Far from being misguided acts of vandalism, these protests weighed heavy on the minds of the perpetrators.

Following Mary Richardson's infamous attack, the National Gallery closed pending an inquiry into what precautions should be taken against future incidents;[13] other institutions followed suit, including Tate, the National Portrait Gallery and the Wallace Collection.[14] During this two-week period only students were permitted entry, provided they had letters of recommendation. Nonetheless, Suffragette action continued with a flurry of similar such acts not long after museums and galleries were reopened. The Royal Academy of Arts in London bore the brunt of these actions, with the opening of the popular annual Summer Exhibition in May 1914. Mary Wood committed the most sensational of these on opening day, 4 May. She is described as an older woman, 'of distinctly peaceable appearance',[15] who pulled out a cleaver and hacked at John Singer Sargent's portrait of the writer Henry James, leaving three slashes across the canvas (ills 90, 91). A later statement suggested that she had caused the damage because she 'wish[ed] to show the public that they have no security for their

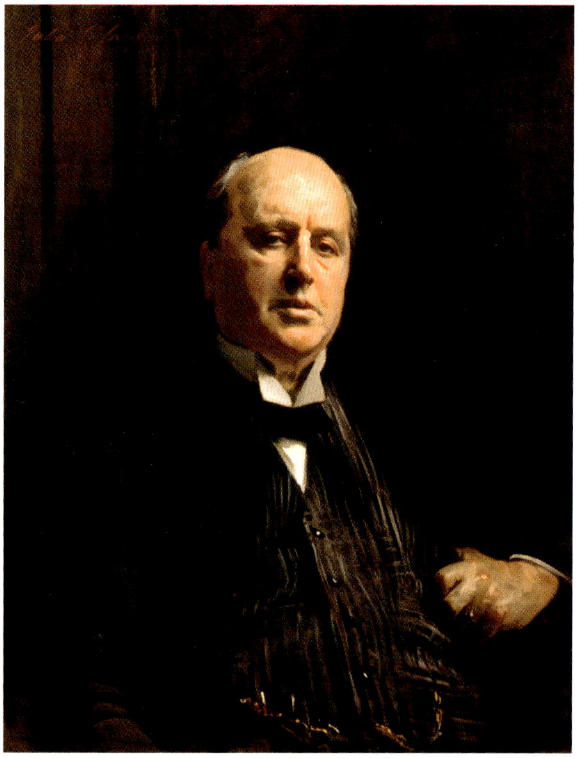

90
John Singer Sargent (1856–1925)
Henry James, 1913
Oil paint on canvas
85.1 × 67.3
National Portrait Gallery, London

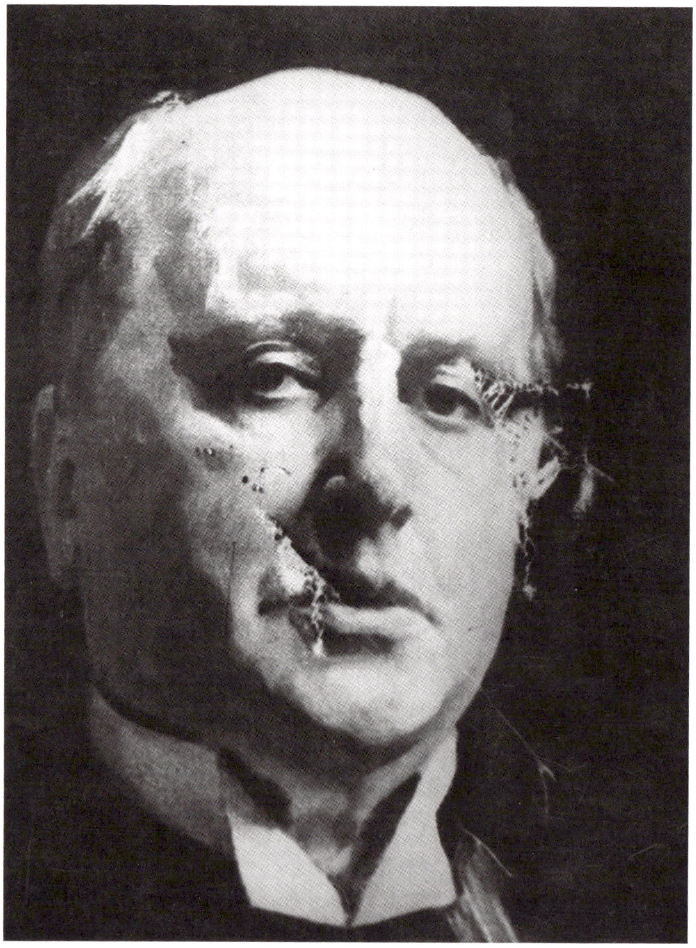

91
Documentation photograph of the damage to the portrait of Henry James 1914
National Portrait Gallery, London

property nor for their art treasures until women are given political freedom'.[16] Her attack was twofold, targeting the owners of the artwork (the public, in their widespread – albeit certainly not unanimous – lack of support for female suffrage) and the subject of the painting (Henry James), both symbols of authority obstructing the freedom of herself and her sisters-in-arms. It is claimed that Wood was unaware of Henry James' prolific literary reputation. The event was, however, exploited by contemporary opinion-makers to illustrate the power of the iconoclasm to create a ripple effect across society. The press declared the attack on a beloved literary figure to be an attack on British tradition. James himself professed to feel disturbed by the action, feeling 'very scalped and disfigured, but ... I seem to be pronounced curable'.[17] There is a clear correlation between the body itself and its representation here: 'scalped' and 'disfigured' suggest actual harm suffered by the sitter. For this reason the portrait was a bold choice for the Suffragettes, by association cutting a familiar public figure rather than merely the canvas of a painting. It is irrelevant whether Mary Wood appreciated the significance of this particular

92
Newspaper photograph documenting the space left on the wall following the removal of the damaged portrait of Henry James
1914
Museum of London

individual: it was enough that he was a figure of authority who presented a unique opportunity for her to make a point.

Once performed, the act of iconoclasm has the power to move beyond the experience of the attacker. The visitor, confronted by the blank space on the gallery wall (ill.92), was forced to imagine what should be there and what its absence represented, making its very lack a potent image in itself – the act of removal part of Woods' iconoclastic gesture. At her trial Woods is said to have highlighted the discrepancy between the genders by stating that the portrait would not have been as valuable if it had been painted by a woman. As with Mary Richardson's attack, Mary Wood's drew attention to a political and economic inequality ultimately imposed by the state and upheld by the public via the gallery space.

Sargent's restoration of his portrait of Henry James, like the swift mending of the *Rokeby Venus* canvas, encouraged the Suffragette action to be seen as minor 'blips' in the lives of the two paintings. In fact, the attacks were an embarrassment to the institutions and the damage viewed with alarm and horror. This is of course to be expected: the role of the museum is to maintain the works entrusted to its care. What is more interesting, perhaps, is the erasure that occurs even now, a century later: there is little mention in either gallery of these iconoclastic acts to the fabric of works in their ownership. This has the effect of negating the fact that the Suffragettes added layers of significance to the works and contributed to their relevance and value to the public. The piercing of the canvases and the scratches to the panels are now virtually impossible to detect, and with the lack of reference to the events it is almost as if they never happened.

One of the last attacks before war broke in 1914 (at which point Emmeline Pankhurst called a halt to the militant actions) occurred in the National Gallery. On 22 May Freda Graham, using a cane, attacked five paintings then attributed to Giovanni

SURELY A SUFFRAGETTE WOULD HAVE RESPECTED A PORTRAIT OF HENRY JAMES.

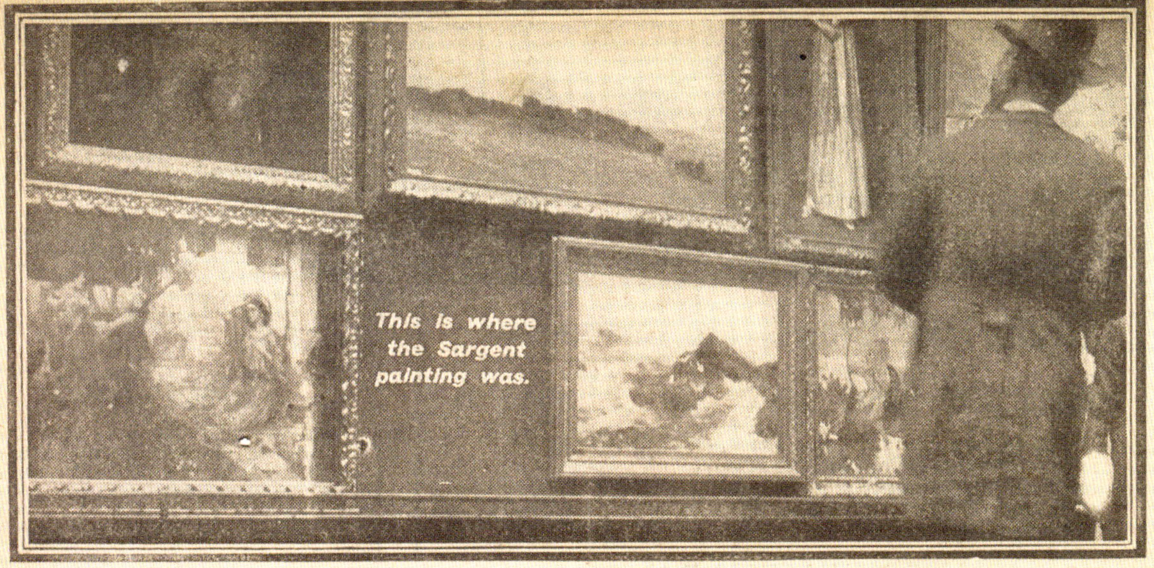

Of course, after the attack the slashed picture was removed.

Why the elderly suffragette, who gave the name of Mrs. Wood, should have chosen Mr. Sargent's portrait of Henry James, the famous author, for her wild attack in the Royal Academy yesterday is one of those things the woman can best explain herself. The visitors to the Academy at the time of the incident showed, at any rate, what they thought of her conduct, before a gallery attendant rescued her to take her to the police station.

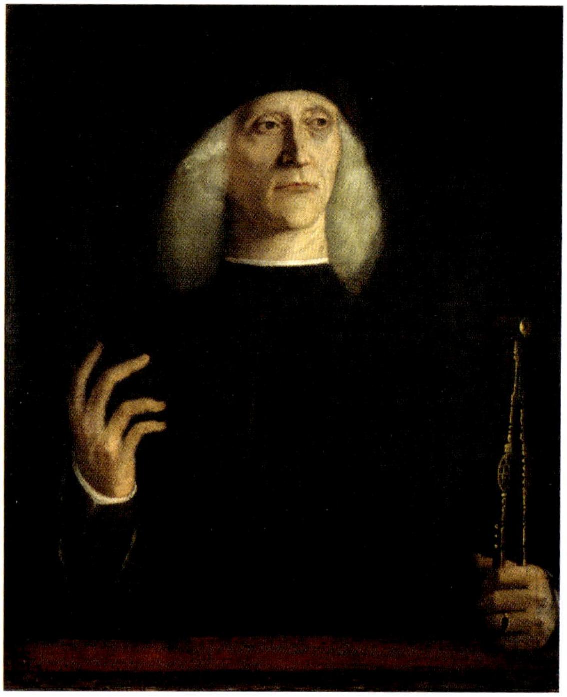

93
Attributed to Gentile Bellini (active *c.*1460–1507)
*A Man with a Pair of Dividers (?) c.*1500
Oil paint on canvas
69.2 × 59.1
National Gallery, London

Bellini, including *A Man with a Pair of Dividers (?)* (ill.93), in a protest against what Graham described as 'King George's illegal and unconstitutional action'.[18] The Renaissance artist's works were held in high regard, revered by many for their beauty and religious subject matter, and the damage inflicted on them resulted in the gallery closing for three months. The attack was later defined as an assault on 'the helpless beauty of five Bellinis'.[19] The adulation accorded such idealised inanimate objects outraged the Suffragettes and was a key reason for their targeting of artworks in galleries. Suffragette Ethel Smyth declared: 'There is to me something hateful, sinister, sickening in this heaping up of art treasures, this sentimentalising over the beautiful, while the desecration and ruin of bodies of women and little children by lust, disease, and poverty are looked upon with indifference.'[20]

Although many galleries were anxious to play down the significance of the actions of the Suffragettes, their lasting effect is nonetheless evident. Indeed, their process of destruction was replicated by an unknown person who defaced the picture of Christabel Pankhurst on the cover of a copy of her *Militant Methods Handbook* (ill.95). Such was the influence of the Suffragette's actions that their detractors themselves turned to the same powerful methods of protest.

Demanding that women should have the right to vote was a significant moment in British history and had a dramatic impact on the development of the subsequent socio-political landscape. Rather than iconoclasm being about destruction, it was a creative process. Far from taking anything away, as Annie Hunt proclaimed, these works have indeed been 'honoured by the attention of a militant'.

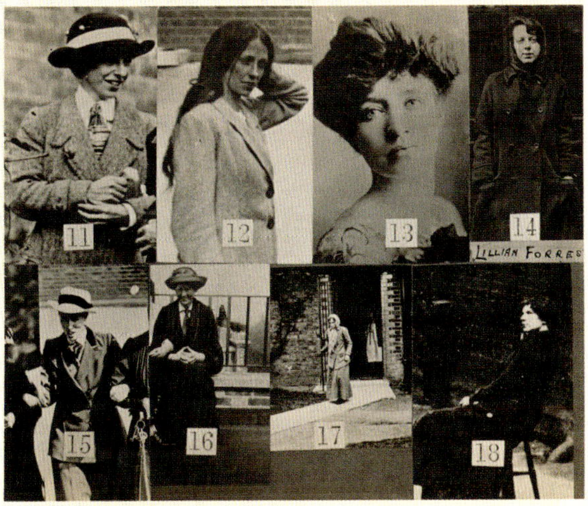

KEY TO ABOVE PHOTOGRAPHS OF KNOWN MILITANT SUFFRAGETTES.

Fig.	Name	Year Born	Height Ft. In.	Eyes	Hair.	C. R. O. Number.	Crime.
11.	Richardson Mary	1883	5.5½	Brown.	Brown.	S.168429.	Arson.
12.	Dennis May @ Lilian Lenton.	1891.	5.2¾	Brown.	D. Brown	S.167399.	Arson.
13.	Marion Kitty.	1872	5.5¼	Blue	Auburn	S.168044.	Arson.
14.	Forrester Lillian.	1880.	5.3½	Grey.	Brown.	S.167641.	Damage.
15.	Johansen Miss.	1881	5.5½	Blue.	Brown tg.grey	S.170195.	Damage.
16.	Giveen Clara.	1887.	5.4.	Blue.	Fair.	S.168045.	Arson.
17.	Baines Jennie.	1864.	4.10½	Brown.	D.Brown	S.165980.	Damage.
18.	Pratt Miriam.	1890.	5.7½	Blue.	Lt.Brn.	S.172271.	Arson.

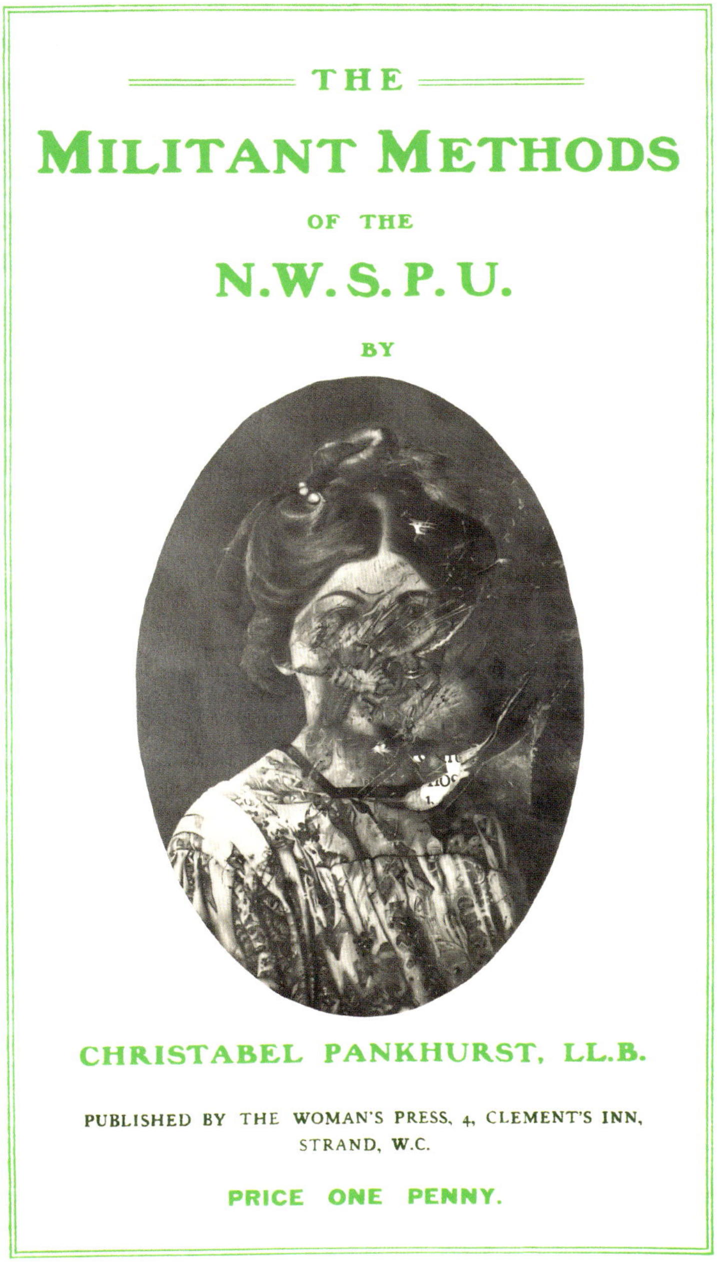

94
Surveillance photographs of
militant suffragettes
Silver print mounted onto
identification sheet
National Portrait Gallery, London

95
Kate Davis (b.1977)
Reversibility (Militant Methods) 2011
Graphite and screenprint on paper
135 × 80 × 3 (framed)
Based on the front cover of the leaflet by
Christabel Pankhurst, 'Militant Methods
of the N.W.S.P.U', 1908
Glasgow Life (Glasgow Museums) on
behalf of Glasgow City Council

Mary Richardson and *The Rokeby Venus*

On 10 March 1914 Mary Richardson decided to take advantage of one of the 'free days' at the National Gallery in London. With a meat chopper hidden up her sleeve, she moved around the gallery, conscious of the throng of visitors, guards, and those whom she suspected to be undercover detectives. Anxious, she sketched while biding her time so as not to look suspicious. When the gallery began emptying at lunchtime and the guards appeared distracted, she launched her attack, the sound of shattering glass causing the detectives to look up at the skylight where workmen had been making repairs. A guard, running towards Richardson, slipped on the polished floor. This gave her time to strike several times more, causing deep gashes in the surface of Diego Velázquez's famous work, *The Toilet of Venus* (*The Rokeby Venus*).

The ensuing hubbub is well documented, as are Richardson's words as she was led away to Vine Street Police Station: 'Yes, I am a Suffragette. You can get another picture but you cannot get another life, as they are killing Mrs Pankhurst.'[21] Her devotion to the cause – and Emmeline Pankhurst's imprisonment for her association with the WSPU – was the defining intent behind this violent act. The connection between the violent act and the painting is profound: the goddess Venus represented 'absolutely pure'[22] idealised beauty, fulfilling the fantasy of many an artist and viewer. This patriarchal conception of femininity is something that, although not directly or specifically rejected by the Suffragettes, was certainly a concern of many of those within the movement. In fact, despite Richardson's fine art education, she is reported to have said that she did not like the work very much, which made it easier for her to destroy.[23]

In contrast to Venus, the Suffragettes were often accused of being 'ugly and sexless'.[24] Such a description served their cause, but also provided the perfect image for exploitation by the press in their depiction of the purity of the benign female body against the ugliness and violence of 'Slasher Mary' the Suffragette.

The damage to the painting was shocking evidence of the ferocity of Richardson's attack, the slashes to the surface of the canvas appearing as gashes on the skin of this youthful female body. Thus the act of violence here is not simply against a prized artwork, but also against the construction by society of the imagined female form. When Richardson was arrested she contrasted this with the real and very visceral experience that Emmeline Pankhurst was undergoing, her body weak from starvation and the torture of being force-fed, her body *actually* being torn apart. That there was less concern for her than for a mythical character represented in a painting was disturbing to many Suffragette activists. The value of human life had to be greater than that of the value of a painting.

In fact, the market value of the damage is something that Richardson underscored in her memoirs some six decades after the event. She caused enough damage to devalue the painting by an estimated £10,000 to £15,000.[25] This sum was made all the more intolerable to some as the painting had only recently been purchased for the public by the National Art-Collections Fund. This had been established in 1903, with the intention of saving works of art for the nation. In its first ten years the sum of £45,000 had by been raised from donors, from wealthy benefactors to poverty-stricken students, all of whom wanted to contribute something to the preservation of art.[26] As a result there was a sense of common ownership over artworks such as *The Rokeby Venus*. To have it slashed by a Suffragette was therefore perceived almost as a personal affront – an iconoclastic act against personal property and sensibilities. LM

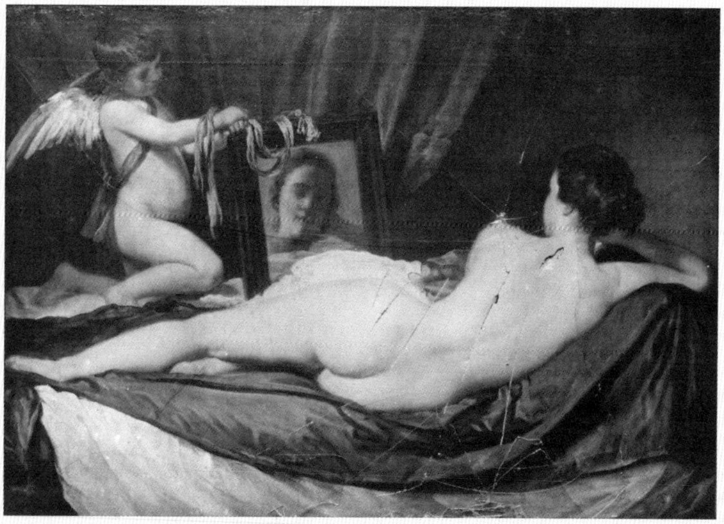

96
Documentation photograph of the damage to the *Rokeby Venus*, 1914
National Portrait Gallery, London

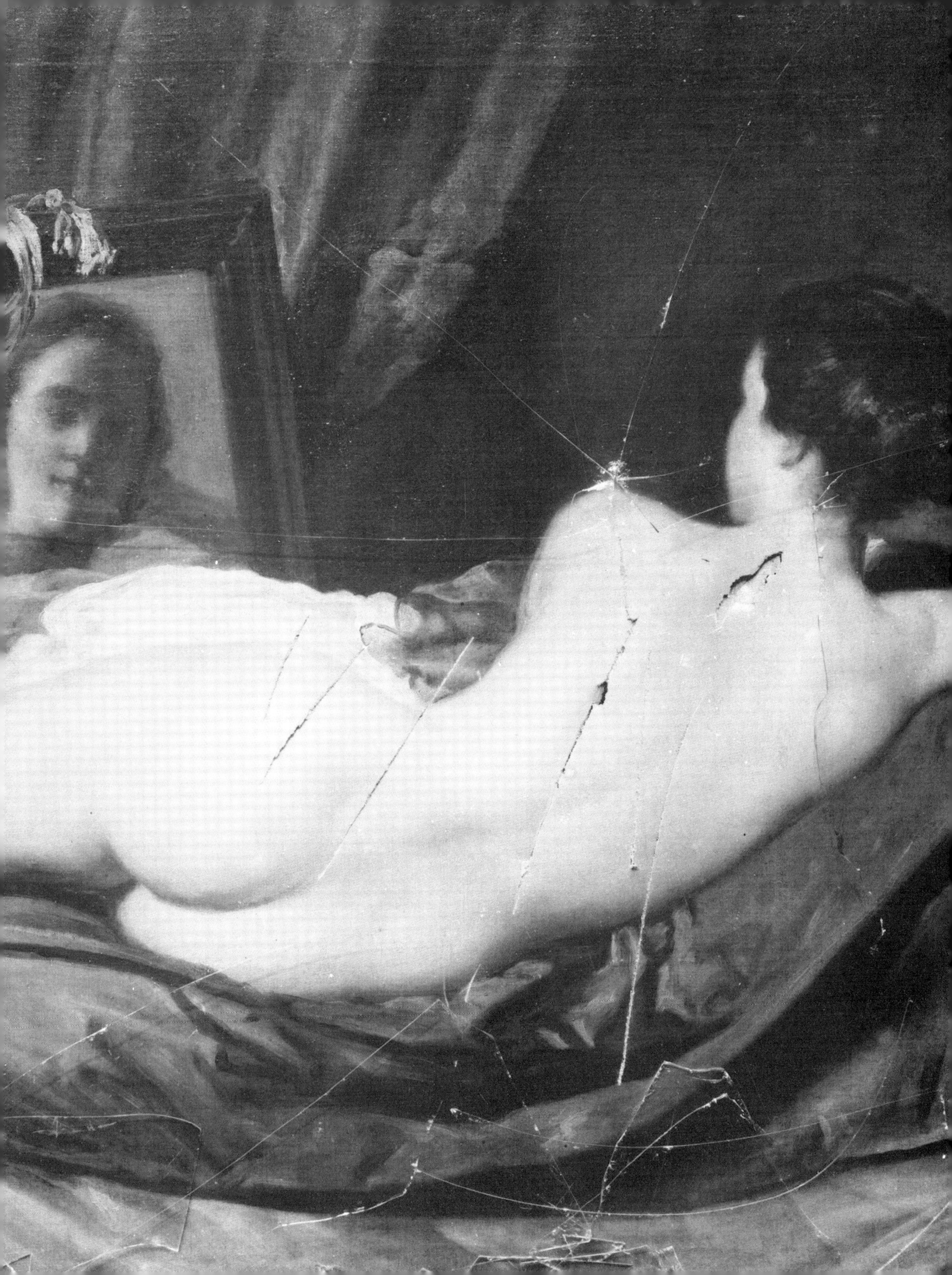

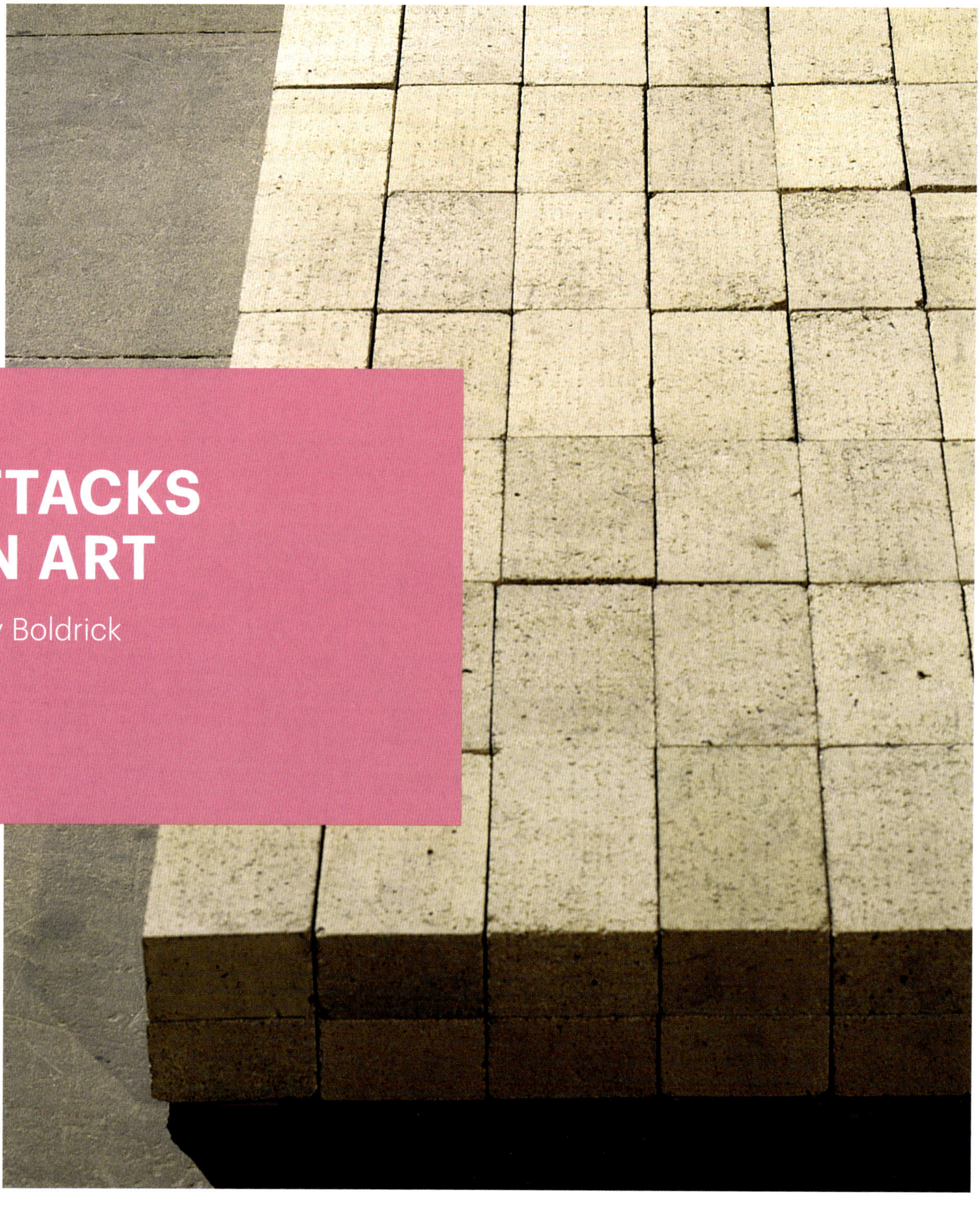

6 ATTACKS ON ART

Stacy Boldrick

> People are sexually aroused by pictures and sculptures; they break pictures and sculptures, they mutilate them, kiss them, cry before them, and go on journeys to them; they are calmed by them, stirred by them, and incited to revolt. They give thanks by means of them, expect to be elevated by them, and are moved to the highest levels of empathy and fear. They have always responded in these ways; they still do.[1]

David Freedberg begins his book *The Power of Images: Studies in the History and Theory of Response* by defining his subject in broader historical and cultural terms than that of today's experience in a museum or gallery: he considers the different forms of responses to art objects throughout history and how those responses were or are understood or, more often, misunderstood. Any forceful action towards a work of art in a public collection is often cast in scholarly and media-based discourse as crude, shocking or even embarrassing because of the social norms it transgresses. As a result, Freedberg argues, more physical or emotional responses to art can be considered uninteresting as scholarship and are repressed. When attacks on art in museums and galleries – violent or destructive actions – become stories in the press, they are seized upon for their notoriety, sensationalised, and often misrepresented. In a different way from scholarship, the media contributes to the repression of iconoclastic acts by amplifying the dramatic or controversial aspects of the story, indirectly encouraging future attacks rather than addressing the complex or unknowable aspects of the situation.[2]

Any form of written or verbal discourse generated by an attack on art can, and often does, mythologise the original circumstances.[3] The narrative centres around the action of the unauthorised attack on the work. The art work itself may be anthropomorphised (viewed in lifelike terms), compared to a human body that 'suffers' or is 'assaulted'.[4] (Even the word 'attack' is questionable.) More often the artwork is described in terms of its market value; sometimes the contrast between the work's market value and the cost of its raw materials is highlighted. Motives for attacks may be the object of ridicule or outrage, depending on the apparent public consensus of the work. An individual who damages a particularly historic or iconic work is often labelled as psychologically unstable. In many cases, when more recent contemporary art is defaced or damaged, the press may take an interest in understanding the motive behind the attack, especially if the work is abstract or considered to be aesthetically challenging. (Often the attack has been fuelled by overblown criticism of the art work in the press in the first place.) If living, the artist may be cast as a shadowy figure in the background. The majority of individual attacks on art on public display involve a series of participants and a number of relationships inside and outside the gallery: relationships between the work of art, its owners and its audience; between institutions and artists, the media and the art world; and most importantly between artists and audiences.

Much writing about attacks on art takes the form of listing descriptions of the scenarios according to motive, or the tools or forms of iconoclasm. The protagonists are described as vandals and their actions are acts of vandalism or art vandalism. Richard Clay discusses the pejorative nature of the term for scholars, with its etymological source in the Vandals, the Germanic tribe regarded as barbaric who sacked Rome in AD 455. Its first recorded use, *vandalisme*, was found in a report on the preservation of France's cultural heritage written in 1793 by a member of the Committee of Public Instruction, Joseph Lakanal, and popularised by his contemporary, Abbé Henri Grégoire, who claimed to have coined the term in order to kill the action.[5] Since then the term vandalism has come to refer to unsanctioned acts of marking on or destroying anything held in the public commons, from public buildings to public objects, as illegal actions.[6] Derogatory associations accompany the term: 'mindless vandalism' is perhaps most commonly used to refer to random or meaningless acts of violence perpetrated by individuals, who are thus dehumanised. Many scholars (including Richard Clay, Dario Gamboni, Alfred Gell and James Simpson) reject this term due to its narrow definition and the associations with the concept of labelling someone 'other' as barbaric as ignorant or of a lower status.[7] In its etymological origins, the word 'vandal' implies that the individual is not able to think clearly about actions and behaviour, so that the perpetrators are unable to take responsibility either for their action or for themselves.[8] In order to consider the longer history of physical actions and attitudes towards art, and to look at specific cases and their historical contexts, 'iconoclasm' is the preferred term in the present publication.

The issue of ownership determines the legal consequences of an attack on, or alteration of, a work of art or architecture. Graffiti is perhaps the most familiar form of iconoclasm that is classified as criminal damage, and one of the most cogent (although not the most common) forms of responses to public art and architecture.[9] The gradual rise of street art has resulted in works by artists such as Banksy acquiring the status of public art, although it can be argued that sanctioned or commissioned street art contests in a less direct way the notions of property ownership.

When artists alter or attack their own work or work by other artists in their ownership, or when the owners sanction such actions, no law is broken. Early twentieth-century international art movements had demanded the destruction of old art for new, and this manifested itself in many ways, including the making of 'auto-destructive' artworks, intentionally made to deteriorate through physical use or handling. The archetypal example of a self-destroying artwork is Marcel Duchamp's readymade, a slightly modified manufactured or mass-produced object which he designated as art, but which he also suggested could be used for any purpose. One of Duchamp's earliest references to the readymade in relation to work by other artists can be found in notes written between 1911 and 1915 for his work *Green Box*, in which he described a found object as a 'Reciprocal Readymade / Use a Rembrandt as an ironing board'.[10] In 1919 Duchamp made L.H.O.O.Q., by drawing a moustache on a postcard of the *Mona Lisa*; he made several further versions over the course of his lifetime, later describing it as 'a combination [of] Readymade and iconoclastic Dadaism'.[11] An example of another type of destructible work, designed more for the purposes of anthropomorphising an object so that the person may take pleasure in its destruction, is *Object to Be Destroyed (Indestructible Object)* 1923 (destroyed 1957, remade several times), made by Duchamp's friend Man Ray, and accompanied by the following instructions: 'With a hammer well aimed, try to destroy the whole with one blow.'[12] Although these artists were never based in Britain and are therefore not included in the present survey, their work and ideas have become part of an international cultural framework through which artists operate.

Radical alterations to works of art or buildings have long been described by their authors as 'improvements'. The eighteenth-century architect James Wyatt, known as 'the Destroyer', described his changes to the fabric and monuments of Salisbury Cathedral as improvements and innovations, although contemporary and later critics took issue with his alterations, which involved changing the floor levels and demolishing and moving chantry chapels and other monuments. In a similar way, the artists Jake and Dinos Chapman consistently refer to their practice of adding to the work of other artists such as Goya or Hogarth as 'rectification' or as 'improving' the work by impoverishing it.[13] The Chapmans cite in their defence Robert Rauschenberg's *Erased de Kooning Drawing* 1953, a work made when the artist requested a drawing from de Kooning for the sole purpose of erasing it.[14] Rauschenberg wanted to find out if he could make a work of art with an eraser by both 'unmaking' and removing the visible marks.[15] De Kooning himself used erasers in his drawings, which may have made Rauschenberg's actions seem more in keeping with the original work, its undoing merely an extension of its making.[16]

Arists who are invited to work with an art gallery's collection or to stage interventions are engaged in a different role from those who physically interact with or purposefully damage a work of art without support.[17] An intervention can involve the artist repositioning or presenting in an original way an existing work of art or a collection, often accompanied by some material remnant of an action. With institutional support, an intervention is a sanctioned response that becomes an artwork in itself, not categorised as an act of unwarranted violence or violation. Some interventions take the form of idiosyncratic or politically radical exhibitions, such as Hans Haacke's presentation of works from the Victoria and Albert Museum in his 2001 exhibition *Mixed Messages* at the Serpentine Gallery. Other actions take the form of research projects, such as Simon Starling's *Drop Sculpture (Atlas)* 2007 for the New Conservation Department at the Rijksmuseum, Amsterdam, which involved dropping, repairing and redisplaying a replica of a seventeenth-century sculpture of Atlas by Artus Quellinus, and his *Infestation Piece (Musselled Moore)* 2006–8, which involved the submersion of a replica of Henry Moore's *Warrior with Shield* 1953–4 in Lake Ontario, where it became infested with mussels over a period of eighteen months.[18] In these types of interventions, curators and artists do not tend to alter original works of art; they work with replicas or change their contexts, but not their material states.

Although artists have long made work for physical engagement, few artists have addressed the possibility of abject or violent physical interactions with their own work. In 1950 Duchamp showed his work *Fountain* 1917 mounted right side up so that it could be used as urinal in *Challenge and Defy*, a group exhibition held at the Stanley Janis Gallery in New York.[19] More recently, in 2012, the London-based artist Eva Rothschild made a Children's Art Commission film, *Boys and Sculpture*, at Whitechapel Gallery, in which a group of boys aged under twelve are left alone in a gallery full of her sculptures. Eventually quiet looking turns to gentle touching, and then more forceful wobbling, until one of the sculptures, a stack of round forms, collapses. Some of the boys kick the spherical forms with glee and others make new sculptures. Rothschild wanted to bring to her sculptures 'ideas of faith, death, magic, things that are all very messy...'.[20] Without conventional gallery rules of controlled movement and 'no touching', the boundaries between space and artwork disappear, becoming open to acts of play and invention, and slapstick messiness; at the same time, the relationship between the work of art and the viewer is turned upside down, undermined to the point of anarchy and exhaustion.

Sanctioned interventions can become targets for unsanctioned ones. In instances of the latter, artists believe either that they are improving works of art or that they are expressing frustration with it, despite (or because of) the fact that they have no claim to individual (as opposed to common) ownership of the work. In a new commission for Tate Britain (and therefore sanctioned) the artist Cornelia Parker wrapped in string Rodin's marble sculpture *The Kiss (Le Baiser)* 1901–4 to make *The Distance: A Kiss with Added String* 2003. Soon after it was on display, Piers Butler, a 'Notting Hill Stuckist' opposed to conceptual art and Cornelia Parker's action, cut the string. In May 1994 Mark Bridger poured black ink into Damien Hirst's *Away from the Flock*, and in 1999 Yuan Chai and Jian Jun Xi jumped on Tracey Emin's *My Bed* 1998 in a performance they called *Two Naked Men Jump into Tracey's Bed*. At Tate Modern in 2012, Vladimir Umanets wrote his name and the words 'a potential piece of yellowism' on the bottom right-hand corner of Mark Rothko's *Black on Maroon* 1958, a work he selected at random.

In most cases physical displays of engagement – whether flamboyant or clandestine – transgress codes of gallery conduct. Their motives may be diverse and multivalent, described as a simple artistic expression, even a compliment to the artist of the original work, or may be motivated by jealousy, anger and frustration, and a contempt for more challenging contemporary art, along with a desire to put themselves in the public eye. These unsanctioned interventions inadvertently make a claim to individual as opposed to public ownership, as the hands (or bodies) of individual artists alter works of art belonging to the public, and not solely to them, in ways that may damage artworks beyond repair.[21]

When physical interaction is not allowed, when an individual without claims to artistic intervention or improvement damages the work in an unsanctioned situation, motivations vary more widely. All iconoclasts want to have some kind of control over the work. For some individuals the work represents a living thing, for some a dead relation.[22] Expressions of outrage at representations of religious figures lie behind many attacks on art. When Chris Ofili's *The Holy Virgin Mary* 1996 was shown at the Brooklyn Museum of Art in 1999 as part of Charles Saatchi's exhibition *Sensation* (originally presented at the Royal Academy in 1997), Dennis Heiner smeared white paint over it (ill.97) and several other forms of protest took place outside the building in response to the work, considered by religious individuals to be blasphemous.[23] In 1961 Salvador Dalí's *Christ of St John of the Cross* 1951 at Kelvingrove Art Gallery and Museum, Glasgow, was attacked by a visitor armed with a stone who smashed the surface and ripped the canvas in the face of what he considered to be a blasphemous depiction of Christ from above; the same reason informed an attack in 1980, when the painting was shot at with an airgun.[24]

It is often impossible to isolate a single rationale for an attack on art. Political, environmental, aesthetic and personal sensibilities, as well as verbal criticism from the press targeted at controversial works, are often enmeshed within motivations that lead to physical attacks. Henry Moore's public sculptures have been the subject of numerous attacks – including *King and Queen* 1953 in Glenkiln, Scotland, beheaded in 1995 in light of written protests against the sculpture's symbolic and aesthetic forms, criticised as 'hideous bits of metal and the like' in the landscape.[25] After a great deal of controversy generated by the press in advance of its exhibition as part of *Sensation*, Marcus Harvey's painting *Myra* 1995, a monumental painting of Myra Hindley's police mugshot painted with the plaster cast of a child's hand, two visitors threw ink and eggs at it.[26] In the case of David Mach's *Polaris*, a public sculpture made of thousands of used tyres

97
Dennis Heiner smearing paint over Chris Ofili's *The Holy Virgin Mary* 1996 at the exhibition *Sensation*, 16 December 1999, Brooklyn Museum of Art. The act was photographed by Philip Jones Griffiths

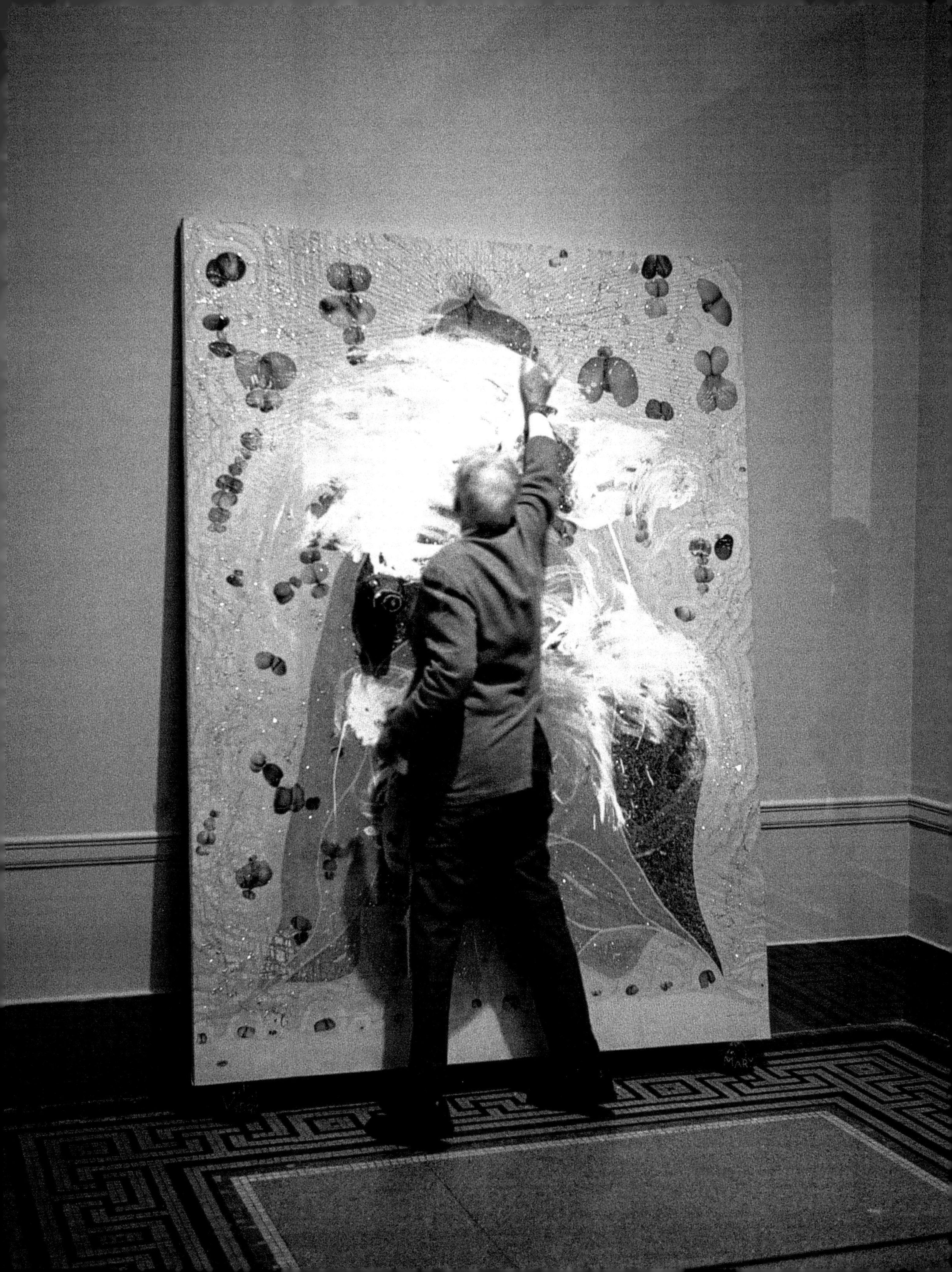

displayed on the walkway behind the Hayward Gallery at London's South Bank in 1983, one viewer, James Gore-Graham, poured petrol over it and set it alight; the work exploded and eventually killed him.[27] The rationale behind the act was never known.

Within the last decade, writers, artists and scholars have addressed attacks on art in galleries in imaginative and intelligent ways, although the issue still remains outside the scope of interest for most art historians. Motives have been analysed, 'art vandals' categorised and the tools of the iconoclast listed.[28] Helen Scott has conducted research into the forms of recorded attacks on art and the motivations behind them, considering examples such as Tony Shafrazi's attack on Picasso's *Guernica* at the Museum of Modern Art in New York in 1974, when he spray-painted the incomprehensible phrase 'KILL LIES ALL' on the painting in order to, in his words, 'retrieve the work from art history, and to bring it up to date'.[29] Brian Dillon identifies the vandal as essentially another, more unusual type of art lover, citing Shafrazi's spray-painted phrase to suggest that both artist and iconoclast in different ways 'leave us at a loss to translate their utterances into terms we fully comprehend'.[30]

Although each attack on an art object is often impossible to understand fully, all take place within a network of people, material things and ideas – art work, institution, attacker and audience, as well as the discourse generated among scholars and critics – and in the context of a particular point in time. The survey in this chapter presents three sculptures in the Tate collection, Reg Butler's *Maquette for the 'Unknown Political Prisoner'* 1951–2, Carl Andre's *Equivalent VIII* 1966 and Allen Jones' *Chair* 1969, all of which have been deliberately subjected to physical attacks by individuals and a period of verbal attack in the press. They have been chosen to represent historic attitudes to art in three decades – the 1950s, the 1970s and the 1980s. In each case the rationale for attack is rational not only for the one who is committing the act, but also for others, including other social groups.

To return to Freedberg, the most powerful images and objects can compel individuals and groups to respond with passionate, violent acts of anger as well as praise. Over time, outrage can be transformed into admiration as the perception of the significance or meaning of images and artworks changes. One of the best examples of such a work is Jacob Epstein's *Tomb of Oscar Wilde* 1912 (ill.98). In the first half of the twentieth century Epstein made sculptures that attracted virulent controversy from the press and public for over thirty years, most notably his sculptures made in 1908 for the British Medical Association building in the Strand, London (although threatened by censorship, these were in reality only physically damaged by erosion and the excising of overhanging parts deemed dangerous), and the W.H. Hudson Memorial (*Rima* 1925) in Kensington Gardens.[31] With its enlarged genitalia, the *Tomb of Oscar Wilde*, considered indecent by its commissioners, was censored by a provisional bronze plaque when it was first unveiled at Père Lachaise cemetery in Paris; the tomb was covered until the outbreak of the First World War.[32] Once uncovered, the sculpture began to attract graffiti and the testicles gained a sheen; in 1961 they were hacked off (and were rumoured to have been kept in the gatekeeper's cottage).[33] Over the years, a tradition of kissing the sculpture developed, although over the course of time layers of lipstick damaged its surface. In 2011 the sculpture was cleaned, restored and is now protected under glass, removed from physical contact.[34] Debates about the idea that iconoclasts are artists are well rehearsed; only recently have scholars begun to ask whether conservation may in itself constitute a form of iconoclasm.[35]

98
Jacob Epstein's *Tomb of Oscar Wilde* 1912, Père Lachaise Cemetary, Paris, France

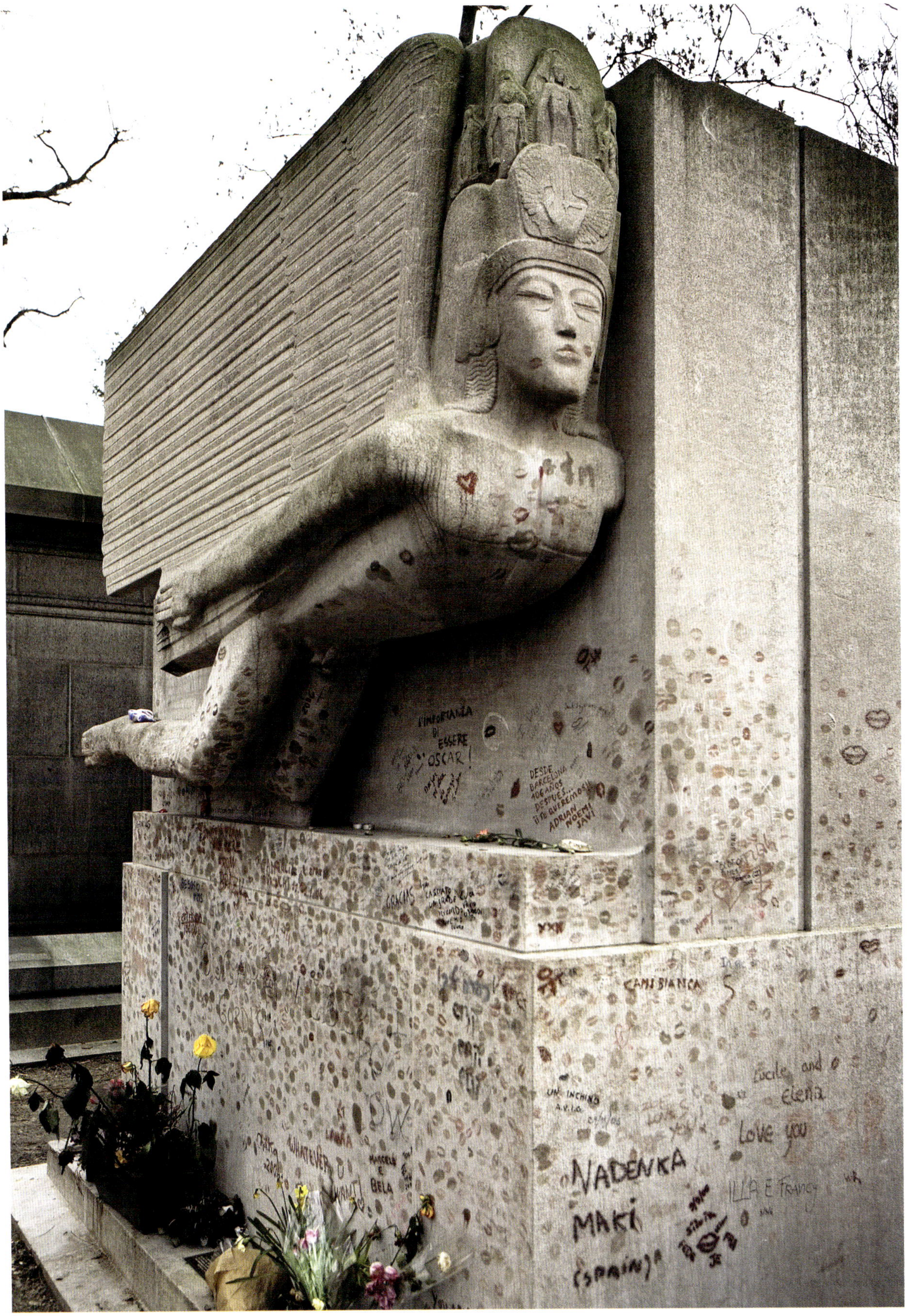
L'IMPORTANZA DI ESSERE OSCAR!
GRACIAS
WHATEVER
Lucile and Elena
Love you
NADENKA
MAKI
(SPAIN)

Reg Butler's maquette for *The Unknown Political Prisoner*

Made in 1951–2, Reg Butler's original maquette for the Unknown Political Prisoner competition consisted of a stone base, three small bronze female figures and an abstract form made of brass sheet and wire, shaped and soldered into a three-tiered structure comprising a cage-like base on three legs and a spire, elements described by the artist as the rock, the watchers and the tower.[36] Although the referent for the Unknown Political Prisoner was broadly defined by the competition's organisers, Butler interpreted the identity of the subject as a prisoner in a concentration camp, the spire symbolising the transcendence of the human spirit or intellect over the physical imprisonment.[37] The version included here is made of soldered bronze sheet and wire on the original stone base, a replica of the sculpture Butler made to replace the damaged original.

The object of the Unknown Political Prisoner competition, organised by Anthony Kloman and supported by the Institute for Contemporary Art in London, was to commission a public monument dedicated to 'all those unknown men and women who in our time have been deprived of their lives or their liberty in the cause of human freedom'.[38] The winners were announced at the international exhibition which opened at the Tate Gallery on 14 March 1953, with the Grand Prize awarded to Reg Butler. The next day, László Szilvassy, a 28-year-old Hungarian refugee, deliberately damaged Butler's maquette and handed to a gallery attendant the following statement: 'Those unknown political prisoners have been and still are human beings. To reduce them – the memory of the dead and the suffering of the living – into scrap metal is just as much a crime as it was to reduce them into ashes or scrap. It is an absolute lack of humanism.'[39] Szilvassy's objection was simple: that political prisoners should not take the form of 'scrap metal'.

In the newspapers, conflicting reports arose about Szilvassy's nationality, refugee status and occupation, the manner in which he damaged the work, the value of the work, its aesthetic value, its materials and the future site of the monument. Even before Szilvassy's damage, opinions were divided about the maquette and some press reports were critical of its form: 'How is its tangled construction to be accounted for, and is the long rod pointing upward from it an aerial or not?'[40] After the damage, more condemnatory headlines followed: 'An abstract work . . . wore an even more abstract look last night. It was squashed out of shape by a man visiting the Tate Gallery'; 'How about this for the first sight of England?'.[41] It was also the butt of jokes: 'Woman leaving the UPP competition at the Tate Gallery yesterday: "But how could they tell that that one *was* crushed out of shape?"'[42] A few months later, *LIFE* magazine included a photograph of Szilvassy – not Butler – at the top of the article, and images of the maquette, intact and damaged, with the headline 'A Big Row for a Big Prize'.[43]

Most press coverage of the damage described Szilvassy walking around the work, taking hold of the sculpture and bending it out of shape, throwing it on the floor, uttering words and walking away, but the accounts differ in their detail. One newspaper alleged that he pushed through people to get at the maquette; another, that he was smiling throughout. Reports of Szilvassy's utterances varied, with him quoted as saying 'Your prizewinner is Kaput', or 'That's the end of that,' or 'Now, it's finished. I am a Hungarian and have been a political prisoner.'[44] Papers variously reported that he bent, broke, squashed, crushed or smashed the work. The press closely followed the course of the trial, which ended with Szilvassy spending a month in jail and paying a fine. Critical attitudes toward the sculpture continued to appear, aligning newspapers with opposing political perspectives.[45] Decades later, Szilvassy distanced himself from the incident and his motives, denying his claim that his parents had died at the hands of communists or that he was opposed to abstract art.[46]

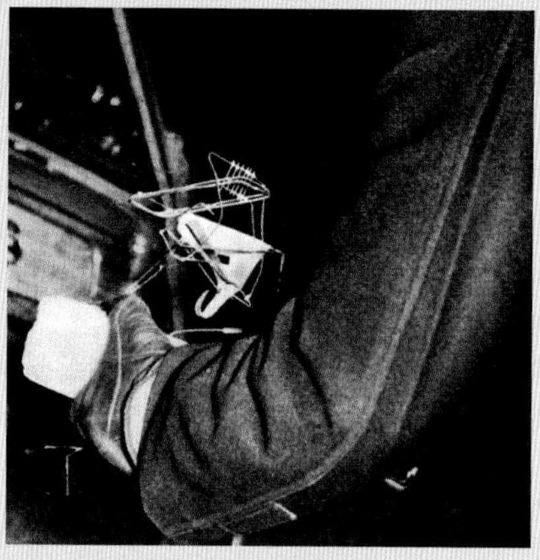

99
Documentation photograph of the destroyed maquette, 1953
Tate Gallery Archive

Rather than condemn the action, Butler responded with interest: 'It shows the model has something . . . You take about a shilling's worth of wire and bend it about in a certain way, and it becomes a symbol powerful enough to make someone want to destroy it.'[47] The artist's reference to the value of its material elements led to questions about the value of the piece as a whole. Newspapers drew attention to Butler's inexpensive materials and the relationship of their form to television aerials – a relatively new addition to the British domestic landscape – as a way of devaluing the maquette, yet television aerials and towers, and science fiction imagery were all formal sources acknowledged by Butler.[48]

Controversy arose as a result of confusion over the potential siting of the monument on the white cliffs of Dover (although it had always been destined for Berlin) when Butler's comment about its scale were misunderstood by the press, prompting forty Tory members of parliament to sign a petition against it.[49] Szilvassy's damage may have provided a focus for residual popular feelings about modernism in the early 1950s, but over time writing about the maquette has been dominated by views on its anti-communist associations and funding of the competition by the US government through the CIA, and about the opposing political alliances of abstraction and figuration.[50] SB

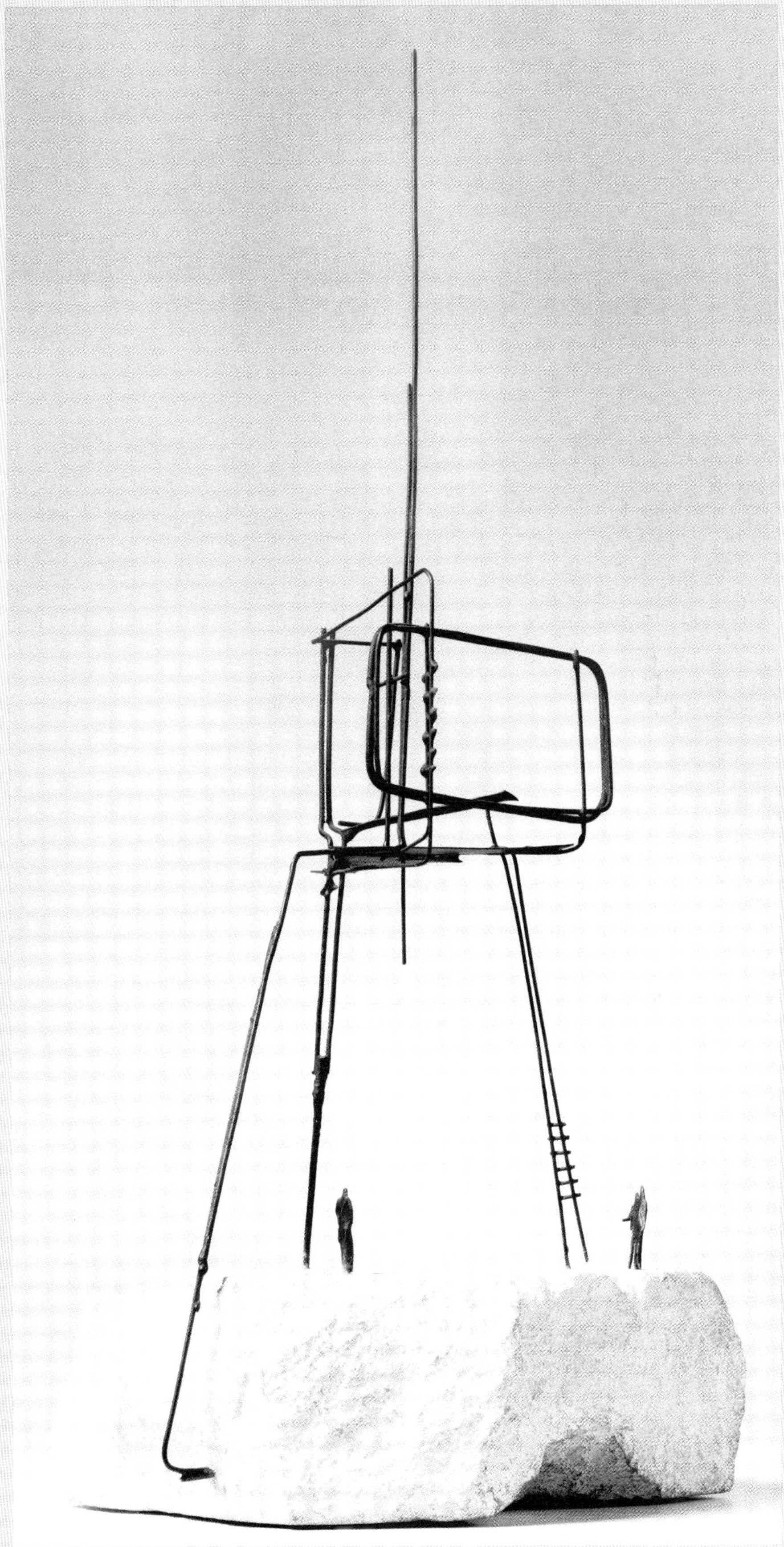

100
Reg Butler (1913–81)
Maquette for *The Unknown Political Prisoner* 1951–2, remodelled 1953
Painted stone and painted bronze
44.5 × 20.5 × 16.5
Tate. Lent by the Estate of Reg Butler 1986

Carl Andre's *Equivalent VIII*

Carl Andre's sculpture *Equivalent VIII* has never had an easy time in Britain. Even its entry into the country was fraught, its arrival coinciding with a dockers' strike, resulting in its retrieval from the ship being delayed. One of the first notes in the acquisition files begins: 'Bricks arrived 22 May at container depot, Dagenham. Unable to get work released because of pickets.'[51]

A sculpture made up of 120 sand-lime firebricks arranged in two stacks of rows of six by ten bricks, *Equivalent VIII* was first shown in 1966 at the Tibor de Nagy Gallery in New York. It was one of eight works made from the same number of bricks, but in different shapes and therefore 'equivalent'; it was remade in 1969 and purchased by Tate in 1972.[52] Although it had been publicly displayed before, attention in the press only arose when Douglas Cooper wrote against its purchase with public funds after the work was listed and illustrated in the Tate Gallery's *Biannual Report of Acquisitions*.[53] Controversy abounded about the validity and value of *Equivalent VIII* in light of its purchase during an economic slump in Britain, and a period of serious inflation, when an article criticising the Tate's government funding and its expenditure on acquisitions was published in the business section of the *Sunday Times* on 15 February 1976.[54] Although Andre's work is discussed alongside other acquisitions, the largest image in the piece is a photograph of *Equivalent VIII*, headed by the strapline 'How the Tate Gallery spent £1m in two years'. The framing of the image with '£1m' suggests, if not an equivalency, an association. A deluge of negative press coverage and cartoons immediately followed, culminating in the *Daily Mirror*'s front page headline: 'Whichever way you look at Britain's latest work of art . . . WHAT A LOAD OF RUBBISH'. This was accompanied by an image of the work right way up, upside down and on its side, as if it were a painting with no point of orientation.[55]

Not long after the *Daily Mail* front page, on 23 February, the attacks went from being verbal and visual to physical when a visitor deliberately splashed the work with a bottle of blue food dye. Notes from the conservation files mention the press coverage in a description of the event:

> Following publicity in the press a member of the public threw the contents of a bottle of blue food dye over the bricks whilst they were on exhibition in gallery 19. The bottle of dye was recovered from the member of the public – it was Marshall's Food Colours Clear Blue produced by A.B. Marshall Ltd., Shaftesbury Road, London N18.[56]

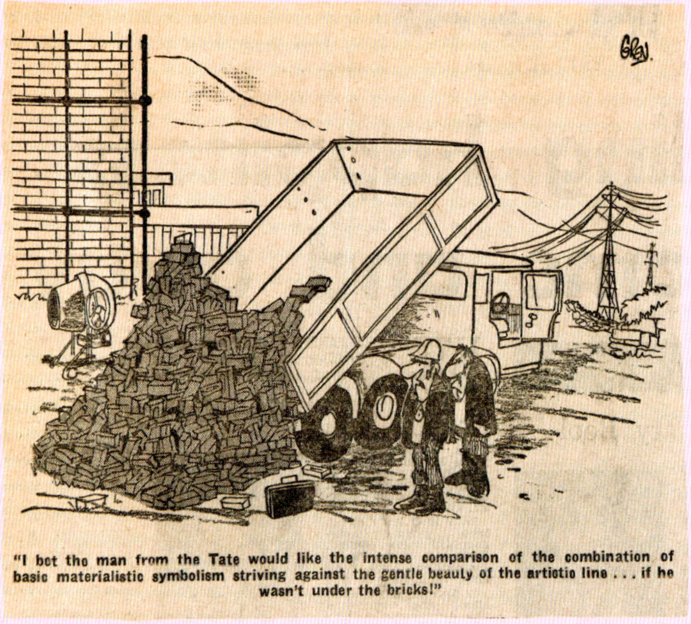

101
Cartoon from the *South Wales Echo*, 17 February 1976
Tate Gallery Archive

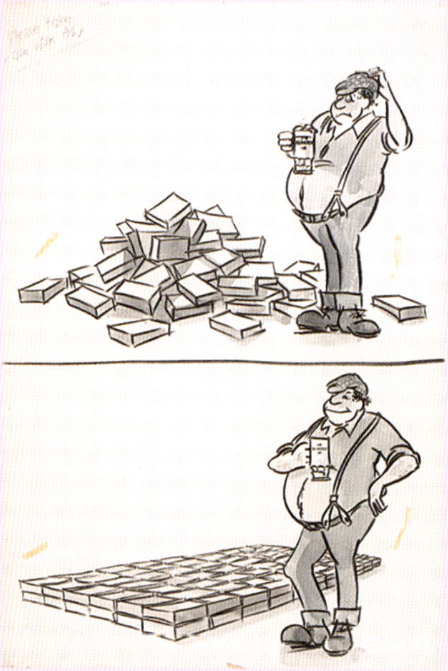

102
Carl Andre (b.1935)
Postcard made from Heineken beer advertisement and sent to artist's friends, 1976. The name of the beer and the slogan 'Refreshes the parts other beers cannot reach' have been taken out.
Tate Gallery Archive

The work was quickly removed and subjected to different types of treatments, with varying degrees of success. Conservation took many months.[57] Press reports about the attack initially describe a 'city toff' and 'well-dressed man', later named as Peter Stowell-Phillips, a chef and 'amateur painter' who recounted: 'The people standing around all clapped . . . except for two old ladies who said: "You are a silly person", and went off to fetch somebody.'[58] Stowell-Phillips was reported as stating: 'I'm a taxpayer. I'm incensed that this pile of bricks was bought with public money. This is my protest'.[59] Newspaper headlines anthropomorphised the work with 'Splash! Those arty bricks get the blues', 'Tate's bricks are off colour', 'Tate bricks take a bath', and even 'Tate bricks disfigured'.[60] Responding to the *Burlington Magazine*'s diatribe against Andre's work, Richard Morphet defended its art-historical significance and the gallery's acquisition of it in a lengthy illustrated response.[61]

The main criticisms against *Equivalent VIII* related to its material value and its lack of visible craftsmanship – or evidence of the hand of the artist – but the subsequent explosion of controversy is equally fascinating.[62] The art historian Alistair Rider most closely assesses the development of vitriol in the press, the economic context for the outrage and the dynamic between the parodies featuring bricklayers in the media (ill.101) and the egalitarian aspects of Andre's work, along with attempts to recast him as a craftsperson.[63] Rider's attention to the papers' wildly inaccurate figures for the cost of the work as being between £400 and £12,000 (when in fact it was purchased for £2,297) represents the extent to which fiction outweighed fact.[64] In May 1977, after its conservation, *Equivalent VIII* was displayed in an exhibition focusing on the work of Andre and his contemporaries (including Donald Judd and Robert Morris) in an attempt to place the piece in its historic context.[65]

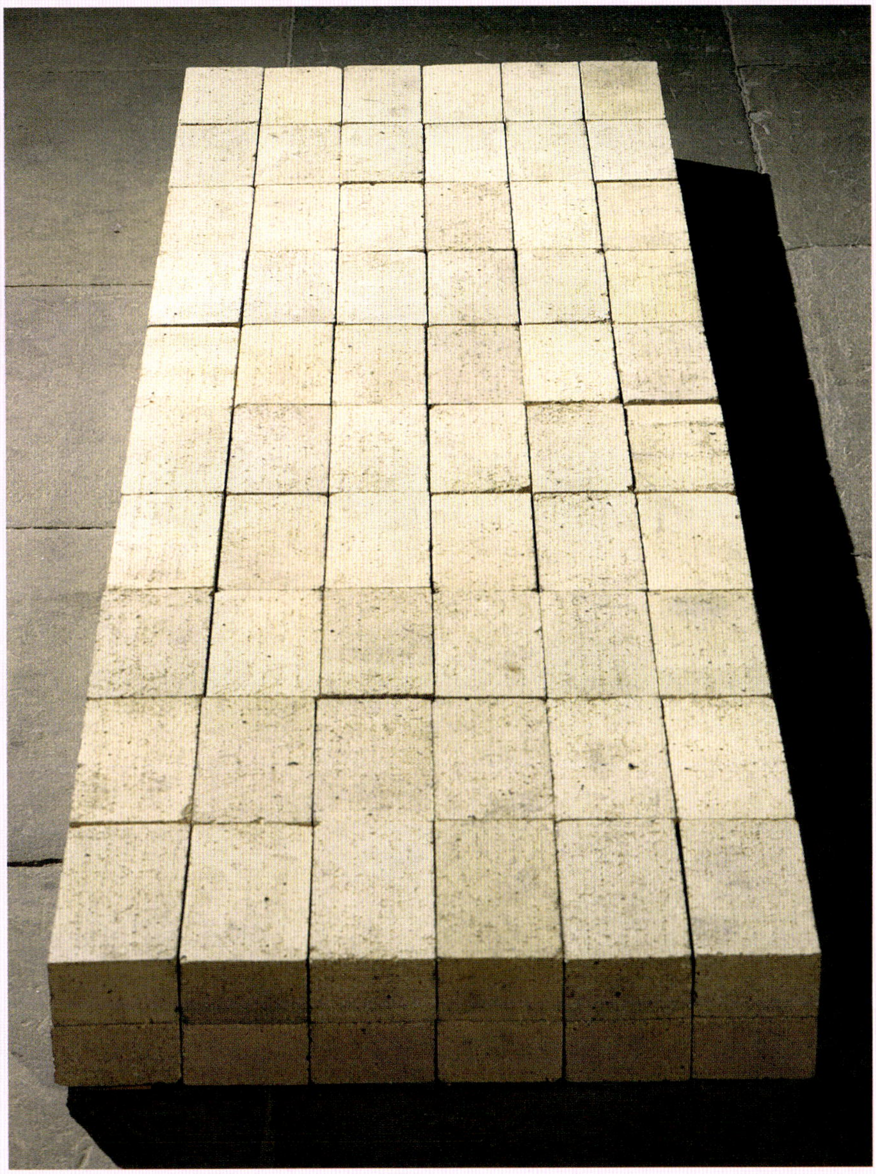

103
Carl Andre (b.1935)
Equivalent VIII, 1966
Firebricks 12.7 × 68.6 × 229.2
Tate. Purchased 1972

Spare bricks accompanied the sculpture when it arrived in Britain in 1972: 'Carl says that a few spares will be coming with the sculpture, and that as far as he knows these firebricks are still in production and available from stock.'[66] Several more were sought after the attack, but the legacy of 'The Bricks' – as one of the most popular targets of abuse for contemporary art, and 'a major feature in our contemporary folk-lore' – remains.[67] As *Equivalent VIII* approaches its half-century and settles in to its place in the art historical canon, the controversy itself has become a subject for other artists, among them Claire Fontaine, an artists' collective that has translated the cartoons and newspaper articles into individual paintings on canvas, one of which was exhibited at Frieze Art Fair in 2012.[68] Unsurprisingly, the painting reproduced the *Daily Mirror*'s front page: 'WHAT A LOAD OF RUBBISH'. SB

Allen Jones' *Chair*

One of a number of erotic sculptures Jones made of figures of women as forms of furniture,[69] *Chair* comprises a female figure lying on her back, her knees pulled up to the chest and a cushion fixed on the back of her thighs and secured by a belt wrapped around the waist, her calves positioned to form a backrest. She is clad in black leather hotpants and thigh-high leather stiletto boots. The figure was modelled in clay by Dick Beech under the supervision of the artist, and cast in acrylic and painted by Gems Wax Models Ltd. from Jones' designs. His ideas were fuelled by non-fine art references and the street scene of the King's Road, where he lived during the 1960s.[70]

When it was acquired by the Tate Gallery in 1981 *Chair* was valued for breaking new ground as an anti-canonical depiction of the female form, one that resonated with the mass-produced images of pop art, and yet remained a figurative sculpture unlike any other. Jones wanted the work to challenge preconceptions of fine art, and Tate's acquisitions committee members held it in high regard. *Chair* and similar sculptures attracted controversy for different reasons, but questions about its relationship to pornography were persistent.[71] Debates about Jones' sculptures had been ongoing since the 1970s. Feminist theorists such as Laura Mulvey and Lisa Tickner took issue with what they considered to be his objectification of women's bodies, writing at length about its contested status as a work that Jones described as erotic and appealing to a broad public, but one which they saw as having problematic implications for women.[72]

On 4 March 1986 a visitor wrote a letter to the Director of the Tate Gallery,[73] singling out *Chair*, on display as part of the exhibition *Forty Years of Modern Art*, for particular criticism:

> ... I found the sculpture deeply offensive to my womanliness and to my sex. As a part-time lecturer in Art and Design I feel responsible to react in some way, my immediate response (I wanted to kick it to small pieces and destroy it) was one of great anger ... The obscenity of the piece shows extreme insensitivity towards women and I would like to see it removed from the exhibition.[74]

Four days later, on 8 March (International Women's Day, then in its seventy-fifth year), two women poured 'viscous paint stripper' over the face of the woman in the sculpture. The damage to the surface of the sculpture – the 'skin' – exposed the polyester resin underneath (ill.104). The *Mail on Sunday* referred to the work as '"Porn" chair', reporting that 'Women demonstrators hurled acid at a controversial Tate Gallery "sculpture" yesterday ... Two women rushed up to the exhibition and threw acid over its face before fleeing, shouting that their action was to coincide with International Women's Day.'[75] The attackers were never caught. The letter to the Director was not considered a warning or a threat, despite its arrival just before the attack.[76]

According to the conservator Lyndsey Morgan, '30 per cent of the visible surface was damaged'. The conservation work required to repair the sculpture was extensive and challenging, taking three months and requiring the assistance of the artist.[77] Since the attack, ideas about women's bodies have changed for many as feminism itself has changed, and attitudes to sexuality have expanded, with fetish culture and sadomasochism now a part of mainstream culture.[78]

Like Carl Andre's *Equivalent VIII*, views about Jones' sculpture have also changed over time. Tate's *Chair* is one of three sculptures held in the collections of national institutions, and the works are consistently celebrated in international exhibitions as important contributions to pop art. Most recently *Chair* appeared in Tate Liverpool's 2013 exhibition *Glam: The Performance of Style*, in a section exploring artifice and eroticism in the early 1970s. Elected a Royal Academician in 1986, Jones is an established figure in the art world and his work has left a considerable legacy. SB

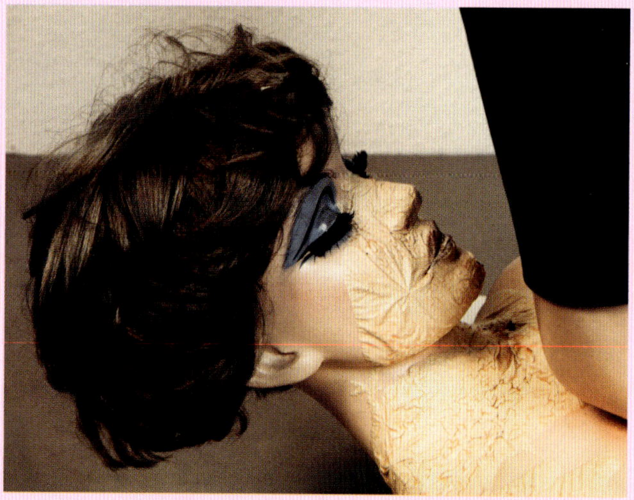

104
Documentation photograph of *Chair* 1969, showing damage caused by the paint stripper attack in 1986

105
Allen Jones (b.1937)
Chair 1969
Acrylic paint on glass fibre and resin with Perspex and leather
77.5 × 57.1 × 99.1
Tate. Purchased 1981

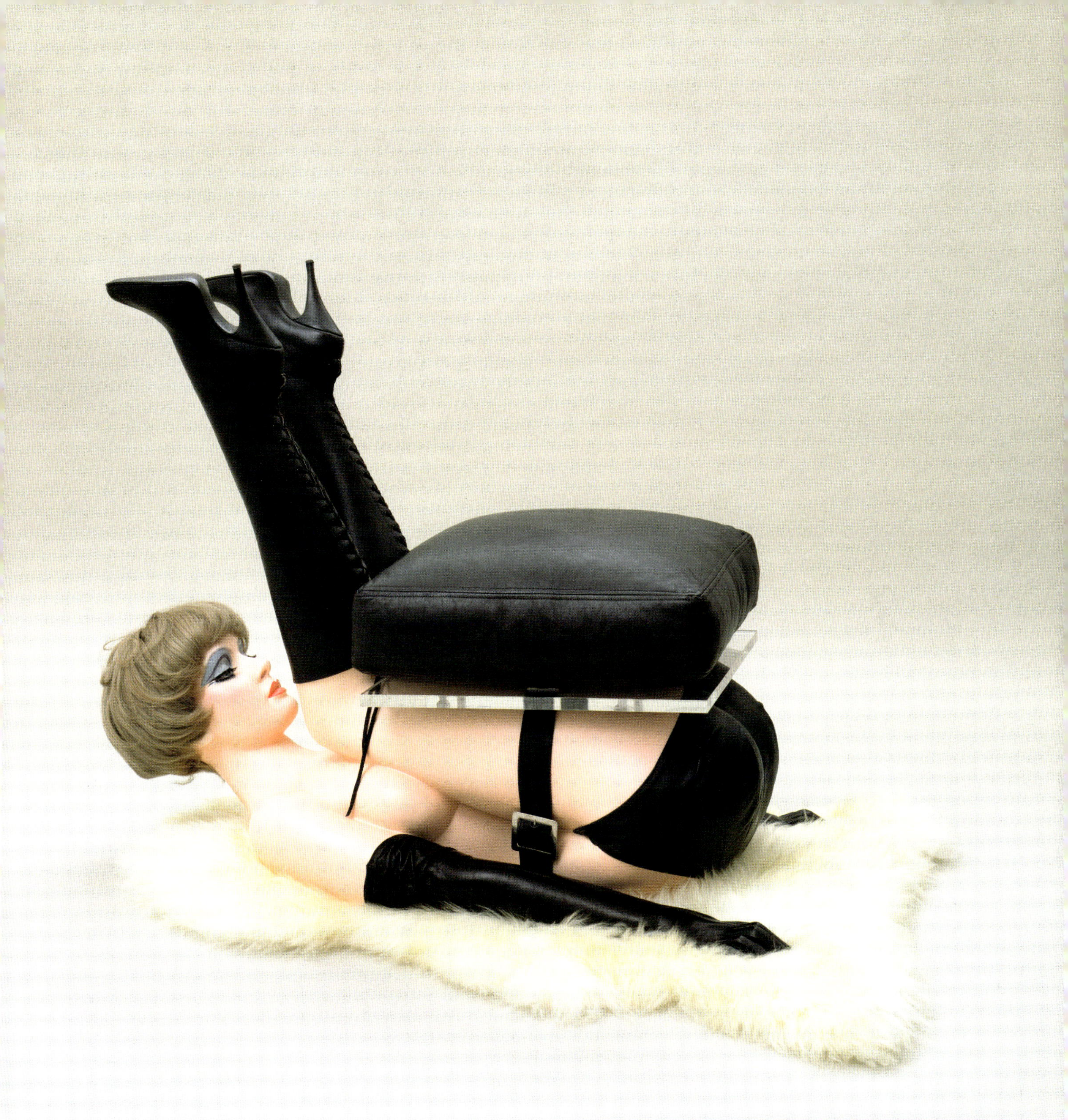

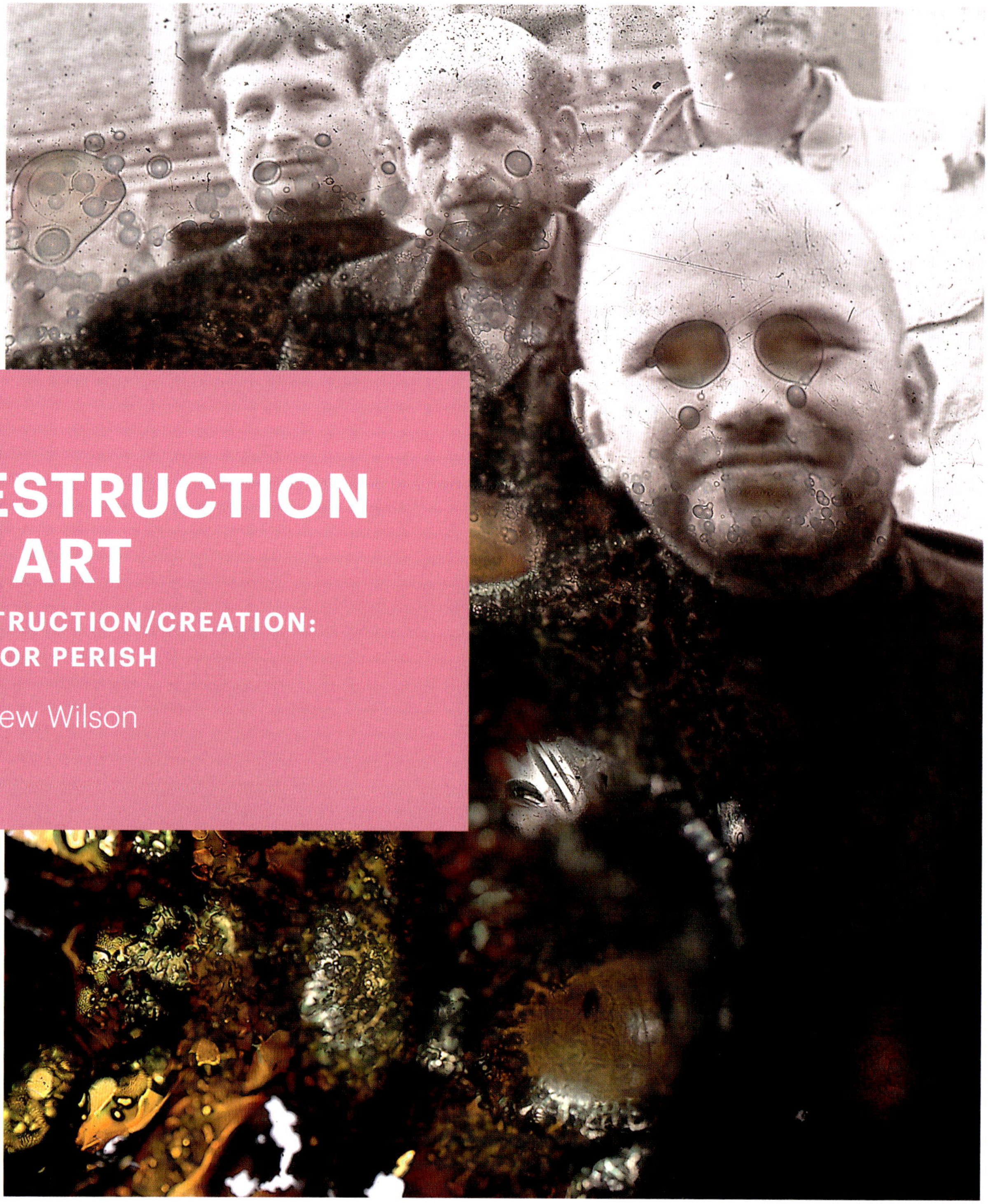

7 DESTRUCTION IN ART

DESTRUCTION/CREATION: ACT OR PERISH

Andrew Wilson

It was a moment heavy in Lutheran symbolism when Bertrand Russell on 18 February 1961 pinned a notice to the door of the Ministry of Defence in London. The notice's urgent and apocalyptic tone suggested that, given its capacity for annihilation through nuclear weapons, time was perhaps running out for the human race. It declared that

> Hitler had tried to wipe out a whole people. Today the nuclear tyrants of East and West threaten the entire human race with extinction ... Our action today is the first step in a campaign of non-violent civil disobedience. We hereby serve notice on our Government that we can no longer stand aside while they prepare to destroy mankind.[1]

Russell was accompanied by over 4,000 people who, inspired by the stance taken by the Committee of 100, sat down for four hours outside the ministry (ill.106). Among the founders of the Committee of 100 the previous year was the artist Gustav Metzger, who had developed an art that was born of its own destruction – what he had termed, in 1959, 'auto-destructive art' – and which was inseparable from his own social and political beliefs and activism.

In Edinburgh at the International Writers' Conference in August 1962, the novelist Alexander Trocchi stated that

> All art can be considered as man's expressive reaction to his state of being in the world ... Modern art begins with the destruction of the object. All other creation is on the other side of nihilism. It begins after Nietzsche, and after Dada.[2]

Trocchi's words gave credence to the 'death of the novel' – a notion that was widely recognised by many of the conference delegates to be the prevailing condition of the contemporary novel, and which prefigured the later post-structuralist notion of the death of the author. This characteristic could be identified in a number of ways, but for Trocchi and William Burroughs, his fellow 'cosmonaut of inner space',[3] it was through their understanding of narrative form being written through a fragmentation that was determined by space rather than the orthodox unfolding of time. However, Trocchi made clear that for him this 'destruction of the object' was a direct result of the artist or writer's engagement with social and political change. In a world in which nuclear brinkmanship – 'Bomb Culture'[4] – suggested the inevitable possibility of global holocaust,[5] an art that began with the 'destruction of the object' appeared as the only possible response.

Metzger's childhood experiences are suggestive of a similar inevitability to his own creation of an art of destruction. Born in Nuremberg, Metzger had arrived in Britain as a child in 1939 with his brother through the assistance of the Children's Refugee Committee; during the war most of his family perished in the Holocaust. Towards the end of the war, while living at an anarchist commune in Bristol, he decided, aged eighteen, not to become a revolutionary but instead to pursue the life of an artist, a life that he understood, from his reading of Eric Gill, to have a directly social and political purpose. To this end, in 1945 he enrolled in classes at the Borough Polytechnic in London, where David Bomberg taught, studying closely with him between 1945 and 1948 and again from 1950 to 1953. In 1953 he had helped Bomberg found the Borough Bottega as a way of trying to encourage a workshop practice, though he left the group in December and Bomberg broke off relations with him. This rupture ultimately led Metzger to leave London for King's Lynn and to stop painting for three years.

In Antwerp in 1948 he had painted images of the cathedral, one of which in particular conveyed

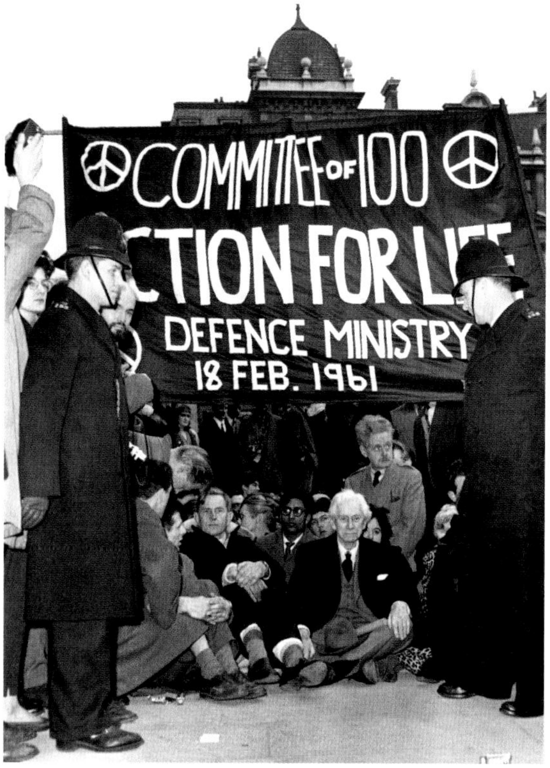

a sense of the world falling apart, of holocaust, death and destruction – an atom-bomb cloud hanging over the cathedral dome. When he resumed painting again in 1956, he did so under the shadow of destruction. In the summer of 1957 Metzger organised an exhibition of sculpture borrowed from churches in Norfolk and Suffolk, *Treasures from East Anglian Churches*; this was almost entirely made up of sculptures that had been assaulted in some way during the Reformation or the later Puritan backlash of the mid-seventeenth century. In the catalogue of the exhibition Metzger wrote plainly that

> much Church Art was destroyed in the period between the Reformation and the end of the Commonwealth. 'Lord! what work was here! what clattering of glasses! what beating down of walls! what tearing up of monuments!' Bishop Hall gives a painfully vivid account of events at Norwich in May 1644.[6]

Metzger's attention here towards religious artefacts that had borne the brunt of iconoclasm and a description of processes of destruction might in retrospect be thought to be indicative of his later formulation of auto-destructive art, however the course of his activities as an artist and as an activist provide a better understanding of the role he came to accord destruction within his work. In the months following the *Treasures from East Anglian Churches* exhibition Metzger not only became active in the King's Lynn Committee for Nuclear Disarmament, and later the following year in the Direct Action Committee Against Nuclear War (DAC), but also organised an unsuccessful protest that attempted to save the ancient fisherman's quarter of King's Lynn from demolition.

However, Metzger's involvement with the DAC and its rocket base protests in Norfolk and elsewhere intensified at a time when his painting was starting to change radically too. Heavily textured paintings of a round worktable took on the unmistakable form of a mushroom cloud, recalling his earlier painting of Antwerp Cathedral. Abstract tachiste paintings on canvas and board gave way to paintings on mild steel and plastic; these surfaces were attacked, scratched and carved into by palette knife, and alongside oil paint Metzger applied pigment and unfixed chalk to emphasise a fragile and ephemeral state. In 1959 he moved back to London and the following year helped found the Committee of 100 alongside Russell, Ralph Schoenman and Michael Scott.[7] The DAC's field secretary, Pat Arrowsmith, writing about Metzger in 1960 – following his first public demonstration of auto-destructive art, for which he presented his acid on nylon painting alongside

106
Sit-down by the Committee of 100, outside the Ministry of Defence building, London, 18 February 1961

107
Gustav Metzger (b.1926)
South Bank Demonstration: Acid Action 1961

a model for auto-destructive monuments – gives an indication of how intertwined Metzger's activism and art had become. She described Metzger as

> an active campaigner for nuclear disarmament. I myself walked into London beside him at the end of last year's Aldermaston March. He took part in the Stevenage campaign against missile manufacture a year ago, and back in the early days of the campaign stood up on a soap box to address the stall-holders of Watton market. Inevitably the art of such a person carries a social message ... Metzger may well be right when he says that this sort of art would shock the general public. For in a symbolic way it would demonstrate the current state of society: a society whose basic ingredients are such that it seems all too likely to end up destroying itself.[8]

In November 1959 Metzger arrived at his formulation of a theory of auto-destructive art. Distributed as a manifesto, this first text was suggestive of both aesthetic and social potential, identifying auto-destructive art as 'primarily a form of public art for industrial societies'.[9] Once he had, the following year, arrived at a means of demonstrating these ideas through the act of painting with acid on nylon, subsequent texts elaborated on its aesthetic characteristics but, more pertinently, on its wider aims – as he made clear, it 'is not limited to theory of art and the production of art works. It includes social action. Auto-destructive art is committed to a left-wing revolutionary position in politics, and to struggles against future wars.'[10] Or as he succinctly explained, 'Auto-destructive art is an attack on capitalist values and the drive to nuclear annihilation'.[11]

In the autumn of 1961, as a prologue to demonstrations planned for Battle of Britain day on 17 September, Metzger, along with thirty-one fellow members of the Committee of 100, refused to be bound over to keep the peace and were imprisoned for periods of up to two months. Prior to being taken away to start his jail sentence, Metzger read out a statement to the court that underlines the extent to which his ideals as an active member of the Committee of 100 were formed out of his own experiences:

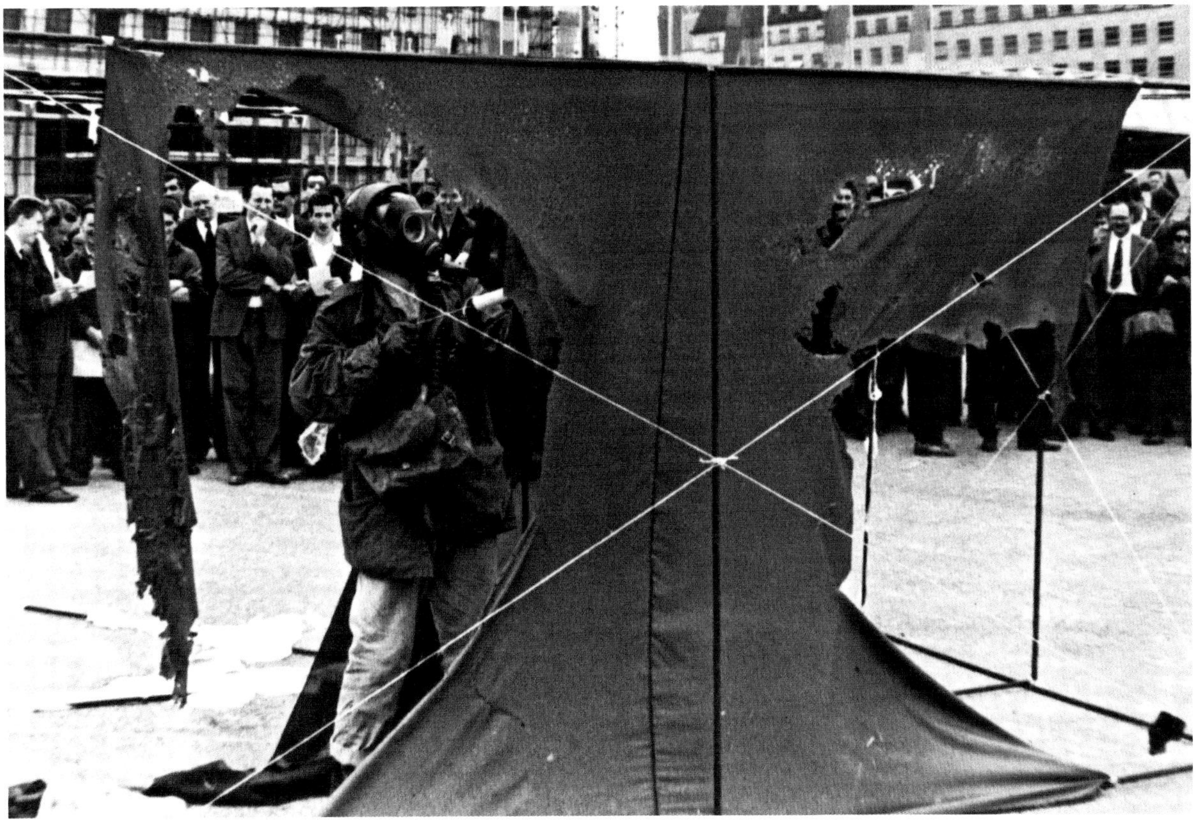

> I came to this country from Germany when 12 years old, my parents being Polish Jews, and I am grateful for the Government for bringing me over. My parents disappeared in 1943 and I would have shared their fate. But the situation is now far more barbarous than Buchenwald, for there can be absolute obliteration at any moment. I have no other choice than to assert my right to live, and we have chosen, in this committee, a method of fighting which is the exact opposite of war – the principle of total non-violence.[12]

If this statement makes clear the extent of Metzger's commitment and engagement in undertaking such political action, it should also be clear that its words were also embodied within the very fabric of his work, neither as an illustration of ruins nor as a metaphor for social sickness, but by the very presentation of a clear, unfettered and progressively destructive force.

The title *Art under Attack* suggests that art is placed in danger of harm; iconoclasm entails the destruction of art, a destruction that is wilful, intentioned and directed. As such, the act of iconoclasm recognises the power that can be held by images and the position of art within society. Iconoclasm is an outward sign of, more usually, a politically or religiously directed motivation or belief. In this respect, an affinity can be recognised between iconoclasm and Metzger's elaboration of auto-destructive art as a clear expression of his social and political beliefs. However, he is no iconoclast.[13] He does not destroy art but, recognising its social authority, instead constructs a situation where destructive forces can be shown for what they are and also be turned in on themselves, both to stimulate a creative physical and material change in a specific work and also in a broad sense to reflect the possibility for moral change in the world. Destruction and creation are for Metzger different sides of the same coin; his theories of auto-destructive art prioritise the different transformations that can be manipulated and followed in the act of creation, rather than the well-defined physicality adopted by an object and its reduction into product. Such ideas coursed through his manifestos of auto-destructive art and were directly signalled in the title of his third and fifth manifestos: *Auto-Destructive Art, Machine Art, Auto-Creative Art* in 1961 and *On Random Activity in Material / Transforming Works of Art* in 1964. Similarly, they also provide nuance to the otherwise straightforward exhortation in the first publicity pamphlets for the Committee of 100, designed by Metzger, that proclaimed 'Act or Perish'. Ultimately, however, the effect of auto-destructive art is realised through what Metzger terms an 'aesthetic of revulsion',[14] whereby within an essentially public arena the artwork can reveal 'by elimination of matter the amount of time left to us'.[15]

Metzger's vision of an auto-destructive art as a public art was one that he hoped would exploit the resources and technology that would destroy the planet and harness them to deliver a 'pharonic vision' of monuments 'to the power of man to destroy life'.[16] It was in the pursuit of this socially and politically engaged public art that in 1966 he initiated the 'Destruction In Art Symposium' (DIAS), a month of events by a wide and diverse range of artists with a three-day symposium as its focus; some fifty avant-garde artists from ten countries took part, as well as scientists, philosophers and psychoanalysts, to link theoretical issues of destruction with actual instances of destruction taking place in society, in science as well as art (ill.108). As a result DIAS necessarily threw its net wide, taking in 'atmospheric pollution, creative vandalism, destruction in protest, planned obsolescence, popular media, urban sprawl/over-crowding, war ... biology, economics, medicine,

108
Seventh session of the three-day 'Destruction in Art' (DIAS) symposium, 11 September 1966: 'Reading of Texts from their Publications'. On the podium, left to right: Gustav Metzger (chair), Wolf Vostell, Al Hansen, Juan Hidalgo.
Photograph by Tom Picton
Tate Archive

physics, psychology, sociology, space research.'[17] Even so, despite this ambition, the majority of the contributors to DIAS were artists, and the event's continuing significance can be recognised in the extent to which it provides a marker for an art that categorically rejected the objectified image in favour of the dynamics of the event, and by so doing underscored a multifaceted engagement with social and political forces. The three-day symposium and the month-long sequence of related events were as a result freewheeling in both the scope and diverse range of approaches to destruction that were presented.

Within an understanding of iconoclasm, DIAS stands at a mid-century pivot point where a shift occurs from iconoclasm being carried through as the result of political, social or religious beliefs and towards iconoclasm being defined as an artistic or aesthetic strategy. However, within DIAS many of the participants pursued destruction as a strategy that even so embodied engagement with political or social issues. But just as Metzger was not in the strict sense an iconoclast (he did not destroy art), similarly, DIAS was not the Destruction *Of* Art Symposium but the Destruction *In* Art Symposium. Nevertheless, in his close identification of auto-destructive art with his political and social activism and beliefs, Metzger's theories and work can indeed be associated with the motivating principle behind iconoclasm, even though art objects are never wilfully destroyed. This paradox was signposted by the front cover of the August 1966 issue of the magazine *Art & Artists*. Devoted to auto-destructive art and published the month before DIAS, its cover bore an image of Velázquez's *Rokeby Venus*, its protecting glass smashed and the canvas cut into and ripped by a meat cleaver, following Mary Richardson's attack on it on 10 March 1914 in

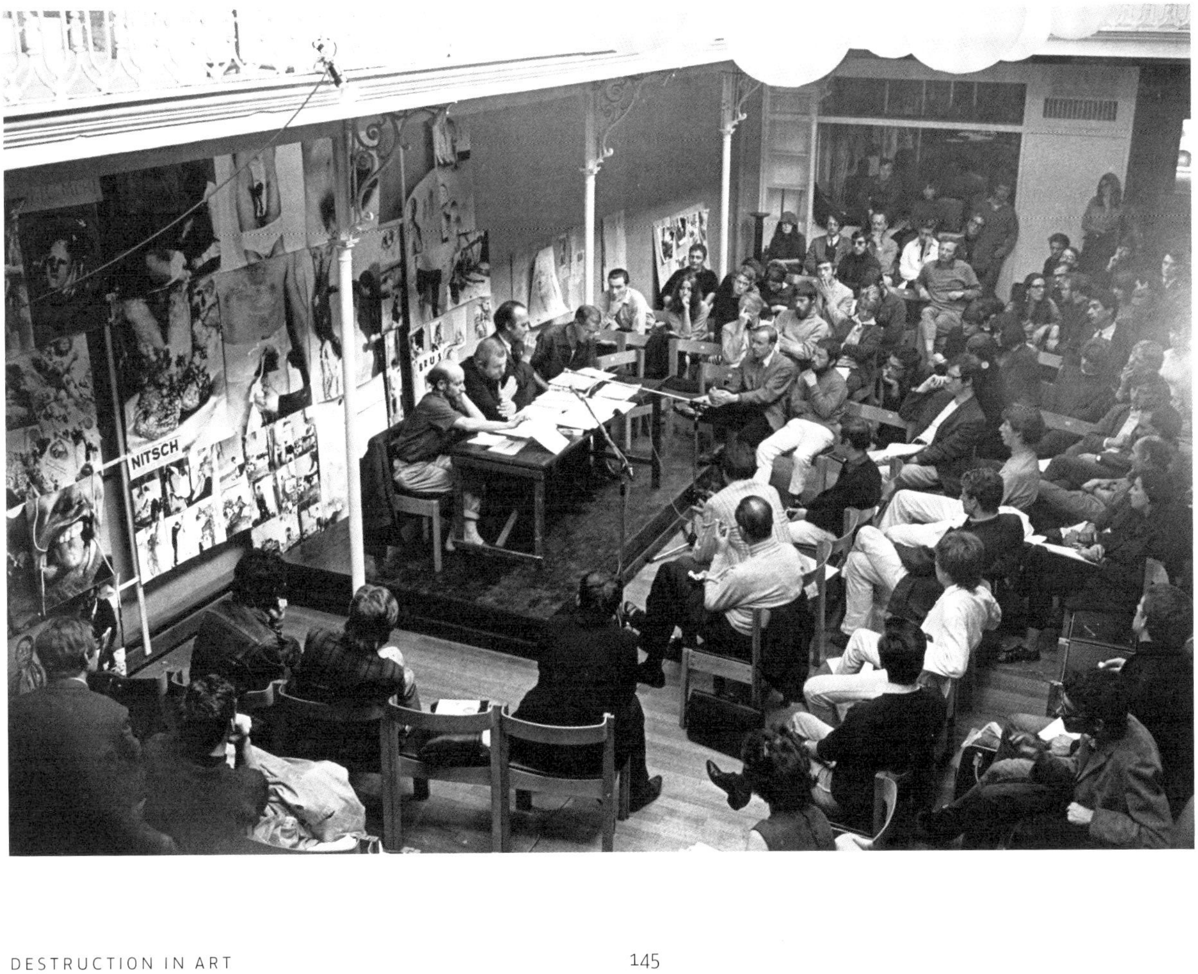

South Africa, or Vietnam, or perhaps Watts. 'Burn, baby, burn', the chants reverberate and engulf one's mind as Stravinsky's chords in the *Rite of Spring*. All is flame and movement. A mad tango. A medieval smell.[25]

Berke's incantation was born of his experience treating schizophrenia in ways that erased the boundaries between patient and doctor, as regression stimulates the search for productive catharsis. For the Viennese Institute of Direct Art – newly formed by Brus, Mühl, Nitsch, filmmaker Kurt Kren and critic Peter Weibel – the unlocking of repression, the confrontation with taboos and the triggering of cathartic response underpinned their actions and use of destructive forces within them. Brus took himself to the limit in his solitary 'Self-Mutilation Actions' – both physically and mentally, whether repeatedly banging his head on the lectern in front of him in *Head Destruction* or jumping up and down with Mühl in *Breath Exercises*. However, his close collaboration with Mühl exchanged his solitary material aestheticism for an interaction between the artists taking part that also served to break down barriers with the audience. Actions such as *Vietnamparty* 1966, just prior to DIAS, or *Ten Rounds for Cassius Clay* performed in London, met sexual taboo head-on and confronted political orthodoxies.

Nitsch was engaged in similar confrontations, although his actions were more ritualised in construction. For his *21st Action*, the crucifixion of an eviscerated lamb was juxtaposed with a film projection of a man's penis being manipulated by strings over a cow's brain. This matrix of degradation and taboo ultimately led the police to charge both Metzger and his fellow DIAS organiser John Sharkey with indecency.

The presence of Yoko Ono offered a direct contrast to the aggression and excess of the Viennese and many of the other participants in DIAS – almost all of

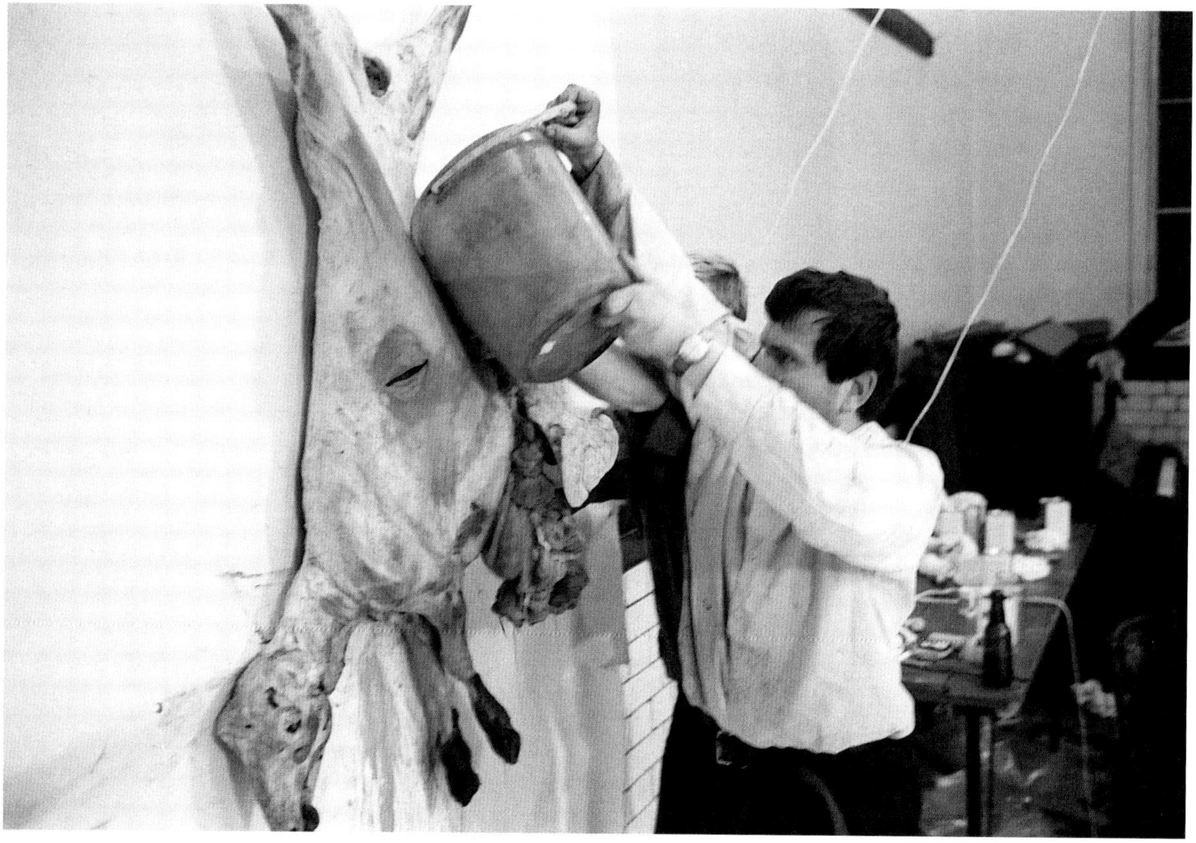

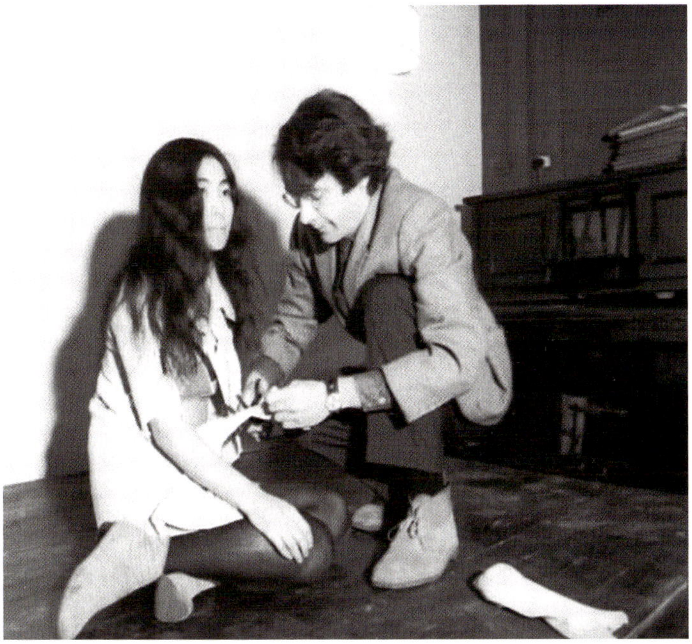

111
Still from a film showing Yoko Ono performing *Cut Piece* with Anthony Cox, part of *Two Evenings with Yoko Ono*, 28 and 29 September 1966, at the Africa Centre.
British Pathé Ltd

112
Fragment of the Biba dress worn by Yoko Ono for *Cut Piece* 1966
Tate Archive

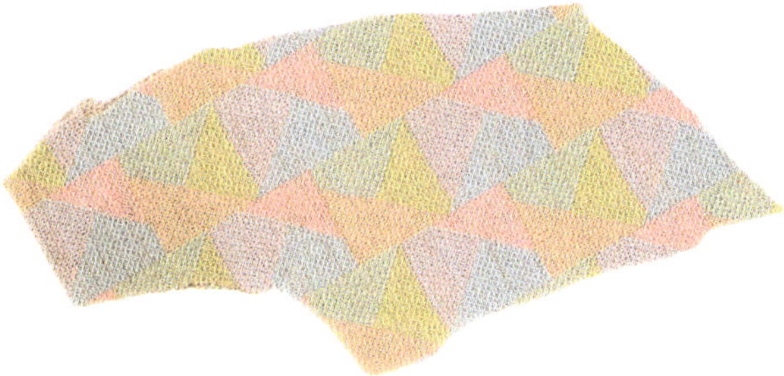

whom were men. The quiet and reflective composure with which Ono sat down and waited for members of the audience to cut off her clothes in *Cut Piece* (ills 111, 112) recalled the manner in which the Vietnamese nun had calmly set herself alight after fellow Buddhists had 'reverently emptied the contents of an American five-gallon jerry can of gasoline' over her.[26] *Cut Piece* brought together the fragility of human existence with the capacity for violence of each audience member just as much with their capacity to do nothing and watch. Equally, the manner in which she drew the outlines around the prone bodies of fellow artists who lay down on a sheet spread over the waste ground of the Free School Playground (a bomb site) directly recalled the imprint of victims of the Hiroshima and Nagasaki bombs. Ono was the embodiment of Fluxus at DIAS, a grouping of artists who, though they drew their inspiration from a pranksterish vaudevillian outlook, had a serious intent that was made clear by the presentation of George Maciunas' statement for DIAS at the start of the symposium. Entitled *USA Surpasses all the Genocide Records!* 1966, it comprised an image of an American flag overprinted with text comparing proportions of people killed by Kublai Khan, Stalin, the Nazis and America: 'America Massacres 6.5% of South Vietnamese & 75% of American Indians'.

John Latham's use of destruction in his works was not so much to reflect social or political issues as to indicate the scientific theories of creation that he was evolving. For Latham, destruction only formed one aspect of his work. The events he presented for DIAS – the burning down by incendiary devices of a number of 'Skoob' towers (Babel-like towers with books attached to a metal armature; ills 113, 114) and *Film*, in which participants moved around 'dressed' in 'soft skoobs' – question the grammar of knowledge and known reality,

110
Herman Nitsch (b.1935)
21st Action: OM Theatre (5th Abreaktionsspiel)
performed at St Bride Institute 16 September 1966
Photograph by Tom Picton
Tate Archive

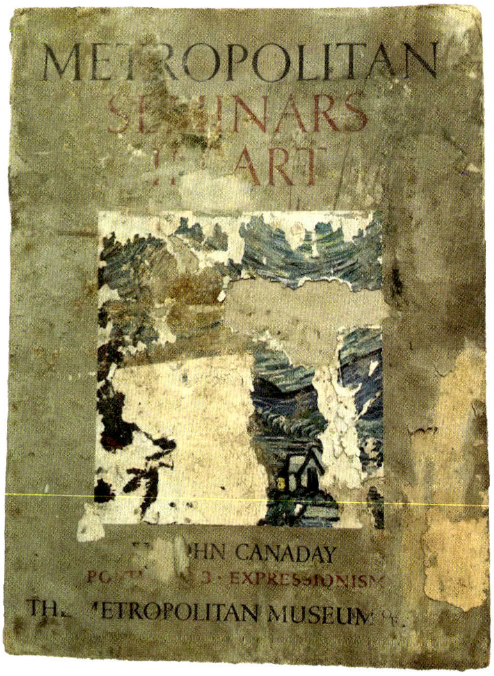

113
John Latham (1921–2006)
Partially burnt copy of *Metropolitan Seminars in Art*, a fragment remaining from a Skoob Tower Ceremony enacted during the Destruction in Art Symposium 1966
25 × 33 × 1.5
John Latham Foundation

114
John Latham (1921–2006)
Skoob Tower Ceremony: National Encyclopedias, Bloomsbury
24 September 1966
Photograph by John Prosser
John Latham Foundation

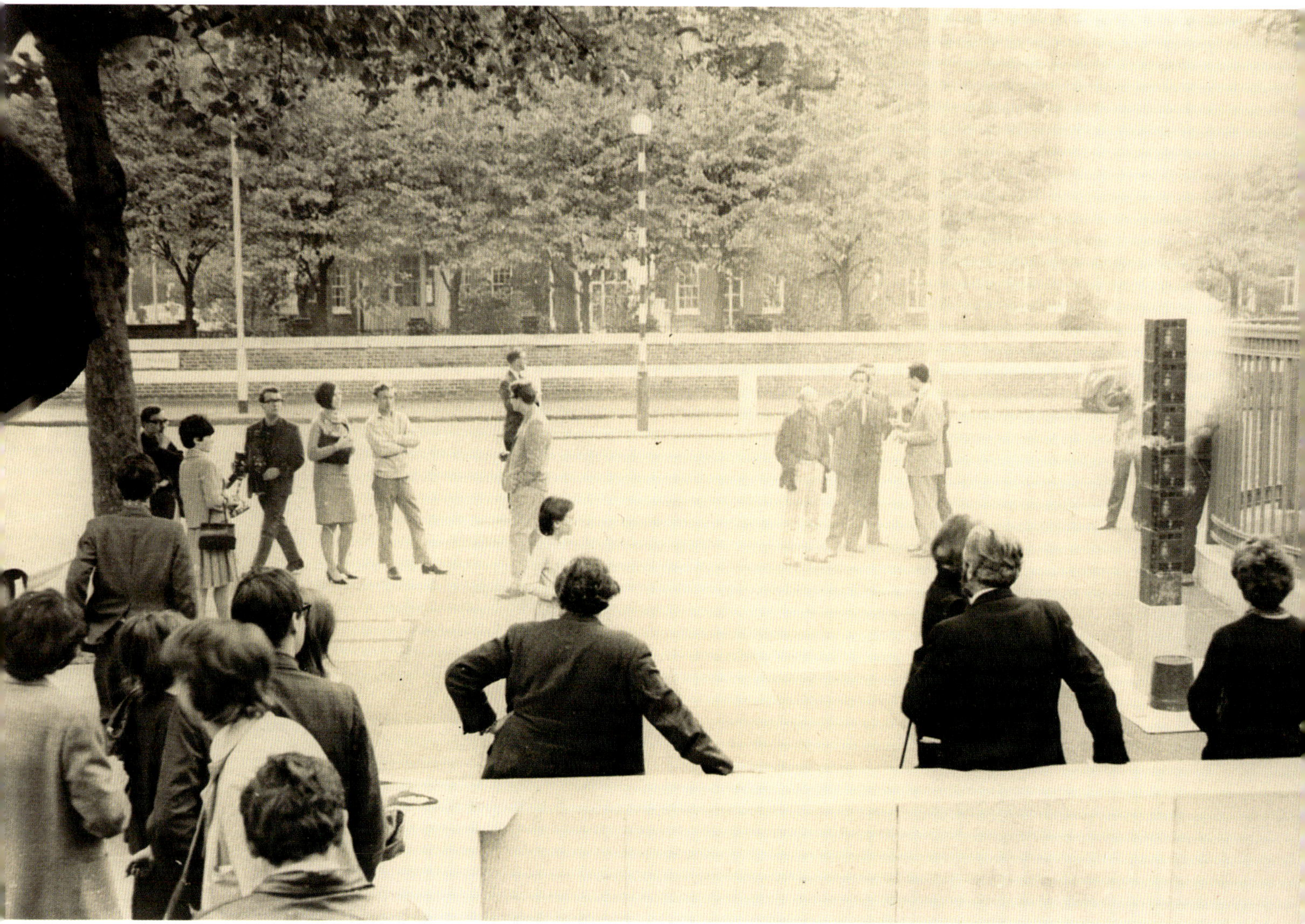

showing it to constitute a dislocated and artificial set of untruths. Underpinning this was Latham's obsession with the determining metaphysics of time. For a writer like Trocchi, the 'destruction of the object' meant breaking the structure of orthodox literary narrative by prioritising space over time. Latham took the opposite approach in his work. He was less preoccupied with the notion of destruction as with the invalidation or dematerialisation of objects in favour of processes of cognition carried out in time rather than locked in space. A previously accepted understanding of knowledge and its status, for which books stand as metaphorical and actual containers, was questioned and dismantled, with the realisation that the languages by which we live our lives evolve and function through time, even though this might often be denied in their form and appearance as a collection of words or images.

In this respect Latham is, however, close to the other half of Metzger's theories of auto-destructive art: being an auto-creative art. This aspect also connects with these artists' need to realise the world – as a set of changing entities – within their work. And this, in turn, is the basis of the work of Mark Boyle and Joan Hills, whose events effectively opened and closed DIAS. Boyle and Hills emphasised that their work aimed to express a totality of existence, rather than just isolate destruction. With DIAS in mind, Boyle wrote: 'I don't think I'm especially interested in "destruction in art". I'm interested in destruction as an aspect of everything ... Things are created and survive only by the destruction of other things.'[27]

For the launch of DIAS, Boyle and Hills presented *Son et Lumière for Insects, Reptiles and Water Creatures*. This was the second such event in a trilogy that aimed to show the elements of the world; the creatures that live in the air, earth and water; and the workings of the human body and its functions, 'aware that whether we watch or not the process of destruction/creation continues everywhere in our universe and in ourselves'.[28] For the closing event of DIAS they presented a slide projection sequence of portraits of DIAS participants and their accompanying events. Each slide was incinerated by the heat of the projector's lamp so that, one by one, the image of each DIAS artist was destroyed on screen (ill.115). Thus Boyle and Hills were not only throwing the issue of destruction back in the faces of their fellow artists (themselves included), but also criticising the fact that the personality and ego of the artist was often reflected in the presentation of such event-based work. For them, as for Metzger, the dialogue of creation/destruction was an inherent process that had little to do with artistic posturing and much more to do with a change of perception: that 'the most complete change an individual can effect in his environment, short of destroying it, is to change his attitude to it'.[29]

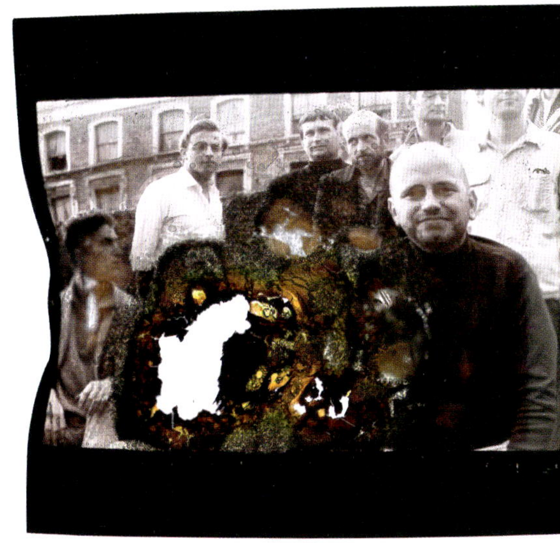

115
Boyle Family
Melted slide from 'Projections'
1966, printed 2013
Photograph, colour print on paper (from a melted slide)
109 × 84
The Boyle Family

From left to right: Peter Weibel, Ferdi Bonnomi, Jean-Jacques Lebel (foreground, in front of Bonnomi), Hermann Nitsch, Gutsav Metzger, Kurt Kren, Otto Mühl (behind Kren), Ivor Davies

Raphael Montañez Ortiz' *Duncan Terrace Piano Destruction Concert*: *The Landesmans' Homage to 'Spring can really hang you up the most'*

> The rest of us were holding ropes lowering the piano down to the basement when it rolled up on end and got stuck about a third way down the steps between the steps and the ceiling … I announced there is an aesthetic reason why the piano chose to be stuck there. The stairwell will act as a funnel projecting the sound with amplification into the basement. The first hit of the axe proved my theory, the sound resonated as I have never heard before, and in addition to the drama of the sound, the sounds of pieces of the piano, which would otherwise however far they flew just land on the floor, played a much more dramatic role in the sound of the concert as they tumbled down the steps in an orchestration with the piano's amplified sound of resonating strings … With a final axe swing the harp came loose and tumbled down the stairs, I remember standing the harp of the piano up, tilting it out of the pile of splintered wood that was once its art nouveau façade, bits and pieces of axe-sliced black and white piano keys were scattered everywhere I looked.[30]

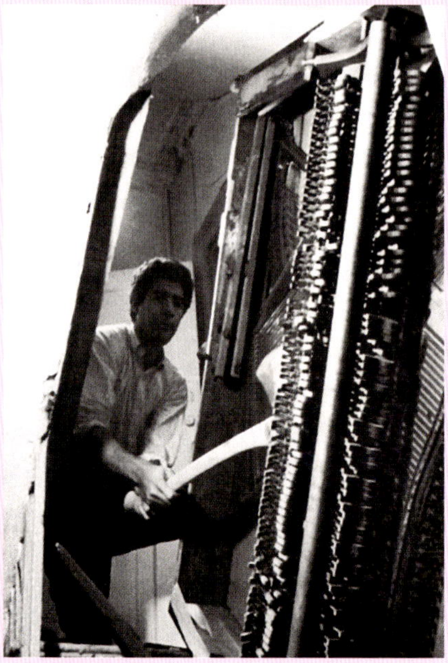

116
Raphael Montañez Ortiz (b.1934)
Duncan Terrace Piano Destruction Concert 1966
Photograph by John Prosser

Raphael Montañez Ortiz's own account of the *Duncan Terrace Piano Destruction Concert* is dramatic. The relatively short sacrifice ritual was intense and concentrated, its violence a contrast to the instruction he had given prior to the event to Jay and Fran Landesman, the piano's owners, to ensure that it be tuned. This contrast underpinned the marriage of the different potentialities of destruction and creation or violence and aesthetics within Ortiz's work. His attention to the harmonics of sound made through the process of destruction or 'un-making' – for this event the sound was recorded – provided one aspect of the redemptive power of this destruction concert.[31]

Invited to participate in DIAS (Destruction In Art Symposium; see p.144) on 9–11 September 1966, Ortiz was one of the first artists to arrive in London at the end of August in order to arrange his contributions to the symposium and the events that would continue through September. The first of his staged ritual events was one of DIAS's first – a chair destruction ritual for the symposium's initial press conference. Reports of that event – visceral and dislocating for the viewer – set the tone for public response to DIAS in terms of shock and outrage.

It may well be that Ortiz first encountered the American expatriate writer Jay Landesman at that press conference, as Landesman was to write about DIAS for the underground newspaper *International Times*.[32] Sometime

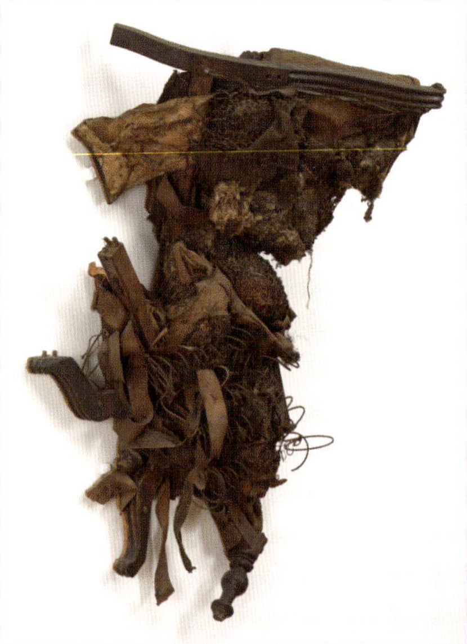

117
Raphael Montañez Ortiz (b.1934)
Duncan Terrace Chair Destruction 1966
Wood, metal and fabric
124.5 × 83.8
Accepted by HM Government in lieu of tax and awaiting permanent allocation

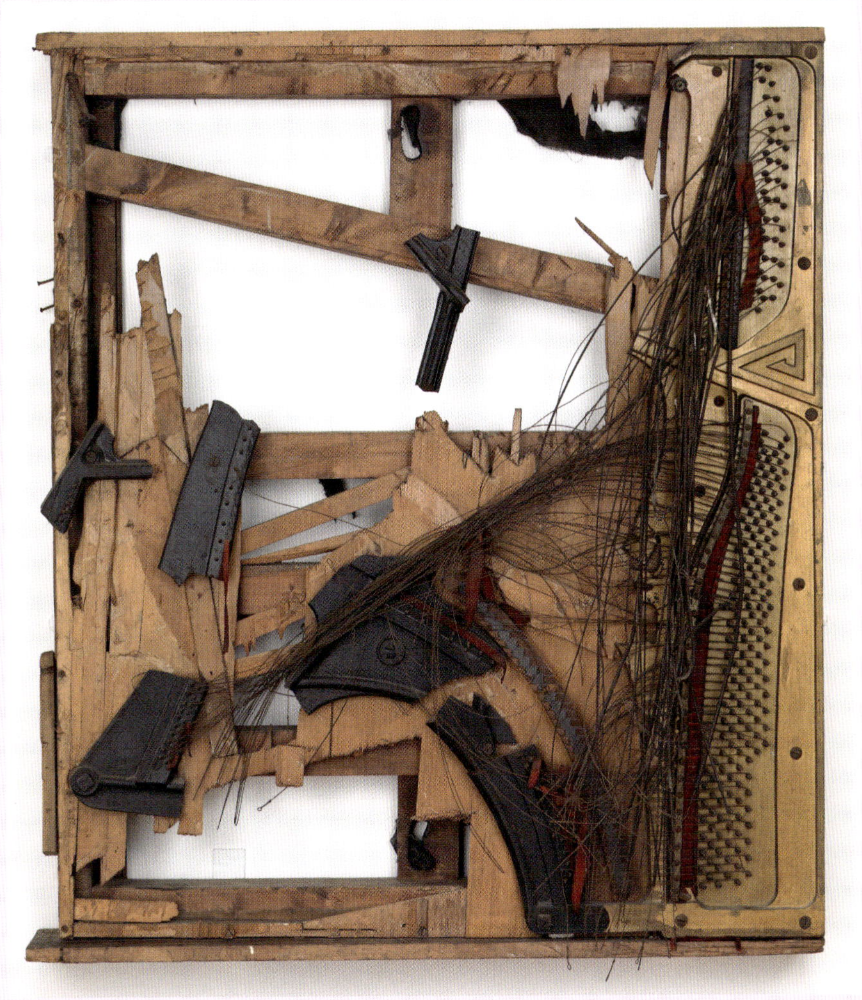

118
Raphael Montañez Ortiz (b.1934)
Duncan Terrace Piano Destruction Concert: The Landesmans' Homage to 'Spring can really hang you up the most' 1966
Wood and metal
142.2 × 124.7
Accepted by HM Government in lieu of tax and awaiting permanent allocation

in mid-September Ortiz arranged to carry out a piano destruction concert as well as two other destruction events (*Duncan Terrace Mattress Destruction*, which no longer exists, and *Duncan Terrace Chair Destruction*, ill.117) at his Islington home. During the last week of September Ortiz carried out the chair and mattress destructions, and though the piano destruction concert had been planned to take place at the same time, it was delayed until 10 October when it could be carried out in front of an invited audience, including two curators from the Tate Gallery (Ronald Alley and Richard Morphet) and a photographer (John Prosser). The piano was one that Fran Landesman had used to compose a number of her popular musicals, including the hit for which she wrote the words *Spring Can Really Hang You Up The Most* 1955, as well as the lyrics for her husband's recent comedy musical, *Dearest Dracula* 1965. This was the third piano destruction concert that Ortiz had created for DIAS, the other two having been filmed respectively by the BBC (for which the 'wrong piano'[33] was unfortunately destroyed) and ABC.

For Ortiz the experience of DIAS encouraged a shift not only in his attitude to destruction, but also in the way he approached his work. Prior to DIAS his work had been constructed in a studio or otherwise controlled conditions; the symposium encouraged him to engage directly with audiences and conceive of his work as equally ritualised event staged for a public and sculptural end result – both states having communicative power and significance. Its meaning was grasped through its symbolism: Ortiz was not blurring the boundaries between art and life (there being a difference between destruction as part of an art practice and destruction enacted in life or society). Nevertheless, where the symbolism of his pre-DIAS sculptures was the result of an interiorised process derived in part from the language of action painting, his destruction rituals at and after DIAS looked outwards to connect with wider social concern. This was emphasised in his second manifesto of 'Destructivism', circulated at DIAS, where he states:

> It is generally understood that destruction is essential to the nature of things and that without it nothing could be. Destruction is built into our species. If we could not destroy we would not survive for one moment. Our species destroys in the most fundamental sense to live, we destroy in the more human sense to realize ourselves. Our lungs destroy, our blood destroys, our stomachs destroy. We slaughter cattle, cut down forests and smash atoms all in order to be.[34]

AW

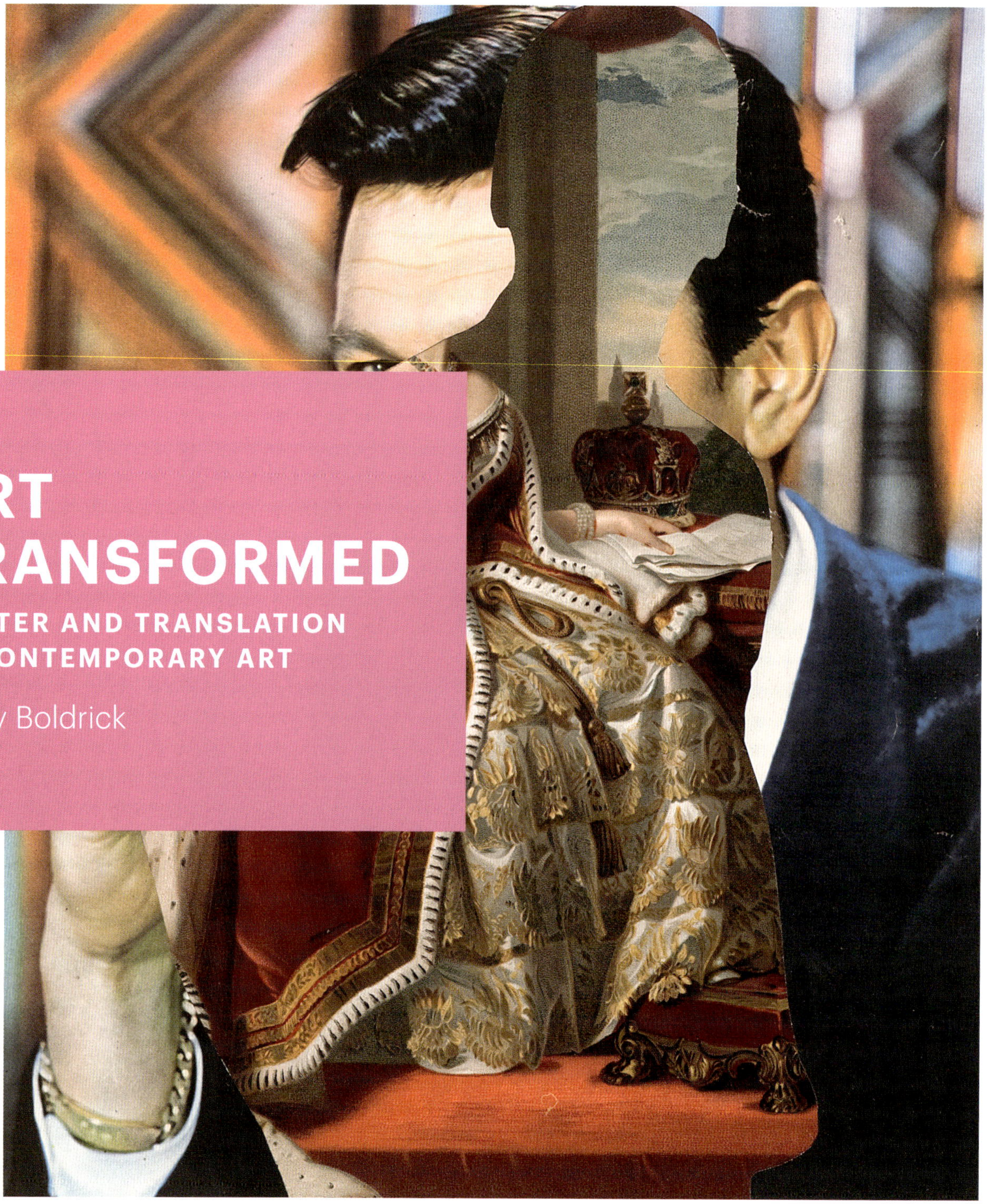

8
ART TRANSFORMED
MATTER AND TRANSLATION IN CONTEMPORARY ART

Stacy Boldrick

You can't shine if you don't burn.
(Kevin Ayers) [1]

Fire is one of the most primal and magical tools of the iconoclast, a sign in itself, associated with celebrations and reverie, purification and punishment. It is also the most deadly. In the words of the philosopher Gaston Bachelard, 'It shines in Paradise. It burns in Hell.'[2]

The curator Francis McKee cites Bachelard in order to explore the contradictory double-edged nature of Douglas Gordon's series of works entitled *Self-Portrait of You + Me*, made from burned posters of Andy Warhol prints. McKee approaches the series and Gordon's practice through the lens of the Reformation, particularly the image wars of the 1520s to 1560s, proposing that we might see in his work 'a faint trace of the aftershock'.[3] Gordon agrees that the works are 'in part a homage and in part a desecration' to and of Warhol, not unlike Mark Boyle's and Joan Hills' burning slides that were part of the performance at the end of the Destruction In Art Symposium (DIAS) in September 1966, an image of which is included in this survey (ill.115).[4] If left to burn out completely, both the slides and the posters would be lost to oblivion. Yet in both cases, the artists' control over the fire and their preservation of the material (the saving of the remains) retains enough visual material for each to be recognisable: images are fragments, defaced and scarred, but not obliterated.

As Andrew Wilson explains in Chapter 7, artists associated with DIAS championed destruction *in* art, not the destruction *of* art, but the destruction *in* and *of* art have both come to loom large in art today. The selection of contemporary work presented here is not a comprehensive survey of iconoclasm in modern and contemporary practice, but rather a small sampling largely concentrating on figuration and the body – and is confined to artists based in Britain. Perhaps surprisingly, the selection focuses neither solely on the erased or unseen in art, nor on the appropriation of other artworks.[5] Rather, the artworks all share similar exploratory attitudes to materials, the subversion of images and an understanding of their capacity to defy understanding: all are visual and physical responses to images that generate new works. There are no features associated with iconoclasm in contemporary British art to distinguish it as a movement. Unlike most of the other sections in the present survey, this form of iconoclasm does not align with a historical period of iconoclasm or political group in Britain. The international foundations of iconoclasm in modern and contemporary art provide a background to the selection of works by artists who come from or have come to be based in Britain, and to the inclusion of their works into this survey.

Calls for the destruction of the art of the past and its replacement with the art of the present and future came early in the nineteenth century, to be cultivated by later philosophers such as Nietzsche.[6] In twentieth-century manifestos the futurists, constructivists, vorticists and dada all championed the deliberate destruction of art and architecture. In 1934 Picasso described his paintings not as a 'sum of additions' but rather 'a sum of destructions'.[7] The legacy of aesthetic practices that incorporate acts of destruction or the destructive transformation of art or images is substantial, integral to the avant-garde, and part of the critical foundations of modernity.[8] Icons of modernist iconoclasm include Marcel Duchamp's readymades and Robert Rauschenberg's *Erased de Kooning Drawing* 1953, discussed in Chapter 6. The rise in visibility of image breaking and destruction in early twentieth-century and postwar art can certainly be understood as a response to the rise of the artwork as an autonomous object, but it should also be understood in relation to larger historical changes, ranging from the development of weapons of mass destruction during the First and Second World Wars to the devastated cities and landscapes of the postwar period and the fears of nuclear devastation brought by the Cold War.[9]

Destruction in Britain before and after the World Wars affected artists in different ways. As war artists Paul Nash and John Piper's work was dissimilar, with Nash taking on subjects such as aerial views and aeroplane-littered landscapes such as *Totes Meer (Dead Sea)* 1940–1 and Piper depicting bombed buildings, as in *St Mary le Port Bristol* 1940. By the 1950s artists associated with the Independent Group, such as Richard Hamilton, Nigel Henderson and Eduardo Paolozzi, who were concerned with exploring all material in contemporary culture as 'found', made collage and assemblage important elements of their practice.[10] By the end of that decade Stuart Brisley was using collage and assemblage to make works such as *Untitled* c.1960 out of reclaimed building materials that were then attacked; by the end of the 1960s he began to dedicate himself to performance, using his body to capture the 'morbid symptoms' of capitalist culture'.[11]

In the same year, outside Britain another strand of destruction in art was developing. Jean Tinguely, a Swiss artist who made kinetic sculptures such as *Machine for Breaking Sculpture* 1960, attracted international attention with the performance of his large-scale self-destructing sculpture *Homage to New York* in the sculpture garden of The Museum of Modern Art in New York. On 17 March 1960 *Homage* whirred into action and caught fire; Tinguely stopped the performance when the fire became dangerous. The work was destroyed but a film and other documentary imagery survive: its loss made the work all the more visible. The artist Michael Landy came to know about Tinguely's work through its remains.[12] He wanted to try to make another version of *Homage to New York*, sourcing as many original fragments as he could, because Tinguely's 'failed to fail'.[13] Landy's drawings depict the sculpture at rest and in explosive action. His drawing H.2.N.Y. *If the saw saws the saw and if the saw which saws the saw which saws the saw there is a metallic suicide Marcel Duchamp* 2007 (ill.119) takes its title from Marcel Duchamp's written response to Tinguely's *Homage*, a dada-esque play on words referencing Tinguely's Swiss nationality: the self-destructing sculpture is a 'Suissecide' or 'Swiss-icide'.[14]

Landy may be best known for *Break Down* 2001, an artwork consisting of the destruction of all of his material possessions. He conducted his project neither with fire nor uncontrollable force, but rather through an orderly, systematic process of sorting and dismantling, complete with conveyer belts, disposal machines and administration. Based in a former C&A store, *Break Down* set into reverse the automotive actions of production and consumption. Throwing away things may be an unconscious act, but sending into oblivion all of one's possessions (7,227 of them in Landy's case) – including works of art – is a profound act of anti-consumerism, a negation of material life. As with Tinguely's *Homage*, nothing remained from *Break Down* apart from documentation: an inventory, publications, a short film and drawings.[15] Yet *Break Down*'s invisibility, its lack of any relic or tangible object underscores its status as a work of art more powerful than what was destroyed. Much of Landy's work is grounded in the idea that 'the pleasure of consumption can lie in its destruction', and it is this attitude to material things that links his work with Gustav Metzger, auto-destructive art and the DIAS artists (see chapter 7).[16]

Shock and controversy are inherent in iconoclasm, although it does not always relate to damaging images.[17] The example offered by the

119
Michael Landy (b.1963)
H.2.N.Y. If the saw saws the saw and if the saw which saws the saw which saws the saw there is a metallic suicide Marcel Duchamp 2007
Oil stick on paper
122 × 152.5
Courtesy the artist and Thomas Dane Gallery, London

activities of the Situationist International through the late 1950s and 1960s, or by those artists who gathered for DIAS in 1966, reveals how transgressive acts of destruction and aggression moved from the sphere of the visual arts into music and the wider cultural field. By 1977 Jamie Reid's design for the Sex Pistols' single *God Save the Queen* shattered royal symbols and bondage trousers changed the way people walked.[18] Out of the ethos of punk came films like Derek Jarman's *Jubilee* 1978, made in the wake of the Queen's Silver Jubilee, set in the postwar ruins of London and full of violent, nihilistic acts, equivocally breaking and remaking images, literally and metaphorically – from defacing images in books to subverting 'Rule Britannia'. In art galleries, abject, used or ruined materials and transgressive representations of female bodies were seized upon by the press as controversial stories. Reports on Mary Kelly's 1976 exhibition *Post Partum Project* focused on the faecal stains in nappies rather than on her feminist work; at the ICA exhibition *Prostitution*, blood-stained tampons were the newsworthy item from COUM Transmissions, along with their extreme performances.[19]

Such moments of literal and metaphorical image breaking informed the art that was to follow. Unlike much of the art discussed in Chapter 7, the destructive act itself is most often not the work of art: destruction is used to transform or translate an image or artwork into something else, a new creation that generates new meanings.

The field of contemporary iconoclasm takes a broad range of forms. Most of these artists start with a reproduction or mass-produced image, although some start with original works of art, editing, degrading, dismantling or dematerialising and reusing the material; many artists explore the nature of the materiality of the work. They are

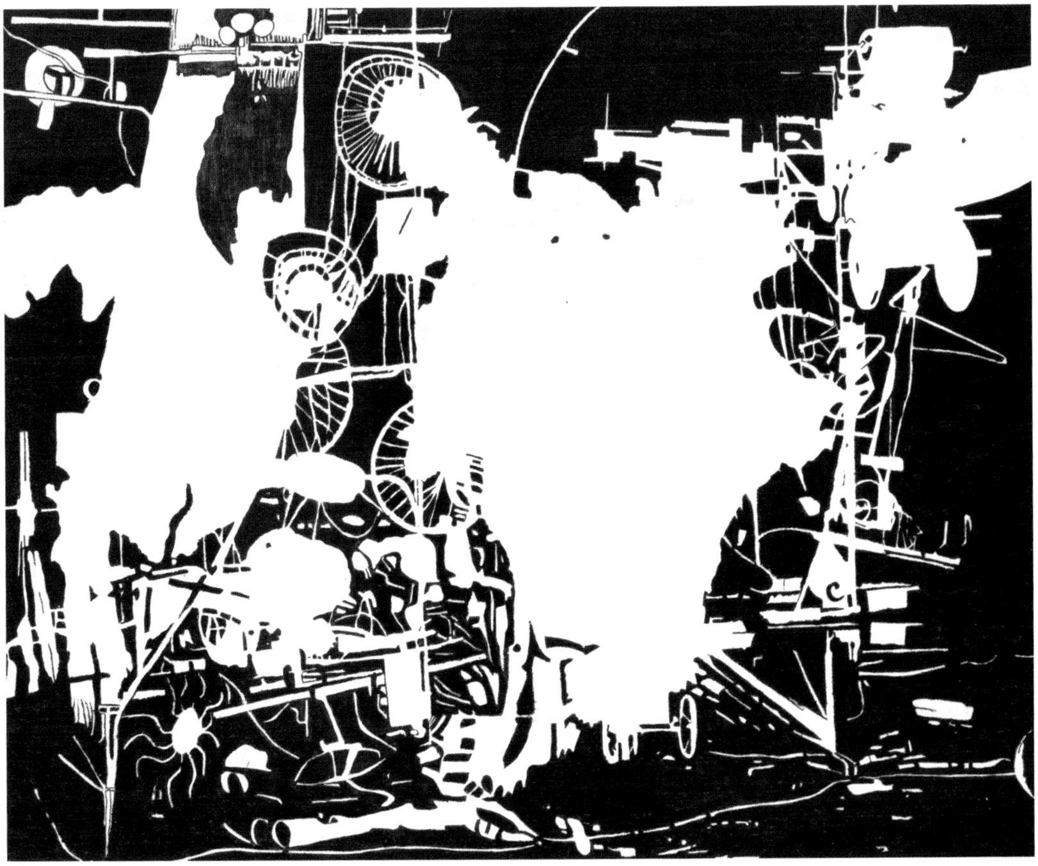

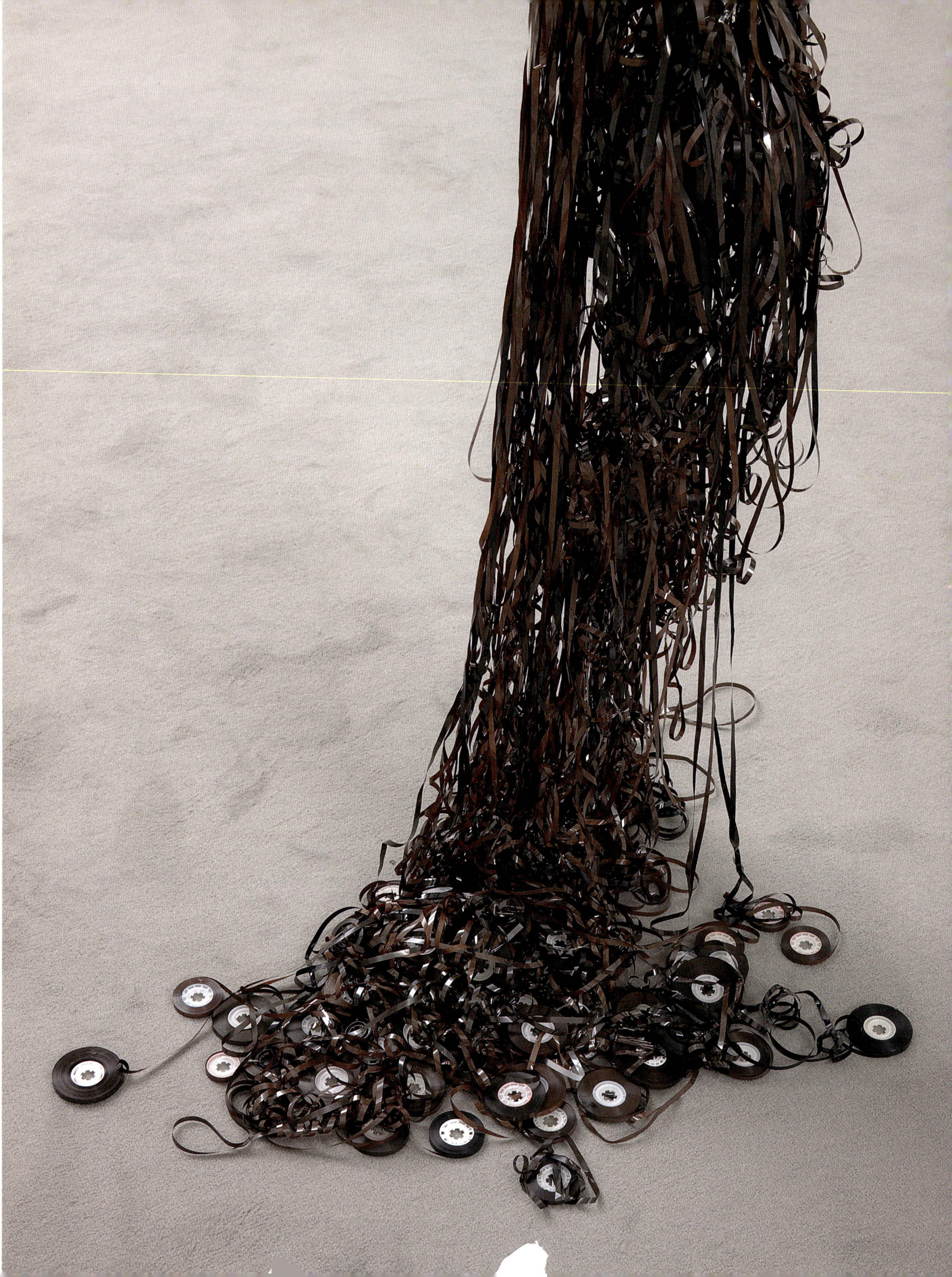

against a Paolozzi sculpture, implying that the viewer has the opportunity to be an iconoclast. His understanding of the artwork as capable of taking on the projections of the viewer is visible throughout his practice. In *Feature Film* 1999 he separated the imagery of Hitchcock's *Vertigo* from a filmed performance of the film's score; in *Domestic (as long as it lasts)* 2002, a video camera films as it is kicked around a flat until its view pixellates into dissolution. In his installation *30 Seconds Text* 1996 Gordon uses illumination and darkness to obscure and reveal a text about decapitation and the last moments of consciousness.

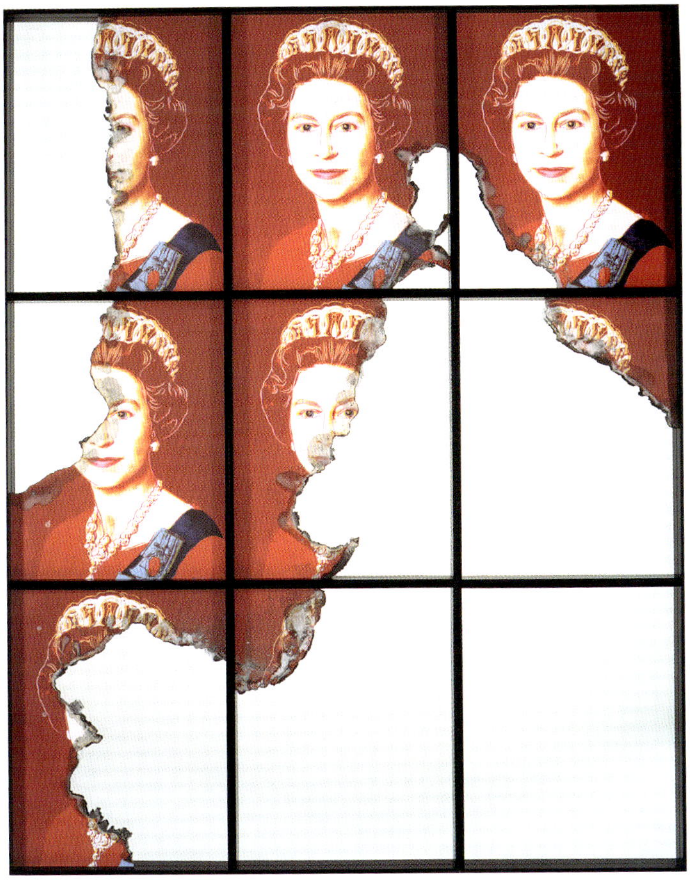

121
Michael Wilkinson (b.1965)
Untitled 2009
Audiotape
Courtesy the artist and The Modern Institute / Toby Webster Ltd., Glasgow

122
Douglas Gordon (b.1966)
Self-Portrait of You + Me (9 piece QEII) 2008
Smoke and mirror 253.2 × 203.4 × 5 (framed)
Courtesy the artist and Gagosian Gallery

In his series *Self-Portrait of You + Me*, Gordon's listing of his materials as 'smoke and mirror' deflect from the everyday materials of poster, mirror and glass, along with the other materials he used, including candles, a blowtorch, blood, sugar, flour and eggs.[32] For his earlier series, *Blind Stars* 2002, he cut out the eyes in photographs of Hollywood icons and replaced them with white or black paper or mirror, an attempt to kill the image staring back at the viewer.[33] In *Self-Portrait of You + Me (9-piece QEII)* 2008 (ill.122) he takes this still further. The burnt edges of eight posters of Warhol's screenprints of the Queen are presented with mirrors behind them to capture the reflections of the viewer and animate the image so that the viewer's projection – the image returning the gaze – becomes the work. Burning bestows an effect of violence on ordinary materials like a poster. Its iconoclasm may be seen as political, aesthetic and material in form: the image of the Queen is regarded as an icon and Warhol's image of her is iconic. The posters survive in varying states of devastation: two are nearly whole, but others have been almost completely destroyed, now only reflecting other images. Likewise, in smaller works such as *Self-Portrait of You + Me (Roger Daltrey)* 2007, icon and viewer coalesce, with the Christological pose and fragmented body harking back to broken medieval images of Christ.[34]

The fragmented and remade body is central to John Stezaker's work. In *Third Person* 1988–90 (ill.123) three images come together in one: an image of the British film star Laurence Harvey, a portrait of Queen Victoria by Franz Xaver Winterhalter, and a distorted silhouette of another figure. Any of these could be the 'third person' of the title.[35] Stezaker's *Untitled* 1989 and *Mask XIV* 2006 (ill.124) are from the series begun in the early 1980s, *Masks*, which combine a photographic 'film portrait' with a postcard obscuring the face, often featuring an opening such as a cave, a grotto or a ruined gateway. In discussing his work Stezaker has spoken of his admiration for Elias Canetti and Maurice Blanchot's ideas of 'image death' or 'death's space', where he 'sees it [his work] as a series of deaths that the image has to go through in order to become visible and disconnected from its ordinary referent'.[36]

Mark Wallinger's *Via Dolorosa* 2002 (ill.125) features the almost complete obscuring of part of Franco Zeffirelli's film *Jesus of Nazareth* 1977. The view of the action is moved digitally from the centre to the edges, blacking out 90 per cent of the image and restricting the view to a narrow rectangular strip. The *Via Dolorosa*, or the way of grief, is the path Christ took to his cruxificion and death; the ending of Christ's life is also the climax of Zeffirelli's film featured in Wallinger's work. Without sound or a central focus the narrative becomes incomprehensible: robed figures, distant, blurred faces, sky, and the edges of a cross can just be made out. The artist has spoken about being struck by the beauty of Zeffirelli's imagery but also about being interested in 'how we become attuned to cinematic language in a way that's probably akin to how people used to read devotional paintings'.[37] Inevitably, *Via Dolorosa* generates a particular meaning for the individual viewer: it addresses the relationship between religious belief and the lack of it, and suggests the inaccessibility of spirituality. As Martin Herbert suggests, 'One might not only recognize our deep affiliation to a specific religion but also have a melancholy sense of something blocked or

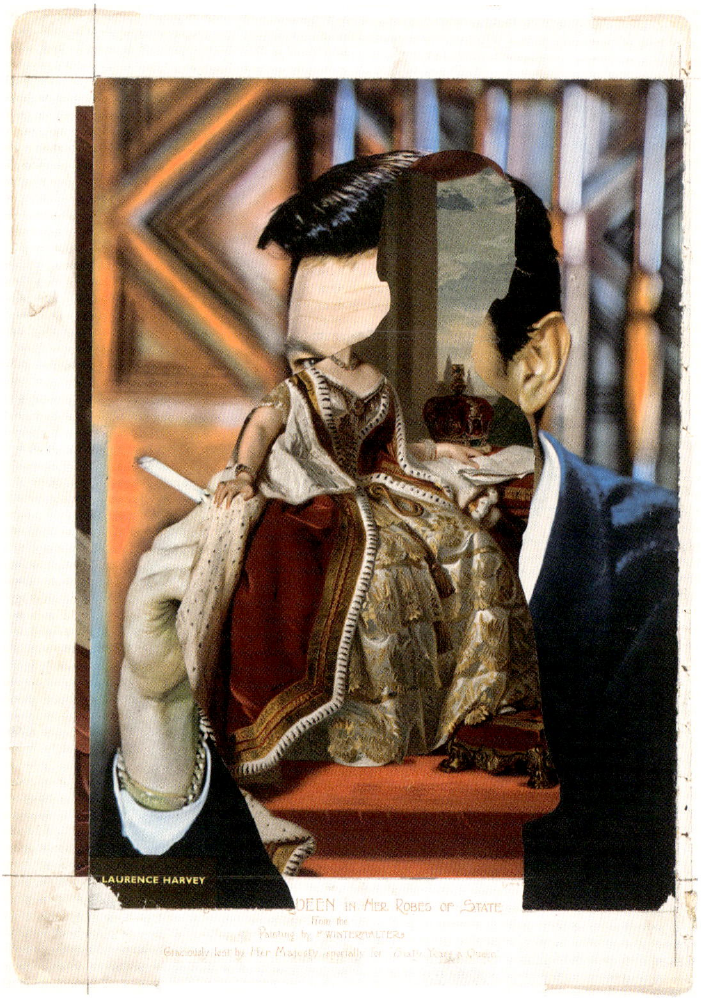

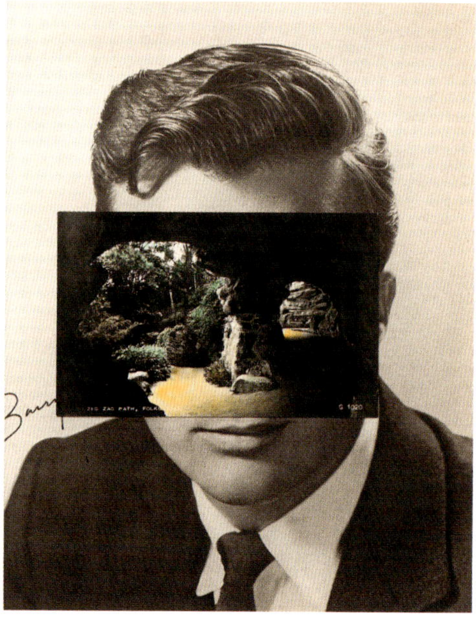

123
John Stezaker (b.1949)
Third Person 1988–9
Photo-etching on paper and printed paper
27 × 20
Tate

124
John Stezaker (b.1949)
Mask XIV 2006
Photo-etching and postcard on paper
24 × 20
Tate

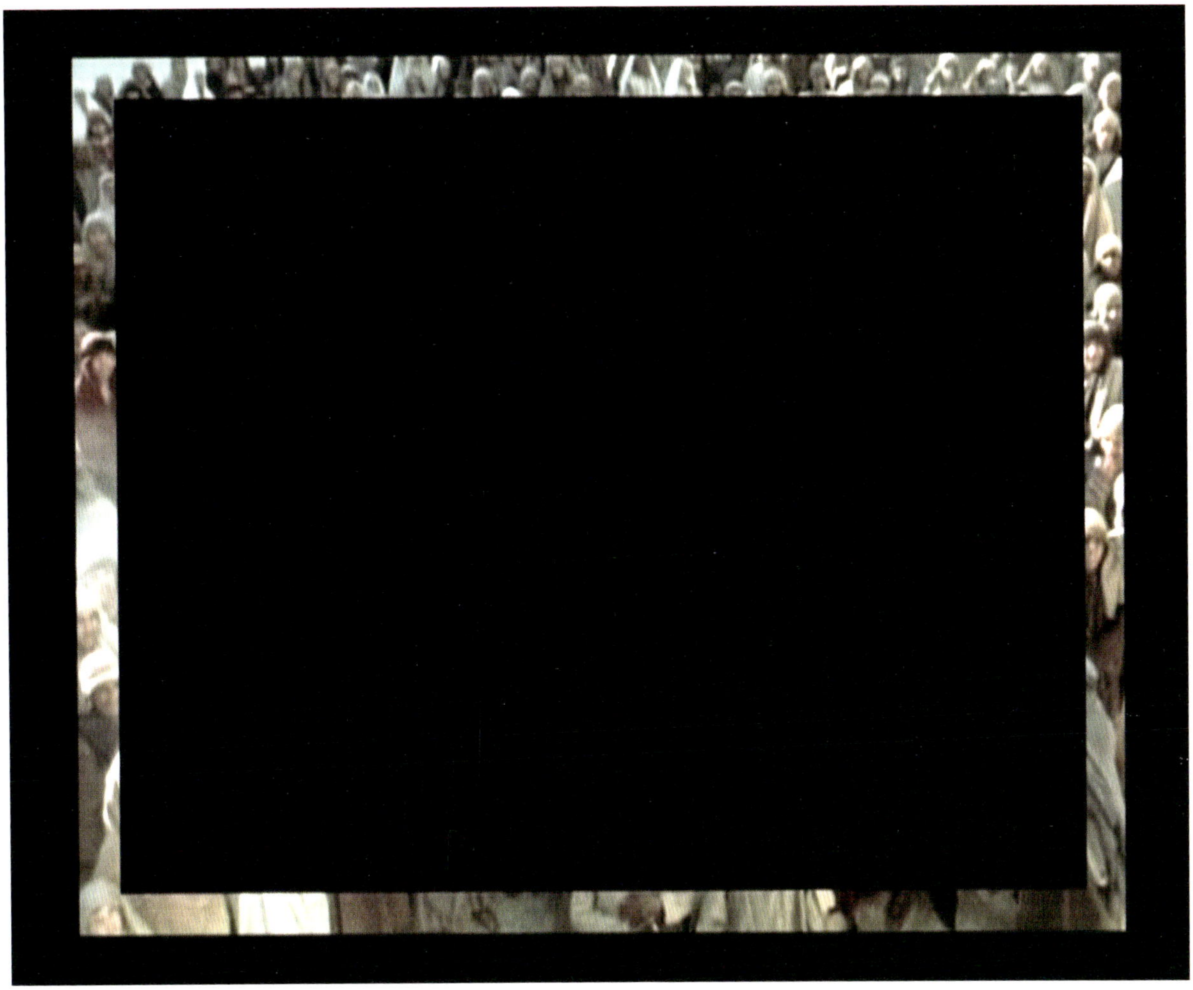

inaccessible'.[38] An image may be marked, broken, rearranged, reconstituted, blocked or negated, but the encounter with the work encourages a state of looking that also makes us unravel our thinking about what we see. From *Where There's Muck* 1985 to *State Britain* 2007 and *I am Innocent* 2010, Wallinger's work is, like all the contemporary work in this survey, 'a ceaseless looking ... for the *other* of something'.[39]

A pencil, a paintbrush, sugar and fire, fingertips, blades, a punch, and software are all used by artists not solely to destroy or damage, but to transform images and artworks into new works with new meanings. Where the Chapmans and Davis engage with additive iconoclasm to regenerate the image by adding elements, Gordon, Skaer and Stezaker remove parts of the image. Where Wilkinson dismantles a video and changes its form, Wallinger digitally manipulates a film and changes its shape. Adding and subtracting, taking the work apart – categorising or constraining the methods of iconoclasm is ultimately futile when obscuring and revealing produce effects that are, in the end, so similar. Material transformations can release images from their constraints.

125
Mark Wallinger (b.1959)
Via Dolorosa 2002
Projected video installation
18 minutes 8 seconds
Edition of 3 plus 1 AP
Courtesy the artist and Anthony Reynolds Gallery, London

Lucy Skaer: *Me*

Lucy Skaer's acts of iconoclasm subvert the physical and material properties of iconic works of art and found objects and images. She uses a number of different strategies to do this, often reproducing them out of very different materials, and then abstracting, fragmenting, scratching, punching holes in or hiding them. Some of her artworks are resistant to interpretation, difficult to see or understand at first sight, or consist of imagery that is not immediately recognisable, or a narrative that is associative rather than diachronic (progressing in time). Isla Leaver-Yap has suggested that Skaer's interest in reproducing original objects and works of art lies in 'eliciting a certain experience of reality absent in the primary source: the moment of encounter between image and observer'.[40]

In Skaer's 2009 installation *The Siege*, its constituent parts were displayed as individual works hidden behind a formidable cinderblock wall, including *Black Alphabet*, twenty-six coal and resin sculptures of Constantin Brancusi's *Bird in Space* 1923–36, nineteen standing and seven stacked in a pile on the floor, like bombs or dead bodies.[41] Unlike Brancusi's bronze and marble originals, these objects neither shine nor glow, nor sit on a plinth: the materials and form of display disturb recognition of the iconic form. Likewise, the series of C-prints, *Blanks Towards Harlequin* 2011, feature groups of silhouettes and backgrounds from images of Renaissance portraits at the National Gallery, London, arranged facing out like playing cards without tops or bottoms and overlaid or blanked out with screenprinted coloured lozenges. Abstracted and fragmented, devoid of the portraits themselves and placed on the floor, the work operates like the harlequin as joker, inverting forms and contexts, disorienting perception; the frames survive the portrait sitters.

In a similar way, Skaer's collaborations with Rosalind Nashashibi defy recognition, even when images are presented within their contexts. In their film *Flash in the Metropolitan* 2006, the artists blind ancient and medieval sculptures in light and enshroud them in complete darkness, animating the inert objects. In *Our Magnolia* 2009 Nashashibi and Skaer begin and end the film with a filmed image of Paul Nash's painting *Flight of the Magnolia* 1944, the last few frames deliberately abraded until the image fades away. *Our Magnolia* brings together several associative images and sounds, including a whale carcass, a civil servant positioned at a computer terminal, the ransacked Baghdad Museum, a scream, a photograph of Margaret Thatcher and taxiing airplanes to present an unsettling, elegiac vision of iconoclasm and death.

Skaer's interest in fragmenting images and in interrupting the relationship between perception and cognition led her to make *Film for an Abandoned Projector* 2011, which could only be played on an old Kalee projector in the disused Lyric Cinema in Leeds. Skaer describes *Film* as 'the imagined subconscious of the projector'. The fate of the short film, shown continuously on a loop, was for it to gradually erode, becoming increasingly marked by time through the wear of its own projection, its own subconscious 'thinking'. The following year Skaer punched out the centres of each individual celluloid frame in the strip of film, from edited cut to edited cut, and made the film into entirely new works – the film *Margin of July* 2012, and the series *Me* 2012.

The group of works entitled *Me* come from this transformation of *Film* to *Margin of July*. Each lozenge contains the remains of the process: punched-out centres of each individual frame of the film, recast into solid resin. Each collection of images is a hoard of fragments, each cut centre showing a scene from the film, and one location, bringing together the space and time of film. Skaer notes that although the *Me* works 'may be the residue of this cancelling out of the film, it is also a kind of move back from the illusion of film to the first hand of sculpture, now containing that piece of time that I originally shot in an inaccessible form'.[42]

Pieces cut out of other films are infrequent – and appear as momentary flickers rather than continuous gaps when the films are playing. In the installations *Kenneth, Hilda* 2011 and *Rachel, Caitlin, Peter, John* 2010 Skaer brings together punched films and sculptural objects that reference the form of the punch itself, made of cast glass and porcelain, pewter, bronze, copper, Burmese blackwood and plaster (respectively), and displayed on a plinth; the tools of iconoclasm and its products materially and aesthetically operate at the same level. Somehow, by breaking images, the artist shows how sculpture and film can be perceived in relation to each other, with three-dimensional forms crossing into the realm of the moving image, and vice versa. Skaer's ambitions are to 'pit materials and ideas against each other' and to 'upset the boundaries of where the art begins and ends'.[43] Her iconoclasms persist. SB

126
Lucy Skaer (b.1975)
Me 2012
Resin and celluloid
23.5 × 15.5 × 0.4
Courtesy the artist and Murray Guy, New York

Jake and Dinos Chapman

Etchings by Goya, watercolours by Hitler, prints by Hogarth, children's colouring books, historic portrait paintings by unknown artists: all of these works of art are rich repositories for the artists Jake and Dinos Chapman. Perhaps the Chapmans' best-known act of iconoclasm is their reworking of Francisco de Goya's portfolio of etchings *The Disasters of War* 1810–20. Unpublished during Goya's lifetime, *The Disasters of War* were printed several times from 1863 through to the twentieth century, resulting in over a thousand sets of prints.[44] The Chapmans' additions to the series of etchings, described as 'reworked and improved' and entitled *Insult to Injury* 2003, followed by another version, *Insult to Insult to Injury* 2004, were subsequently derided and celebrated by both the press and the public.[45] The artists later reworked and improved another series of Goya etchings, *Los Caprichos* 1797–8, in *Like a Dog Returns to its Vomit* 2005.

In the Chapmans' understanding of Goya's work, their markings are aligned with Goya's artistic principles, particularly his treatment of the monstrous and its complex intertwined horror and humour.[46] Goya's *Disasters of War* have long been a source for the Chapmans, who first transformed the etched images into groups of tiny painted figures in their *Disasters of War* 1993, later followed by nearly life-sized sculptures of single scenes such as *Great Deeds Against the Dead* in 1994.[47] The curator Simon Baker has suggested that the Chapmans' relationships with the work of other artists can be understood in relation to their own working relationship with each other – a form of collaboration that is antagonistic – and part of their larger dedication to improving or 'rectifying', often by impoverishing, the original image.[48] The artists describe the relationship as competitive rather than collaborative: '... so you end up with artworks that are beaten-up objects. And if you're both scratching away at it, hopefully the final work won't be like either of you thought it would be.'[49]

Two associated iconoclastic aspects integral to the Chapmans' practice are reviewed here: 'improvements' to historic works acquired by the artists, and their playfully adversarial collaborations with other living artists. The first aspect is represented by three portrait paintings they reworked as

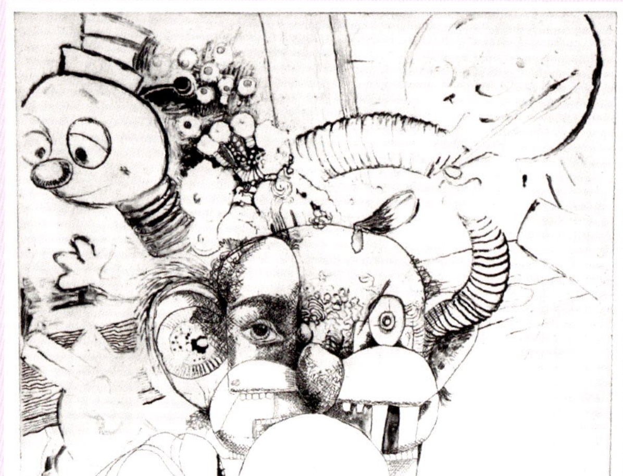

127
Jake and Dinos Chapman (b.1966 and 1962)
One Day You Will No Longer Be Loved II (No. 6)
2008
Oil paint on canvas
30 × 25
Courtesy the artists and White Cube, London

128a–d
Jake and Dinos Chapman (b.1966 and 1962), George Condo (b.1957) and Paul McCarthy (b.1945)
George-Dinos-Jake-Paul (Portrait) 2006
Etchings on paper, 4 parts
Each 127 × 91
Courtesy the artists and RS&A Ltd, London

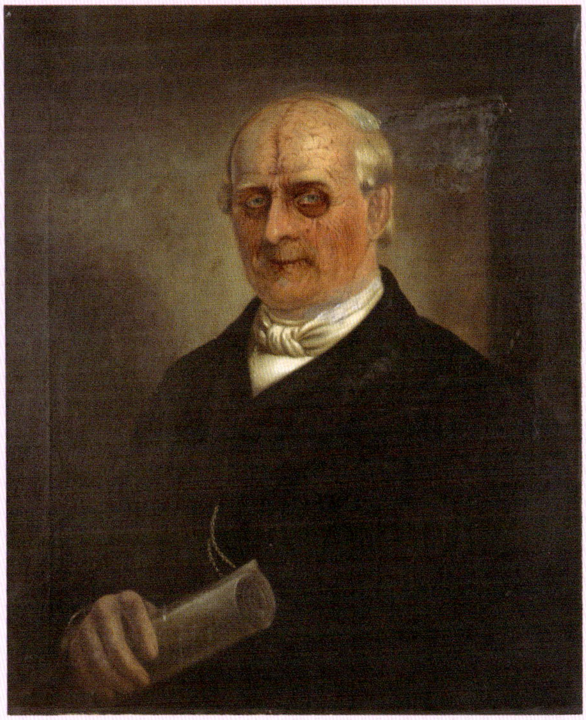

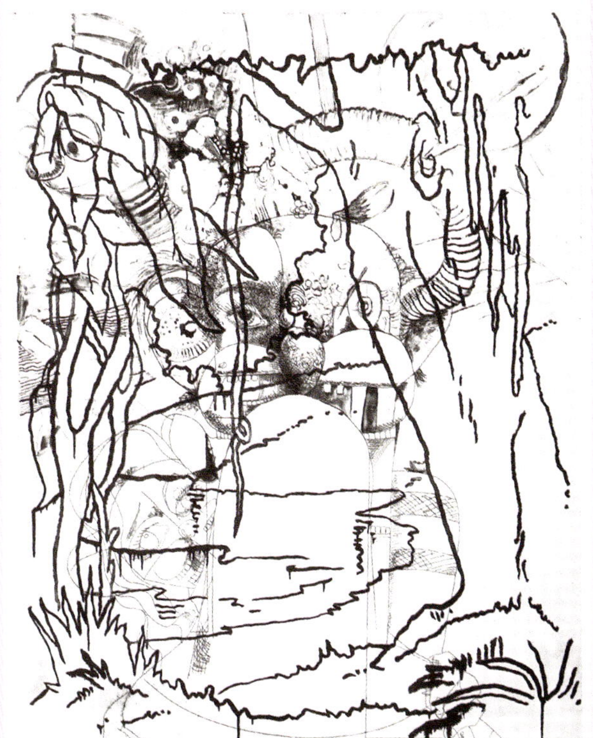

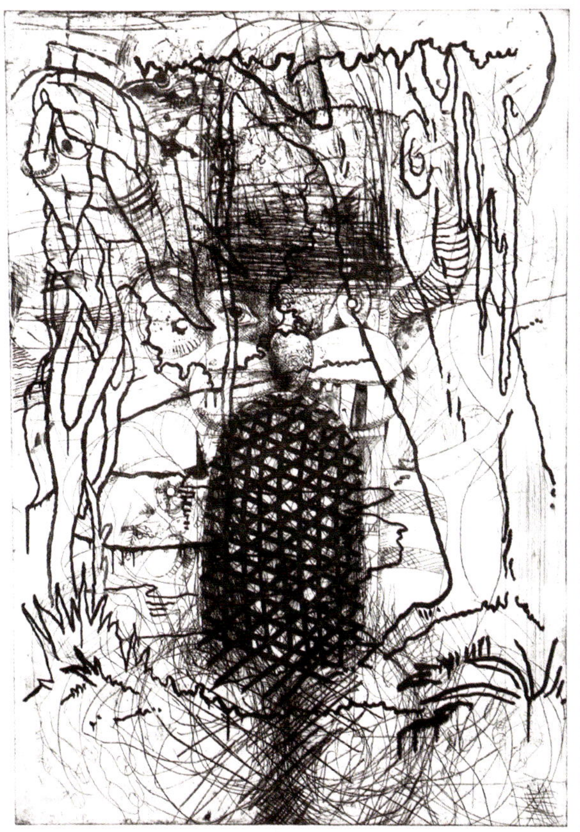

part of the series *One Day You Will No Longer Be Loved* 2006–ongoing (ill.127). Together they present visual aspects of bodily decay in order to convey a sense of the sitter's fate: decomposition.[50] This alteration subverts portraiture's traditional concern with capturing the likeness of the sitter in life, but it also undermines the pretentions of the historic painted portrait, as images made for people who could afford them yet share the ultimate fate of all people.[51] The Chapmans have 'rectified' or 'improved' the paintings by drawing attention to the ephemeral and reversible nature of status and beauty: a century or more after the commissioning of the portraits, no one now loves these individuals enough to look after the portraits. The artists' overpainting is so technically attuned to the original works that it can be difficult to distinguish the hand of the original painter from the added brushstrokes. The gruesome alterations may simultaneously amuse, fascinate and unsettle the viewer, but ultimately the Chapmans' intention is to rectify in their own ways the fictions of the original portrait painters.

Similarly, the Chapmans' iconoclastic collaborations with living artists can also be understood as 'improvements', but conflict and contest here take more visible forms. *With the Artists* was a project organised by the RS&A gallery, in which Jake and Dinos Chapman invited the artists George Condo and Paul McCarthy to collaborate in a series of works somewhat similar to the game 'Exquisite Corpse'.[52] But instead of appending separate parts to an initial image to make a whole with four distinguishable parts, the artists responded in turn to each other's compositions, 'defacing, removing, painting over, cutting up and otherwise interfering with' each other's markings made on canvases and etching plates of various sizes passed between the artists in four different permutations. In the body of work the artists respond by variously subtly and violently adding to and altering images at each stage: shading, cross-hatching, reshaping, blocking, defacing, often scrawling graffiti. The etching entitled *George-Dinos-Jake-Paul* (*Portrait*) 2006 (ill.128a–d) began with a couple of finely etched, sinister faces by George Condo; this was sent to Dinos Chapman, who embellished the central face and added a cartoon snake; then to Jake Chapman, who covered the entire scene with a thickly rendered, banal landscape; and finally to Paul McCarthy, whose series of scratches and bold hatchings resolved into a phallic form. The four parts, as illustrated, capture each stage of production, distinguishing each artist's superimposed contribution to the final etching. The hand of each artist can be identified through differences in draughtsmanship and iconography, content and form, but in each instance the building up of layers and masses produces an image with a remarkable range of markings and depths. In *Portrait*, one steely eye stares through a ruined landscape, terrifying and beautiful, comedic and base, its masculinity characterised by playful aggression.[53]

Baker analyses the destructive character of the Chapmans' collaborations through the writings of Georges Bataille, who described children's drawings as art that proceeds through stages of depiction, interpretation and destructive transformation, a series of 'successive destructions'.[54] The successive destructions of Jake and Dinos Chapman conflate and amplify the violent and seductive tenors of images, complicating enmeshed responses of attraction and repulsion.[55] SB

NOTES

ICONOCLASMS PAST AND PRESENT

1 Mitchell 2005, p.9, cites the art historian Tom Cummins.
2 Jeremy Dimmick, James Simpson and Nicolette Zeeman, 'Introduction', in Dimmick et al. 2002, p.1.
3 Freedberg 1989; Gell 1998.
4 Elkins 1996, p.11; Didi-Huberman 2005; Mitchell 2005; Simpson 2010; Bynum 2011; Koerner 2004; Belting 1994.
5 Marks 2004, pp.4, 251, 314 n. 116, links the fragments to a will and dates them to c.1520. Land 2011, pp.272–3, dates the fragments to 1450–75. See also Duffy 2010, pp.62–3; Anderson 2004, pp.47–58; Middleton 1888–91.
6 Richard Marks, 'An Age of Consumption: Art for England *c.*1400–1547', in Marks and Williamson 2003, p.14; Phillip Lindley, 'From Romanesque to Reformation', in Deacon and Lindley 2001, pp.39–53; Cooper 2001, p.274; Duffy 2005; Phillips 1973; Strong 1990.
7 See pp.106–7 in the present volume.
8 Christov-Bakargiev 2012.
9 Flood 2002; Virgina Chieffo Raguin, 'Introduction: Art and Religion: Then and Now', in Raguin 2010, pp.1–21. See also Hal Foster, 'The Last Column', *London Review of Books*, vol.33, no.17, 8 September 2011; Dorrian 2004; Noyes 2013.
10 Arjun Appadurai, 'Introduction: Commodities and the Politics of Value', in Appadurai 1988, pp.3–63; Igor Kopytoff, 'The Cultural Biography of Things: Commoditization as Process', in Appadurai 1988, pp.64–94; Taussig 1999; Tamen 2004; Bynum 2011.
11 Mitchell 2005, p.18. See also Flood and Strother 2005; Storr 2010; Michalski 1998.
12 The attacked Churchill monument may be a familiar example. See http://www.guardian.co.uk/uk/2000/may/08/mayday.world and the artist Sam Durant's website http://samdurant.net/defaced_monuments/Pages/London/london.html. The veteran jailed for bloodying the statue with red paint distanced himself from 'mindless rioters'. Several protesters added graffiti to the stone plinth, and attacks with red paint and graffiti followed in 2007 and 2010. The monument was installed in 1973; Ivor Roberts-Jones made the bronze statue.
13 Elkins 2004. On the complex nature of motivation and the term *iconoclash*, see Latour and Weibel 2002. See also Latour and Weibel 2005.
14 On anthropomorphism and prosopopoeia, see 'Notes from the Field: Anthropomorphism', *Art Bulletin*, vol.94, no.1, March 2012, pp.10–31, especially contributions by Caroline van Eck (pp.16–20) and Finbarr Barry Flood (pp.18–20) and Powell 2012, pp.103–20; Tamen 2004, pp.77–86.
15 McKim-Smith 2002; Lindley 2001; see also pp.66–7 in the present volume.
16 See pp.134–5 in the present volume.
17 See pp.174–5 in the present volume.
18 Graves 2008, p.37; Warnke 1977. See also Groebner 2004.
19 Aston 1993, p.268. See also Deacon and Lindley 2001, p.29; Satz 2007.
20 Spraggon 2003, pp.42–6; Cressy 2000b, pp.234–50.
21 See the British Museum's stall plate belonging to William Parr, Marquess of Northampton (a member of the Order of the Garter from 1552), broken in two when Parr committed an act of treason: Trigg 2012, p.139; Blick 2013.
22 Clanchy 1993, pp.308–17; Bedos-Rezak 2010, p.70; Cherry 2002.
23 Gilchrist 2012, p.242; Chapman 2000.
24 John Morrill, 'William Dowsing and the Administration of Iconoclasm', in Cooper 2001, pp.1–28.
25 On the institutionalisation of art as iconoclasm as 'a provincial nostalgia of totality', see Tamen 2004, pp.63–4.
26 McRoberts 2012, pp.151–2.
27 Cane and Ashley-Smith 2013.
28 Bradley 1990.
29 Cane and Ashley-Smith 2013.
30 Brilliant and Kinney 2011.
31 Camille 1989, p.27, from the Douai-Reims Bible, New York 1953.
32 Aston 1988; Duffy 2005; Marks 2004; Spraggon 2003, pp.1–31. On *dulia* and *latria*, see Camille 1989, pp.203–20; Ellenbogen and Tugendhaft 2011. See also Nagel 2012.
33 Kessler 2004, p.19; Stanbury 2007.
34 Duffy 2005; Marks 2007.
35 Duffy 2005, pp.xxii–xxviii; on the Lollards, see Aston 1988, pp.96–159; Simpson 2010, pp.57–64.
36 Aston 1988, pp.125–6. See also Powell 2012, pp.103–20, 312–13, nn.4, 6; Camille 1989, pp.40–1.
37 Aston 1988, p.137.
38 Deacon and Lindley 2001; Powell 2012, pp.81–101, 191–209.
39 Aston 1988, p.109; Aston 1984, p.174 n.135, Logan 1968, pp.52, 190.
40 Simpson 2010, p.63.
41 Stanbury 2002, p.135.
42 Stanbury 2002.
43 Simpson 2010, p.70 n.44, cites Martin Bucer, *A treatise declaring and showing . . . that pictures and other images . . . are in no wise to be suffered in the temples or churches*, London 1535, in *Short-Title Catalogue*, 2nd edn., rev. W.A. Jackson et al., 3 vols., Bibliographical Society 1976–91, 24239, image 49. My thanks to James Simpson for this reference.
44 Duffy 2005, p.407.
45 Duffy 2006.
46 Aston 1988, pp.246–342; Marks 2004, pp.255–75; Simpson 2010, pp.60–4.
47 Aston 2003; Virginia Chieffo Raguin, 'You Are What You Wear (and Use, and See): The Form of the Reform in England', in Raguin 2010, pp.65–81.
48 Spraggon 2003, pp.61–98; on the destruction of funerary monuments, see Llewellyn 2001 and Lindley 2007.
49 Simpson 2010, p.15.
50 Bynum 2011, pp.122–3.
51 Powell 2012 explores the ideas of Adorno and Baudrillard on dead things and Ad Reinhardt's 'dead paintings'. See also Groys 2008
52 On materiality as 'the meeting of matter and imagination', see Michael Ann Holly 2013, pp.15–17. See also Butler 2011.
53 Walsham 2010, p.17.

IDOLATRY, ICONOCLASM AND THE REFORMATION'S LONG LEGACY

1 John Griffiths (ed.), *The Two Books of Homilies Appointed to be Read in Churches*, Oxford 1859, p.246.
2 For idolatry in general, see Aston 1988, especially chapter 7, 'The Sin of Idolatry: The Teaching of the Decalogue'; Freedberg 1989, especially chapter 14, 'Idolatry and Iconoclasm'.
3 Aston 1988, p.343.
4 Aston 1988, p.467.
5 See Hamling and Williams 2007, introduction pp.1–13.
6 Haynes 2006, pp.112–19; Haynes 2006b.
7 'St Margaret's Westminster', in Walford 1878, pp.567–76 (http://www.british-history.ac.uk); Esdaile 1950.
8 Aston 1988, p.406; William Hole, with an introduction by Thomas Wilson, *The Ornament of Churches Considered: with a particular view to the late decoration of the parish church of St Margaret, Westminster*, Oxford 1761
9 Haynes 2006, pp. 74–101. For the Enlightenment's neutralising of images, see also Simpson 2010, pp.116–54.
10 Charles Kingsley, *Alton Locke: Tailor and Poet. An Autobiography*, London 1850.
11 *Gentleman's Magazine*, October 1782, pp.476–8; James Northcote, *The Life of Sir Joshua Reynolds*, 1819, vol.1, pp.305–15.
12 Carr 1980.
13 Haydon 1998, p.49.
14 'Golden Square Area: Warwick Street', *Survey of London*, vols. 31 and 32: *St James Westminster*, pt 2 (1963), pp. 167–73; http://www.british-history.ac.uk; Haywood and Seed 2012, pp.4, 148–9.
15 Janes 2009, pp.15–16, 33–6, and for the legal cases, 78–86; Yates 1999, pp.91–4.
16 Janes 2010.
17 J.C. Ryle, 'Idolatry', chapter 8 in *Knot's Untied: Being Plain Statements on Disputed Points in Religion from the Standpoint of an Evangelical Churchman*, London 1877.
18 Giebelhausen 2000; Grieve 1969, pp.292–5.
19 John Milton, *Eikonoklastes*, 1649, p.85.
20 Carlyle, *On Heroes, Hero-Worship and the Heroic in History*, London 1840.
21 Thomas Carlyle, 'Hudson's Statue', no.VII in 'Latter-Day Pamphlets', 1850, in *Thomas Carlyle's Collected Works*, vol.19, London 1870, p.316; Smith 2001, pp.177–8.
22 Aston 1988, pp.257, 319.
23 Spraggon 2003, p.83.
24 See Elsner 2003.
25 Waller 2011, p.22; Erasmus [1526] 1997, pp.619–74.
26 Coleman and Elsner 1999, pp.207–8.
27 Janes and Waller 2010, pp.10–12.
28 Hare 1991, pp.158–9.
29 *Catholic Herald*, 12 September 1941.
30 Catholic Archdiocese of Birmingham Archives, P99/14/1-21.
31 Davidson 2007, p.43.

1 DISSOLUTION

Susan Harrison thanks Richard Mason for sharing and discussing ideas, Stuart Harrison for commenting on the draft paper, and Kevin Booth for his support.

1 Woodward 1966, p.4.
2 Ibid., p.6.
3 The Ancient Monuments Consolidation and Amendment Act 1913. Many are now in the National Collection in the care of English Heritage.
4 Ultimately succeeded by English Heritage.
5 Morrison and Harrison 1999.
6 Copinger 1895.
7 Howard Leithead, 'Cromwell, Thomas, Earl of Essex', *Oxford Dictionary of National Biography* (http://www.oxforddnb.com/index/101006769/Thomas-Cromwell accessed 28/03/2013), p.21.
8 Copinger 1895.
9 Hope and Brakspear 1911, p.305. The penalty for treason was execution by hanging, drawing and quartering.
10 Harrison, Wood and Newman 1998, pp.29–30.
11 '. . . eighteen score and five fodders, with thirty-four fodders and a half that were

there before…' (Hope and Brakspear 1911, p.307).

12 Ibid.

13 Youings 1971, p. 13.

14 In a letter to Cromwell by the Duke of Norfolk (Hope and Brakspear 1911, p.307).

15 Giovanni Portinari, an Italian engineer, was employed by Cromwell to pull down Lewes Priory, Sussex. He took with him three carpenters; two smiths; two plumbers, one who keeps the furnace; and seventeen labourers (Graham 1952). They were from London and less likely to be inhibited by any local sympathies for an old familiar building (Aston 1973, p.239).

16 Aston 1973, p.238.

17 Ibid.

18 Personal communication, Stuart Harrison.

19 Sir John Williams, 'Sundry Jewels and plate which came by occasion of the defacing and taking down of shrines and other vain and famed things called Reliques and other superfluous plate found…made for the avoiding the abuse of Idolatry', in Williams 1886.

20 Following the surrender on 3 December 1538. Fergusson and Harrison 1999, p.175.

21 The de facto practical arrangement seems to have been to pull down the crossing tower to ruin the church but it was not always done, as Whitby Abbey and Kirkstall Priory and some other sites show, but Fountains, Byland and Rievaulx all seem to have had their towers felled. Personal communication, Stuart Harrison.

22 Fergusson and Harrison 1999, pp.175, 226; Coppack 1986. William Blythman was the Augmentations Clerk who accompanied the Commissioners to Rievaulx and other local sites.

23 Williams 1886.

24 Find no.154, English Heritage accession no.81065623, cloister arcade, on pavement 4ft west of Chapter House, 4 July 1923.

25 Find no.155, accession no.81065624, cloister arcade, on pavement 2ft west of Chapter House.

26 From a survey of the buildings made c.1539 for Thomas, Earl of Rutland: 'the particions, the imagys and tables gyldyd that cam out of the church, the portal karvyd' (Fergusson and Harrison 1999, p.230.

27 Find no. 140, accession no.81300428, outside Galilee Porch, 12ft above doorstep to south of west door opening, 12 January 1923.

28 Fergusson and Harrison 1999, pp.74–6.

29 To whom all Cistercian churches were dedicated.

30 Stuart Harrison, 'Gisborough Priory Stone Collection Overview', unpublished report for English Heritage, 2008.

31 Gilyard-Beer 1984, p.7.

32 Accession no.88280267, dated c.1300.

33 Accession no.88257777.

34 John Richard Walbran, 'On the excavation now in progress at Fountains Abbey: A paper read before the Yorkshire Architectural Society, at a meeting held at Skipton-in Craven, 31 May 1854', Yorkshire Architectural Society 13th Report, in *Reports and Papers read at the meetings of the Architectural Societies of the Archdeanery of Northampton, the County of York, the Dioceses of Lincoln and Worcester and the Architectural and Archaeological Society of Bedford during the year 1854*, vol.3, London 1854, p.65 (http://archive.org/stream/reportspapers ofa31asso#page/54/mode/2up). The Virgin and child sculpture was found in amongst the rubble of the Galilee Porch, and therefore seems contemporary with Dissolution activity.

35 Accession nos.81065614 and 81065603.

36 Such as the fragmentary painted angel (accession no.81300248) and soldier (accession no.81300341).

37 Aveling 1952, p.101.

38 Fergusson 1999, p.29.

39 For example the Gisborough Priory Bible, now in St John's College, Cambridge (MS C.24), bears traces on the flyleaf of the erased *ex libris* inscription *Liber sancte marie de gyseburn*. The inscription below states that the book was borrowed in 1594 for the pawn of a gold angel.

40 Cross 1989, pp.28–90.

41 Ker 1941, p.89.

42 Michael Sherbrooke witnessed the aftermath of the despoliation of Roche Abbey as a small child but his father and uncle were eyewitnesses to the event itself. Dickens 1959.

43 Site finds book, 1920s.

44 Find no.102A, accession no.765385, in drain, reredorter, 27 August 1925.

45 Find no.27, accession no.765347, annunciation plaque, in drain by south wall at junction, 4 May 1925.

46 See p.38.

47 Copinger 1895.

48 John Richard Walbran, *On the excavation now in progress at Fountains Abbey, A paper read at the joint meeting of the Architectural Societies of Yorkshire and Lincolnshire, at a meeting held at Ripon, 17th June 1851, in Yorkshire Architectural Society 10th Report in Reports and Papers read at the meetings of the Architectural Societies of the Archdeanery of Northampton, the County of York, the Dioceses of Lincoln and Worcester and the Architectural and Archaeological Society of Bedford during the year 1851*, London 1851, p.25.

49 J. Buglass, 'The Infirmary, Fountains Abbey, North Yorkshire, Archaeological Investigation', unpublished report, 2012.

50 Find no.133, accession no.765343, pillar between the twin bridges at outfall.

51 Accession no.81065654, almost sixty examples have been recovered from both Rievaulx and Fountains Abbey.

52 John Richard Walbran, paper read 1854 on the excavation of Fountains Abbey, Yorkshire Architectural Society (see note 34), p.60.

53 Thornton Abbey finally closed in 1547; it had been re-founded as a college following the Suppression but, despite the delay of a few years, it too shared the same methods of despoliation and destruction as witnessed in other foundations.

54 Accession no.78206195.

55 The panel at Rievaulx Abbey is in situ above the entrance to the Abbot's Lodging, a building remodelled from the Abbey Infirmary in the late fifteenth century by Abbot John Burton. They may be by the same sculptor and it is likely that the panel from Fountains Abbey also occupied a similar position, although it was found by Walbran in one of the southern chapels. Carter 2009, pp.1–22.

56 T.P. O'Connor, 'Five human skeletons from the Chapter House of Jervaulx Abbey, North Yorkshire', *Ancient Monuments Laboratory Report* (old series), no.4893, 1986.

57 Peers recorded this coffin as empty and without a cover (Peers 1929, p.23). The human remains are not as interpreted in Fergusson, Harrison and Coppack (2006) 2010, where the remains are suggested to be those of two workmen trapped during demolition work. Mason forthcoming.

58 Oxford Archaeology North, unpublished report, 'Furness Abbey Presbytery, Cumbria: Archaeological Post-excavation Assessment', 2011.

59 Walbran 1875, p.125.

60 Gilyard-Beer and Coppack 1986, p.164.

61 This may have been due to lead furnaces being set up in the nave, in or on graves. (Fairbank 1885, p.396).

62 Accession no.81300227, rebus panel of John Burton, Abbot of Rievaulx 1489–c.1513: an eagle (symbol of Saint John) depicted above a barrel (ton).

63 Rievaulx Abbey Finds Book, find no.30, accession no.81065663, near west door at floor level, 23 April 1920.

64 At Jervaulx 400 fothers were removed (Hope and Brakspear 1911, p.307).

65 Rievaulx Abbey Finds Book, find no.48, 23 March 1920. Coal was found on the tile floor at the north nave wall.

66 Walbran 1875, pp.104–5.

67 Ibid., pp.106–7.

68 Dickens 1959.

69 Fairbank 1885, p.396.

70 Aston 1973, p.231.

71 Parliamentary Act 31 Henry VIII c.13.

72 Woodward 1966, p.101.

CHRIST IN MAJESTY

73 Find no. 380, 81065601, Infirmary, January 1931, dated c.1260–90.

74 Such as the Eleanor Percy tomb at Beverley Minster.

75 Remodelled from the Abbey Infirmary in the later fifteenth century by Abbot John Burton.

76 No other recorded iconic statues were recovered from this location in the 1930s. Other damaged stones found in there included the rebus pinnacle (accession no.81065666) and rebus panel of Abbot John Burton (accession no.81300227), friezes (accession nos.81065604 and 81065605) and grotesque label stops (accession nos.81300277 and 81300383), all of which originated from that building.

WINDOW GLASS

77 At Fountains Abbey all the glass was removed from the windows, so no more than a handful was found (Walbran 1875, pp.104–5).

78 Aston 1973, p.238; Ellis 1824–46, pp.131–2.

79 Fergusson and Harrison 1999, p.229; see also note 22.

80 Walbran 1854 (see note 34), p.25.

81 Accession no.960132.2. Similar crowned letters are evident in the windows of the Antechapel at New College, Oxford, c.1380. My thanks to A. Eavis for this identification and comparison.

82 Accession no.88092169.

83 Little is known about the medieval glazing at Furness Abbey except that John Petty, a York-based glazier, worked at the Abbey from c.1470 until his death, a period contemporary with the production of the angel panel. Jasmine Allen, 'An Excavated Angel from Furness', online publication, *Vidimus*, no.31 (http://vidimus.org/issues/issue-31/); and Hegbin-Barnes 2009, pp.118–19.

84 Accession no.88257662.

85 Thomas 2006, p.205.

86 Accession no.671509, mother and child roundel.

87 Coppack 1988, p.26.

SHRINES, PILGRIMAGE AND THE CULT OF BECKET

88 Nilson 1998, p.149; Binski 2004.

89 Crook 2011, pp.213–18.

90 Blick 2011, pp.21–58. Nilson 1998, pp.147–54.

91 Crook 2011, p.217.

92 Ibid., pp.217–18; Eamon Duffy in Doran 2009, p.207 no.205; Urry 1975, pp.195–209. Mason 1920, p.113, cites the discovery of some fragments in 1885.

93 Tatton-Brown 2002, p.96, cites his 'The Two Great Marble Pavements in the Sanctuary and Shrine Areas of Canterbury Cathedral and Westminster Abbey', in Fawcett 1998, and 'The Trinity Chapel and Corona Floors', *Canterbury Cathedral Chronicle*, vol.75, 1981, pp. 51–6. See also Binski 2004, pp.3–7, 292.

94 Binski (2004, pp.3–7) also assesses the marble in relation to the creamy white limestone in the Trinity Chapel, a play on the rose and lily.

95 Crook 2011, p.214, cites Matthew Paris, *Historia Anglorum (alias Historia Minor)*, ed. F. Madden, 3 vols., Rolls Series 44, 1866–9, vol.2, p.241.

96 Crook 2011, pp.213, 229.

97 Blick 2005, p.405; Crook 2011, p.300.

98 Crook 2011, p.300; Duffy 2009, p.207 no.205; Butler 1995, pp.109–33; Mayer 2007, pp.126–43.

99 Duffy 2009, p.207, no.205; Roberts 2002, pp.225–7.

100 Duffy 2006, pp.149–50.

101 Ibid., pp.150–8.

102 Ibid., pp.155–8.

103 Ibid., pp.152, 163–4. My thanks to Julian Luxford for conversations about these manuscripts.

104 Butler 1995, in 'Prologue: Raiders in the Night', cites the 1990 arrest in the Cathedral precinct of two young men determined to find Becket's bones, pp.ix–xii.

105 Urry 1975, pp.204–5.

2 REFORMATION

1 Michalski 1993; Wandel 1995.
2 Duffy 1992; Marks 2004.
3 Duffy 2006a.
4 Aston 1988, pp.239–43.
5 Ibid., pp.262–3, 300–2 ; Aston 1993a.
6 Aston 1988, pp.323–36.
7 Duffy 1992, pp.377–593.
8 Ibid., pp.478–503.
9 Latour and Weibel 2002.
10 KSH & Co. Ltd, 'Painted Medieval Screen (fragment) at St Mary's Church, Gressenhall Norfolk', condition report for Tate Britain, 2013.
11 Aston 1988; Phillips 1973.
12 Storer and Greig 1807, vol.1, unpaginated.
13 Williams 2003.
14 Gamboni 1997.
15 Boldrick and Clay 2007, p.3.
16 Andreas Bodenstein von Karlstadt, *On the abolishing of the images, and that there should be no beggars among Christians* (1522).
17 Freedberg 1989.
18 Latour and Weibel 2002, p.15.
19 Freedberg 1985.
20 Lindley 1989; Lindley 1993.
21 Deacon and Lindley 2001, pp.25–53.
22 Tait 1964; Duffy 1992, pp.448–503.
23 Bate and Thornton 2012, p.26.
24 Goodison 1977, pp.24–6.
25 Bruno Latour, 'What is Iconoclash? Or is there a World Beyond the Image Wars?', in Latour and Weibel 2002, pp.14–37.
26 Cheetham 1984.
27 Duffy 1992; Duffy 1997.
28 Pema Konchok, 'Buddhism as a Focus of Iconoclasm in Asia', in Latour and Weibel 2002, pp.40–59.
29 Frere and Kennedy 1910, p.116.
30 Lindley 1989, p.605.
31 Williams 2005.
32 Latour and Weibel 2002, p.14.
33 Marks and Williamson 2003, p.462; Duffy 1997, p.160.
34 Lasko and Morgan 1973, pp.37–8; KSH & Co. Ltd, 'Small Crucifixion at Norwich Cathedral', conservation report for Tate Britain, 2012.
35 Freedberg 1985, pp.33–6.
36 K. Woods, 'The Mercers' Christ re-examined', in Marks 2006, pp.57–69. On sculptures of the Dead Christ more generally, see also Powell 2012.
37 Aston 1988, pp.405–8.
38 Freedberg 1985, p.35.
39 Maniura and Shepherd 2006.
40 Joseph Koerner, 'The Icon as Iconoclash', in Latour and Weibel 2002, pp.164–213; Graves 2008, pp.35–57.
41 Aston 1988, pp.323–4; Haugaard 1970, pp.188–9.
42 Freedberg 1985, p.7.

THE DEAD CHRIST

43 Woods 2006.
44 Evans and Cook 1955.
45 Woods 2006, p.58.
46 My thanks to Tabitha Barber for suggesting this (the removal of lower legs, arms and the Crown of Thorns suggests the deliberate targeting of imagery), and to Stacy Boldrick for bringing to my attention the similar pattern of defacement in the Utrecht statue.
47 Duffy 1992, pp.238–48, 397.
48 Patina Art Collection Care Limited, 'Statue of Christ', condition report for the Mercer's Company, 2012 (we are grateful to Jane Ruddell for sharing this with us).
49 Van Os 1994.
50 Woods 2006, p.57; Patina Art Collection Care Limited (2012).
51 Woods 2006, p.59.
52 Graves 2008.
53 Marks 2004, p.3.

THE GREAT SCREEN OF WINCHESTER CATHEDRAL

54 Lindley 1993, p.797.
55 Lindley 1989, p.604 n.2.
56 Lindley 1993, pp.797–807.
57 Stone 1972, p.225.
58 Lindley 1989, pp.607–12; Marks and Williamson 2003, pp.358, 461.
59 Sandra Deighton, 'Madonna and Child from the Great Screen, Winchester Cathedral', condition report for Tate Britain, 2012.
60 Lindley 1989, pp.604–5.
61 Ibid, p.605.
62 Ibid, p.611.

THE PAINTED SCREEN AT ST MARY'S, GRESSENHALL

63 Baker 2011, p.158.
64 Duffy 1997.
65 KSH & Co. Limited, 'The Painted Medieval Screen at St Mary's Church, Gressenhall Norfolk', condition report for Tate Britain, 2013.
66 Duffy 1992, pp.110–13, 157–60; Duffy 1997.
67 Duffy 1997.
68 KSH & Co. Limited (2013).
69 Duffy 1997, pp.152–3.
70 Ibid, pp.158–62; Duffy 1992, pp.568–77.

3 PURITAN ICONOCLASM

1 S. Gunton, *The History of the Church of Peterborough*, London 1686, p.337, cited in Aston 1988, p.65.
2 Nuttall 1933–6.
3 Spraggon 2003, pp.50–2.
4 John Cleveland's satirical attack on Cromwell, *The Character of a London Diurnal*, 1645. See Knoppers 2000, p.13.
5 In particular see Spraggon 2003, Cooper 2001 and Aston 1996.
6 For Parliamentary legislation against images see Spraggon 2003, pp.61–98 and appendix I, pp.257–61.
7 See Fincham and Tyacke 2007, pp.274–7, and Parry 2006.
8 Spraggon 2003, p.145.
9 Cited in Spraggon 2003, p.33.
10 Parry 2006, pp.1–2.
11 Richard Culmer, *Cathedrall newes from Canterbury*, London 1644, p.18.
12 Culmer 1644, p.17; Longstaffe-Gowan and Knox 2006.
13 Spraggon p.85 and n.65.
14 Eales 1989, p.150.
15 Spraggon 2003, p.83.
16 Ibid., pp.88–93.
17 Richard Culmer, *Cathedrall newes from Canterbury*, London 1644, p.23.
18 For a comprehensive edition of Dowsing's journal see Cooper 2001.
19 John Morrill, 'William Dowsing and the administration of iconoclasm in the Puritan revolution', in Cooper 2001, pp.1–28.
20 Marks 1993, p.218.
21 Aston 1988, p.404.
22 Marks 1993, p.218.
23 William Hinde, *A Faithfull Remonstrance of the Holy Life and Happy Death of John Bruen*, London 1641, pp.78–9; see also Spraggon 2003, p.41.
24 *Mercurius Britanicus*, July 1644, cited in Spraggon 2003, p.98.
25 Joseph Hall, Bishop of Norwich negotiated this solution for the figures of bishops in the windows of his episcopal chapel. See Aston 1988, p.69.
26 *Mercurius Rusticus: or The Countries Complaint of the barbarous Outrages committed by the Sectaries of this late flourishing Kingdom*, 1685 edn, p.154.
27 For iconoclasm in cathedrals see Lehmberg 1996, pp.25–56; Spraggon 2003, pp.177–216; Aston 1988, pp.63–74.
28 John Milton, *Of Reformation*, 1641, in *Complete Prose Works of John Milton*, ed. D. Wolfe, vol.1: *1624–1642*, New Haven 1953, p.557.
29 *Mercurius Rusticus*, 1685 edn, pp.119–20.
30 *Mercurius Rusticus*, 1685 edn, pp.148–9. Ryves's account was based on that of Thomas Paske, subdean of the cathedral.
31 Loomie 1998, pp.680–2; Thurley 2002, p.249.
32 For the history and demolition of the cross see Cressy 2000; Spraggon 2003, pp.42–6; and Aston 1993, pp.284–8.
33 *The Pope's proclamation … whereunto is added Six articles exhibited against Cheapside Crosse, whereby it stands guilty of high treason*, London 1641.
34 Cressy 2000, p.245.
35 *Articles of High Treason Exhibited against Cheapside Crosse, with the last Will and Testament of the said Crosse*, 1642; *The remarkable funeral of Cheapside-Crosse in London*, 1642 (OS).
36 Loewenstein 1990, pp.65–9; Simpson 2010, pp.117–19.
37 John Milton, *Eikonoklastes*, London 1649, pp.B4–5.
38 An inscription on the book's fly-leaf by Zachary Cradock, English preacher in Lisbon, records its history and the command for its correction according to the 'Rules of the Index Expurgatorius'. He presented it to Lambeth Palace Library in 1678.
39 Palmer and Brown 2010, p.130.

IMAGE AND TEXT AT LITTLE GIDDING

40 For the textual reordering see Dyck and Williams 2008.
41 *The Arminian Nunnery*, London 1641.
42 For the Little Gidding community and their use of images, see Aston 2007; Henderson 1982.
43 Henderson 1982, p.193.
44 Ransome 1992.
45 See Henderson 1982; Parry 2006, pp.129–30.
46 Parry 2006, pp.43–5.
47 Aston 2007, p.101.
48 Smyth 2012.

CHARLES I AND SYMBOLS OF THE STUART REGIME

49 *Mercurius Rusticus*, 1685 edn, pp.38–8.
50 Parry 2006, p.53.
51 *Mercurius Rusticus*, 1685 edn, pp.149–51.
52 Letter in the cathedral archives. I am grateful to Jo Bartholomew for giving me a copy of this document.
53 Spraggon 2003, p.81 and appendix II, pp.262–3.
54 Howarth 1989, p.92.
55 Smith 2001, pp.73–5.
56 He is also said to have capitalised on his trophy by making bronze-handled cutlery for both Royalists and Parliamentarians eager to possess a piece of the king.
57 Smith 2001, p.78.

RICHARD CULMER AND THE GLASS OF CANTERBURY CATHEDRAL

58 Richard Culmer, *Cathedrall newes from Canterbury*, 1644, pp.19–20. For Culmer, see Aston 1988, pp.84–92, and Spraggon 2003, pp.182–5.
59 Spraggon 2003, p.183.
60 Culmer 1644, pp.21–2.
61 Caroe 1911.
62 Sparks 2001.
63 Spraggon 2003, p.184.
64 For the history of the windows, see Caviness 1977; Caviness 1981.
65 Caviness 1977, p.13; Caviness 1981, p.87.
66 Caviness 1981, p.50. For losses to the glass in areas with iconoclastic activity depicted by Johnson, see pp.10, 64 and 152. My thanks also to Leonie Seliger, Director of the Stained Glass Studio, Canterbury Cathedral, for bringing this to my attention and sharing her first-hand knowledge of the window restoration.
67 Culmer 1644, p.22.

THE PAINTED GLASS OF CHRIST CHURCH, OXFORD

68 For the discovery, identification and history of the fragments and the van Linge glazing scheme, see Power and Shortland 2009; and Scott, Shortland and Power 2012.
69 Parry 2006, pp.59–76; Faludy 2005.
70 College Chapter Minutes. My thanks to Matthew Power for giving me a copy of this document.
71 Wood 1786, vol.2, part 2, p.649.
72 Fincham and Tyacke 2007, p.274.
73 Parry 2006, pp.70–2.
74 Parry 2006, pp.74, 137.
75 Spraggon 2003, p.246 n.98.
76 Bachrach and Collmer 1981, p.112.
77 For reform in Oxford see Spraggon 2003, pp.231–49.
78 Spraggon 2003, p.246.
79 See Spraggon 2003, p.240.
80 Scott et al. 2012.

4 POLITICS AND PUBLIC SPACE

1 'The Destruction of the Statue of James II at Newcastle', depositions heard before the Mayor of Newcastle, 23 May 1689, published 1847 by M.A. Richardson, Newcastle, in *Reprints of Rare Tracts: Chiefly Illustrative of the History of the Northern Counties*, vol.4, Newcastle 1849. Summaries are in the *Calendar of State Papers* (1895) 1969, and in Toynbee 1951, pp.108–17.
2 Toynbee 1951, p.112; Sullivan 2005.
3 See especially Whelan 2002; Thompson 1991, esp. 'Rough Music', pp.467–538.
4 *Biographical Dictionary of Sculptors in Britain* (http://www.henry-moore.org/hmi/library/biographical-dictionary-of-sculptors-in-britain).
5 Toynbee 1951, passim.
6 Toynbee 1951, pp.109–10.
7 *Calendar of State Papers* (1895) 1969, 21 May 1689, HO Letterbook (Secretarys), 1, p.81.
8 *Biographical Dictionary of Sculptors in Britain* (http://www.henry-moore.org/hmi/library/biographical-dictionary-of-sculptors-in-britain).
9 Chastel-Rousseau 2011; see also Baker forthcoming.
10 *Biographical Dictionary of Sculptors in Britain* (http://www.henry-moore.org/hmi/library/biographical-dictionary-of-sculptors-in-britain); Chastel-Rousseau 2011.
11 McParland 1987.
12 1769, quoted in McParland 1987, p.187.
13 G.N. Wright, *An Historical Guide to Ancient and Modern Dublin*, London 1821, quoted in Whelan 2002, p.518.
14 Murphy 2010, p.9.
15 Howley Hayes Architects, February 2009.
16 Charles Knight (ed.), *London*, vol.6, 1844, p.72. The author goes on to advocate a 'purification of our public statues', leaving no works standing 'that do not fulfil the conditions which Morality and Art are alike interested in demanding from the men whose effigies are to adorn our high places'.
17 The best summary of which is to be found in Read 1982, pp.82–128.
18 *Biographical Dictionary of Sculptors in Britain* (http://www.henry-moore.org/hmi/library/biographical-dictionary-of-sculptors-in-britain).
19 Yarrington et al. (1994), pp.299–300.
20 'Blow up the Duke Of Sutherland, but leave his limbs among the heather', *Independent*, 9 October 1994; 'Attempts to topple Duke of Sutherland statue', *BBC News*, 29 November 2011.
21 Hansard, *House of Commons Debate*, 19 May 1854, vol.133, cc.656–7.
22 *Biographical Dictionary of Sculptors in Britain* (http://www.henry-moore.org/hmi/library/biographical-dictionary-of-sculptors-in-britain).
23 *The Builder*, 11 January 1851, p.22.
24 'Leicester Square Area: Leicester Estate', in Sheppard 1966, pp.416–40.
25 *The Graphic* (London), Saturday, 4 July 1874; *Daily News* (London), Friday 10 March 1865.
26 McParland 1987, p.195.

GRINLING GIBBONS' EQUESTRIAN STATUE OF WILLIAM III, COLLEGE GREEN, DUBLIN

27 Green 1964, p.136; Beard1989, p.89; *Biographical Dictionary of Sculptors in Britain* (http://www.henry-moore.org/hmi/library/biographical-dictionary-of-sculptors-in-britain).
28 Robert Pool and John Cash, *Views of the Most Remarkable Public Buildings, Monuments and other edifices in the city of Dublin*, Dublin 1780, pp.10–11; Whelan 2002.
29 *London News-Letter*, London, Saturday 25 February 1716.
30 Whelan 2002.
31 *Daily Courant*, London, Friday 1 September 1710.
32 *Daily Courant*, London, Tuesday 31 January 1716.
33 Whelan 2002.
34 *Post Man and the Historical Account*, London, 6 November 1714 – 9 November 1714.
35 *News-Letter*, London, Saturday 25 February 1716.
36 Quoted in Whelan 2002.
37 *The Times*, Tuesday 12 April 1836.
38 Whelan 2002.
39 *The Times* (quoting *Saunders NewsLetter*), Monday 11 April 1836.
40 Ibid.
41 Wednesday 13 April 1836; Monday 18 April; Tuesday 19 April; Friday 22 April; Monday 25 April 25.
42 Copied in *The Times*, Monday 4 July 1836.
43 Strickland 1913, vol.2, p.485.
44 *The Times*, Saturday 16 July 1836.
45 Whelan 2002.
46 Murphy 2010, p.9.
47 Green 1964, p.136.
48 Whelan, op cit; *The Times*, Monday 12 November 1928
49 *The Times*, Tuesday 12 April 1836.

JOSEPH WILTON'S EQUESTRIAN STATUE OF WILLIAM III, BOWLING GREEN, NEW YORK

50 No longer extant. The Berkeley Square statue collapsed under its own weight in the early nineteenth century and had to be removed in 1827. 'Joseph Wilton', in *A Biographical Dictionary of Sculptors in Britain 1660–1851* (www.henry-moore.org/hmi/library/biographical-dictionary-of-sculptors-in-britain, accessed 12 April 2013).
51 In fact, it seems likely that New York received the statue destined for Berkeley Square, for despite being commissioned two years later, the New York monument was dedicated two years before its London counterpart. See Marks 1981.
52 Oliver Wolcott Papers, Connecticut Historical Society Museum, quoted in 'The Tale of the Horse. Spinning Litchfield's Revolutionary Stories', an anonymous essay (http://www. litchfieldhistorical-society.org/musuem/exhibit6.php).
53 Letter from Lieutenant Cadwalader Colden to the Earl of Hillsborough, 18 August 1770, quoted in Coutu 2006, p.224.
54 Coutu 2006, p.231.
55 According to an 1845 statement made by Capt. Oliver Brown of Wellsburg, West Virginia, who was in command of the troops at the time. 'King George's Head', *Sons of the American Revolution Magazine*, Winter 1998 (www.connecticut-sar.org/articles/king_georges_head.htm, accessed 12 April 2013).
56 Hutchinson 1886, p.167. The whereabouts of the head are no longer known.
57 A bullet mould used for this purpose was discovered in the orchard of the Wolcott House (Litchfield Historical Society, Connecticut, USA).
58 Oliver Wolcott Papers, Connecticut Historical Society Museum.
59 Letter from Ebenezer Hazard to Horatio Gates, New York, 12 July 1776, New York Historical Society, Gates Papers.

SIR FRANCIS CHANTREY'S STATUE OF WILLIAM PITT, HANOVER SQUARE, LONDON

60 Yarrington et al. (1994), pp.195–6.
61 'Notes from Cunningham's Handbook for London', *Notes and Queries*, Saturday 4 May 1850, pp.436–7.
62 Yarrington et al. (1994), p.195.
63 *The Examiner*, Sunday 18 September 1831.
64 *The Morning Chronicle*, Tuesday 1 May 1832.
65 Penny 1991; Sullivan 2013.

NELSON'S PILLAR, DUBLIN

66 Alderman Cope quoted in Henchy 1948, p.53.
67 Murphy 2010, p.10.
68 O'Brien 2007, p.15.
69 Whelan 2001.
70 Thomas Bodkin, speech given December 1955, quoted in Ó Riain 1998, p.24 (http://www.historyireland.com/volumes/volume6/issue4/features/?id=190, accessed 5 April 2013).
71 *Irish Times*, 8 March 1966.
72 *Irish Times*, 9 March 1966 and *Irish Independent*, 9 March 1966.
73 *Irish Independent*, 9 March 1966.
74 Dublin City Library and Archive, file Ar/add/ 50.

DEFACED COINS

75 *The Lord Mayor of London*, published by Birt, Printer, 39 Great St Andrews Street, Seven Dials, National Library of Scotland (Balcarres Heritage Trust material), Crawford.EB.2666.
76 Sheppard 1922, pp.109–10; Scott;1975, p.6.
77 Scott 1975, p.8.

5 SUFFRAGETTES

1 *The Suffragette*, 31 July 1914, p.122.
2 This term was first used in 1906 by the *Daily Mail* journalist Charles E. Hands. Crawford 1999, p.452.
3 Correspondence with the Viscount Dillon, 12 February 1913, National Portrait Gallery Archives.
4 National Gallery Archive, NG 1/8, pp.148–67.
5 *The Suffragette*, 13 March 1914, p.491.
6 Tony Bennett, 'Useful Culture', in Boswell and Evans 1999, p.382. See also Leahy 2012.
7 MacLeod 2006, p.47.
8 Bennett 1995, p.66.
9 This is not always the case, of course. Manchester Art Gallery in particular is keen to mark this aspect of its history, having highlighted it in various online materials and during its centenary celebrations.
10 *The Manchester Guardian*, 4 April 1914.
11 National Gallery Archive, NG 1/8, 145.
12 'To Suffragettes', *BLAST*, no. 1, 20 June 1914, p.151.
13 National Gallery Archive, NG 1/8, p.173.
14 *The Times*, 12 March 1914, p.6.
15 *The Times*, 5 May 1914.
16 Fowler 1991, p.115.
17 Edel 1984, p.712.
18 Plender and Reeve 2010.
19 MacLeod 2006, p.46.
20 *Wonder Women*, Manchester Art Gallery (http://www.manchestergalleries.org/the-collections/wonder-women/).

MARY RICHARDSON AND *THE ROKEBY VENUS*

21 *The Times*, 11 March 1914, p.9. See also Gell 1998, pp.62–5.
22 'The Masterpiece Described', in *The Times*. Quoted in Fowler 1991, p.112.
23 Richardson 1953, p.165.
24 Fowler 1991, p.112.
25 Estimated by Hawes Turner, Keeper and Secretary of the National Gallery, in Fowler 1991, p.111.
26 Ibid.

6 ATTACKS ON ART

1 Freedberg 1989, p.1.
2 Scott 2013 (forthcoming). On transgression in the museum, see also the excellent Leahy 2012, pp.127–52.
3 Rider 2011, p.173 describes the verbal attacks on Andre's *Equivalent VIII* as 'a phenomenon that has been so successfully mythologized and become so much a part of British popular folklore regarding modern art in general that it is tempting to … dismiss it out of hand'.
4 McKim-Smith 2002.
5 Clay 2007, pp.7–8 n.31. Clay cites Deloche and Leniaud 1989, p.34 n.15 and pp.80–1. On Gregoire, see Gamboni 1997, p.18.
6 Ward 1973. Goldstein 1996. See also Tamen 2001, pp.50–75.
7 See Gamboni 1997, pp.18–19ff.; Clay 2007, pp.7–11; Simpson 2010, pp.3–5; Gell 1998, pp.62–5.
8 See Stanley Cohen, 'Property Destruction: Motives and Meanings', in Ward 1973, pp.23–53, p.40.
9 See Oliver and Neal 2010; Fleming 2001.
10 Gamboni 1997, p.261.
11 Ibid. On readymades, see Ades, Cox and Hopkins 1999, pp.146–71; for more on *LHOOQ* see ibid., pp.131–2.
12 Gamboni 1997, p.282. See also Powell 2012, pp.95–101 on Duchamp, readymades and Man Ray.
13 Christopher Turner, *Tate Etc.*, issue 8, August 2006: 'The Chapmans were condemned in some corners of the press for this act of vandalism. They answered their critics with the "canonical defence",

this time citing Robert Rauschenberg's *Erased de Kooning Drawing* of 1953 ... to justify their attempt to eclipse Goya. The Chapmans' "rectification", or "improvement", as they termed their adaptation, revealed their ambivalent relation to the master...'. On Wyatt, see A. Buchanan, "Wyatt the Destroyer": a Vandal at Salisbury Cathedral?' in Boldrick and Clay 2007, pp.123–43.

14 On 'auto-erasure', see Baker 2010, pp.27–8. See also Krčma 2012.
15 See http://www.sfmoma.org/explore/collection/artwork/25846.
16 Krčma 2012. On erasure, see also Galpin 1998.
17 Scott 2013 (forthcoming).
18 Starling describes the work as 'counter-entropic': see '*Drop Sculpture (Atlas)*, A Project for the New Conservation Department, Rijksmuseum, Amsterdam', in Starling 2007.
19 Gamboni 1997, p.280.
20 See http://www.whitechapelgallery.org/exhibitions/childrens-art-commission-eva-rothschild-boys-and-sculpture.
21 Scott 2013 (forthcoming) categorises such interventions as 'artistic iconoclasm'.
22 McKim-Smith 2002.
23 See http://www.artsjournal.com/issues/Brooklyn.htm.
24 Severin Carrell, 'Surreal case of the Dali images and battle over artistic licence', *Guardian*, 27 January 2009 (http://www.guardian.co.uk/artanddesign/2009/jan/27/salvador-dali-art-design-scotland); Polly Smith, 'How to Restore a Salvador Dali Masterpiece' (http://www.youtube.com/watch?v=xsabULGXuuY).
25 Gamboni 1997, p.184 n.43, p.369; David Lee, 'The End of Henry Moore in Public?', *The Jackdaw*, October 2012 (http://www.thejackdaw.co.uk/?p=986).
26 Walker 1999, p.212.
27 Ibid, pp.126–7. Sarah Kent, 'Why Sculptor Mach Must Keep His Nerve', *Glasgow Herald*, November 1983.
28 Goss 2001; Dillon 2004.
29 On Shafrazi, see Gamboni 1997, p.192. See Scott's *Responding to Art Vandalism*, a detailed survey of vandalism in UK museums and galleries in Scott 2010, pp.11–24; Scott 2013 (forthcoming).
30 Dillon 2004. His categories include: the religious iconoclast, the radical (political and aesthetic), the bourgeois (civic and aesthetic judgment), the connoisseur, the avant-gardist, the failed artist and the madman.
31 See Sarah Crellin, 'Let There Be History: Epstein's BMA House Sculptures', in Curtis and Wilson 2011, pp.36–42; Wagner 2005, pp.31–57, pp.193–7.
32 Gamboni 1997, pp.153–4. Farr 1981, p.11.
33 Gamboni 1997, p.154. Wagner 2005, pp.68–9.
34 Dalya Alberge, 'Oscar Wilde's Refurbished Tomb Ends Lip Disservice', *Guardian*, 30 November 2011. John Tagliabue, 'Walling Off Oscar Wilde's Tomb from Admirer's Kisses', *New York Times*, 15 December 2011.
35 Cane and Smith 2013 (forthcoming).

REG BUTLER'S MAQUETTE FOR *THE UNKNOWN POLITICAL PRISONER*

36 Catalogue entry, *Working Model for the Unknown Political Prisoner Competition* 1955–6 (T02332), in *Tate Gallery* 1981 (http://www.tate.org.uk/art/artworks/butler-working-model-for-the-unknown-political-prisoner-t02332/text-catalogue-entry). This entry for another version of the sculpture, the larger 'Working Model', offers the most comprehensive account of the sculpture and its additional versions. See also Butler's 1958 BBC Television interview (http://www.bbc.co.uk/archive/sculptors/12801.shtml).
37 Catalogue entry in *Tate Gallery* 1981.
38 *International Sculpture Competition, The Unknown Political Prisoner*, exh. cat., Tate Gallery, London 1953, p.2.
39 Catalogue entry in *Tate Gallery* 1981; statement reported in *Times*, 17 March 1953; Burstow 1989; Burstow 1997; Calvocoressi 1981; Gamboni 1997, p.128.
40 T.W. Earp, *Daily Telegraph*, 13 March 1953.
41 'Man Crushes Prizewinning Sculpture', *Daily Telegraph*, 16 March 1953; 'How about This for The First Sight of England?', *Daily Sketch*, 18 March 1953.
42 'Puzzle Corner', *Daily Telegraph*, 17 March 1953.
43 'A Big Row for a Big Prize', *LIFE*, 1 June 1953, pp.39–42.
44 *Daily Herald*, 16 March 1953; 'A Wrecker in the Tate Gallery', *Daily Sketch*, 16 March 1953; 'Drama at the Tate – No. 1 Exhibit Smashed', *Daily Mirror*, 16 March 1953.
45 Burstow 1997, p.71; Walker 1999, p.35.
46 Burstow 1989, p.492, n.16. In Burstow's 1984 interview, Szilvassy disowned authorship of the article accredited to him: 'Art or Mockery?', *Sunday Pictorial*, 19 March 1953.
47 Butler quoted in *Daily Herald*, 16 March 1953.
48 Burstow 1989, pp.484–6; Walker 1999, p.35.
49 Walker 1999, p.35.
50 Calvocoressi 1981; Burstow 1989; Burstow 1997; Lapp 1998.

CARL ANDRE'S *EQUIVALENT VIII*

51 Memorandum, 24/5/72, Tate Public Records, Acquisitions File, Carl Andre TG 4/2/17/1, p.146 A.10.
52 Rider 2011, p.173. Curtis and Wilson 2011, p.194, no.86.
53 Ibid; Gilmour 1977; Cooper 1976; *Tate Gallery Biannual Report and Illustrated Catalogue of Acquisitions, 1972–1974*, London 1975. Gilmour also cites Bernard Denvir's 1975 essay in the *Times Educational Supplement*.
54 Rider 2011, p.174; Colin Simpson, 'The Tate Drops a Costly Brick', *Sunday Times*, 15 February 1976, p.53.
55 Rider 2011, p.174. Philip Mellor, 'Whichever Way You Look at Britain's Latest Work of Art... WHAT A LOAD OF RUBBISH', 16 February 1976, p.1; Mulholland 2003, pp.5–10. For Andre's response to the press coverage, see 'The Bricks Abstract: A Compilation by Carl Andre', *Art Monthly*, October 1976, vol.1, p.24, published in Meyer 2005, p.36.
56 'Notes Relating to the Vandalism', Tate Conservation File, 1973.
57 Rider 2011, p.173.
58 'Toff Tips Blue Dye on Tate's Bricks', *Sun*, 24 February 1976; Nicholas Comfort, 'Blue Dye Blacks out the Tate's Bricks', *Daily Telegraph*, 24 February 1976.
59 Ronald Ricketts, 'Splash! Those Arty Bricks Get the Blues', *Daily Mirror*, 24 February 1976.
60 Ricketts 1976; 'Tate's Bricks are Off Colour', *Morning Telegraph Sheffield*, 24 February 1976; 'Tate Bricks Take a Bath', *Western Morning News*, 24 February 1976; 'Tate Bricks Disfigured', *Times*, 24 February 1976.
61 Morphet 1976.
62 Rider 2011, pp.173–6, 191–3. Scott 2010b, p.34; Walker 1999, pp.73–8.
63 Rider 2011, pp.191–4.
64 Ibid., pp.174 n.11, 256; Gilmour 1977; Bailey 2011.
65 William Packer, 'Carl Andre's Bricks', *Financial Times*, 3 May 1977; Rider 2011, p.256 n.5.
66 Sandy Nairne, note to Richard Morphet, 10 May 1972, Tate Public Records, Acquisitions File, Carl Andre TG 4/2/17/1.
67 Sandy Nairne, letters to Dick Eshbaugh, Tate Conservation File, July 1977 and March 1978, Tate Public Records, Acquisitions File, Carl Andre TG 4/2/17/1; Packer 1977.
68 Claire Fontaine also showed a work in the form of *Equivalent VIII* at Galerie Chantal Crousel, Frieze Art Fair, in 2008. My thanks to Alistair Rider for this reference.

ALLEN JONES' *CHAIR*

69 Morgan 1999, pp.73–4.
70 Catalogue entry, *Tate Gallery* 1984 (http://www.tate.org.uk/art/artworks/jones-chair-t03244).
71 Walker 1999, pp.144–9.
72 Ibid, pp.147–8; Mulvey 1973; Tickner 1979.
73 Roger Ackland/Roy Perry, internal memorandum: Re. Damage to Allen Jones's Chair, Tate Conservation File, 17 March 1986.
74 Ackland/Perry, attached letter dated 4 March 1986.
75 '"Porn" Chair is Damaged', *Mail on Sunday*, 9 March 1986.
76 Ackland/Perry 1986.
77 Morgan 1999, p.75.
78 Attwood 2009.

7 DESTRUCTION IN ART

1 The full text is printed in *Peace News*, 24 February 1961. The paper pinned to the door of the Ministry was immediately destroyed.
2 Alexander Trocchi, statement, typewritten and duplicated transcript of the *International Writers' Conference*, Edinburgh, session for 24 August 1962, p.11.
3 Ibid., p.18.
4 This phrase was coined by Jeff Nuttall and used by him as the title for his memoir first published in 1968. In it he explains: 'To a certain degree the Underground happened everywhere spontaneously. It was simply what you did in the H-bomb world if you were, by nature, creative and concerned for humanity as a whole ... concerned for the business of being human in whatever happened to be the conditions surrounding humanity, convinced that the business of being human and the continuation of that business is intrinsically, not relatively, important, possessed by a sense of warm and sensuous well-being in one's membership of everybody else' (Nuttall 1971 p.160).
5 This outlook is well expressed by David McReynolds writing in *Peace News* (9 September 1960, p.5): 'I believe the Bomb has had a profound effect on the Beat generation. This is the first time in our history when we knew there might not be any future at all ... Today we know the future may vanish at any moment, time itself becomes a stillness, and the earth silent. Technology, which cut us off from the past by destroying the old sense of community has also cut us off from the future by giving us the hydrogen bomb.'
6 Gustav Metzger, 'Introduction', *Treasures from East Anglian Churches*, The Crypt, Clifton House, King's Lynn 1957, unpaginated. A copy of this ephemeral publication was recently discovered by Mathieu Copeland, and I am grateful to him for generously bringing it to my attention.
7 Detail regarding Metzger's anti-nuclear activities can be found in Andrew Wilson, 'papa what did you do when the nazis built the concentration camps? My dear, they never told us anything', in Metzger 1996, pp.64–73.
8 Pat Arrowsmith, 'Auto-Destructive Art', *Peace News*, 22 July 1960, p.11.
9 Gustav Metzger, 'Auto-Destructive Art', 4 November 1959, reprinted in Metzger 1996, p.59.
10 Gustav Metzger, *Auto-Destructive Art, Metzger at AA*, London 1965, p.1, reprinted in Metzger 1996, p.25.
11 Gustav Metzger, 'Auto-Destructive Art, Machine Art, Auto-Creative Art', 23 June 1961, reprinted in Metzger 1996, p.60.
12 'Quotes from Bow Street', *Peace News*, September 15, 1961, p.7. Metzger was imprisoned for one month.
13 In Gustav Metzger, *Auto-Destructive Art, Metzger at AA*, London 1965, p.1, reprinted in Metzger 1996, p.25, Metzger writes that 'auto-destructive art is not simply the therapeutic instrument of a frustrated iconoclast – but a coherent, a necessary phase in the development of modern art'.
14 Ibid., p.44.
15 Gustav Metzger, untitled statement, *Art and Artists*, August 1966, p.22.
16 Ibid.
17 Gustav Metzger, 'Excerpts from Selected Papers Presented at the 1966 "Destruction In Art Symposium"', *Studio International*, December 1966, p.282.
18 Cover caption, *Art & Artists*, August 1966, p.3.
19 Raphael Montañez Ortiz, letter to the author, 24 May 2012.
20 Ralph Ortiz (Raphael Montañez Ortiz), 'A letter to *Art & Artists*, June 1966' as part

of 'Ralph Ortiz', *Art & Artists*, August 1966, p.62.

21 The only strictures DIAS had placed on participating artists were that the events should place no one, audience or artists, in danger, that animals should not be killed and that all artists should take legal responsibility for their actions. In the first week of DIAS events, Ortiz had himself ritualistically killed a chicken and read its entrails, yet this was an event removed from the official programme of DIAS.

22 A fuller transcript of this symposium, giving an account of the demonstrations by Metzger as well as the following discussion between Metzger, Houédard, Ivor Davies, Mark Boyle and the audience, was published by Metzger soon after DIAS.

23 Publicity flyer for the Dialectics of Liberation Congress, July 1967.

24 Ralph Ortiz (Raphael Montañez Ortiz), 'Destructivism', handout distributed at DIAS, reprinted without title in Gustav Metzger, 'Excerpts from Selected Papers Presented at the 1966 "Destruction In Art Symposium"', December 1966, p.282.

25 Joe Berke, 'Man as Self-Destroying Art', excerpt printed without title, ibid., p.283.

26 'South Vietnam: The Light That Failed', *Time*, 10 June 1966.

27 Mark Boyle, 'Appendix 8, Animal', in *Journey to the Centre of the Earth: Mark Boyle's Atlas and Manual*, London 1970, unpaginated.

28 Ibid.

29 Mark Boyle, untitled statement in *Control*, no.1, 1965, unpaginated.

RAPHAEL MONTANEZ ORTIZ, *DUNCAN TERRACE PIANO DESTRUCTION CONCERT: THE LANDEMANS' HOMAGE TO 'SPRING CAN REALLY HANG YOU UP THE MOST'*

30 Personal communication, 24 May 2012.

31 The piano destruction concert was recorded by a friend of the Landesmans who had encouraged the New York radio station WBAI to air it.

32 Jay Landesman, 'Two Views of DIAS; September is the Cruellest Month', *International Times*, no.1, 14–27 October 1966, p.9. For an account of Landesman's recollection of DIAS see his *Jaywalking* (Landesman 1992), pp.43–5.

33 Jay Landesman, *International Times*, ibid. Ortiz had mistakenly destroyed a baby grand piano that had been newly purchased by the BBC.

34 Raphael Montañez Ortiz, 'Destructivism', one-sheet privately printed handout distributed at DIAS, reprinted without title in Gustav Metzger, 'Excerpts from Selected Papers Presented at the 1966 "Destruction In Art Symposium"', *Studio International*, December 1966, p.282. His first manifesto of 'Destructivism', circulated in 1962, is reprinted in Ortiz and Stiles 1988, p.52.

8 ART TRANSFORMED

1 Note found by Ayers's bedside after he died in his sleep, 18 February 2013. Sean O'Hagan, 'Kevin Ayers Obituary', *Guardian*, 20 February. 2013. Ayers was a founding member of the band Soft Machine.

2 Bachelard 1964, p.7.

3 McKee 2008, p.7.

4 Cooke and Gordon 2008, p.18.

5 Rugoff and Luckett 2012.

6 Gamboni 1997, p.255. Nietzsche 2009 edn.

7 Gamboni 1997, p.264, cites Christian Zervos, 'Conversations avec Pablo Picasso', *Cahiers d'art*, vol.10, nos.7–10, 1935, pp.173–8, p.173.

8 Gamboni 1997, pp.257–9. Groys 2008 and Lütticken 2009. See also the Hirshhorn Museum's exhibition *Damage Control: Art and Destruction since 1950* coinciding with this survey.

9 Noyes 2013 (forthcoming).

10 Massey 1995.

11 Roberts 1981.

12 Sillars 2009.

13 Ibid, p.23, cites Calvin Tomkins, *The Bride and the Bachelors: Five Masters of the Avant Garde*, New York 1965.

14 Gamboni 1997, p.273. See also Tomkins and Schwabsky 2007.

15 Inventory in *Michael Landy: Break Down Inventory*, Manchester 2002. *Michael Landy: Break Down*, Artangel, London 2001. See also http://www.artangel.org.uk/projects/2001/break_down

16 Sillars 2009, p.27.

17 Beech 2006.

18 Stolper and Wilson 2004.

19 Walker 1999, pp.83–93. COUM Trans-missions became Throbbing Gristle in 1976.

20 These concerns are distinct from those about identity and power associated with appropriation art (see Welchman 2001) and have more of an affinity with Hal Foster's 'archival impulse'. Foster 2004. On destruction in contemporary art more broadly, see Christov-Bakargiev 2012.

21 Such as *Relics* 1972–ongoing (ashes from burned paintings in glass containers) and *Painting Books and Painting Blocks* 1972–84 (paintings reconfigured in books and blocks).

22 See Toren 2012.

23 See Taylor 2013; Rancière 2007.

24 On the post-Reformation rise of portraiture in relation to iconoclasm, see Simpson 2010, pp.134–5, 137. See also Pointon 2013.

25 Groys 2008.

26 Personal communication, 2013.

27 Dominic Paterson, 'Not Just the Perfect Moment', exhibition text, Drawing Room, London; see also Davis 2010.

28 Pelevin and Weinreich 2012, p.47. In the 1990s the Western press linked hanging tapes with hanging bodies, associating the action with the killing of music shop owners, but this symbolic meaning was neither necessarily intentional nor accurate; Jamal Elias and James Noyes, personal communication.

29 Personal communication with Michael Wilkinson, 2012.

30 Fisher 2011, p.112, first published in *Michael Wilkinson 'Lions after Slumber'*, exh. cat., Modern Institute, Glasgow 2009.

31 Fisher 2011, p.109.

32 Cooke and Gordon 2008, pp.14–15: 'I thought that mixing the drama of perverse ritual with Warhol's Catholicism could add a nice refrain.'

33 Cooke and Gordon 2008, pp. 13–14. Thanks to Katy Pallister for information about Gordon's work.

34 Mark Francis, 'Repeat after Me', in Cooke and Gordon 2008, p.5, links Gordon with Gustav Metzger and the DIAS artists. Pete Townsend, Daltrey's fellow band member in The Who, was inspired by Gustav Metzger to destroy his guitar in a public performance.

35 Bracewell 2010, p.12. See also Company 2011 and Stezaker 2011. The original portrait painted by Franz Xaver Winterhalter in 1859 and now in the Royal Collection (at Buckingham Palace) was reproduced as a frontispiece for a biography of Queen Victoria. As as child, Stezaker was drawn to the image and scribbled on it, later incorporating the image into this work. Thanks to Eugene Barilo von Reisberg for identifying this work, and to Alison McQueen for providing direction. See Elizabeth Manchester's text for Stezaker's comments about the image: http://www.tate.org.uk/art/artworks/stezaker-third-person-t12349/text-summary.

36 Léith 2008, p.12. Bracewell 2010, p.17. John Stezaker in conversation with Christophe Gallois and Daniel F. Herrmann in 'The Third Meaning', Stezaker 2010, pp.34–45.

37 Herbert 2011, p.142.

38 Ibid., p.145.

39 Ibid., p.234.

LUCY SKAER

40 Leaver-Yap 2008, p.92.

41 Fiduccia 2009, p.32.

42 Personal communication with the artist, 2013.

43 Zakaitis 2012, pp.30–1.

JAKE AND DINOS CHAPMAN

44 Turner 2006.

45 Baker 2013 (forthcoming); Baker 2010.

46 Turner 2006; Barson 2006; Adams 2010. See also Kristeva 1982.

47 Baker 2010, pp.29–35 Adams 2010, p.58.

48 Baker 2010, pp.28–9.

49 Barrett and Chapman 2007, pp.2–8, pp.3–4.

50 Will Self writes about the series in relation to hallucinogenic states of perception and 'hectomorphism', whereby images change shape in hundreds of ways (http://will-self.com/2008/08/14/interview-with-the-chapman-brothers/).

51 Pointon 2013.

52 Sanders 2007. Denise Hawrysio's group exhibition *15/1* held in 1992 explored this idea through installation.

53 Hopkins 2007.

54 Baker 2010, p.47. See also Bataille 1988.

55 Grunenberg 2006.

BIBLIOGRAPHY

Parveen Adams, 'Hanged, Drawn and Quartered or Goya after the Chapmans', in *Inside the Death Drive: Excess and Apocalypse in the World of the Chapman Brothers*, ed. J. Harris, Tate Liverpool Critical Forum, no.11, Liverpool 2010, pp.55–75

Dawn Ades, Neil Cox and David Hopkins, *Marcel Duchamp*, London 1999

William Anderson, 'Re-discovery, Collecting and Display of English Medieval Alabasters', *Journal of the History of Collections*, vol.16, no.1, 2004, pp.47–58

Arjun Appadurai (ed.), *The Social Life of Things: Commodities in Cultural Perspective*, Cambridge 1988

Margaret Aston, 'English ruins and English history: the dissolution and the sense of the past', *Journal of the Warburg and Courtauld Institutes*, vol.36, 1973, pp.231–55

Margaret Aston, *Lollards and Reformers: Images and Literacy in Late Medieval England*, London 1984

Margaret Aston, *England's Iconoclasts: Laws Against Images*, Oxford 1988

Margaret Aston, *Faith and Fire: Popular and Unpopular Religion 1350–1600*, London 1993, pp.267–71

Margaret Aston, 'Puritans and Iconoclasm 1560–1660', in *The Culture of English Puritanism 1560–1700*, eds. C. Durston and J. Eales, Basingstoke 1996, pp.92–121

Margaret Aston, 'Public Worship and Iconoclasm', in *The Archaeology of Reformation 1480–1580*, eds. D. Gaimster and R. Gilchrist, Leeds 2003, pp.9–28

Margaret Aston, 'Moving Pictures: Foxe's Book of Martyrs and Little Gidding', in *Agent of Change: Print Culture Studies after Elizabeth L. Eisenstein*, eds. S. Alcorn Baron, E. Lindquist and E.F. Shelvin, Massachusetts 2007, pp.84–104

Feona Attwood, *Mainstreaming Sex: The Sexualisation of Western Culture*, London 2009

Dom Hugh Aveling, 'The Rievaulx community after the dissolution', *Ampleforth Journal*, no.57, 1952, p.101

Gaston Bachelard, *The Psychoanalysis of Fire*, trans. A.C.M. Ross (originally *La Psychanalyse du Feu*, 1938), Boston 1964

A.G.H. Bachrach and R.G. Collmer, *Lodewijck Huygens: The English Journal, 1651–1652*, Leiden 1981

Martin Bailey, 'Revealed: Secrets of the Tate Bricks', *Art Newspaper*, no.224, May 2011 (http://theartnewspaper.com/articles/Revealed%3A+secrets+of+the+Tate+bricks/23578)

Simon Baker, 'Quartered, Drawn and Hung (Chapman, Chapman, Condo and McCarthy)', in *Inside the Death Drive: Excess and Apocalypse in the World of the Chapman Brothers*, ed. J. Harris, Tate Liverpool Critical Forum, no.11, Liverpool 2010, pp.27–54

Simon Baker, 'The Cruel Practice of Art', in *Striking Images, Iconoclasms Past and Present*, eds. S. Boldrick, L. Brubaker and R. Clay, Farnham 2013 (forthcoming)

Malcolm Baker, *The Marble Index: Roubiliac and Sculptural Portraiture in Eighteenth-Century Britain* (forthcoming)

David Barrett and Jake and Dinos Chapman, 'Interview', in *Jake and Dinos Chapman: New Art Up-Close 3*, London 2007, pp.2–8

Tanya Barson, 'Powers of Laughter', in *Jake and Dinos Chapman: Bad Art for Bad People*, eds. C. Grunenberg and T. Barson, exh. cat., Tate Liverpool 2006, pp.66–85

George Bataille, 'Attraction and Repulsion I: Tropisms, Sexuality, Laughter and Tears', and 'Attraction and Repulsion II: Social Structure', in *The College of Sociology (1937–39)*, ed. D. Hollier, trans. B. Wing, Minneapolis 1988

Jonathan Bate and Dora Thornton, *Shakespeare: Staging the World*, exh cat British Museum 2012.

Geoffrey Beard, *The Work of Grinling Gibbons*, London 1989

Brigitte Bedos-Rezak, *When Ego Was Imago: Signs of Identity in the Middle Ages*, Leiden 2010

Dave Beech, 'Shock: A Report on Contemporary Art', in *Jake and Dinos Chapman: Bad Art for Bad People*, eds. C. Grunenberg and T. Barson, exh. cat., Tate Liverpool 2006, pp.98–110

Hans Belting, *Likeness and Presence: A History of the Image before the Era of Art*, trans. Edmund Jephcott, Chicago 1994

Tony Bennett, *The Birth of the Museum*, London 1995

Paul Binski, *Becket's Crown: Art and Imagination in Gothic England, 1170–1300*, New Haven and London 2004

A Biographical Dictionary of Sculptors in Britain 1660–1851, eds. I. Roscoe, E. Hardy and M.G. Sullivan, New Haven and London 2009

Sarah Blick, 'Reconstructing the Shrine of St. Thomas Becket', in *Art and Architecture of Late Medieval Pilgrimage in Northern Europe and the British Isles (Texts)*, eds. S. Blick and R. Tekippe, *Studies in Medieval and Reformation Traditions*, vol.104, Leiden and Boston 2005, pp.405–41

Sarah Blick, 'Votives, Images, Interaction and Pilgrimage to the Tomb and Shrine of St Thomas Becket, Canterbury Cathedral', in *Push Me, Pull You: Art and Devotional Interaction in Late Medieval and Renaissance Art*, eds. S. Blick and L.D. Gelfand, Leiden and Boston 2011, vol.2, pp.21–58

Sarah Blick, 'Bent Coins', *Encyclopedia of Medieval Pilgrimage*, online publication (http://www.encquran.brill.nl/entries/encyclopedia-of-medieval-pilgrimage/bent-coins-SIM_00017), Brill Online, 2013

S. Boldrick and R. Clay (eds.), *Iconoclasm: Contested Objects, Contested Terms*, Aldershot 2007

S. Boldrick, L. Brubaker and R. Clay (eds.), *Striking Images, Iconoclasms Past and Present*, Farnham (forthcoming)

D. Boswell and J. Evans, *Representing the Nation: A Reader, Histories, Heritage and Museums*, Routledge 1999

Michael Bracewell, Paul Stolper and Andrew Wilson, *No Future: SEX, Seditionaries and the Sex Pistols*, exh. cat., The Hospital, London 2004

Michael Bracewell, 'Behind the Lines: the Art of John Stezaker', in *John Stezaker*, exh. cat., Whitechapel Gallery, London 2010, pp. 10–19

Richard Bradley, *The Passage of Arms: An archaeological analysis of prehistoric hoards and votive deposits*, Cambridge 1990

Sabine Breitwesser, Justin Hoffmann, Kristine Stiles and Andrew Wilson, *Gustav Metzger: History History*, exh. cat., Generali Foundation, Vienna 2005

Richard Brilliant and Dale Kinney, *Reuse Value: Spolia and Appropriation in Art and Architecture from Constantine to Sherrie Levine*, Farnham 2011

Robert Burstow, 'Butler's Competition Project for a Monument to "The Unknown Political Prisoner Competition": Abstraction and Cold War Politics', *Art History*, vol.12, no.4, December 1989, pp.472–96

Robert Burstow, 'The Limits of Modernist Art as a "Weapon of the Cold War": Reassessing the Unknown Patron of the Unknown Political Prisoner Competition', *Oxford Art Journal*, vol.20, no.1, 1997, pp.68–80

John Butler, *The Quest for Becket's Bones*, New Haven and London 1995

Rex Butler (ed.), *Jeremy Gilbert-Rolfe: Art after Deconstruction*, Brisbane 2011

Caroline Walker Bynum, *Christian Materiality: An Essay on Religion in Late Medieval Europe*, New York 2011

Calendar of State Papers Domestic: William and Mary, 1689–90, ed. William John Hardy, London (1895) 1969

Richard Calvocoressi, 'Public Sculpture in the 1950s', in *British Sculpture in the Twentieth Century*, eds. S. Nairne and N. Serota, exh. cat., Whitechapel Art Gallery, London 1981, pp.134–53

Michael Camille, *The Gothic Idol: Ideology and Image-making in Medieval Art*, Cambridge 1989

David Campany, 'Two Images and a Reflection', in *John Stezaker Film Still: Collages since 1979*, London 2011, pp.7–13

Simon Cane and Jonathan Ashley Smith, 'Iconoclasm as Conservation, Concealment and Subversion', in *Striking Images, Iconoclasms Past and Present*, eds. S. Boldrick, L. Brubaker and R. Clay, Farnham 2013 (forthcoming)

W.D. Caroe, 'Canterbury Cathedral Choir during the Commonwealth and after, with special reference to two oil paintings', *Archaeologia*, no.62, 1911, pp.353–66

Gerald Carr, 'Benjamin West's Altar Paintings for St Marylebone Church', *Art Bulletin*, vol.62, no.2, June 1980, pp.293–303

Michael Carter, 'Late medieval relief sculptures of the annunciation to the Virgin from the Cistercian abbeys of Rievaulx and Fountains', *Cîteaux: Commentarii Cistercienses*, no.60, 2009, pp.1–22

Madeline H. Caviness, *The Early Stained Glass of Canterbury Cathedral circa 1175–1220*, Princeton 1977

Madeline H. Caviness, *Corpus Vitrearum Medii Aevi, Great Britain*, vol.2: *Christ Church Cathedral Canterbury*, London and New York 1981

John Chapman, *Fragmentation in Archaeology: People, Places and Broken Objects in the Prehistory of South-Eastern Europe*, London and New York 2000

Charlotte Chastel-Rousseau 'Originals or replicas? Royal equestrian monuments in eighteenth-century Great Britain and Ireland', in *Reading the Royal Monument in Eighteenth-Century Europe*, ed. C. Chastel-Rousseau, Farnham 2011, pp.153–72

John Cherry, 'The Breaking of Seals', *Middelalderlige segl-stamper i Norden*, eds. M. Andersen and G. Tegnér, Roskilde 2002, pp.81–96

Carolyn Christov-Bakargiev, 'On the Destruction of Art – or Conflict and Art, or Trauma and the Art of Healing', in

The Book of Books: dOCUMENTA (13), exh. cat., vol.1, Ostfildern 2012, pp.282–95
M.T. Clanchy, *From Memory to Written Record, England 1066–1307*, 2nd edn, Oxford 1993
Richard Clay, 'Contested Objects, Contested Terms', in *Iconoclasm: Contested Objects, Contested Terms*, eds. S. Boldrick and R. Clay, Aldershot 2007, pp.5–14
Michael W. Cole and Rebecca E. Zorach (eds.), *The 'Idol' in the Age of Art: Objects, Devotions and the Early Medieval World*, Farnham 2009
Simon Coleman and John Elsner, 'Pilgrimage to Walsingham and the Re-Invention of the Middle Ages', in *Pilgrimage Explored*, ed. J. Stopford, Woodbridge 1999, pp.189–214
Lynne Cooke and Douglas Gordon, 'Interview: Lynne Cooke in Conversation with Douglas Gordon', in *Douglas Gordon: self-portrait of you + me, after the factory*, with texts by Mark Francis, Francis McKee, Lynne Cooke, exh. cat., Gagosian Gallery, New York 2008, pp.13–22
Douglas Cooper, 'Painters of Light and Mood. 2', in *Books and Bookmen*, no.21, January 1976, p.16
Trevor Cooper (ed.), *The Journal of William Dowsing: Iconoclasm in East Anglia during the English Civil War*, Woodbridge 2001
Walter Arthur Copinger, *The Laboryouse Journey and serche of John Leyland for England's antiquities*, Manchester 1895
Glyn Coppack, 'Some descriptions of Rievaulx Abbey in 1538–9: the disposition of a major Cistercian precinct i n the early sixteenth century', *Journal of the British Archaeological Association*, no.139, 1986, pp.101–33
Glyn Coppack, *Abbeys: Yorkshire's Monastic Heritage*, London 1988
Joan Coutu, *Persuasion and Propaganda: Monuments and the Eighteenth-Century British Empire*, Montreal, London and Ithaca 2006
Elizabeth Crawford, *The Women's Suffrage Movement: A Reference Guide, 1866–1928*, London 1999
David Cressy, *Travesties and Transgressions in Tudor and Stuart England: Tales of discord and dissension*, Oxford 2000, pp.234–50
David Cressy, 'The Downfall of Cheapside Cross: Vandalism, Ridicule and Iconoclasm', in D. Cressy, *Agnes Bowker's Cat: Travesties and Transgressions in Tudor and Stuart England*, Oxford 2001
John Crook, *English Medieval Shrines*, Woodbridge 2011
C. Cross, 'A Medieval Yorkshire Library', *Northern History*, no.25, 1989
Penelope Curtis and Keith Wilson (eds.), *Modern British Sculpture*, exh. cat., Royal Academy of Arts, London 2011
Peter Davidson 'The Solemnity of the Madonna Vulnerata, Valladolid, 1600', in *Triumphs of the Defeated*, eds. P. Davidson and J. Bepler, Wiesbaden 2007, pp.39–54
Kate Davis, *Role Forward*, exh. cat., Centre for Contemporary Arts, Glasgow 2010
Bernard Deloche and Jean-Michel Leniaud, eds., *La culture des sans-culottes: Le premier dossier du patrimoine 1789–1798*, Paris and Montpellier 1989
A.G. Dickens (ed.), *Tudor Treatises*, Yorkshire Archaeological Society Record Series, vol.125, Wakefield 1959
Georges Didi-Huberman, *Confronting Images: Questioning the Ends of a Certain History of Art*, trans. J. Goodman, University Park, PA 2005
Brian Dillon, 'Seven Faces of the Art Vandal', *Tate Etc.*, no.2, autumn 2004 (http://www.tate.org.uk/context-comment/articles/seven-faces-art-vandal)
Jeremy Dimmick, James Simpson and Nicolette Zeeman (eds.), *Images, Idolatry and Iconoclasm in Late Medieval England: Textuality and the Visual Image*, Oxford 2002
Susan Doran (ed.), *Henry VIII: Man and Monarch*, exh. cat., British Library, London 2009
Mark Dorrian, '9/11, Three Years On', *arq: Architectural Research Quarterly*, vol.8, no.1, 2004, pp.84–8
Eamon Duffy, *The Stripping of the Altars: Traditional Religion in England 1400–1580*, New Haven and London 1992 (2nd edn 2005)
Eamon Duffy, 'The parish, piety, and patronage in late medieval East Anglia: The evidence of rood screens', in *The Parish in English Life 1400–1600*, eds. K. French, G. Gibbs and B. Kümin, Manchester 1997, pp.133–62
Eamon Duffy, *Marking the Hours: English People and their Prayers 1240–1570*, New Haven and London 2006
Eamon Duffy, 'The Reformation and the Alabastermen', in *Object of Devotion: Medieval English Alabaster Sculpture from the Victoria and Albert Museum*, ed. P. Williamson, Alexandria, VA 2010, pp.54–65
Paul Dyck and Stuart Williams, *Towards an Electronic Edition of an Early Modern Assembled Book*, online publication (http://projects.chass.utoronto.ca/chwp/CHC2007/Dyck_Williams/Dyck_Williams.htm), 2008
Jacqueline Eales, 'Sir Robery Harley, KB (1579–1656) and the "character" of a puritan', *British Library Journal*, no.15, 1989, pp.134–57
Leon Edel (ed.), *The Letters of Henry James*, vol.4: *1895–1916*, Cambridge MA 1984
James Elkins, *The Object Stares Back: On the Nature of Seeing*, New York 1996
James Elkins, *Pictures and Tears: A History of People Who Have Cried in Front of Paintings*, New York and London 2004
Josh Ellenbogen and Aaron Tugendhaft (eds.), *Idol Anxiety*, Stanford, CA 2011
H. Ellis, *Original Letters Illustrative of English History*, London 1824–46, vol.3
Jaś Elsner, 'Iconoclasm and the Preservation of Memory', in *Monuments and Memory: Made and Unmade*, eds. R.S. Nelson and M. Olin, Chicago 2003, pp.209–32
Desiderius Erasmus, 'A Pilgrimage for Religion's Sake' [1526], in *Collected Works of Erasmus: Colloquies*, trans. Craig R. Thomson, vol.40, Toronto 1997
Katharine Esdaile, 'Changes at St Margaret's Westminster, 1761', *Church Quarterly Review*, no.300, July/September 1950, pp.230–44
J. Evans and N. Cook, 'A Statue of Christ from the ruins of Mercers' Hall', *Archaeological Journal*, no.111, 1955, pp.168–80
F.R. Fairbank, 'Roche Abbey: Further report on the excavations there', *Associated Architectural Societies Reports and Papers*, vol.19, 1885, pp.392–7
Alexander Faludy, 'Linge, Bernard van', in *Oxford Dictionary of National Biography*, May 2005
Dennis Farr, 'The Patronage and Support of Sculptors', in *British Sculpture in the Twentieth Century*, eds. S. Nairne and N. Serota, exh. cat., Whitechapel Art Gallery, London 1981, pp.9–37
Jane Fawcett, *Historic Floors: Their History and Conservation*, Oxford 1998
Peter Fergusson, *Roche Abbey*, London (1990) 1999
Peter Fergusson and Stuart Harrison, *Rievaulx Abbey: Community, Architecture, Memory*, New Haven and London 1999
Peter Fergusson, Stuart Harrison and Glyn Coppack, *Rievaulx Abbey*, London (2006) 2010
Joanna Fiduccia, 'Fathoming Gestures', in *Lucy Skaer – A Boat Used as a Vessel*, exh. cat., Kunsthalle, Basle 2009, pp.31–3
Kenneth Fincham and Nicholas Tyacke, *Altars Restored: The Changing Face of English Religious Worship 1547–c.1700*, Oxford 2007
Mark Fisher, untitled essay in *Michael Wilkinson, 1979–*, London 2011
Juliet Fleming, *Graffiti and the Writing Arts of Early Modern England*, London 2001
Finbarr Barry Flood, 'Between Cult and Culture: Bamiyan, Islamic Iconoclasm and the Museum', *The Art Bulletin*, vol.84, no.4, 2002, pp.641–59
Finbarr Barry Flood and Zoë Strother, 'Editorial: Between Creation and Destruction', *Res*, 48, 2005, pp.5–10
Finbarr Barry Flood, 'Notes from the Field: Anthropomorphism', *Art Bulletin*, vol.94, no.1, March 2012, pp.10–31
Hal Foster, 'An Archival Impulse', *October*, vol.110, autumn 2004, pp.3–22
Rowena Fowler, 'Why Did Suffragettes Attack Works of Art?', *Journal of Women's History*, vol.2, no. 3, winter 1991, pp.109–25
David Freedberg, *The Power of Images: Studies in the History and Theory of Response*, Chicago 1989
Richard Galpin, *Erasure in Art: Destruction, Deconstruction and Palimpsest*, online publication (http://www.richardgalpin.co.uk/archive/erasure.htm), February 1998
Dario Gamboni, *The Destruction of Art: Iconoclasm and Vandalism since the French Revolution*, London 1997
Alfred Gell, *Art and Agency: An Anthropological Theory*, Oxford 1998
Michaela Giebelhausen, 'Academic Orthodoxy and Pre-Raphaelite Heresy: debating religious painting at the Royal Academy 1840–1850', in *Art and the Academy in the Nineteenth Century*, eds. C. Trodd and R. Denis, Manchester and London 2000, pp.164–78
Roberta Gilchrist, *Medieval Life: Archaeology and the Life Course*, Woodbridge 2012
Pat Gilmour, 'Trivialisation of Art by the Press', *Arts Review*, January 1977
R. Gilyard-Beer, *Gisborough Priory*, London 1984
R. Gilyard-Beer and G. Coppack, 'Excavations at Fountains Abbey, North Yorkshire, 1979–80: The early Development of the Monastery', *Archaeologia*, no.108, 1986, pp.147–88
Arnold P. Goldstein, *The Psychology of Vandalism*, New York 1996
Steven Goss, 'A Partial Guide to the Tools of Art Vandalism', *Cabinet*, no.3, 2001 (http://www.cabinetmagazine.org/issues/3/toolsofartvandalism.php)
R. Graham, 'A history of the buildings of the English Province of the Order of Cluny after the suppression of some priories and the general dissolution of the monasteries', *Journal of the British Archaeological Association*, 3rd series, vol .15, 1952, pp.17–18
C.P. Graves, 'From an Archaeology of Iconoclasm to an Anthropology of the Body: Images, Punishment, and Personhood in England, 1500–1660', *Current Anthropology*, vol.49, no.1, February 2008, pp.35–57
David Green, *Grinling Gibbons: His Work as a Carver and Statuary 1648–1721*, London 1964
Alastair Grieve, 'The Pre-Raphaelite Brotherhood and the Anglican High Church', *Burlington Magazine*, vol.111, no.794, May 1969, pp.292–5
John Griffiths (ed.), *The Two Books of Homilies Appointed to be Read in Churches*, Oxford 1859
Valentin Groebner, *Defaced: The Visual Culture of Violence in the Late Middle Ages*, trans. P. Selwyn, New York 2004
Boris Groys, 'Iconoclasm as Artistic Device', in *Art Power*, Cambridge, MA 2008, pp.67–81
Christoph Grunenberg, 'Attraction-Repulsion Machines: The Art of Jake and Dinos Chapman', in *Jake and Dinos Chapman: Bad Art for Bad People*, eds. C. Grunenberg and T. Barson, exh. cat., Tate Liverpool 2006, pp.11–28
Tara Hamling and Richard L. Williams (eds.), *Art Re-formed: Re-assessing the Impact of the Reformation on the Visual Arts*, Cambridge 2007
C. Hare, *Historic Worthing: The Untold Story*, Adlestrop 1991

S. Harrison, J. Wood and R. Newman, *Furness Abbey*, London 1998

Colin Haydon, '"I love my King and my Country, but a Roman Catholic I hate": anti-catholicism, xenophobia and national identity in eighteenth-century England', in *Protestantism and National Identity: Britain and Ireland c.1650–c.1850*, eds. T. Claydon and I. McBride, Cambridge 1998, pp.33–52

Clare Haynes, *Pictures and Popery: Art and Religion in England 1660–1760*, Aldershot 2006

Clare Haynes, 'The Politics of Religious Imagery in the Late Seventeenth Century', in *Fear, Exclusion and Britain in the 1680s*, ed. J. McElligott, Aldershot 2006b, pp.49–63

Ian Haywood and John Seed (eds.), *The Gordon Riots: Politics, Culture and Insurrection in Late Eighteenth- Century Britain*, Cambridge 2012

Penny Hegbin-Barnes (ed.), *The Medieval Stained Glass of Lancashire (Corpus Vitrearum Medii Aevi, Great Britain)*, Oxford 2009

Patrick Henchy, 'Nelson's Pillar', *Dublin Historical Record*, vol.10, no.1, spring 1948, p.53

George Henderson, 'Bible Illustration in the Age of Laud', *Transactions of the Cambridge Bibliographical Society*, vol.8, no.2, 1982, pp.173–216

Martin Herbert, *Mark Wallinger*, London 2011

Michael Ann Holly, 'Notes from the Field: Materiality', *Art Bulletin*, March 2013, vol.94, no.1, pp.10–37

W.H. St John Hope and H. Brakspear, 'Jervaulx Abbey', *Yorkshire Archaeological Journal*, vol.83, 1911

David Hopkins, *Dada's Boys: Masculinity after Duchamp*, New Haven and London 2007

David Howarth, 'Charles I, Sculpture and Sculptors', in *The Late King's Goods*, ed. A. MacGregor, Oxford and London 1989, pp.73–113

Peter Orlando Hutchinson (ed.), *The Diary and Letters of his Excellency Thomas Hutchinson Esq*, vol.2, London 1886

Dominic James, *Victorian Reformation: The Fight over Idolatry in the Church of England, 1840–1860*, Oxford 2009

Dominic James, 'The Cultural Context of the Riots at St George-in-the-East, London', seminar paper given on 18 March 2010, St George-in-the-East, published online (www.sgite.org.uk)

Dominic James and Gary Waller (eds.), *Walsingham in Literature and Culture from the Middle Ages to Modernity*, Farnham 2010

N.R. Ker, *Medieval Libraries of Great Britain: A list of surviving books*, London 1941

Herbert Kessler, *Seeing Medieval Art*, Peterborough, Ontario 2004, pp.19–42

Laura Knoppers, *Constructing Cromwell: Ceremony, Portrait and Print 1645–1661*, Cambridge 2000

David Knowles, *Bare Ruined Choirs*, Cambridge 1976

Joseph Leo Koerner, *The Reformation of the Image*, London 2004

Ed Krčma, 'The Rub: De Kooning, Rauschenberg and Erasure in Post-War Drawing', author's draft, 2012

Julia Kristeva, *Powers of Horror: An Essay on Abjection*, New York 1982

Karin Land, *Die Englischen Alabastermadonnen des Späten Mittelalters*, Dusseldorf 2011

Jay Landesman, *Jaywalking*, London 1992

Axel Lapp, 'The Freedom of Sculpture – The Sculpture of Freedom: The International Sculpture Competition for a Monument to the Unknown Political Prisoner, London, 1951–3', *Sculpture Journal*, vol.2, 1998, pp.113–22

Bruno Latour and Peter Weibel (eds.), *Iconoclash: Beyond the Image Wars in Science, Religion and Art*, exh. cat., Zentrum für Kunst und Medientechnologie, Karlsruhe and Cambridge, MA 2002

Bruno Latour and Peter Weibel (eds.), *Making Things Public: Atmospheres of Democracy*, Karlsruhe 2005

Helen Rees Leahy, *Museum Bodies: The Politics and Practices of Visiting and Viewing*, Farnham 2012

Isla Leaver-Yap, 'Lucy Skaer's "Black Drawings": Encounter and Aftermath', in *Lucy Skaer*, exh. cat., The Fruitmarket Gallery, Edinburgh 2008, pp.92–9

Stamford E. Lehmberg, *Cathedrals under Siege: Cathedrals in English Society 1600–1700*, Exeter 1996

Caoimhín Mac Giolla Léith, 'Stezaker's Masks', in *John Stezaker: Masks*, exh. cat., The Approach, London 2008, pp.7–14

Phillip Lindley, 'The Great Screen of Winchester Cathedral, I, *Burlington Magazine*, vol.131, 1989, pp.604–15

Phillip Lindley, 'The Great Screen of Winchester Cathedral, II: style and date', *Burlington Magazine*, vol.135, no.1089, December 1993, pp.796–807

Phillip Lindley, *Tomb Destruction and Scholarship: Medieval Monuments in Early Modern England*, Donington 2007

Phillip Lindley and Richard Deacon (eds.), *Image and Idol: Medieval Sculpture*, exh. cat., Tate, London 2001

Nigel Llewellyn, *Funeral Monuments in Post-Reformation England*, Cambridge 2001

F.D. Logan, *Excommunication and the Secular Arm in Medieval England*, Toronto 1968

Todd Longstaffe-Gowan and Tim Knox, 'One rare piece of novelty', *Apollo*, July 2006, pp.49–57

Albert J. Loomie, 'The Destruction of Rubens's *Crucifixion* in the Queen's Chapel, Somerset House', *Burlington Magazine*, vol.140, no.1147, October 1998, pp.680–2

Sven Lütticken, *Idols of the Market: Modern Iconoclasm and the Fundamentalist Spectacle*, Berlin 2009.

Francis McKee, 'Possessions', in *Douglas Gordon: self-portrait of you + me, after the factory*, with texts by Mark Francis, Francis McKee and Lynne Cooke, exh. cat., Gagosian Gallery, New York 2008, pp.6–10

Gridley McKim-Smith, 'The Rhetoric of Rape: The Language of Vandalism', *Woman's Art Journal*, vol.23, no.1, spring–summer 2002, pp.29–36

Suzanne MacLeod, 'Civil disobedience and political agitation: the art museum as a site of protest in the early twentieth century', *Museum and Society*, vol.5, no.1, July 2006, pp.44–57

Edward McParland, 'A Note on George II and St Stephen's Green', in *Eighteenth-Century Ireland*, vol.2, 1987, pp.187–95

David McRoberts, *Lost Interiors: The Furnishings of Scottish Churches in the Later Middle Ages*, ed. S.M. Holmes, Edinburgh 2012

Arthur S. Marks, 'The Statue of King George III in New York and the Iconology of Regicide', *The American Art Journal*, vol.13, no.3, summer 1981, p.62

Richard Marks, *Stained Glass in England during the Middle Ages*, Toronto 1993

Richard Marks, *Image and Devotion in Late Medieval England*, Stroud 2004

Richard Marks (ed.), *Late Gothic England: Art and Display*, Donington 2007

Richard Marks and Paul Williamson (eds.), *Gothic: Art for England 1400–1547*, exh. cat., Victoria and Albert Museum, London 2003

Arthur James Mason, *What Became of the Bones of St Thomas?*, Cambridge 1920

R. Mason, 'Reinterpreting the dissolution: recent work on the Rievaulx Abbey archive', *Church Archaeology*, forthcoming

Anne Massey, *The Independent Group: Modernism and Mass Culture, 1945–59*, Manchester 1995

Thomas H. Mayer, 'Becket's Bones Burnt! Cardinal Pole and the Invention and Dissemination of an Atrocity', in *Martyrs and Martyrdom in England c.1400–1700*, eds. T.S. Freeman and T.F. Mayer, Woodbridge 2007, pp.126–43

Gustav Metzger, *damaged nature, auto-destructive art*, London 1996

James Meyer, *Minimalism: Art and Polemics in the Sixties*, London (2000) 2005

Sergiusz Michalski, *Public Monuments: Art in Political Bondage 1870–1977*, London 1998.

John H. Middleton, 'On Fragments of Alabaster Retables from Milton and Whittlesford', *Proceedings of the Cambridge Antiquarian Society*, vol.7, 1888–91, pp.106–11

W.J.T. Mitchell, *What Do Pictures Want? The Lives and Loves of Images*, Chicago 2005

Lyndsey Morgan, '*Chair* 1969 Allen Jones', in *Material Matters: The Conservation of Modern Sculpture*, London 1999, pp.72–81

Richard Morphet, 'Carl Andre's Bricks', *Burlington Magazine*, vol.118, no.88, 4 November 1976, pp.762–7

A. Morrison and S. Harrison, 'Collections from Clearance Excavations at Whitby and Rievaulx Abbeys', in J. Bryant (ed.), *Collections Review*, vol.2, London 1999

Neil Mulholland, *The Cultural Devolution: Art in Britain in the Late Twentieth Century*, Aldershot 2003

Laura Mulvey, 'You Don't Know What Is Happening Do You Mr Jones?' *Spare Rib*, no.8, February 1973, pp.13–16, 30

Paula Murphy, *Nineteenth-Century Irish Sculpture: Native Genius Reaffirmed*, New Haven and London 2010

Alexander Nagel, *Medieval Modern: Art out of time*, London 2012

Friedrich Nietzsche, *The Twilight of the Idols, or How to Philosophize with a Hammer*, trans. D. Large, Oxford 2009

Ben Nilson, *Cathedral Shrines of Medieval England*, Woodbridge 1998

James Noyes, *The Politics of Iconoclasm: Religion, Violence and the Culture of Image-breaking in Christianity and Islam*, London 2013

James Noyes, 'Iconoclasm in the Twentieth Century: Machines, Mass Destruction, and Two World Wars', in *Striking Images: Iconoclasms Past and Present*, eds. S. Boldrick, L. Brubaker and R. Clay, Farnham 2013 (forthcoming)

Geoffrey Nuttall, 'Was Cromwell an Iconoclast?', *Transactions of the Congregational History Society*, no.12, 1933–6, pp.51–66

Jeff Nuttall, *Bomb Culture*, London 1971

Andrew O'Brien, 'The History of Nelson's Pillar', *Dublin Historical Record*, vol.60, no.1, spring 2007, pp.21–5

Jeff Oliver and Tim Neal, *Wild Signs: Graffiti in Archaeology and History*, London 2010

Micheál Ó Riain, 'Nelson's Pillar: A controversy that ran and ran', *History Ireland*, vol.4, no.6, winter 1998, pp.21–5

Raphael Montañez Ortiz and Kristine Stiles, *Rafael Montañez Ortiz Years of the Warrior 1960, Years of the Psyche 1988*, exh. cat., El Museo del Barrio, New York 1988

Graham Parry, *Glory, Laud and Honour: The Arts of the Anglican Counter Reformation*, Woodbridge 2006

Charles Reed Peers, 'Rievaulx Abbey: The Shrine in the Chapter House', *Archaeological Journal*, no.86, 1929, pp.20–8

Mikhail Pelevin and Matthias Weinreich, 'The Songs of the Taliban: Continuity of Form and Thought in an Ever-Changing Environment', *Iran and the Caucasus*, vol.16, 2012, pp. 45–70

Nicholas Penny, 'Chantrey, Westmacott and Casts after the Antique', *Journal of the History of Collections*, vol.3, no.2, 1991, pp.255–64

John Phillips, *The Reformation of Images: Destruction of Art in England, 1535–1660*, Berkeley and Los Angeles 1973

Olivia Plender and Hester Reeve, *The Suffragette as Militant Artist: Suffragette artists and suffragette attacks on works of art*, online publication (http://shura.shu.ac.uk/4605/22/Reeve_Suffragette_as_Militant_Artist_2010_(6).pdf), Emily Davison Lodge 2010

Audrey Baker, *English Panel Paintings 1400–1558: A survey of figure paintings on East Anglian rood screens*, edited,

updated and extented by Pauline Plummer and Ann Ballantyne, London 2011
Marcia Pointon, *Portrayal and the Search for Identity*, London 2013
Amy Knight Powell, *Depositions: Scenes from the Late Medieval Church and the Modern Museum*, New York 2012
Matthew Power and Andrew J. Shortland, 'Van Linge glass in the cathedral of Christ Church, Oxford', *Annales du 17e Congrès de l'Association Internationale pour l'Histoire du Verre*, Antwerp 2009, pp.473–7
Virgina Chieffo Raguin (ed.), *Art, Piety and Destruction in the Christian West, 1500–1700*, Farnham 2010
Jacques Rancière, 'Are Some Things Unrepresentable?', in Jacques Rancière, *The Future of the Image*, trans. G. Elliott, London 2007, pp.109–38
David Ransome, *The Ferrar Papers 1590–1790 in Magdalene College, Cambridge*, microform publication (http://www.microform.co.uk/guides/R97513.pdf), 1992
Benedict Read, *Victorian Sculpture*, New Haven 1982
Mary Richardson, *Laugh a Defiance*, London 1953
Alistair Rider, *Carl Andre: Things In Their Elements*, London 2011
John Roberts, 'Stuart Brisley', in *Stuart Brisley: A Retrospective*, ed. Sandy Nairne, exh. cat., ICA, London 1981, pp.11–14
Peter Roberts, 'Politics, Drama and the Cult of Thomas Becket in the Sixteenth Century', in *Pilgrimage: The English Experience from Becket to Bunyan*, eds. Colin Morris and Peter Roberts, Cambridge 2002, pp.199–237
Ralph Rugoff and Helen Luckett, *Invisible: Art about the Unseen 1957–2012*, exh. cat., Hayward Gallery, London 2012
Mark Sanders, *With The Artists/Meet The Artists: Jake Chapman, George Condo, Paul McCarthy and Dinos Chapman*, exh. cat., Deitch Projects and RS&A, New York and London 2007
Aura Satz, 'Attacks on Automata and Eviscerated Sculptures', in *Iconoclasm: Contested Objects, Contested Terms*, eds. S. Boldrick and R.Clay, Aldershot 2007, pp.35–49
J. Gavin Scott, *British Countermarks on Copper and Bronze Coins*, London 1975
Helen E. Scott, 'Responding to Art Vandalism in British Museums and Galleries: A Survey of the Situation', *The Journal of Art Crime*, vol.3, no.1, spring 2010, pp.11–24
Helen E. Scott, '"Wholly Uninteresting?" The Motives Behind Acts of Iconoclasm', in *Perspectives on Power: An Inter-Disciplinary Approach*, eds. H.M. Morgan, J.L. Černič and L. Milligan, Newcastle 2010b, pp.21–40
Helen E. Scott, 'Iconoclasm as Art: Creative Gestures and Criminal Acts inside Museums and Galleries', in *Art and Destruction*, ed. Jenny Walden, Newcastle 2013 (forthcoming)
Rebecca Scott, Andrew Shortland and Matthew Power, 'The Interpretation of Compositional Groupings in 17th- Century Window Glass from Christ Church Cathedral, Oxford', *Annales du 18e Congrès de l'Association Internationale pour l'Histoire du Verre*, Thessaloniki 2012, pp.425–9
Rebecca Scott, Andrew Shortland, Patrick Degryse, Matthew Power, Kelly Domoney, Sara Boyen and Dennis Braekmans, 'In situ analysis of ancient glass: 17th-century painted glass from Christ Church Cathedral, Oxford and Roman glass vessels', *Glass Technology: European Journal of Glass Science and Technology*, April 2012, vol.53, no.2, pp.65–73
F.H.W. Sheppard (ed.), *Survey of London*, vols.33, 34: *The Parish of St Anne Soho*, London 1966
Thomas Sheppard, *Catalogue of Love Tokens and other engraved pieces in the Hull Museum, Hull Museum Publications*, no.126, Hull 1922
Laurence Sillars (ed.), *Joyous Machines: Michael Landy and Jean Tinguely*, exh. cat., Tate Liverpool 2009
James Simpson, *Under the Hammer: Iconoclasm in the Anglo-American Tradition*, Oxford 2010
Nicola Smith, *The Royal Image and the People*, Aldershot 2001
Adam Smyth, '"Shreds of holinesse": George Herbert, Little Gidding and Cutting up Texts in Early Modern England', *English Literary Renaissance*, vol.42, no.3, 2012, pp.452–81
Margaret Sparks, 'The Refitting of the Quire of Canterbury Cathedral 1660–1716: Pictorial and Documentary Evidence', *Journal of the British Archaeological Association*, vol.154, 2001, pp.170–90
Julie Spraggon, *Puritan Iconoclasm during the English Civil War*, Woodbridge 2003
Sarah Stanbury, 'The Vivacity of Images: St Katherine, Knighton's Lollards, and the Breaking of Idols', in *Images, Idolatry and Iconoclasm in Late Medieval England: Textuality and the Visual Image*, eds. J. Dimmick, J. Simpson and N. Zeeman, Oxford 2002, pp.131–50
Sarah Stanbury, *The Visual Object of Desire in Late Medieval England*, Philadelphia 2007
Simon Starling, 'Replication: Some Thoughts, Some Works', *Tate Papers*, no. 8, online publication (http://www.tate.org.uk/download/file/fid/7383), autumn 2007
John Stezaker, 'Film Stills, Still', pp.15–25 in *John Stezaker Film Still: Collages since 1979*, London 2011
L. Stone, *Sculpture in Britain: The Middle Ages*, London 1972
Robert Storr, *September: A History Painting by Gerhard Richter*, London 2010
W.G. Strickland, *A Dictionary of Irish Artists*, Dublin and London 1913
Roy Strong, *Lost Treasures of Britain: Five Centuries of Creation and Destruction*, London 1990
M.G. Sullivan, 'Brass sculpture and the ideology of bronze in Britain 1660–1851', *Sculpture Journal*, vol.14, 2005, pp.30–40
M.G. Sullivan *Sir Francis Chantrey and the Ashmolean Museum*, Oxford 2013
Miguel Tamen, *Friends of Interpretable Objects*, Cambridge 2001 (2004)
Tate Gallery 1978–80: Illustrated Catalogue of Acquisitions, London 1981
Tate Gallery 1980–82: Illustrated Catalogue of Acquisitions, London 1984
Tim Tatton-Brown, 'Canterbury and the Architecture of Pilgrimage Shrines in England', in *Pilgrimage: The English Experience from Becket to Bunyan*, eds. Colin Morris and Peter Roberts, Cambridge 2002, pp.90–107
Michael Taussig, *Defacement: Public Secrecy and the Labor of the Negative*, Stanford 1999
Michael Taylor (ed.), *Thinking is Making: Presence and Absence in Contemporary Sculpture*, London 2013
J. Thomas, 'Evidence for the Dissolution of Thorney Abbey: Recent excavations and landscape analysis at Thorney, Cambridgeshire', *Medieval Archaeology*, no.50, 2006, pp.179–241
E.P. Thompson *Customs in Common*, London 1991
Simon Thurley, 'The Stuart Kings, Oliver Cromwell and the Chapel Royal 1618–1685', *Architectural History*, vol.45, 2002, pp.238–74
Lisa Tickner, 'Allen Jones in Retrospect: A Serpentine Review', *Block*, no.1, 1979, pp.39–45
Calvin Tomkins and Barry Schwabsky, *Michael Landy: H2NY*, London 2007
Amikam Toren, 'Artist's Page: Porno Romo', *Third Text*, no.118, September 2012, pp.545–9
M.R. Toynbee 'Fresh light on William Larson's statue of James II at Newcastle upon Tyne', *Archaeologia Aeliana*, 4th series, vol.29, 1951, pp.108–17
Stephanie Trigg, *Shame and Honor: A Vulgar History of the Order of the Garter*, Philadelphia 2012
Christopher Turner, 'Great Deeds Against Dead Artists: How the Chapman Brothers Nearly Changed their Name to Goya', in C. Grunenberg and T. Barson (eds.), *Jake and Dinos Chapman: Bad Art for Bad People*, exh. cat., Tate Liverpool 2006, pp.37–53
William Urry, 'Some Notes on the Two Resting Places of St Thomas Becket at Canterbury', *Thomas Becket: Actes du Colloque International de Sédières 19–24 Août 1973*, ed. R. Foreville, Paris 1975, pp.195–209
Henk van Os, *The Art of Devotion in the Late Middle Ages in Europe 1300–1500*, London 1994
Anne Wagner, *Mother Stone: The Vitality of Modern British Sculpture*, New Haven and London 2005
John Richard Walbran, *A guide to Ripon, Fountains Abbey, Harrogate and Bolton Priory and several places of interest in their vicinity*, 12th edn, Ripon 1875
Edward Walford, *Old and New London: A Narrative of its History, its People, and its Places*, vol.3, 1878
John A. Walker, *Art and Outrage: Provocation, Controversy and the Visual Arts*, London 1999
Gary Waller, *Walsingham and the English Imagination*, Farnham 2011
Alexandra Walsham, 'Introduction: Relics and Remains', in *Relics and Remains, Past and Present*, Supplement 5, Oxford 2010
Colin Ward (ed.), *Vandalism*, London 1973
Martin Warnke, 'Durchbrochene Geschichte? Die Bilderstürme der Wiedertäufer in Münster, 1533–34', in *Bildersturm: Die Zerstörung des Kunstwerks*, ed. M. Warnke, Frankfurt 1977, pp.159–67
John C. Welchman, *Art After Appropriation: Essays on Art in the 1990s*, San Diego 2001
Yvonne Whelan, 'Symbolising the State – the iconography of O'Connell Street and environs after Independence (1922)', *Irish Geography*, vol.34, no.2, 2001, pp.135–56
Yvonne Whelan, 'The Construction and Destruction of a Colonial Landscape: Monuments to British monarchs in Dublin before and after Independence', *Journal of Historical Geography*, vol.28, no.4, 2002, pp.508–33
Sir John Williams, *Account of the monastic treasures confiscated at the dissolution of the various houses in England by Sir John Williams, knight, late master and treasurer of the jewels to His Majesty King Henry VIII*, ed. W.B.D.D. Turnbull, Edinburgh 1886
Anthony Wood, *The History and Antiquities of the University of Oxford*, ed. J. Gutch, 2 vols., Oxford 1786
Kim Woods, 'The Mercers' Christ re-examined', in *Late Gothic England: Art and Display*, ed. R. Marks, Donnington 2006, pp.57–69
G.W.O. Woodward, *The Dissolution of the Monasteries*, London 1966
A. Yarrington, I. Lieberman, Alex Potts and Malcolm Baker, 'An Edition of the Ledger of Sir Francis Chantrey, RA, at the Royal Academy, 1809–41', *Walpole Society*, vol.56, 1991–2 (1994)
Nigel Yates, *Anglican Ritualism in Victorian Britain 1830–1910*, Oxford 1999
Joyce A. Youings, *The Dissolution of the Monasteries*, London 1971
Jonas Zakaitis, 'Interview: Jonas Zakaitis talks with Lucy Skaer', *The Federal*, no.3, November 2012, pp.29–32

LIST OF EXHIBITED WORKS

Note The information given in this listing was correct at the time of going to press. Measurements of artworks are given in centimetres, height before width.

DISSOLUTION

Girolamo da Treviso (active *c*.1497–1544), *A Protestant Allegory* *c*.1538–44 (ill.23)
Oil paint on panel
68 × 84 (unframed)
Royal Collection Trust/HM The Queen

Two fragments from the shrine of Thomas Becket *c*.1220 (ill.30)
Marble
10 × 12.8 × 12.5 and 7.5 × 16.5 × 12.6
The Dean and Chapter of Canterbury Cathedral

Book of Hours, 1450–75 (ill.32)
Harley 2985, open at ff 29v–30
21.5 × 15
The British Library

Book of Hours, c.1390–1400 (ill.33)
Sloane 2683, open at ff 16v–17
19.5 × 12
The British Library

Letter 'M' from a tomb inscription 13th century (ill.22)
Copper alloy
5.1 × 4.4
English Heritage, Fountains Abbey

Section of tomb inscription 14th century (not illustrated)
Copper alloy
23.7 × 3.9
English Heritage, Fountains Abbey

Letter 'S' from a tomb inscription 13th century (ill.21)
Copper alloy
4 × 2.9
English Heritage, Fountains Abbey

Window came date unknown (ill.28)
Lead
10 × 10.2
English Heritage, Fountains Abbey

Window came date unknown (ill.27)
Lead
English Heritage, Rievaulx Abbey

Papal bulla of Pope Innocent IV 1243–54 (ill.19)
Lead
3.6 × 3.6 × 0.4
English Heritage, Roche Abbey
Plaque, possibly a book fitting *c*.1500 (ill.17)
Copper alloy
3.3 × 3
English Heritage, Roche Abbey

Book boss or stud date unknown (not illustrated)
Copper alloy
3.3 × 3
English Heritage, Roche Abbey

Book clasp early 12th century (ill.16)
Copper alloy
2.6 × 3.8 × 4
English Heritage, Roche Abbey

Window glass fragment: crowned letter 'J', 1360–1400 (ill.25)
Painted glass
8.2 × 6 × 0.2 mm
English Heritage, Rievaulx Abbey

Annunciation panel late fifteenth century (ill.20)
Limestone
66 × 111 × 20
English Heritage, Fountains Abbey

Christ in Majesty *c*.1260–90 (ill.24)
Stone
69.6 × 43.3 × 29.2
English Heritage, Rievaulx Abbey

Niche canopy from the pulpitum screen, Rievaulx Abbey 15th century (ill.15)
Stone
69 × 58 × 40
English Heritage, Rievaulx Abbey

Fragment from the upper section of the pulpitum screen, Rievaulx Abbey 15th century (not illustrated)
Stone
41 × 41 × 15 mm
English Heritage, Rievaulx Abbey

Window ventilator panel 14th century (ill.18)
Lead
9.8 × 7.8
English Heritage, Rievaulx Abbey

Finial cross from the Galilee Porch, Rievaulx Abbey 15th century (ill.13)
Stone
28 × 38.5 × 19.5
English Heritage, Rievaulx Abbey

Window glass fragment: head of an angel 1475–1500 (ill.26)
Painted glass
14 × 10 mm
English Heritage, Furness Abbey

A pile of window glass fragments date unknown (ill.29)
English Heritage, Rievaulx Abbey

Enthroned figure 1300–50 (ill.14)
Sandstone
Legs 65 × 45 × 35; torso 53 × 50
English Heritage, Gisborough Priory

REFORMATION

The Crucifixion, *c*.1380–1400 (ill.47)
Oil paint and mixed media on panel
71 × 50 × 4.5
The Dean and Chapter of Norwich Cathedral

The Dead Christ, *c*.1500–20 (ill.49)
Limestone
197 × 68.6
The Mercers' Company

Section of a painted screen late 15th century (ill.51)
Oil paint and gilding on carved oak panel
152.5 × 116.8 × 24.2
Church of St Mary, Gressenhall, Norfolk

Figure of Christ, 1475–1525 (ill.45)
Wood with traces of pigment
16.5 × 4.1 × 2.5
On loan from the British Museum, London

The Stonyhurst Salt, 1577–78 (ill.43)
Silver-gilt and rock crystal with gemstones
26.3 × 9.4
On loan from the British Museum, London

Christ before Pilate, *c*.1400–25 (ill.42)
Tempera and gilding on panel
33 × 29.8
Fitzwilliam Museum, Cambridge

Christ bearing the Cross *c*.1400–25 (not illustrated)
Tempera and gilding on panel
33.1 × 29.9
Fitzwilliam Museum, Cambridge

Retable fragments *c*.1520 (ill.44)
Alabaster with traces of pigment and gilding
Church of St Mary and St Andrew, Whittlesford, Cambridgeshire

Head of God the Father late 15th century (ill.38)
Limestone with traces of pigment
28 × 26 × 16
The Dean and Chapter of Winchester Cathedral

A Gloved Hand late 15th century (ill.39)
Limestone
10.4 × 17.5 × 9
The Dean and Chapter of Winchester Cathedral

Head of a King or Bishop late 15th century (ill.40)
Limestone
22 × 15 × 17.5
The Dean and Chapter of Winchester Cathedral

The Virgin and Child late 15th century (ill.50)
Limestone with traces of pigment
48 × 38 × 20
The Dean and Chapter of Winchester Cathedral

THE WORD

Triptych painted with the Ten Commandments 16th century (ill.34)
Oil paint on panel
125 × 201 (open)
Preston St Mary Parochial Church Council

Triptych painted with arms of Elizabeth I, and on the exterior wings text sermonising against images and idolatry (shown closed) (ill.35)
117 × 990 (closed) Preston St Mary Parochial Church Council

Section of a painted rood screen with *Christ as the Man of Sorrows* *c*.1500, later whitewashed and overpainted with biblical text *c*.1540–53 (ill.46)
Oil paint on oak panel
80 × 24
Priory Church of St Mary and the Holy Cross, Binham, Norfolk

King Edward VI and the Pope, *c*.1570 (ill.36)
Oil paint on panel
62.2 × 90.8
Lent by the National Portrait Gallery, London

Little Gidding Harmony, *Acta Apostolorum Elegantis Monochromatis Delineata* c.1635–40 (ill.55)
Pasted book
The British Library

After Maarten van Heemskerck (1498–1574), plate from the late 16th century Lord's Prayer series (Ferrar print no.122) (ill.56)
Engraving on paper (with excision)
The Master and Fellows of Magdalene College, Cambridge

Anonymous print, thought to be published byTheodoor Galle (1571–1633), *Oratio* (Ferrar print no.50) (not illustrated)
Engraving on paper (with excision)
The Master and Fellows of Magdalene College, Cambridge

Anonymous print, with scenes of the Creation (Ferrar print no.488) (not illustrated)
Engraving on paper (with excisions)
The Master and Fellows of Magdalene College, Cambridge

After Maerten de Vos (1532–1603), *The Last Judgement* c.1580 (Ferrar print no.213) (ill.57)
Engraving on paper (with excisions)
The Master and Fellows of Magdalene College, Cambridge

PURITAN ICONOCLASM

The Presentation in the Temple, c.1180 (ill.60)
Stained glass
69.5 × 70 × 0.7
The Dean and Chapter of Canterbury Cathedral

Christ Leading the Gentiles from Pagan Gods, c.1180 (ill.61)
Stained glass
69.5 × 70 × 0.7
The Dean and Chapter of Canterbury Cathedral

Abraham van Linge (active 1623–42), fragments of painted glass (mounted into three panels), 1630s (see ill.64 for some of the fragments)
92 × 52 × 0.7; 92.3 × 5.2 × 0.7; 92.5 × 52.4 × 0.7
The Dean and Chapter of Christ Church, Oxford

Abraham van Linge (active 1623–42), *The Deposition* 1629 (ill.52)
Painted and stained glass
81.3 × 41.9
Victoria and Albert Museum, London. Given by Wilfred Drake

Hubert Le Sueur (c.1580–after 1658), *Charles I*, 1638–9 (ill.58)
Bronze with gilding
190 × 80 × 120 (with mace)
The Dean and Chapter of Winchester Cathedral

Thomas Johnson (active 1634–76), *Canterbury Cathedral Choir*, 1657 (ill.59)
Oil paint on canvas
83.5 × 95 (with frame)
Private collection

Basilika: The Works of King Charles the Martyr 1662 (ill.54)
Printed book, expurgated by the Portuguese Inquisition
36.8 × 25 × 8.5
His Grace the Archbishop of Canterbury and the Trustees of Lambeth Palace Library

John Milton, *Eikonoklastes* 1649 (not illustrated)
Printed book
The British Library

POLITICS AND PUBLIC SPACE

British School 17th century, *Oliver Cromwell* (ill.3)
Oil paint on canvas
75 × 62 × 1.5
Inverness Museum and Art Gallery

After William Larson (d.1692), Equestrian statuette of King James II, c.1686 (ill.65)
Bronze
64 × 40 × 22.5
National Gallery of Ireland, Dublin

John Smyth (c.1773–1840), Head of William III, 1836 (ill.74)
Lead
34 × 31 × 35
Private collection

Francis Johnston 1760–1829
Fragment from the column of Nelson's Pillar 1808–9 (not illustrated)
Granite
6 × 15 × 9
Professor Jim Bennett

Francis Johnston 1760–1829
Fragment from the column of Nelson's Pillar 1808–9 (not illustrated)
Granite
5 × 10 × 2.2
The Little Museum of Dublin

Sir Henry Cheere (1702–81) and John Cheere (1709–87), Head of the Duke of Cumberland 1747 (ill.66)
Lead
34 × 92 (circumference)
On loan from the Hunt Museum's Trust

Joseph Wilton (1722–1803), fragment of the equestrian statue of George III 1770–6 (ill.77)
Lead
21.6 × 48.3 × 33
Lent by the New-York Historical Society

Sir Francis Legatt Chantrey (1781–1841), Head from the colossal statue of the Rt Hon William Pitt 1831 (ill.79)
Plaster
55 × 41 × 46
Ashmolean Museum, Oxford

Grinling Gibbons (1648–1721), fragment from the plinth of the equestrian statue of William III 1701 (ill.73)
Marble
100 × 80 × 10.8
Dublin City Council

The defaced statue of George I, Leicester Square
Newspaper photograph, taken 17 October 1866, reprinted in *The Sketch*, 14 September 1898
Private collection

After Sir Joshua Reynolds (1723–92), *William Augustus, Duke of Cumberland* c.1758–60 (ill.68)
Oil paint on canvas
87.6 × 59.1
Lent by the National Portrait Gallery, London

John Bull and his Favourite Statue of Bronze!!, 1802 (ill.9)
Hand-coloured etching
35.6 × 25.1
On loan from the British Museum, London

The Brazen Image erected on a Pedestal wrought by Himself 1802 (ill.10)
Hand-coloured etching
41.1 × 25.3
On loan from the British Museum, London

Francis Wheatley 1747–1801
The Dublin Volunteers on College Green, 4th November 1779, 1779
Oil paint on canvas
221 x 364.5
National Gallery of Ireland, Dublin

Victoria copper penny 1841 (ill.86)
The queen shown smoking a pipe and inscribed 'I love' in her hair and 'shag' across her face
Timothy Millett

George III copper halfpenny 1799 (ill.85)
The king with a noose around his neck and inscribed 'Poor John Bull' on the reverse
Timothy Millett

George III copper Cartwheel penny 1797 (not illustrated)
Inscribed 'Gibbs Ld Mayor pelted with Rotten Eggs'
Timothy Millett

Unidentified coin, probably a George II copper halfpenny (not illustrated)
Inscribed 'Pitt's Deserts' and 'No Triple Tax'
Timothy Millett

George III copper Cartwheel penny 1797 (not illustrated)
Inscribed 'Down with the Catholics'
Timothy Millett

George III copper Cartwheel penny 1797 (not illustrated)
Inscribed 'Willm 4th The Idiot King'
Timothy Millett

George IV copper penny 1826 (not illustrated)
Inscribed 'The Fine English Gentleman. Patron of Vice and Frivolity'
Timothy Millett

George III copper Cartwheel penny 1797 (not illustrated)
Inscribed 'Down with Prince Albert'
Timothy Millett

George III copper halfpenny, date removed (ill.84)
Modified to depict a coffin and an axe with a jackboot and female figure hanging from a gibbet on the reverse
Timothy Millett

William III copper halfpenny (not illustrated)
Inscribed 'Down with the Rump 1747'
Timothy Millett

Unidentified coin (not illustrated)
Inscribed 'Room for Cuckolds here comes my Lord Mayor'
Timothy Millett

George III copper Cartwheel penny (ill.83)
Inscribed 'The man who did this was born without a shirt 1849'
Timothy Millett

THE SUFFRAGETTES

James Singer Sargent (1856–1925), *Portrait of Henry James* 1913 (ill.90)
Oil paint on canvas
85.1 × 67.3
Lent by the National Portrait Gallery, London. Bequeathed by Henry James 1916

Documentary photograph of the damage to the portrait of Henry James 1914 (ill.91)
Lent by the National Portrait Gallery, London

Surveillance photographs of militant suffragettes (ill.94)
Silver print mounted onto identification sheet
Lent by the National Portrait Gallery, London

Mary Raleigh Richardson and Catherine Wilson (not illustrated)
Criminal Record Office memorandum, issued 24 April 1914
Lent by the National Portrait Gallery, London

Lillian Forrester and Evelyn Manesta
(not illustrated)
Criminal Record Office memorandum, issued 24 April 1914
Lent by the National Portrait Gallery, London

Sir Edward Coley Burne-Jones, Bt (1833–98), *Sibylla Delphica* c.1886 (ill.87)
Oil paint on panel
152.8 × 60.3
Manchester City Galleries
Sir George Frederick Watts (1817–1904), *May Prinsep: Prayer* 1867–87 (ill.88)
Oil paint on canvas
102.6 × 69.6
Manchester City Galleries

Kate Davis (b.1977), *Reversibility (Militant Methods)* 2011 (ill.95)
Graphite and screenprint on paper
135 × 80 × 3 (framed)
Lent by Glasgow Life (Glasgow Museums) on behalf of Glasgow City Council

Christabel Pankhurst (1880–1958), *The Militant Methods of the N.W.S.P.U.* c.1908
(not illustrated)
Printed pamphlet
Dimensions
Lent by Glasgow Life (Glasgow Museums) on behalf of Glasgow City Council

Attributed to Gentile Bellini (active c.1460–1507), *A Man with A Pair of Dividers (?)*, c.1500 (ill.93)
Oil paint on canvas
69.2 × 59.1
The National Gallery, London. Bought 1886

Toffee hammer c.1911 (not illustrated)
Iron alloy
19 × 6.2 × 1.8
Museum of London

Surveillance photograph of Mary Richardson 1914 (not illustrated)
13.8 × 14.6
Museum of London

Newspaper cutting dated Thursday 4 June 1914 referring to the suffragette attack on artworks at the Doré Gallery, London (ill.89)
Museum of London

Newspaper cutting referring to the suffragette attack on the Sargent portrait of Henry James at the Royal Academy 1914 (ill.92)
Museum of London

ATTACKS ON ART

Reg Butler (1913–81), Maquette for *The Unknown Political Prisoner* 1951–2, remodelled 1953 (ill.100)
Painted stone and painted bronze
44.5 × 20.5 × 16.5
Tate. Lent by the Estate of Reg Butler 1986

Carl Andre (b.1935), *Equivalent VIII* 1966 (ill.103)
Firebricks
12.7 × 68.6 × 229.2
Tate. Purchased 1972

Allen Jones (b.1937), *Chair* 1969 (ill.105)
Acrylic paint on glass fibre and resin with Perspex and leather
77.5 × 57.1 × 99.1
Tate. Purchased 1981

DESTRUCTION IN ART

Destruction In Art Symposium 1966
(not illustrated)
Print on paper with writing; poster designed by John Sharkey
77 × 50
Ivor Davies Archive

Gustav Metzger (b.1926), *Manifesto World* 1962 (not illustrated)
Print on paper
Private collection

John Latham (1921–2006), *Skoob Tower Ceremony* 1966 (not illustrated)
Print on paper
62 × 49
Ivor Davies Archive

Yoko Ono (b.1933), *Cut Piece* 1966
(see ill 111 for film still)
16mm film, silent, digitally transferred
British Pathé Ltd

Harold Liversidge, *Auto-Destructive Art – The Activities of G. Metzger* 1963
(not illustrated)
16mm film, black and white, silent, transferred to video
Contemporary Films Ltd

Michael Landy (b.1963), *H.2N.Y. If the saw saws the saw and if the saw which saws the saw which saws the saw there is a metallic suicide Marcel Duchamp* 2007
Oil stick on paper
122 × 152.5
Courtesy the artist and Thomas Dane Gallery, London

Raphael Montañez Ortiz (b.1934)
Duncan Terrace Piano Destruction Concert: The Landesmans' Homage to 'Spring can really hang you up the most' 1966 (ill.118)
Wood and metal
142.2 × 124.7
Accepted by HM Government in lieu of tax and awaiting permanent allocation

Raphael Montañez Ortiz (b.1934)
Duncan Terrace Chair Destruction 1966 (ill.117)
Wood, metal and fabric
124.5 × 83.6
Accepted by HM Government in lieu of tax and awaiting permanent allocation

Raphael Montañez Ortiz born 1934
Duncan Terrace Piano Destruction Concert: The Landesman's Homage to 'Spring can really hang you up the most' 1966 (not illustrated)
Audio recording
c:intermedium records 2008

Boyle Family
Melted slide from 'Projections' 1966, printed 2013 (ill.115)
Photographic print from a colour slide
109 × 84
Boyle Family, London

Gustav Metzger (b.1926), *Manifesto SDA Self Destructive Art* 19 October 1959
(not illustrated)
Handwritten draft manifesto
Private collection

Gustav Metzger (b.1926)
Auto-Destructive Art 4 November 1959
(not illustrated)
Printed manifesto
Private collection

Auto-Destructive Art Demonstration by G. Metzger 23 June 1961 (not illustrated)
Printed manifesto
Private collection

On Random Activity in Material/Transforming Works of Art 30 July 1964 (not illustrated)
Printed manifestos
Private collection

Machine, Auto-Creative and Auto-Destructive Art 1962 (not illustrated)
Article from *Ark* magazine
Private collection

Auto-Destructive Art: Metzger at AA 1965
(not illustrated)
Booklet
Private collection

Auto-Destructive edition of *Art & Artists*, August 1966 (not illustrated)
Magazine, open at spread on Gustav Metzger
Ivor Davies Archive
Publicity list of participants for DIAS, September 1966 (not illustrated)
Ivor Davies Archive

Programme for DIAS *Conclusion* event, Mercury Theatre, 30 September 1966
(not illustrated)
Private collection

Invitation letter for DIAS 1966 (not illustrated)
Ivor Davies Archive

Press release for DIAS September 1966
(not illustrated)
Ivor Davies Archive

Letter from Gustav Metzger to Ivor Davies July 1966 (not illustrated)
Ivor Davies Archive

Auto-Destructive edition of *Art & Artists*, August 1966
Magazine
Private collection

DIAS planning document 1966
(not illustrated)
Ivor Davies Archive

DIAS Preliminary Report 1967
(not illustrated)
Published programme
Private Collection

London Life 8 October 1966 (not illustrated)
Magazine, open at article 'Destruction in Art …What are they trying to prove?'
Ivor Davies Archive

Art & Artists October 1966 (not illustrated)
Magazine, open at 'DIAS Report Destruction In Art'
Ivor Davies Archive

Studio International December 1966
(not illustrated)
Magazine, open at article 'Excerpts from Selected Papers Presented at the 1966 "Destruction In Art Symposium"'
Ivor Davies Archive

Life 17 April 1967
Magazine, open at article 'The Other Culture'
Ivor Davies Archive

Ivor Davies (b.1935), *Explosions in House*, performed at the London Free School Playground 13 September 1966 (ill.109)
Archive photographic prints (two)
Ivor Davies Archive

Raphael Montañez Ortiz (b.1934), *Destructivism* 1966 (not illustrated)
Printed manifesto
Private collection

Programme for *Two Evenings with Yoko Ono* 28 and 29 September 1966 (not illustrated)
Tate Archive

Fragment of a Biba dress worn by Yoko Ono for *Cut Piece*, performed at *Two Evenings with Yoko Ono* September 1966 (ill.112)
Tate Archive

Yoko Ono (b.1933), *Shadow Piece*, performed at the London Free School Playground 13 September 1966 (not illustrated)
Photographer: Tom Picton
Tate Archive

Hermann Nitsch (b.1938), *21st Action: OM Theatre (5th Abreaktionsspiel)*, performed at St Bride Institute 16 September 1966 (ill.110)
Photographer: Tom Picton
Tate Archive

John Latham (1921–2006), partially burnt copy of *Metropolitan Seminars in Art*, a fragment remaining from a *Skoob Tower Ceremony* enacted as part of DIAS 1966 (ill.113)
25 × 33
Courtesy John Latham Foundation

John Latham (1921–2006), announcement card *Attention Unit Real Estate / Encyclopedias over London* 27 September 1966 (not illustrated)
Courtesy John Latham Foundation

John Latham (1921–2006), *Skoob Tower Ceremony (Metropolitan Seminars in Art)* (not illustrated)
Photographer: John Prosser
Courtesy John Latham Foundation

John Latham (1921–2006), *Skoob Tower Ceremony: Exploding Encyclopedias*, South Bank June 1966 (not illustrated)
Photographer: John Prosser
Courtesy John Latham Foundation

John Latham (1921–2006), *Skoob Tower Ceremony: National Encyclopedias*, Bloomsbury 24 September 1966 (ill.114)
Photographer: John Prosser
Courtesy John Latham Foundation

ART TRANSFORMED

George Condo (b.1957), Jake Chapman (b.1966), Dinos Chapman (b.1962) and Paul McCarthy (b.1945)
George – Dinos – Jake – Paul (Portrait) (first stage) 2006 (ill.128a)
Etching on paper
127 × 91 mm
RS&A Ltd

George Condo (b.1957), Jake Chapman (b.1966), Dinos Chapman (b.1962) and Paul McCarthy (b.1945)
George – Dinos – Jake – Paul (Portrait) (second stage) 2006 (ill.128b)
Etching on paper
127 × 91 mm
RS&A Ltd

George Condo (b.1957), Jake Chapman (b.1966), Dinos Chapman (b.1962) and Paul McCarthy (b.1945)
George – Dinos – Jake – Paul (Portrait) (third stage) 2006 (ill.128c)
Etching on paper
127 × 91 mm
RS&A Ltd

George Condo (b.1957), Jake Chapman (b.1966), Dinos Chapman (b.1962) and Paul McCarthy (b.1945)
George – Dinos – Jake – Paul (Portrait) (fourth stage) 2006 (ill.128d)
Etching on paper
127 × 91 mm
RS&A Ltd

Lucy Skaer (b.1975), *Me* 2012 (ill.126)
Resin and celluloid
23.5 × 15.5 × 0.4
Courtesy the artist and Murray Guy, New York

Mark Wallinger (b.1959), *Via Dolorosa* 2002 (ill 125)
Projected video installation, DVD transfer, 18 mins 8 seconds
Courtesy Anthony Reynolds Gallery, London

Kate Davis (b.1977), *Disgrace V* 2012 (not illustrated)
Graphite on found image
30 × 21
Courtesy the artist and Galerie Kamm, Berlin

Kate Davis (b.1977), *Disgrace VI* 2012 (ill.120)
Graphite on found image
30 × 21
Courtesy the artist and Galerie Kamm, Berlin

Kate Davis (b.1977), *Disgrace VII* 2012 (not illustrated)
Graphite on found image
30 × 21
Courtesy the artist and Galerie Kamm, Berlin
Kate Davis (b.1977), *Disgrace VIII* 2012 (not illustrated)
Graphite on found image
30 × 21
Courtesy the artist and Galerie Kamm, Berlin

Jake and Dinos Chapman (b.1966 and 1962), *One Day You Will No Longer Be Loved XVII* 2008 (not illustrated)
Oil paint on canvas
53.6 × 42
Private collection, courtesy White Cube, London

Jake and Dinos Chapman (b.1966 and 1962), *One Day You Will No Longer Be Loved (that it should come to this) V*, 2010 (not illustrated)
Oil paint on canvas
76 × 64
Courtesy the artists
Jake and Dinos Chapman (b.1966 and 1962), *One Day You Will No Longer Be Loved II (No.6)*, 2008 (ill.127)
Oil paint on canvas
76.2 × 63.5
Courtesy the artists and White Cube, London

Douglas Gordon (b.1966), *Self-portrait of You + Me (9 piece QEII)* 2008 (ill.122)
Smoke and mirror
253.2 × 203.4
Courtesy the artist and Gagosian Gallery

Douglas Gordon (b.1966), *Self-Portrait of You + Me (Roger Daltrey)* 2007 (not illustrated)
Smoke and mirror
63.2 × 53
Courtesy the artist and Gagosian Gallery

Michael Wilkinson (b.1965), *Untitled*, 2013 (see ill.121 for earlier version)
Videotape
Courtesy the artist and The Modern Institute/ Toby Webster Ltd., Glasgow

John Stezaker (b.1949), *Third Person* 1988–9 (ill.123)
Photo-etching on paper and printed paper
27 × 20
Tate

John Stezaker (b.1949), *Mask XIV* 2006 (ill.124)
Photo-etching on paper and printed paper
24 × 20
Tate

John Stezaker (b.1949), *Mask XIII*, 2006 (not illustrated)
Postcard and photograph, black and white, on paper
24 × 19
Tate

PICTURE CREDITS

Every effort has been made to obtain image permissions. Any omissions are entirely unintentional and should be addressed to the publishers.

AP Photo/Adam Butler 6
AP Photo/POOL via APTN p.8
© Ashmolean Museum, University of Oxford 79
Photo Javier Ayarza. Courtesy Royal English College, Valladolid, Spain p.22 and no.11

Image courtesy Paul Barber 70
© The British Library p. 14 and nos. 7, 31, 32, 33, 55
© The Trustees of the British Museum 43, 45, 53
Footage supplied by British Pathé 111

Reproduced with permission from Canterbury Cathedral 30, 60, 61, 62, 63
Photograph by Robert Carter 74
Image courtesy Christ Church Cathedral, Oxford 64
The Department of Conservation and Technology. The Courtauld Institute of Art and Gallery 48
Photograph © John Crook. Reproduced by kind permission of The Dean & Chapter of Winchester Cathedral 2013 37, 38, 39, 40, 50

Courtesy the artist and Thomas Dane Gallery, London 120
Ivor Davies Archives/Photo: Michael Brooms 109
Photo: S.L. Deighton, Conservator 52
Photo by Sam Drake/Tate Photography 59

Reproduced by permission of English Heritage 26, 69
English Heritage/Alun Bull 16, 17, 19
English Heritage/James Davies 20
English Heritage/Bob Smith 13, 15, 24

Image courtesy Donal Fallon/ www.comeheretome.com 81
© The Fitzwilliam Museum, Cambridge 42

© Clement Guillaume/The Bridgeman Art Library 98
Courtesy of the artist and Murray Guy, New York 126

Photo © Neil Holmes/The Bridgeman Art Library 46
Courtesy of the Hunt Museum, Ireland 66
Copyright © Paul Hurst. All rights reserved 48

Photo: Independent Newspapers (Part of the NPA National Photographic Archives & Independent Newspapers Ireland) 82
Copyright of Inverness Museum and Art Gallery 3
Image courtesy Isis Gallery 5

© Philip Jones Griffiths/Magnum Photos 97

Courtesy of the artist & Galerie Kamm, Berlin 95
Photo by Keystone/Hulton Archive/Getty Images 107

His Grace the Archbishop of Canterbury and the Trustees of Lambeth Palace Library 54
Image courtesy Lafayette College, Pennsylvania 78
Courtesy John Latham Foundation 113, 114
Photo by Marcus Leith/Tate Photography 14, 18, 21, 22, 27, 28, 29

The Master and Fellows of Magdalene College, Cambridge 56, 57
© Manchester City Galleries 87, 88
Courtesy Church of St Mary, Gressenhall, Norfolk 51
Courtesy The Mercer's Company 1, 49
Courtesy the artist and The Modern Institute/Toby Webster Ltd, Glasgow 121
Photo by Dr Richard Murray 2
© Museum of London 89, 92

© The National Gallery, London 93
Photo © National Gallery of Ireland, Dublin 65, 72
National Library of Ireland 75

© National Portrait Gallery, London 36, 90, 91, 93
Photograph © National Portrait Gallery, London; collection National Gallery, London 96
©National Trust Images/Joe Cornish 12
Collection of The New-York Historical Society 77

The Pepys Library, Magdalene College, Cambridge 8
Photograph by Tom Picton 108, 110
© 2013 The Friends of Preston St Mary Church 34, 35
Photograph by John Prosser 114, 116

Courtesy the artist and Anthony Reynolds Gallery, London 125
REUTERS/Reuters Television/Pool 4
Supplied by Royal Collection Trust/© HM Queen Elizabeth II 2013 p.30 and no.23
Image courtesy RS&A Ltd (London) 128a–d
Courtesy of Robert Russell/Wilton Historical Heritage Museum 76

Photograph: Alastair Smeaton/Dublin City Council 73
© Studio lost but found / Douglas Gordon / VG Bild-Kunst, Bonn, 2013. Image courtesy Gagosian Gallery 122

© Tate Photography 119, 123, 124
Photo by Rod Tidnam/Tate Photography 70, 101, 102, 104, 112
Photo by Rod Tidnam and David Lambeth/ Tate Photography. Courtesy Timothy Millett 83, 84, 85, 86
Photo: Todd-White Art Photography. Courtesy White Cube 127
Topham/AP/Topfoto 106

© Victoria and Albert Museum, London 52, 71
View Pictures Ltd / SuperStock

Winchester Cathedral Archives. Photo: John Crook, 2013 41

COPYRIGHT CREDITS

© Carl Andre. DACS, London/VAGA, New York 2013
© Boyle Family. All rights reserved, DACS 2013
© The estate of Reg Butler
© George Condo, Dinos Chapman, Jake Chapman, Paul McCarthy
© Jake and Dinos Chapman
George Condo – © ARS, NY and DACS, London 2013
© Kate Davis
© Ivor Davies
Douglas Gordon © DACS 2013
© Allen Jones
© Michael Landy
© Estate of John Latham
© Raphael Montañez Ortiz
Herman Nitsch © DACS 2013
© Yoko Ono
© Tom Picton/Tate, London 2013
© Sex Pistols Residuals
© Lucy Skaer
© John Stezaker
© Mark Wallinger
© Michael Wilkinson

INDEX

Page numbers in *italic* type refer to illustrations; **bold** type refers to main entries.

SUPPORTING TATE

Tate relies on a large number of supporters – individuals, foundations, companies and public sector sources – to enable it to deliver its programme of activities, both on and off its gallery sites. This support is essential in order for Tate to acquire works of art for the Collection, run education, outreach and exhibition programmes, care for the Collection in storage and enable art to be displayed, both digitally and physically, inside and outside Tate. Your donation will make a real difference and enable others to enjoy Tate and its Collection both now and in the future. There are a variety of ways in which you can help support Tate and also benefit as a UK or US taxpayer. Please contact us at:

Development Office
Tate
Millbank
London SW1P 4RG

Tel 020 7887 4900
Fax 020 7887 8098

Tate Americas Foundation
520 West 27 Street Unit 404
New York, NY 10001
USA

Tel 001 212 643 2818
Fax 001 212 643 1001

Donations, no matter the size, are gratefully received, either to support particular areas of interest, or to contribute to general activity costs.

Gifts of Shares
We can accept gifts of quoted share and securities. All gifts of shares to Tate are exempt from capital gains tax, and higher rate taxpayers enjoy additional tax efficiencies. For further information please contact the Development Office.

Gift Aid
Through Gift Aid you can increase the value of your donation to Tate as we are able to reclaim the tax on your gift. Gift Aid applies to gifts of any size, whether regular or a one-off gift. Higher rate taxpayers are also able to claim additional personal tax relief. Contact us for further information and to make a Gift Aid Declaration.

Legacies
A legacy to Tate may take the form of a residual share of an estate, a specific cash sum or item of property such as a work of art. Legacies to Tate are free of inheritance tax, and help to secure a strong future for the Collection and galleries. For further information please contact the Development Office.

Offers in lieu of tax
Inheritance Tax can be satisfied by transferring to the Government a work of art of outstanding importance. In this case the amount of tax is reduced, and it can be made a condition of the offer that the work of art is allocated to Tate. Please contact us for details.

Tate Members
Tate Members enjoy unlimited free admission throughout the year to all exhibitions at Tate, as well as a number of other benefits such as exclusive use of our Members' Rooms and a free annual subscription to *Tate Etc.* Whilst enjoying the exclusive privileges of membership, you are also helping secure Tate's position at the very heart of British and modern art. Your support actively contributes to new purchases of important art, ensuring that Tate's collection continues to be relevant and comprehensive, as well as funding projects in London, Liverpool and St Ives that increase access and understanding for everyone.

Tate Patrons
Tate Patrons share a passion for art and are committed to supporting Tate on an annual basis. The Patrons help enable the acquisition of works across Tate's broad collecting remit and also give their support to vital conservation, learning and research projects. The scheme provides a forum for Patrons to share their interest in art and meet curators, artists and one another in an enjoyable environment through a regular programme of events. These events take place both at Tate and beyond and encompass curator-led exhibition tours, visits to artists' studios and private collections, art trips both in the UK and abroad, and access to art fairs. The scheme welcomes supporters from outside the UK, giving the programme a truly international scope. For more information, please contact the Patrons Office on +44(0)20 7887 8740 or at patrons.office@tate.org.uk.

Corporate Membership
Corporate Membership at Tate Modern, Tate Britain and Tate Liverpool offers companies opportunities for corporate entertaining and the chance for a wide variety of employee benefits. These include special private views, special access to paying exhibitions, out-of-hours visits and tours, invitations to VIP events and talks at members' offices.

Corporate Investment
Tate has developed a range of imaginative partnerships with the corporate sector, ranging from international interpretation and exhibition programmes to local outreach and staff development programmes.
We are particularly known for high-profile business to business marketing initiatives and employee benefit packages. Please contact the Corporate Fundraising team for further details.

Charity Details
The Tate Gallery is an exempt charity; the Museums & Galleries Act 1992 added the Tate Gallery to the list of exempt charities defined in the 1960 Charities Act. Tate Members is a registered charity (number 313021). Tate Foundation is a registered charity (number 1085314).

Tate Americas Foundation
Tate Americas Foundation is an independent charity based in New York that supports the work of Tate in the United Kingdom. It receives full tax exempt status from the IRS under section 501(c)(3) allowing United States taxpayers to receive tax deductions on gifts towards annual membership programmes, exhibitions, scholarship and capital projects. For more information contact the Tate Americas Foundation office.

Tate Britain Donors to the Centenary Development Campaign
The Annenberg Foundation
The Asprey Family Charitable Foundation
Ron Beller and Jennifer Moses
Alex and Angela Bernstein
The Charlotte Bonham-Carter Charitable Trust
Lauren and Mark Booth
Ivor Braka
CHK Charities Limited
The Clore Duffield Foundation
Sadie Coles
Giles and Sonia Coode-Adams
Alan Cristea
Thomas Dane
Sir Harry and Lady Djanogly
The D'Oyly Carte Charitable Trust
The Dulverton Trust
Maurice and Janet Dwek
Bob and Kate Gavron
Sir Paul Getty, KBE
Alan Gibbs
Mr and Mrs Edward Gilhuly
Nicholas and Judith Goodison
Richard and Odile Grogan
Pehr and Christina Gyllenhammar
The Heritage Lottery Fund
Jay Jopling
Mr and Mrs Karpidas
Howard and Lynda Karshan
Peter and Maria Kellner
Madeleine Kleinwort
Brian and Lesley Knox
The Kresge Foundation
Catherine and Pierre Lagrange
Mr and Mrs Ulf G Linden
Ruth and Stuart Lipton
Anders and Ulla Ljungh
Lloyds TSB Foundation for England and Wales
David and Pauline Mann-Vogelpoel
Sir Edwin and Lady Manton
Nick and Annette Mason
Viviane and James Mayor
Sir Peter and Lady Osborne
Maureen Paley
William A Palmer
Mr Frederick Paulsen
The Pet Shop Boys
The P F Charitable Trust
The Polizzi Charitable Trust
Sir John and Lady Ritblat
Barrie and Emmanuel Roman
Lord and Lady Sainsbury of Preston Candover
Mrs Coral Samuel, CBE
David and Sophie Shalit
Mr and Mrs Sven Skarendahl
Pauline Denyer-Smith and Paul Smith
Mr and Mrs Nicholas Stanley
The Jack Steinberg Charitable Trust
Charlotte Stevenson
Tate Gallery Centenary Gala
Tate Members
Carter and Mary Thacher
Mr and Mrs John Thornton
The Trusthouse Charitable Foundation
David and Emma Verey
Dinah Verey
Clodagh and Leslie Waddington
Gordon D Watson
Mr and Mrs Anthony Weldon
The Duke of Westminster, OBE, TD, DL
Sam Whitbread

Mr and Mrs Stephen Wilberding
Michael S Wilson
The Wolfson Foundation
and those who wish to remain anonymous

Donors to The Tate Britain Millbank Project
The Deborah Loeb Brice Foundation
Clore Duffield Foundation
The Alan Cristea Gallery
Sir Harry and Lady Djanogly
The Gatsby Charitable Foundation
J Paul Getty Jr Charitable Trust
Paul Green, Halcyon Gallery
The Heritage Lottery Fund
The Hiscox Foundation
James and Clare Kirkman
The Linbury Trust and The Monument Trust
The Manton Foundation
The Mayor Gallery
Ronald and Rita McAulay
Midge and Simon Palley
PF Charitable Trust
The Porter Foundation
The Dr Mortimer and Theresa Sackler Foundation
Mrs Coral Samuel, CBE
Tate Members
The Taylor Family Foundation
David and Emma Verey
Sir Siegmund Warburg's Voluntary Settlement
Garfield Weston Foundation
The Wolfson Foundation
and those who wish to remain anonymous

Tate Britain Benefactors and Major Donors
We would like to acknowledge and thank the following benefactors who have supported Tate Britain prior to 30th April 2013.

29th May 1961 Charitable Trust
The Ahmanson Foundation
The Ampersand Foundation
Ann Stokes Angus
Annenberg Foundation
Klaus Anschel
The Kenneth Armitage Foundation
The Art Fund
Art Mentor Foundation Lucerne
Arts Council England
Arts & Humanities Research Council
David and Liane Aukin
Gillian Ayres
Miroslaw Balka
The Estate of Peter and Caroline Barker-Mill
The Barns-Graham Charitable Trust
Trevor Bell
Anne Best
Big Lottery Fund
Billstone Foundation
Sutapa Biswas
The Charlotte Bonham-Carter Charitable Trust
Louise Bourgeois
Sir Alan and Sarah Bowness
Sophie Bowness
Pierre Brahm
The Estate of Dr Marcella Louis Brenner
British Council
The Estate of Joseph and Ruth Bromberg
Mrs Lucy Carter
Trustees of the Chantrey Bequest
Patricia Phelps de Cisneros
Toby Clarke
The Clore Duffield Foundation
The Clothworkers' Foundation
Ian Collins
Sonia and Giles Coode-Adams
Isabelle and John Corbani
Douglas S Cramer
Jane Crawford
Martin Creed
Alan Cristea Gallery
The Estate of William Crozier
Bilge Ogut-Cumbusyan and Haro Cumbusyan
Thomas Dane Ltd
Richard Deacon
Department for Business, Innovation and Skills
Department for Culture, Media and Sport
Department for Education
Jonathan Djanogly
Anthony and Anne d'Offay
Peter Doig
Jytte Dresing, The Merla Art Foundation, Dresing Collection
The Duerckheim Collection
EDP - Energias de Portugal, S.A.
Maryam and Edward Eisler
The John Ellerman Foundation
European Union
Esmée Fairbairn Foundation
The Estate of Maurice Farquharson
Dan Fauci
The Finnis Scott Foundation
Wendy Fisher
David Fitzsimons
The Estate of Ann Forsdyke
Friends of Heritage Preservation
Galleria Franco Noero
The Estate of Jack Gaster
The Getty Foundation
Ida Gianelli
Milly and Arne Glimcher
Nicholas and Judith Goodison
Goodman Gallery, Johannesburg and Cape Town
Richard Green
The Estate of Alan Green
Margot and George Greig
Konstantin Grigorishin
Calouste Gulbenkian Foundation
The Haberdashers' Company
Paul Hamlyn Foundation
Viscount and Viscountess Hampden and Family
Hauser & Wirth
Desiree Hayter
Heritage Lottery Fund
David Herman and the Herman family
The Hintze Family Charitable Foundation
Damien Hirst
David Hockney
The Estate of Mrs Mimi Hodgkin
Maja Hoffmann/LUMA Foundation
Jenny Holzer
The Estate of Sir Robert Horton
The Idlewild Trust
Cristina Iglesias
Joachim Jacobs
Marc Jacobs
J. Patrick Kennedy and Patricia A. Kennedy
Bharti Kher
Kirby Laing Foundation
Jack Kirkland
Mr and Mrs James Kirkman
Leon Kossoff
Jannis Kounellis
The Kreitman Foundation
Samuel H. Kress Foundation, administered by the Foundation of the American Institute for Conservation
Catherine Lagrange
Pierre Lagrange
David and Amanda Leathers
The Leathersellers' Company Charitable Fund
The Leche Trust
Agnes and Edward Lee
Simon and Carine Lee
Legacy Trust UK
The Leverhulme Trust
Gemma Levine
Mark and Liza Loveday
John Lyon's Charity
The Estate of Sir Edwin Manton
Robert Mapplethorpe Foundation
Lord McAlpine of West Green
Mark McCain
The Andrew W Mellon Foundation
The Paul Mellon Centre for Studies in British Art
Sir Geoffroy Millais
Jean-Yves Mock
The Modern Institute
The Henry Moore Foundation
Peter Moores Foundation
The Estate of Mrs Jennifer Ann Murray
NADFAS
National Heritage Memorial Fund
Netherlands Organisation for Scientific Research (NWO)
Neugerriemschneider
New Art Trust
Tony Oursler and Artangel
Outset Contemporary Art Fund
The Estate of Mr Brian and Mrs Nancy Pattenden
Stephen and Yana Peel
Stanley Picker Trust
The Pilgrim Trust
PINTA Museum Acquisition Programme
Gilberto Pozzi
The Nyda & Oliver Prenn Foundation
Oliver Prenn
Glenstone Foundation, Emily and Mitchell Rales
Jay Smith and Laura Rapp
Frances Reynolds
Yvonne Robinson
Barrie and Emmanuel Roman
Edward Ruscha
The Estate of Simon Sainsbury
Ibrahim El-Salahi
The Sandra Charitable Trust
Anna Marie and Robert F Shapiro
Candida and Rebecca Smith
The Estate of Mrs Freda Mary Snadow
The Stanley Foundation
The Estate of Jiro Takamatsu
Tate Africa Acquisitions Committee
Tate Americas Foundation
Tate Asia-Pacific Acquisitions Committee
Tate International Council
Tate Latin American Acquisitions Committee
Tate Members
Tate Middle East and North Africa Acquisitions Committee
Tate North American Acquisitions Committee
Tate Patrons
Tate Photography Acquisitions Committee
Tate Russia and Eastern Europe Acquisitions Committee
Tate South Asia Acquisitions Committee
Melissa Tecklenberg
Terra Foundation for American Art
The Estate of Mr Nicholas Themans
Robert Therrien
The Tretyakov Family Collection
Tyler Graphics Ltd in honour of Pat Gilmour
The Vandervell Foundation
Waddington Custot Galleries Ltd
Offer Waterman & Co
Wellcome Trust
Welton Foundation
The Estate of Fred Williams
Samuel and Nina Wisnia
Poju and Anita Zabludowicz
and those who wish to remain anonymous

Platinum Patrons
Mr Alireza Abrishamchi
Ghazwa Mayassi Abu-Suud
Mr Shane Akeroyd
Basil Alkazzi
Ryan Allen and Caleb Kramer
Mr and Mrs Edward Atkin, CBE
Beecroft Charitable Trust
Mrs Abeer ben Halim
Mr Harry Blain
Broeksmit Family Foundation
Rory and Elizabeth Brooks (Chair)
The Lord Browne of Madingley, FRS, FREng
Mr Stephane Custot
Miel de Botton
Fares and Tania Fares
Mr David Fitzsimons
The Flow Foundation
Mr Michael Foster
Edwin Fox Foundation
Hugh Gibson
The Goss-Michael Foundation
Mandy Gray and Randall Work
Mrs Nathalie and Mr Luc Guiot-Saucier
Mr and Mrs Yan Huo
Mr Phillip Hylander
Anne-Marie and Geoffrey Isaac
Mrs Gabrielle Jungels-Winkler
Maria and Peter Kellner
Esperanza Koren
Mrs Ella Krasner
Mr and Mrs Eskandar Maleki
Scott and Suling Mead
Gabriela Mendoza and Rodrigo Marquez
Pierre Tollis and Alexandra Mollof
Mr Donald Moore
Mary Moore
Mr and Mrs Paul Phillips
Mariela Pissioti
Maya and Ramzy Rasamny
Frances Reynolds
Simon and Virginia Robertson
Mr and Mrs Richard Rose
Claudia Ruimy
Vipin Sareen and Rebecca Mitchell
Hakon Runer and Ulrike Schwarz-Runer
Mr and Mrs J Shafran
Mrs Andrée Shore
Maria and Malek Sukkar
Mr Vladimir Tsarenkov and Ms Irina Kargina
Mr and Mrs Petri Vainio
Michael and Jane Wilson
Poju and Anita Zabludowicz
and those who wish to remain anonymous

Gold Patrons
Eric Abraham
Kirsty Anson
Jacqueline Appel and Alexander Malmaeus
Katrina Barter
Jenny and Robert Borgerhoff Mulder
Elena Bowes
Ben and Louisa Brown
Nicolò Cardi
Melanie Clore
Beth and Michele Colocci
Bilge Ogut-Cumbusyan and Haro Cumbusyan
Mr Dónall Curtin
Mrs Robin D'Alessandro
Harry G. David
Mr Frank Destribats
Mrs Maryam Eisler
Mala Gaonkar
Kate Groes
Mrs Helene Guerin-Llamas
Mr and Mrs Charles M Hale
Mrs Petra Horvat
Ms Natascha Jakobs
Tiina Lee
Fiona Mactaggart
Paul and Alison Myners
Reem Nassar
Mr Francis Outred
Simon and Midge Palley
Mathew Prichard
Valerie Rademacher
Mr Charles Roxburgh
Carol Sellars
Mrs Dana Sheves
Britt Tidelius
Mr and Mrs Stanley S. Tollman
Emily Tsingou and Henry Bond
Mrs Celia Forner Venturi
Rebecca Wang
Manuela and Iwan Wirth
Barbara Yerolemou
and those who wish to remain anonymous

Silver Patrons
Agnew's
Mrs Malgosia Alterman
Toby and Kate Anstruther
Mr and Mrs Zeev Aram
Mrs Charlotte Artus
Tim Attias
Miss Silvia Badiali
Mrs Jane Barker
Mr Edward Barlow
Victoria Barnsley, OBE
Christopher Bartlett
Jim Bartos
Mr Harold Berg
Lady Angela Bernstein
Ms Anne Berthoud
Madeleine Bessborough
Ms Karen Bizon
Janice Blackburn
David Blood and Beth Bisso
Mrs Sofia Bogolyubov
Nathalie and Daniel Boulakia
Helen Boyan
Mr Brian Boylan
Ivor Braka
Alex Branczik
Viscountess Bridgeman
The Broere Charitable Foundation
Mr Dan Brooke
Michael Burrell
Mrs Marlene Burston
Mrs Aisha Caan
Timothy and Elizabeth Capon
Mr Francis Carnwath and Ms Caroline Wiseman
Lord and Lady Charles Cecil
Dr Peter Chocian
Frank Cohen
Nicola Collard
Mrs Jane Collins
Dr Judith Collins
Terrence Collis
Mr and Mrs Oliver Colman
Carole and Neville Conrad
Giles and Sonia Coode-Adams
Alastair Cookson
Cynthia Corbett
Mark and Cathy Corbett
Mrs Ursula Cornely
Tommaso Corvi-Mora
Mr and Mrs Bertrand Coste
Kathleen Crook and James Penturn
James Curtis
Sir Howard Davies
Mr and Mrs Roger de Haan
Giles de la Mare
Maria de Madariaga
Anne Chantal Defay Sheridan
Marco di Cesaria
Simon C Dickinson Ltd
Ms Sophie Diedrichs-Cox
James Diner
Liz and Simon Dingemans
Ms Charlotte Ransom and Mr Tim Dye
Rafe Eddington
Joan Edlis

Lord and Lady Egremont
Jeffrey and Jennifer Eldredge
John Erle-Drax
Dr Nigel Evans
Stuart and Margaret Evans
Eykyn Maclean LLC
Gerard Faggionato
Ms Rose Fajardo
Richard Farleigh
Mrs Heather Farrar
David Fawkes
Mrs Margy Fenwick
Mr Bryan Ferry, CBE
Mrs Jean Fletcher
Lt Commander Paul Fletcher
Steve Fletcher
Katherine Francey Stables
Elizabeth Freeman
Stephen Friedman
Shoshana Bloch
Carol Galley
Daniela and Victor Gareh
Mrs Lisa Garrison
Ljubica Georgievska
Mr Mark Glatman
Ms Emily Goldner and Mr Michael Humphries
Ms Josefa Gonzalez-Blanco
Mr Jonathan Goodman
Mr and Mrs Paul Goswell
Penelope Govett
Martyn Gregory
Sir Ronald Grierson
Mrs Kate Grimond
Richard and Odile Grogan
Louise Hallett
Richard Hazlewood
Michael and Morven Heller
Richard and Sophia Herman
Miss Judith Hess
Mrs Patsy Hickman
Robert Holden
James Holland-Hibbert
Lady Hollick, OBE
Holtermann Fine Art
Vicky Hughes
John Huntingford
Mr Alex Ionides
Maxine Isaacs
Helen Janecek
Sarah Jennings
Mr Haydn John
Mr Michael Johnson
Jay Jopling
Mrs Marcelle Joseph and Mr Paolo Cicchiné
Mrs Brenda Josephs
Tracey Josephs
Mr Joseph Kaempfer
Andrew Kalman
Jag-Preet Kaur
Dr Martin Kenig
Simon and Jeannette Kenny
Mr David Ker
Nicola Kerr
Mr and Mrs Simon Keswick
Richard and Helen Keys
Mrs Mae Khouri
David Killick
Mr and Mrs James Kirkman
Brian and Lesley Knox
David and Sarah Kowitz
Mr and Mrs Herbert Kretzmer
Linda Lakhdhir
Ms Jacqueline Lane
Mrs Julie Lee
Simon Lee
Mr Gerald Levin
Leonard Lewis
Mrs Cynthia Lewis Beck
Sophia and Mark Lewisohn
Mr Gilbert Lloyd
George Loudon
Mrs Elizabeth Louis
Mark and Liza Loveday
Catherine Lovell
Daniella Luxembourg Art
Anthony Mackintosh
The Mactaggart Third Fund
Mrs Jane Maitland Hudson
Mr M J Margulies
Lord and Lady Marks
Marsh Christian Trust
Mrs Anne-Sophie McGrath
Ms Fiona Mellish
Mr Martin Mellish
Mrs R W P Mellish
Professor Rob Melville
Mr Alfred Mignano
Victoria Miro
Ms Milica Mitrovich
Jan Mol
Lulette Monbiot
Mrs Bona Montagu
Mr Ricardo Mora
Mrs William Morrison
Richard Nagy
Julian Opie
Pilar Ordovás
Sir Richard Osborn
Joseph and Chloe O'Sullivan
Desmond Page
Maureen Paley
Dominic Palfreyman
Michael Palin
Mrs Adelaida Palm
Stephen and Clare Pardy
Mrs Véronique Parke
Mr Sanjay Parthasarathy
Frans Pettinga
Miss Nathalie Philippe
Trevor Pickett
Mr Oliver Prenn
Susan Prevezer, QC
Mr Adam Prideaux
Mr and Mrs Ryan Prince
James Pyner
Ivetta Rabinovich
Mrs Phyllis Rapp
Ms Victoria Reanney
Dr Laurence Reed
Mr and Mrs Philip Renaud
The Reuben Foundation
Sir Tim Rice
Lady Ritblat
Ms Chao Roberts
David Rocklin
Frankie Rossi
Mr David V Rouch
Mr James Roundell
Naomi Russell
Mr Alex Sainsbury and Ms Elinor Jansz
Mr Richard Saltoun
Mrs Amanda Sater
Mrs Cecilia Scarpa
Cherrill and Ian Scheer
Sylvia Scheuer
The Schneer Foundation
Mrs Cara Schulze
Andrew and Belinda Scott
The Hon Richard Sharp
Mr Stuart Shave
Neville Shulman, CBE
Ms Julia Simmonds
Jennifer Smith
Paul and Marcia Soldatos
Mr George Soros
Louise Spence
Mr and Mrs Nicholas Stanley
Mr Nicos Steratzias
Stacie Styles
Mrs Patricia Swannell
Mr James Swartz
The Sylvie Fleming Collection
The Lady Juliet Tadgell
Tot Taylor
Christopher and Sally Tennant
Mr Henry Tinsley
Karen Townshend
Melissa Ulfane
Mr Marc Vandecandelaere
Mrs Cecilia Versteegh
Mr Jorge Villon
Gisela von Sanden
Audrey Wallrock
Stephen and Linda Waterhouse
Offer Waterman
Terry Watkins
Lisa West
Miss Cheyenne Westphal
Walter H. White, Jnr.
Sue Whiteley
Mr David Wood
Mr Douglas Woolf
Anthony Zboralski
and those who wish to remain anonymous

Young Patrons
Vinita Agarwal
Aziz Ahsan
Stephanie Alameida
HH Princess Nauf AlBendar Al-Saud
Ms Maria Allen
Miss Noor Al-Rahim
HRH Princess Alia Al-Senussi (Chair, Young Patrons Ambassador Group)
Miss Sharifa Alsudairi
Sigurdur Arngrimsson
Miss Katharine Arnold
Maria and Errikos Arones
Miss Joy Asfar
Ms Mila Askarova
Miss Olivia Aubry
Flavie Audi
Sarah Bejerano
Josh Bell and Jsen Wintle
Miss Marisa Bellani
Ms Shruti Belliappa
Mr Erik Belz
Mr Edouard Benveniste-Schuler
Miss Margherita Berloni
Raimund Berthold
Dr Brenda Blott
Mrs Sofia Bocca
Ms Lara Bohinc
Miss Camilla Bullus
Miss Verena Butt
Miss May Calil
Miss Sarah Calodney
Matt Carey-Williams and Donnie Roark
Georgina Casals
Alexandra and Kabir Chhatwani
Miss Katya Chitova
Bianca Chu
Mrs Mona Collins
Mrs Laura Comfort
Thamara Corm
Miss Amanda C Cronin
Mr Theo Danjuma
Mr Joshua Davis
Ms Lora de Felice
Countess Charlotte de la Rochefoucauld
Emilie De Pauw
Agnes de Royere
Federico Debernardi
Mira Dimitrova
Ms Michelle D'Souza
Miss Roxanna Farboud
Jane and Richard Found
Mr Andreas Gegner
Mrs Benedetta Ghione-Webb
Miss Dori Gilinski
Jessica Grosman
Olga Grotova and Oleksiy Osnach
Mr Nick Hackworth
Alex Haidas
Sara Harrison
Kira Allegra Heller
Christoph Hett
Mrs Samantha Heyworth
Andrew Honan
Katherine Ireland
Miss Eloise Isaac
Kamel Jaber
Scott Jacobson
Mr Christopher Jones
Ms Melek Huma Kabakci
Miss Meruyert Kaliyeva
Efe and Aysun Kapanci
Nicole Karlisch
Ms Tanya Kazeminy Mackay
Miss Tamila Kerimova
Ms Chloe Kinsman
Ms Marijana Kolak
Alkistis Koukouilou
Miss Constanze Kubern
Miss Marina Kurikhina
Mr Jimmy Lahoud
Ms Aliki Lampropoulos
Ms Anna Lapshina
Isabella Lauder-Frost
Mrs Julie Lawson
Lin Lei
Karen Levy
Miss MC Llamas
Mr Justin Lobo
Alex Logsdail
Charlotte Lucas
Mr John Madden
Ms Sonia Mak
Mr Jean-David Malat
Kamiar Maleki
Zoe Marden
Ms Clémence Mauchamp
Mr John McLaughlin
Miss Nina Moaddel
Mr Fernando Moncho Lobo
Ms Michelle Morphew
Erin Morris
Ali Munir
Mrs Annette Nygren
Katharina Ottmann
Ilona Pacia
Christine Chungwon Park
Ms Camilla Paul
Alexander V. Petalas
Mrs Stephanie Petit
The Piper Gallery
Mr Eugenio Re Rebaudengo
Mr Bruce Ritchie and Mrs Shadi Ritchie
Kimberley and Michael Robson-Ortiz
Mr Simon Sakhai
Miss Tatiana Sapegina
Olga Savchenko
Taya Sawiris
Mr Simon Scheuer
Franz Schwarz
Alex Seddon
Count Indoo Sella Di Monteluce
James Sevier
Henrietta Shields
Ms Heather Shimizu
Mr Paul Shin
Ms Marie-Anya Shriro
Mr Max Silver
Laura Simkins
Tammy Smulders
Miss Jelena Spasojevic
Alexandra Sterling
Mr Dominic Stolerman
Gerald Tan Mr Edward Tang
Miss Georgiana Teodorescu
Miss Inge Theron
Soren S K Tholstrup
Hannah Tjaden
Mr Giancarlo Trinca
Mrs Padideh Trojanow
Mr Philippos Tsangrides
Mr Rupert Van Millingen
Angus Walker
Mr Neil Wenman
Ms Hailey Widrig Ritcheson
Miss Julia Wright
Ms Seda Yalcinkaya
Arani Yogadeva
Mr Fabrizio Zappaterra
Daniel Zarchan
Alma Zevi
and those who wish to remain anonymous

International Council Members
Mr Segun Agbaje
Staffan Ahrenberg, Editions Cahiers d'Art
Doris Ammann
Mr Plácido Arango
Gabrielle Bacon
Anne H Bass
Cristina Bechtler
Nicolas Berggruen
Olivier and Desiree Berggruen
Baron Berghmans
Mr Pontus Bonnier
Frances Bowes
Ivor Braka
The Deborah Loeb Brice Foundation
The Broad Art Foundation
Bettina and Donald L Bryant Jr
Melva Bucksbaum and Raymond Learsy
Mrs Christina Chandris
Richard Chang
Pierre TM Chen, Yageo Foundation, Taiwan
Lord Cholmondeley
Mr Kemal Has Cingillioglu
Mr and Mrs Attilio Codognato
Sir Ronald Cohen and Lady Sharon Harel-Cohen
Mr Alfonso Cortina de Alcocer
Mr Douglas S Cramer and Mr Hubert S Bush III
Mr Dimitris Daskalopoulos
Mr and Mrs Michel David-Weill
Julia W Dayton
Ms Miel de Botton
Tiqui Atencio Demirdjian and Ago Demirdjian
Joseph and Marie Donnelly
Mrs Olga Dreesmann
Mrs Jytte Dresing
Barney A Ebsworth
Füsun and Faruk Eczacibaşi
Stefan Edlis and Gael Neeson
Mr and Mrs Edward Eisler
Carla Emil and Rich Silverstein
Alan Faena
Harald Falckenberg
Fares and Tania Fares
HRH Princess Firyal of Jordan
Mrs Doris Fisher
Mrs Wendy Fisher
Dr Corinne M Flick
Amanda and Glenn Fuhrman
Candida and Zak Gertler
Alan Gibbs
Lydia and Manfred Gorvy
Kenny Goss
Mr Laurence Graff
Ms Esther Grether

Konstantin Grigorishin
Mr Xavier Guerrand-Hermès
Mimi and Peter Haas Fund
Margrit and Paul Hahnloser
Andy and Christine Hall
Mr Toshio Hara
Paul Harris
Mrs Susan Hayden
Ms Ydessa Hendeles
Marlene Hess and James D. Zirin
André and Rosalie Hoffmann
Ms Maja Hoffmann (Chair)
Vicky Hughes
ITYS, Athens
Dakis and Lietta Joannou
Sir Elton John and Mr David Furnish
Pamela J. Joyner
Mr Chang-Il Kim
Jack Kirkland
C Richard and Pamela Kramlich
Catherine Lagrange
Mr Pierre Lagrange and Mr Roubi L'Roubi
Baroness Marion Lambert
Bernard Lambilliotte
Agnès and Edward Lee
Mme RaHee Hong Lee
Jacqueline and Marc Leland
Mr and Mrs Sylvain Levy
Mr Eugenio Lopez
Mrs Fatima Maleki
Panos and Sandra Marinopoulos
Nancy and Howard Marks
Mr and Mrs Donald B Marron
Andreas and Marina Martinos
Mr Ronald and The Hon Mrs McAulay
Angela Westwater and David Meitus
Mr Leonid Mikhelson
Simon and Catriona Mordant
Mrs Yoshiko Mori
Mr Guy and The Hon Mrs Naggar
Mr and Mrs Takeo Obayashi
Hideyuki Osawa
Mrs Kathrine Palmer
Irene Panagopoulos
Young-Ju Park
Yana and Stephen Peel
Daniel and Elizabeth Peltz
Andrea and José Olympio Pereira
Fondation Cartier pour l'art contemporain
Catherine and Franck Petitgas
Sydney Picasso
Mr and Mrs Jürgen Pierburg
Jean Pigozzi
Ms Miuccia Prada and Mr Patrizio Bertelli
Laura Rapp and Jay Smith
Maya and Ramzy Rasamny
Patrizia Sandretto Re Rebaudengo and Agostino Re Rebaudengo
Robert Rennie and Carey Fouks
Mr John Richardson
Michael Ringier
Lady Ritblat
Barrie and Emmanuel Roman
Ms Güler Sabanci
Dame Theresa Sackler
Mrs Lily Safra
Muriel and Freddy Salem
Dasha Shenkman
Uli and Rita Sigg
Michael S. Smith
Norah and Norman Stone
John J Studzinski, CBE
Maria and Malek Sukkar
Mrs Marjorie Susman
David Teiger
Mr Budi Tek, The Yuz Foundation
Mr Robert Tomei
The Hon Robert H Tuttle and Mrs Maria Hummer-Tuttle
Mr and Mrs Guy Ullens
Michael and Yvonne Uva
Mrs Ninetta Vafeia
Corinne and Alexandre Van Damme
Paulo A W Vieira
Robert and Felicity Waley-Cohen
Diana Widmaier Picasso
Christen and Derek Wilson
Michael G Wilson
Mrs Sylvie Winckler
The Hon Dame Janet Wolfson de Botton, DBE
Anita and Poju Zabludowicz
Michael Zilkha
and those who wish to remain anonymous

Africa Acquisitions Committee

Tutu Agyare (Co-Chair)
Bolanle Austen-Peters
Mrs Nwakaego Boyo
Lavinia Calza
Mrs Kavita Chellaram
Salim Currimjee
Harry G. David
Robert Devereux (Co-Chair)
Hamish Dewar
Isis Dove-Edwin and Paul Ellis
Mrs Wendy Fisher
Kari Gahiga
Helene Huth
Andrea Kerzner
Samallie Kiyingi
Matthias and Gervanne Leridon
Nicholas Logsdail
Caro Macdonald
Hoosein Mahomed
Dr Kenneth Montague
Miles Morland
Alain F. Nkontchou
Professor Oba Nsugbe, QC
Pascale Revert Wheeler
Kathryn Jane Robins
Mike and Maria Spink
Emile Stipp
Roelof Petrus van Wyk
Mr Varnavas A. Varnava
Mercedes Vilardell
Tony Wainaina
Alexa Waley-Cohen
Edwin Wulfsohn
and those who wish to remain anonymous

Asia-Pacific Acquisitions Committee

Bonnie and R Derek Bandeen
Andrew Cameron
Mr and Mrs John Carrafiell
Mrs Christina Chandris
Richard Chang
Pierre TM Chen, Yageo Foundation, Taiwan
Adrian Cheng
Katie de Tilly
Mr. Hyung-Teh Do
Ms Mareva Grabowski
Reade and Elizabeth Griffith
Louisa Guinness
Ms Kyoko Hattori
Cees Hendrikse
Mr Yongsoo Huh
Tessa Keswick
Shareen Khattar Harrison
Mr Chang-Il Kim
Ms Yung Hee Kim
Alan Lau
Woong Yeul Lee
Mr William Lim
Ms. Dina Liu
Ms Kai-Yin Lo
Anne Louis-Dreyfus
Mrs Geraldine Elaine Marden
The Red Mansion Foundation
Mr Jackson See
Mr Paul Serfaty
Dr Gene Sherman AM
Leo Shih
Mr Robert Shum
Sir David Tang (Chair)
Mr Budi Tek, The Yuz Foundation
Rudy Tseng (Taiwan)
and those who wish to remain anonymous

Latin American Acquisitions Committee

Monica and Robert Aguirre
Karen and Leon Amitai
Luis Benshimol
Billy Bickford, Jr. and Oscar Cuellar
Estrellita and Daniel Brodsky
Trudy and Paul Cejas
Patricia Phelps de Cisneros
Gerard Cohen
David Cohen Sitton
HSH the Prince Pierre d'Arenberg
Tiqui Atencio Demirdjian (Chair)
Patricia Druck
Lily Gabriella Elia
Angelica Fuentes de Vergara
Mauro Herlitzka
Rocio and Boris Hirmas Said
Anne Marie and Geoffrey Isaac
Nicole Junkermann
Jack Kirkland
Fatima and Eskander Maleki
Becky and Jimmy Mayer
Solita and Steven Mishaan
Catherine and Michel Pastor
Catherine Petitgas
Isabella Prata and Idel Arcuschin
Frances Reynolds
Erica Roberts
Judko Rosenstock and Oscar Hernandez
Guillermo Rozenblum
Alin Ryan Lobo
Lilly Scarpetta and Roberto Pumarejo
Catherine Shriro
Norma Smith
Juan Carlos Verme
Tania and Arnoldo Wald
Juan Yarur Torres
and those who wish to remain anonymous

Middle East and North Africa Acquisitions Committee

HRH Princess Alia Al-Senussi
Abdullah Al Turki
Mehves Ariburnu
Sule Arinc
Marwan T Assaf
Perihan Bassatne
Boghossian Foundation
Ms Isabelle de la Bruyère
Füsun Eczacibaşi
Maryam Eisler (Co-Chair)
Shirley Elghanian
Delfina Entrecanales, CBE
Noor Fares
Maha and Kasim Kutay
Sherine Magar-Sawiris
Nina Mahdavi
Mrs Fatima Maleki
Fayeeza Naqvi
Dina Nasser-Khadivi
Ebru Özdemir
Mrs Edwina Özyegin
Ramzy and Maya Rasamny (Co-Chair)
Mrs Karen Ruimy
Dania Debs-Sakka
Miss Yassi Sohrabi
Maria and Malek Sukkar
Ana Luiza and Luiz Augusto Teixeira de Freitas
Berna Tuglular
and those who wish to remain anonymous

North American Acquisitions Committee

Carol and David Appel
Jackie Appel
Dorothy Berwin and Dominique Levy
Paul Britton
Matt Cohler
Beth Rudin De Woody
James Diner
Glenn Fuhrman
Victoria Gelfand-Magalhaes
Marc Glimcher
Pamela Joyner
Monica Kalpakian
Elisabeth and Panos Karpidas
Christian K Keese
Anne Simone Kleinman and Thomas Wong
Celine and Jacques Lamarre
Marjorie and Michael Levine
James Lindon
Massimo Marcucci
Lillian and Billy Mauer
Liza Mauer and Andrew Sheiner
Nancy McCain
Della and Stuart McLaughlin
Marjorie and Marc McMorris
Stavros Merjos
Gregory R. Miller
Shabin and Nadir Mohamed
Elisa Nuyten and David Dime
Amy and John Phelan
Melinda B and Paul Pressler
Liz Gerring Radke and Kirk Radke
Laura Rapp and Jay Smith
Robert Rennie (Chair) and Carey Fouks
Kimberly Richter
Amie Rocket and Anthony Munk
Donald R Sobey
Robert Sobey
Beth Swofford
Dr Diane Vachon
Christen and Derek Wilson
and those who wish to remain anonymous

Photography Acquisitions Committee

Ryan Allen
Louise Baring Franck
Mr Nicholas Barker
Cynthia Lewis Beck
Marisa Bellani
Veronica and Jeffrey Berman
Pierre Brahm (Chair)
William and Alla Broeksmit
Elizabeth and Rory Brooks
Marcel and Gabrielle Cassard
Nicolas and Celia Cattelain
Beth and Michele Colocci
Fares and Tania Fares
David Fitzsimons
Margot and George Greig
Alexandra Hess
Michael Hoppen
Bernard Huppert
Tim Jefferies, Hamiltons Gallery
Dede Johnston
Jack Kirkland
David Knaus
Mark McCain
Mr Scott Mead
Sebastien Montabonel
Mr Donald Moore
Mr Axel Nordin
Ellen and Dan Shapiro
Saadi Soudavar
Maria and Malek Sukkar
Mrs Caroline Trausch
Michael and Jane Wilson
and those who wish to remain anonymous

Russia and Eastern Europe Acquisitions Committee

Dilyara Allakhverdova
Maria Baibakova
Maria Bukhtoyarova
Mr Pavel Erochkine
Dr Kira Flanzraich (Chair)
Konstantin Grigorishin
Carl Kostyál
Mrs Grażyna Kulczyk
Peter Kulloi
Ms Nonna Materkova
Victoria Mikhelson
Neil K. Rector
Ovidiu Şandor
Zsolt Somlói
Tretyakov Family Collection
Igor Tsukanov
Mrs Alina Uspenskaya
and those who wish to remain anonymous

South Asia Acquisitions Committee

Dr Amin Jaffer
Professor Nirmalya Kumar
Darashaw K Mehta
Yamini Mehta
Mr Rohan Mirchandani
Shalini Misra
Amna and Ali Naqvi
Fayeeza Naqvi
Mrs.Chandrika Pathak
Puja and Uday Patnaik
Lekha Poddar (Chair)
Rajeeb Samdani
Mrs Faiza Seth
Azad Shivdasani
Iwan Wirth
and those who wish to remain anonymous

Tate Britain Corporate Supporters

BP
Christie's
EY
Hildon Limited
J.P. Morgan
Le Méridien
Sotheby's
Vodafone Group
and those who wish to remain anonymous

Tate Britain Corporate Members

AIG
Bank of America Merrill Lynch
Christie's
Clifford Chance LLP
College Group
Deloitte LLP
Deutsche Bank
EY
GAM (UK) Limited
HSBC
The John Lewis Partnership
Kingfisher plc
Linklaters
Mazars
Morgan Stanley
Pearson
The Brooklyn Brothers
Tishman Speyer
Wolff Olins
and those who wish to remain anonymous

First published 2013 by
order of the Tate Trustees
by Tate Publishing, a division
of Tate Enterprises Ltd,
Millbank, London SW1P 4RG
www.tate.org.uk/publishing

on the occasion of the exhibition

ART UNDER ATTACK
Histories of British Iconoclasm

Tate Britain
2 October 2013 – 5 January 2014

A catalogue record for this book is available from the British Library

ISBN 978 1 84976 030 0 (pbk)

Distributed in the United States and Canada by ABRAMS, New York

Library of Congress Control Number applied for

Designed by Philip Lewis
Colour reproduction by DL Imaging Ltd.
Printed and bound in Italy by Elcograf S.p.A.

MIX
Paper from responsible sources
FSC® C015829

FRONT COVER, left to right:

1ST ROW statue of our Lady Vulnerata probably 16th century (detail of ill.11); video grab of statue of Saddam Hussein being toppled, 2003 (detail of ill.4); Douglas Gordon, *Self-Portrait of You + Me (9 piece QEII)* 2008 (detail of ill.122)
2ND ROW statue of Winston Churchill, defaced May 2000 (detail of ill.6)
3RD ROW British School, *Christ Before Pilate* c.1400–25 (detail of ill.42); John Stezaker, *Mask XIV* 2006 (detail of ill.124); British School, *The Crucifixion* c.1380–1400 (detail of ill.47)
4TH ROW head from Nelson's Pillar, Dublin, 'captured' by students in 1966 (detail of ill.81); Jake and Dinos Chapman, *One Day You Will No Longer Be Loved II (No.6)* 2008 (detail of ill.127); fragment of window glass from Furness Abbey (detail of ill.26)

BACK COVER The Virgin and Child late 15th century (ill.50)

TITLE PAGE After Maarten van Heemskerck, engraved plate from Lord's Prayer series late 16th century (detail of ill.56)

Measurements of artworks are given in centimetres, height before width